History of the Popes

Volume I

History of the Popes

Their Church and State
Volume I

LEOPOLD VON RANKE

E. FOWLER, TRANSLATOR

NEW YORK

History of the Popes: Their Church and State, Volume I.
Originally published in German in 1834–1836. This translation
published in 1901 by The Colonial Press.
This edition published by Cosimo Classics in 2020.

Cover copyright © 2020 by Cosimo, Inc.
Cover image from the frontispiece in Volume III,
"Miniature of St. Luke," from a Livre written at Troyes c. 1480. Cover
design by www.heatherkern.com.

ISBN: 978-1-64679-149-1

This edition is a replica of a rare classic. As such, it is possible that
some of the text might be blurred or of reduced print quality. Thank
you for your understanding, and we wish you a pleasant reading
experience.

Ordering Information:
Cosimo publications are available at online bookstores. They may also be
purchased for educational, business, or promotional use:
Bulk orders: Special discounts are available on bulk orders for reading
groups, organizations, businesses, and others.
Custom-label orders: We offer selected books with your customized cover
or logo of choice.

For more information, contact us at www.cosimobooks.com.

SPECIAL INTRODUCTION

L EOPOLD VON RANKE won for himself a position among the historians of the world which he is never likely to lose. Whether we consider the width and depth of his erudition, the impartial spirit in which he conducted his investigations, or the comprehensiveness of his historical views, we must pronounce him to be the type of the scientific historian and the model who may be safely imitated by all his successors. The long list of his compositions bears sufficient testimony to his unwearying industry.

It would hardly be possible to set forth the qualities of this great historian better than was done on the occasion of his death, in May, 1896, by one of the first of our English historians, Dr. S. R. Gardiner. He truly remarks that to speak of Ranke " as the greatest historian of his time is to fail to appreciate his work at its due value. He was more than this. He was a path-maker, and that, too, not in one direction only. . . . He developed instinctively in himself all the tendencies which were to appear in the collective work of a younger generation. It would have been much for any man to lead the way in the conscientious use of manuscript authorities, or in the divorce of history from modern politics, or in the search into the roots of character and action in the mental and moral attainments of each special period. It was Ranke's glory, not only to have pointed the way in all these matters, but in one respect to have reached an achievement which was all his own. No one else has been able to speak with equal authority on the history of so many nations. Grote wrote nothing on the history of Rome, Mommsen has written nothing on the history of Greece. Ranke was equally at home in the Germany of the Reformation, in the France of Louis XIV, and in the England of Charles I and Cromwell."

It can hardly be said to derogate from the peculiar character

and excellency of Von Ranke's work that he lived through the
most eventful period in the history of the world, and that the
state of Germany during his youth almost constrained him to
give his attention to the history of the other nations of Europe;
and it may have arisen as much from his circumstances as from
his temperament that he showed more interest in the doings
of statesmen than in the lives and characters of the actors in
the dramas whose progress he narrates. One advantage at
least results from his lack of enthusiasm, that he does not, like
Macaulay, write under the perpetual bias of political sentiment.
We can always follow him without the slightest fear of being
misled by the prejudices of the writer.

If Ranke had begun his historical investigations at a somewhat later period, his tone might have been different. The fall
of the great Napoleon took place when he was barely twenty
years of age, and he was nearly seventy-five when the second
Napoleon proclaimed war upon Prussia and gave occasion for
the foundation of the new German Empire. The greater part
of his historical work was accomplished in the interval between
these two events.

Ranke was born December 21, 1795, at Wiehe, a small town
of Thüringia, about twenty-seven miles from Merseburg, capital of the government of the same name in Prussian Saxony.
He studied at the Gymnasium of Schulpforta, and subsequently
at the University of Leipzig under the eminent Greek scholar
Hermann, by whom he was guided to the study of the historians of antiquity. On leaving the university in 1818, he was
made professor of history at the Gymnasium of Frankfort-
on-the-Oder, a position in which he was enabled to give the
greater part of his thoughts to the study of history, especially
to the latter part of the fifteenth century and to the sixteenth.
As a result of these studies, he published, in 1824, his first contributions to history, namely, a "History of the Latin and
Germanic Nations" ("Geschichte der romanischen und ger-
manischen Völker") and "Contributions to the Critical Study
of some Modern Historians" ("Kritik neuerer Geschicht-
schreiber"). In the latter work he laid down the true principles of historical composition, the scientific methods which
he was henceforth to inculcate by precept and example. It has
been remarked that these treatises are characterized by a certain

crudeness of style. Germans, as a people, have never greatly excelled in this respect, and German literature had had only a short life when Ranke began to write. It is, however, more worthy of note that, even in these earlier compositions, the historian already displayed the clearness of insight, the scientific instinct, the comprehensiveness of view which he never lost.

The first publications of Ranke were so remarkable, especially as being the work of a man living at a distance from great public libraries, that we cannot wonder that they soon came under the notice of the Minister of Public Education, who lost no time in appointing the author *Professor extraordinarius* in the University of Berlin (1825). In this new post he had much greater facilities for carrying on his historical studies and investigations. At Berlin, in the collection of the Royal Library, he discovered in manuscript the " Secret Relations of the Venetian Ambassadors," giving an account of their diplomatic missions to the various countries of Europe. Ranke immediately perceived the importance of these documents, and embodied much of their contents in a volume on the " Princes and Peoples of Southern Europe in the Sixteenth and Seventeenth Centuries" ("*Fürsten u. Völker von Südeuropa*"), published in 1827, and republished fifty years afterward under the title " The Ottomans and the Spanish Monarchy in the Sixteenth and Seventeenth Centuries." We can hardly overestimate the importance of the work of Ranke in bringing to the light documents hitherto concealed from the public eye. At the present day such collections are for the most part accessible to all students of history; and it is to Ranke more than anyone else that we are indebted for the change.

In 1827 he obtained the means of visiting some of the great libraries and depositories of documents in Southern Europe; so that he was able to spend four years in Venice, Vienna, Rome, and Florence, where he discovered much material available for future use. Returning to Berlin, he gave himself with great devotion to the duties of his chair, while he afforded proofs of the value of his researches in the South by several publications, among others a history of the Servian Revolution ("*Die serbische Revolution, 1829*"). One of his most important undertakings about this time was the " Historical and Political

Journal" ("*Historische-politische Zeitschrift*"), 1832–1836. In this review several valuable studies, on the different forms of government and other subjects, appeared, and were afterward republished in his collected works.

But the work which first gave Ranke his assured place among the great historians of the world was that which is presented in these volumes—"The Popes of Rome, their Church and State, in the Sixteenth and Seventeenth Centuries" ("*Die Romanischen Päbste, ihre Kirche und ihr Staat im XVI und XVII Jahrhundert*"), of which the first volume appeared in 1834 and the third and last in 1837. To this great work we shall presently return, so that here it may suffice to remark that the work was universally recognized as both adequate and impartial, so that it has been translated into the principal languages of Europe, and by three different translators into English. It is truly remarked by a French writer that never before had there proceeded from a Protestant pen an estimate so impartial of the political and religious situation of the epoch of the great crisis of the sixteenth and seventeenth centuries, a picture so striking of the part of the Catholic Church in those times of strife and trouble, or a description so intelligent and sagacious of all those pontiffs who occupied the Holy See during that period, from Leo X to Paul IV and Sixtus V. "It was," the writer remarks, "great history, written by a man who loved truth for itself, one who knew well the heart of man, and who was no less able to set forth, in artistic fashion, the discoveries of the scholar and the judgments of the moralist."

Soon afterward Ranke put forth the first volume of a work which in some measure was complementary to his "History of the Popes," the "History of Germany in the Time of the Reformation" ("*Deutsche Geschichte im Zeitalter der Reformation*"). The work extended to six volumes, published from 1839 to 1847. From this time, although individuals might prefer one or another of the historians of Germany, the general verdict gave to Ranke a place of supremacy among them. Men who were put forward as having a superior claim as historians are now almost forgotten. A whole school of historical writers has sprung from him. He is the father of Neander and Gieseler and of many more. The great Niebuhr gave him the first place; and Döllinger pronounced him to be "*Præceptor Germaniæ*."

The "History of the Popes," had made Ranke Ordinary Professor of history at Berlin, and in 1841 he became historiographer royal. In recognition of this honor he put forth a work of less interest, "Nine [afterward twelve] Books of Prussian History" (*"Neun Bücher preussischer Geschichte"*), in three volumes, 1847–1848. It will be remembered that this was not a time quite favorable for such a publication. This was followed by a history of France principally in the sixteenth and seventeenth centuries (*"Französische Geschichte vornehmlich im XVI und XVII Jahrhundert"*), in five volumes, 1852–1861. When it is remembered that this history covers the period of time that lies between Francis I and Louis XIV, the time of French supremacy in Europe, a supremacy gained by so many doubtful means, it will be understood how arduous and delicate was the task imposed upon himself by a German writer; yet it is confessed that Ranke has marshalled his facts and pronounced his judgments with a calmness and an impartiality which could hardly be excelled. Michelet speaks of it as a work beyond all praise.

The next important work of our historian was one in which English-speaking men and women, whether in Great Britain or in the Western Hemisphere, have a nearer and warmer interest. Ranke's "History of England principally in the Seventeenth Century" (*"Englische Geschichte vornehmlich im XVI und XVII Jahrhundert"*) was published in six volumes (1859–1867), and a later edition in nine (1870–1874). The author had thus taken up in turn the histories of Spain, of Italy, of France, of Germany, and of England, tracing the rise and development of those great nations and examining their mutual influence during the most critical periods of their history. If this great work lacks something of the vivacity of his earlier writings, it is not inferior to them in the vastness of the knowledge which it displays nor yet in the sagacity and fairness of its judgments.

When the last volume of his English history was published, Ranke was in his eightieth year, and might well have claimed the repose which he had so well earned. But he could not yet feel that his work was done, and so he began the issue of a series of treatises on German history intended as supplementary to his previous writings on this subject. Among these may merely be mentioned a " History of Germany between the Religious Peace and the Thirty Years' War " (1868), a " History of Wallenstein" (1869), "The German Powers and the League of Princes " (1872), " Contributions to the History of Austria and Prussia between the Treaties of Aachen and Hubertsburg " (1875), " The Origin and Beginning of the Revolutionary War " (1875), "The Memories of Hardenburg " (1877). But a still grander scheme hovered before the imagination of the aged historian. This was nothing less than the idea of a universal history.

The first volume of this great undertaking appeared in 1880, and year after year saw the appearance of a new volume, reaching to the number of twelve, when death cut short the work, May 23, 1886, while he was occupied with the Middle Ages. The work was not a history in the ordinary sense of the word: it was not a continuous narrative of events connected with particular countries or epochs. It was rather a commentary upon the history of the world and presupposed a considerable knowledge of facts on the part of the reader. It was a review of history by a great savant and a great thinker, who could cast his eye over the large area before him, and speak with the authority of knowledge and wisdom of the men and the events of the past, and give us out of his own fulness a true conception of the philosophy of history.

Few men have labored more assiduously, more devotedly than Ranke. Few men have been more loyal to the idea of life and work which they set before themselves. It may also be said that few men have obtained more generous recognition from their own age and from those in authority. From the government he received every kind of assistance, and by the royal family he was treated as an intimate friend. In 1865 he was raised to the nobility. In 1867 he was made a member of the Order of Merit, and in 1882 a privy councillor. In 1885 his ninetieth birthday was kept as a public holiday, while the Emperor visited him at his house and personally offered his congratulations.

An interesting account of the personal appearance of von Ranke is given by a writer in " Blackwood's Magazine " (August, 1886): "Long ago, about the time of the great war, I often met him, most commonly in the Thiergarten [in Berlin]; the small figure—he was not much over five feet—and the peculiarly finely poised head with the clear outline of the face, readily recognizable from afar. He had a curious old-fashioned way of saluting ladies, even out-of-doors, with a kiss on either cheek, after first asking permission in a formula which carried one back to Minna von Barnhelm and Chodowiecki's drawings. So kindly and so funny, too, it was. He was very small in stature, but few men have made such a majestic impression. The head was superb, finely chiselled, with a great arched forehead, exceedingly mobile lips, covered only during the last few years of his life by a long white beard, and very bright eyes, with an incessantly inquiring and keenly interested look. He seemed to send this look before him, to recognize and to welcome."—(Sophie Weisse.) The same writer tells us that she heard from Ranke of an American who had visited him and asked whether he expected to finish his great undertaking, the "*Weltgeschichte.*" "*Lieber Freund,*" said the great historian, "*ich glaube*"—and here with an implied religious faith—"*und wenn Gott will, dass ich mein werk vollende, so werde ich es vollenden.*" "Yes," he went on, "it is finished, the whole '*Weltgeschichte*' is finished here," touching his head; "but from one's head to the pen is a long way: so many a thing must be gone over again, many facts settled and confirmed, much elaborated [*ausgearbeitet*] as it should be." Being asked whether he did not enjoy his work, he replied: "My work? Oh, surely! It is my life. I live to work. As long as I live, I shall work"—with that magnificent upward look, says the writer, which those who have seen it will not readily forget.

Those who may wish for illustrations of the industry and insight, both almost superhuman, of the great historian, may safely be referred to a most valuable collection of historical and biographical essays ("*Historisch-biographische Studien*") published by him in 1877. These "Studies" deal with several subjects of great difficulty, and are not only monuments of the wonderful patience and perseverance of the antiquary, but are striking exemplifications of the penetrating intelligence of the historian. One example may here be noticed, as a specimen of the acuteness and insight of the historian in discerning the respective authority of historical testimony and solving a problem which had presented great difficulties to previous writers. We refer to the interview between Lorenzo de' Medici and Savonarola, when the former lay dying.

It is well known that two different accounts have been given of the incident, Roscoe and others preferring to follow the testimony of Politian, while Villari and others followed the two biographers of Savonarola, Pico della Mirandola, and Burlamacchi, both friends of the great Frate. The differences had reference to several points; for example, the way in which Savonarola came to visit the dying man at all. According to Roscoe, Savonarola almost forced his presence upon Lorenzo: according to the other side, Lorenzo sent and entreated him to come; and Savonarola reluctantly consented, being persuaded that no good result could be hoped for. Passing over the fact that Roscoe adds considerable details, not contained in his authorities, we note that there were various incidents in the accounts of the interview which could not be reconciled. For example, according to Pico and Burlamacchi, Savonarola demanded of Lorenzo that he should restore " liberty to his native country, as it was in the early days of Florence," and that Lorenzo, while ready to confess his faith in God and his need of divine mercy, and even to restore money which he had wrongfully taken away, resisted this attack upon the pride and ambition of his family, and angrily turned his back upon the friar, refusing to utter another word.

Writers who took the view most favorable to Savonarola had urged, first, that Politian was not present during the whole of the interview. In his letter describing the last days of Lorenzo's life, he states that he several times went into an adjoining chamber; and another witness asserts expressly that, " during the interview, the others left the room." Further, it has been urged that the facts generally must have been communicated by Savonarola himself to his biographers, while their account is intrinsically the more probable. On the whole, the weight of evidence seemed decidedly on the side of Savonarola. Yet the difficulties were so great that writers like Perrens and Milman took the other view, and this to a large extent on account of a passage in the narrative of Burlamacchi.

This writer relates that Lorenzo said he had three sins to confess, for which he asked absolution: the sack of Volterra; the money taken from the Monte delle Fanciulle, whereby a number of orphan girls were reduced to destitution; and the blood shed in punishing those who were implicated in the Pozzi conspiracy.

It has naturally been objected that these circumstances could not have been known without a violation of the secrecy of the confessional; and this was a difficulty not easily surmounted. But here, as in so many historical questions of difficulty, the genius of the historian triumphed. Previous writers had generally assumed that the biography of Burlamacchi, as coming from a member of the Dominican order, must be of greater authority than that of Pico. But Ranke shows conclusively that, if we follow the lead of Pico, most of the difficulties connected with the interview will disappear. In the first place the so-called confession of Lorenzo, recorded by Burlamacchi, falls away, having no place in the story told by Pico. In the second place, the account given by the latter presents no difficulties. It may be well to state the case in Ranke's own words (" *Studien*," s. 350):

" According to Pico, Savonarola declined to hear a formal confession from Lorenzo until he had satisfied him on three points. Above all he must have faith. Next he must restore the money provided as the dower for young girls, which he had appropriated, or else give orders to his heirs to do so. To the first Lorenzo consented, and he promised to take care for the second. Then, it is said, Savonarola brought forward the third point, he must restore her liberty to Florence. ' *Libertatem patriae restitue, ut in statu pristino Florentina respublica collocetur.*' All this is repeated by Burlamacchi, as follows: ' *e necessario che si restituisca Firenze in liberta e nel suo stato populare a uso di repubblica.*' But then he adds a statement which is inconsistent with the narrative of Pico into which he brings it: he represents Lorenzo as confessing three principal sins; referring to the testimony of trustworthy sureties. In this case, however, the testimony is not credible; for in such a case there would be a violation of the secrecy of the confessional. The incident, therefore, as reported by Burlamacchi, is impossible. But there is no such impossibility in

the narrative of Pico. It is quite consistent with what Politian
says, namely, that he exhorted Lorenzo to a virtuous life, to
which it is quite natural that other particulars should be added
of which Politian was not aware; and Savonarola might speak
of such exhortations as were not connected with a regular confession. Even in this view many difficulties remain; and I do
not put forward these suggestions as a complete solution. It
is clear, however, that Pico hands on the original tradition as
it was held by the followers of the Frate, whereas in Burlamacchi there is much that is fabulous and impossible."

Here is an example of careful investigation and penetrating
historical criticism which may be regarded as a model by all
laboring in the same field. It may be mentioned, in regard
to this particular case, that Dr. Bass Mullinger, Professor
of history in the University of Cambridge, who had previously
followed Milman here, after reading von Ranke's essay, declared, in a letter to the present writer, that it was conclusive
in regard to this particular incident, and especially in regard
to the respective merits of the biographers of Savonarola.

And now, turning to the great work before us, the " History
of the Popes, their Church and State; and especially their
conflicts with Protestantism in the Sixteenth and Seventeenth
Centuries," it is obvious to remark that the book, which is
admirably written and well translated, will here tell its own
story. Moreover, its moral has been set forth in the brilliant
pages of Macaulay, in his well known essay on " Von Ranke."
As this essay is within the easy reach of all, we will make
only two extracts from it. In the first place we have Macaulay's judgment of the characteristic merits of this history. It
" is known and esteemed," he says, " wherever German literature is studied, and has been found interesting in a most inac-
curate and dishonest French version. It is indeed the work
of a mind fitted both for minute researches and for large speculations. It is written also in an admirable spirit, equally remote from levity and bigotry, serious and earnest, yet tolerant
and impartial." So much for the general historical character
of the book.

The special teaching of the history is pointed out with equal
force and precision. Macaulay states it in this fashion: " The
subject of this book has always appeared to us singularly in-

esting. How it was that Protestantism did so much, yet did
more, how it was that the Church of Rome, having lost a
ge part of Europe, not only ceased to lose, but actually re-
ned nearly half of what she had lost, is certainly a most
ious and important question ; and on this question Professor
nke has thrown far more light than any other person who
 written on it." This is high praise, and we are not aware
t any critic has ever called it in question.
In regard to the papacy, Ranke struck the true historical
e near the beginning of his history. Speaking of the proc-
 by which the Church came to be constituted on the model
the empire, he remarks : " No long time had elapsed before
 bishops of Rome acquired the supremacy. It is indeed a
n pretence to assert that this supremacy was universally
cnowledged by East and West, even in the first century, or,
leed, at any time, but it is equally certain that they quickly
ned a pre-eminence, raising them far above other ecclesi-
ical dignitaries." So far we discern the calm judgment of
 impartial historian, simply desirous of ascertaining and
ting the truth.
Equally fair and accurate is his statement of the causes which
oduced the state of things in which the Roman pontiffs bene supreme. " Many causes concurred to secure them this
sition; for if the relative importance of each provincial
oital secured to its bishop a corresponding weight and dig-
y, how much more certainly would this result take place as
garded the ancient capital of the empire, that city whence
 whole had derived its name? Rome was, besides, one of
 most illustrious seats of the apostles [if by that the author
ans sees, the seat of an episcopate, we must hesitate to fol-
v him] ; here had the greater number of the martyrs shed
eir blood. The bishops of Rome had displayed the most
daunted firmness throughout the different persecutions, and
d sometimes been scarcely installed in their sacred office be-
e they followed their predecessor in the path of that martyr-
m by which his seat had been vacated." It is an admirable
atement of the process by which the bishops of Rome rose
 their proud pre-eminence in the Church of Christ; and if
e story has now become familiar to us, it is perhaps owing
 Ranke more than to any other writer that it has become so.

Equally excellent is his sketch of the relation of the papacy
to the empire during the Middle Ages.

It is, however, when the historian reaches the period to which
his volumes are specially devoted that we recognize the fulness
of his knowledge, the firmness of his grasp, and his great
power of presentation, by which he sets before us the successive stages in the history of the Church; on the one hand
bringing out the essential character of the period and of the
men who determined the direction of events; on the other
furnishing such details in the life and work of men as lend a
living interest to the story which he narrates. And everywhere we remark the same calm spirit of loyalty to the truth
of history, without a leaning in favor of the side he would
himself espouse or any indication of antagonism to that which
he would condemn. Whether he tells of the great advances
made by the Reformation in its earlier periods, or of the reaction in the Counter-Reformation, when Rome won back much
of that which she had lost, it is the historian that is speaking,
not the partisan.

This is remarkable in Ranke's dealing with the popes. Even
Alexander VI is treated with a kind of courtesy while the plain
truth is told about him. Leo X, the " elegant pagan Pope,"
as Carlyle called him, has full justice done to him, although the
widest charity could hardly speak of him as a Christian in
faith or practice. Some of the popes that follow evoke a keener
interest, but all stand before us as living men whom we know,
and who, we feel sure, are represented to us as they lived,
nothing extenuated, nor aught set down in malice.

Not less remarkable and commendable are those passages
which tell of the relations of the papacy to foreign countries,
of the terrible invasion of Italy, for example, by the German
armies of Charles V, and the sack of Rome, when " the bloodthirsty soldiery, hardened by long privations and rendered savage by their trade, burst over the devoted city." The result
of this terrible invasion is told in a few words which stamp
themselves upon the memory. " How vivid a lustre was cast
over the beginning of the sixteenth century by the splendor
of Rome: it designates a period most influential in the development of the human mind. This day saw the light of that
splendor extinguished forever."

No less striking is the brief but relatively complete account
ven of the loss of England under Elizabeth to the papacy.
fter speaking of the violent and impolitic conduct of Paul
", he adds, " Thus had Elizabeth not been disposed to the
inion of the Protestants, the force of her circumstances would
ve compelled her to adopt that party." In reference to this
d other imprudences of the papacy, the author remarks:
We are warranted in declaring that the popedom seemed
stined to suffer no injury to which it had not itself conduced,
one way or another, by its tendency to interference in polit-
al affairs." As a result of the aggressions of the reforming
rty and the unwisdom of Rome, he remarks: "And now,
we survey the world from the heights of Rome, how enor-
ous were the losses sustained by the Catholic faith! Scandi-
via and Great Britain had wholly departed; Germany was
most entirely Protestant; Poland and Hungary were in fierce
mult of opinion; in Geneva was to be found as important a
ntral point for the schismatics of the Latin nations and of
e West, as was Wittenberg for those of Germanic race and
e East, while numbers were already gathering beneath the
nners of Protestantism in France and the Netherlands."
It seemed as though victory were assured to the Protestant
ith and Europe were lost to Rome. But the history before
s tells another tale. It would be interesting to linger here
ver the pages in which Ranke tells of the means whereby the
de of conquest was rolled back, how practical abuses were met
d remedied by the great Council of Trent; how the mighty
ciety founded by Loyola brought help and strength to the
avering armies of Rome; how Austria, to her own great and
reparable loss, crushed the growing spirit of reform within
er borders, and helped to desolate Germany at large in the
hirty Years' War; how France, at one time almost a reformed
untry, underwent reaction and finally drove some of her
oblest sons, because they were Protestants, from her borders;
d how the endless divisions and conflicts among the Prot-
stants themselves furnished arms to their adversaries and
eakened their own power of aggression, but these things will
e found told in the pages before us; and it is our present busi-
ess to assure the reader that he will not find the details of the
tory wearisome, uninteresting, or uninstructive.

To those who are familiar with other historical writings treating of the same period, it will be a matter of astonishment to observe how little Ranke owes to those who had gone before him, and how little is added to his representation of the subject by those who have come after him. It has often been said that Ranke was the founder of a school, the initiator of a method, in history; and the statement is hardly too strong. At least it is a true verdict which declares that he has here given us history, and not the personal feelings of a partisan, and that he has given us not only history, but literature, showing that the noble language which he wielded was adapted, not merely for setting forth the investigations of science and the speculations of philosophy, but also for clothing human thought and historical facts in garments of grace and beauty.

William Clarke

RANKE'S INTRODUCTION

THE power of Rome in the early and Middle Ages is universally known: in modern times, also, she has exercised renewed influence over the world. After the decline of her importance, in the first half of the sixteenth century, she once more raised herself to be the centre of faith and opinion to the Romanic nations of southern Europe, and made bold, and often successful, attempts to recover her dominion over those of the North.

This period of a revived church-temporal power—its renovation and internal development—its progress and decline—it is my purpose to describe, at least in outline; an undertaking which, however imperfectly it may be performed, could never have been attempted, had I not found opportunity to avail myself of certain materials hitherto unknown. My first duty is to give a general indication of these materials and their sources.

In an earlier work* I have already stated the contents of our Berlin MSS.; but Vienna is incomparably richer than Berlin in treasures of this kind.

Besides its essentially German character, Vienna possesses also an element more extensively European: the most diversified manners and languages meet in all classes, from the highest to the lowest, and Italy in particular is fully and vividly represented. Even the collections in this city present a comprehensiveness of character, attributable to the policy of the state and its geographical position; its ancient connection with Spain, Belgium, and Lombardy; and its proximity to and ecclesiastical relations with Rome. The Viennese have from the earliest times displayed a taste for collecting, possessing, and preserving; whence it arises that even the original and purely national collections of the imperial library are of great value: to these, various foreign collections have since been added. A number of volumes similar to the Berlin *Informazioni* were purchased

*In the Preface to the "Ottoman and Spanish Empires in the Sixteenth and Seventeenth Centuries."

at Modena, from the house of Rangone; from Venice were acquired the invaluable manuscripts of the Doge Marco Foscarini; including his materials for a continuation of his literary undertaking, the " Italian Chronicles," of which no trace is elsewhere to be found; and the bequest of Prince Eugene added a rich collection of historical and political manuscripts, which had been formed, with comprehensive judgment, by that distinguished statesman. The reader is animated by feelings of pleasure and hope, on examining the catalogues, and perceiving the many unexplored sources of knowledge that will enable him to supply the deficiencies manifest in almost all printed works of modern history. A whole futurity of study! And at the distance of a few steps only, Vienna presents literary subsidies still more important. The imperial archives contain, as might be expected, the most authentic and valuable records for the elucidation of German, and general, but particularly of Italian history. It is true that the greater part of the Venetian archives have been restored, after many wanderings, to Venice; but there still remains in Vienna a mass of Venetian manuscripts far from unimportant; despatches, original or copied, and abstracts thereof made for the use of the State, and called " Rubricaries;" reports which, in many instances, are the only copies extant; official registers of public functionaries, chronicles, and diaries. The notices to be found in the present volumes, relating to Gregory XIII and Sixtus V, are for the most part derived from the archives of Vienna. I cannot sufficiently acknowledge the unconditional liberality with which I was permitted to have access to these treasures.

And perhaps I ought here to particularize the many and various aids afforded me in furtherance of my attempt, both at home and abroad, but I feel restrained by a scruple (whether well-founded or not, I am unable to decide), that I should have to mention so many names, some of them of great eminence, as would give my gratitude the appearance of vain-glory; and a work, which has every reason to present itself modestly, might assume an air of ostentation ill suited to its pretensions.

Next to Vienna, my attention was principally directed to Venice and Rome.

It was formerly the almost invariable practice of great houses in Venice to form a cabinet of manuscripts, as an adjunct to

the library. It was in the nature of things that these would
relate principally to the affairs of the republic. They served
to show the part taken by the respective families in public affairs, and were preserved as records and memorials of the
house, for the instruction of its younger members. Some of
these private collections still remain, and I had access to several;
but much the larger number were destroyed in the general ruin
of 1797, or since. If more have been preserved than might
have been expected, the gratitude of the world is due chiefly
to the librarians of St. Mark, who labored to save, from the
universal wreck, whatever the utmost resources of their institution would permit them to secure. Accordingly this library
possesses a considerable store of manuscripts, indispensable to
the history of the city and State, and which are even valuable
aids toward that of Europe. But the inquirer must not expect too much from it: it is a somewhat recent acquisition;
gathered, almost at hazard, from private collections; incomplete and without unity of plan. It is not to be compared with
the riches of the State archives, especially as these are now arranged. I have already given a sketch of the Venetian archives, in my inquiry into the conspiracy of 1618, and will not
repeat what I there said. For my Roman investigations, the
reports of the ambassadors returning from Rome, were above
all desirable; but I had great reason to wish for assistance from
other collections, because none are free from *lacunæ*, and these
archives must necessarily have sustained losses in their many
wanderings. In different places I gathered together forty-
eight reports relating to Rome: the oldest dating from the year
1500; nineteen of the sixteenth, twenty-one of the seventeenth
century; these formed an almost complete series, having only a
few breaks here and there. Of the eighteenth century there
were, it is true, only eight, but these, too, were very instructive
and welcome. In the majority of cases I saw and used the originals. They contain a great number of interesting notices, the
results of personal observation, which had passed out of memory with the generation. It was from these that I first derived the idea of a continued narrative, and these also inspired
me with courage to attempt it.

It will be obvious that Rome alone could supply the means
for verifying and extending these materials.

But was it to be expected that a foreigner, and one professing a different faith, would there be permitted to have free access to the public collections, for the purpose of revealing the secrets of the papacy? This would not perhaps have been so ill-advised as it may appear, since no search can bring to light anything worse than what is already assumed by unfounded conjecture, and received by the world as established truth. But I cannot boast of having had any such permission. I was enabled to take cognizance of the treasures contained in the Vatican, and to use a number of volumes suited to my purpose; but the freedom of access which I could have wished was by no means accorded. Fortunately, however, other collections were thrown open to me, from which I could acquire information, which, if not complete, was very extensive and authentic. In the flourishing times of aristocracy, more particularly in the seventeenth century, it was customary throughout Europe for the great families, who had administered the affairs of state, to retain possession of some of the public documents. This practice prevailed in Rome to a greater extent, perhaps, than in any other State. The reigning kinsmen of the pontiff, who in all ages exercised considerable power, usually bequeathed as an heir-loom to the princely houses they founded, a large part of the state papers accumulated during their administration. These constituted a part of the family endowments. In the palaces which they erected, a few rooms, usually in the upper part of the building, were always reserved for books and manuscripts, which each succeeding generation contributed to enrich. Thus, to a certain extent the private collections of Rome may be regarded as the public ones, as the archives of state were dispersed among the descendants of reigning houses, without any objection being made to the practice; much in the same manner as the redundancy of public wealth was suffered to flow into the coffers of the papal kindred, and certain private galleries, such as the Borghese or Doria, became greatly superior to the Vatican, both in extent and historical importance, though the latter is distinguished by its selection of masterpieces. The manuscripts which are preserved in the Barberini, Chigi, Altieri, Albani, and Corsini palaces, are accordingly of inestimable value, for the aid they give toward a history of the popes, their State and Church. The

state-paper office, recently established, is particularly important
for its collection of registers illustrative of the Middle Ages;
which, as regards that period, will still repay the inquirer; but,
so far as my knowledge extends, I do not believe that much is to
be gained from it for later centuries. Its value sinks into insignificance, unless I have been purposely deceived, when compared with the wealth and magnificence of private collections.
Each of these comprises, as may be readily supposed, that epoch
in which the pope of the family reigned; but as the kindred of
each pontiff usually retained an eminent station; as men are in
general desirous of extending and completing a collection once
begun, and as opportunities were frequent in Rome, from the
literary traffic in manuscripts established there; so the whole
of these private collections possess many valuable documents il-
lustrating other periods, both proximate and remote. The richest of all (in consequence of important bequests), is the Barberini; that of the Corsini Palace has been remarkable from
its commencement for the care and judgment with which it has
been formed. I was fortunately permitted to use all these collections, as well as others of less importance; and in some instances with unrestricted freedom. An unhoped-for harvest
of authentic and suitable materials thus lay before me. As
for example, correspondences of the nuncios *(nunciaturæ)*,
with the instructions given to them, and the reports which were
brought back; circumstantial biographies of different popes,
written with the more freedom, because not intended for the
public; lives of distinguished cardinals; official and private
journals; investigations of particular circumstances and transactions; special opinions and deliberations; reports on the administration of the provinces, their trade and manufactures;
statistical tables, and accounts of receipts and disbursements.
These documents, for the most part entirely unknown, were
prepared by men practically acquainted with their subject, and
of a credibility which, though it does not supersede the necessity for a searching and critical examination, is equal to that
usually accorded to the testimony of well-informed contemporaries. The oldest of these MSS. of which I made use, related to the conspiracy of the Porcari against Nicholas V. Of
the fifteenth century I met with only a few; but on entering the
sixteenth, they became more numerous and more comprehensive

at every step. Though the whole course of the seventeenth century, during which so little is known with certainty respecting Rome, they afford information, the more valuable because of its previous dearth. After the commencement of the eighteenth century, they decrease in number and intrinsic value; but at that time the Roman State and court had already lost much of their influence and importance. I will go through those Roman MSS., as well as the Venetian, in detail, at the end of the work, and will there note, whatever I may find deserving attention, and which I could not well introduce in the course of the narrative. The large mass of materials, both manuscript and printed, which are lying before me, renders a stringent condensation indispensable.

An Italian or Roman, a Catholic, would enter on the subject in a spirit very different from mine. By indulging in expressions of personal veneration, or, perhaps, in the present state of opinion, of personal hatred, he would give to his work a peculiar, and, no doubt, more brilliant coloring; on many points he would be more elaborate, more ecclesiastical, more local. In these respects, a Protestant, a North German, cannot be expected to compete with him. He regards the papal power with feelings of more indifference; and must, from the first, renounce that warmth of expression which arises from partiality or hostility; and which might, perhaps, produce a certain impression in Europe. For mere matters of ecclesiastical or canonical detail, we can have no true sympathy; on the other hand, our position affords us different, and, if I am not mistaken, purer and less partial views of history.* For what is there in the present day that can make the history of the papal power of importance to us? Not its particular relation to ourselves; for it no longer exercises any essential influence, nor does it create in us solicitude of any kind; the times are past in which we had anything to fear; we now feel ourselves perfectly secure. Popery can now inspire us with no other interest than what results from the development of its history and its former influence.

The papal power was, however, not so unchangeable as is commonly supposed. If we consider the question apart from

* Nor has any change been produced in this respect by the events that have occurred since the first edition of this work was published. The author, on reviewing it, has found occasion for only slight additions and alterations, which in no wise affect the essentials of the subject.

those principles upon which its existence depends, and which it cannot abandon without consigning itself to destruction, we shall find it affected, quite as deeply as any other government, and to the very essence of its being, by the various destinies to which the nations of Europe have been subjected. As the history of the world has varied; as one nation or another has gained the ascendancy; as the fabric of social life has been disturbed; so also has the papal power been affected: its maxims, its objects, and its pretensions, have undergone essential changes; and its influence, above all, has been subjected to the greatest variations. If we cast a glance at the long catalogue of names so frequently repeated through successive ages, from Pius I in the second century, to our contemporaries, Pius VII and VIII in the nineteenth, we receive an impression of uninterrupted stability; but we must not permit ourselves to be misled by the semblance of constancy. The popes of different periods are, in fact, distinguished by differences as strongly marked as those existing between the various dynasties of a kingdom. To us, who are lookers-on at a distance, it is precisely these mutations that present the most interesting subject of contemplation. We see in them a portion of the history of the world, and of the general progress of mankind; and this is true, not only of periods when Rome held undisputed sovereignty, but also, and perhaps even more remarkably, of those shaken by the conflicting forces of action and counter-action, such as the times which the present work is intended to comprise—the sixteenth and seventeenth centuries;—times when the papacy was menaced and endangered, yet maintained and fortified itself; nay, even re-extended its influence; striding onward for a period, but at last receding again, and tottering to its fall; times when the mind of the Western nations was pre-eminently occupied by ecclesiastical questions; and when that power, which, abandoned and assailed by one party, was upheld and defended with fresh zeal by the other, necessarily assumed a station of high and universal importance. It is from this point of view that our natural position invites us to consider it, and this I will now attempt.

I think it appropriate to commence by recalling to the memory of my reader the situation of the papal power in the beginning of the sixteenth century, and the course of events which led thereto.

CONTENTS

BOOK I

CHAPTER I

EPOCHS OF THE PAPACY

CHAPTER II

THE CHURCH AND HER TERRITORIES IN THE BEGINNING OF THE SIXTEENTH CENTURY

CHAPTER III

POLITICAL COMPLICATIONS—CONNECTION BETWEEN THESE AND THE REFORMATION

BOOK II

BEGINNING OF A REGENERATION OF CATHOLICISM

xxvi CONTENTS

ILLUSTRATIONS

THE HISTORY OF THE POPES

BOOKS I, II, III AND IV

THE HISTORY OF THE POPES

BOOK I

CHAPTER FIRST

EPOCHS OF THE PAPACY. A.D. 1–1500

Section I.—Christianity in the Roman Empire

IF we examine the condition of the ancient world in its earlier ages, we find it occupied by a great number of independent communities. Seated along the shores of the Mediterranean, and extending themselves inland, so far as their knowledge of the country permitted, they dwelt divided into various tribes, all originally confined within very narrow limits, but all purely free, and each possessing its own peculiar character and institutions. The independence enjoyed by these communities was not merely political; an independent religion also had been established by each: the ideas of God and of divine things had received a character strictly local; deities of the most diversified attributes divided the worship of the world, and the law by which their votaries were governed became inseparably united with that of the state. We may safely declare that this intimate union of church and state, this twofold freedom, limited only by the light obligations arising from identity of race, had the most important share in the civilization of the early ages. Each community was indeed surrounded by narrow limits, but within these the rich fulness of the world's vigorous youth found space to develop itself according to its own unfettered impulse.

How entirely was all this changed as the might of Rome

arose! All the self-governing powers that had previously filled the world are seen to bend one after the other, and finally to disappear. How suddenly did the earth become desolated of her free nations!

In later times, empires have been shaken because religion had lost its power of control. In those days the subjugation of the state necessarily involved the downfall of the national religion. Impelled by the political power, believers in every creed would draw toward Rome; but what significance could remain to these peculiar forms of belief, once torn from the soil whence they had derived their birth? The worship of Isis was doubtless intelligible in Egypt, where it deified the powers of nature, as manifested in those regions. In Rome this worship became a senseless idolatry. No sooner did the various mythologies come in contact than their mutual destruction ensued: it was impossible to discover any theory capable of reconciling their contradictions.

But even had this been possible, it would no longer have sufficed to the necessities of the world.

However deeply we may sympathize with the fall of so many free states, we cannot fail to perceive that a new life sprang immediately from their ruins. With the overthrow of independence fell the barriers of all exclusive nationalities: the nations were conquered—they were overwhelmed together; but by that very act were they blended and united; for, as the limits of the empire were held to comprise the whole earth, so did its subjects learn to consider themselves as one people. From this moment the human family began to acquire the consciousness of its universal brotherhood.

It was at this period of the world's development that Jesus Christ was born.

How obscure and unpretending was his life! His occupation was to heal the sick and to discourse of God in parables with a few fishermen, who did not always understand his words. He had not where to lay his head. Yet, even from the worldly point of view whence we consider it, we may safely assert that nothing more guileless or more impressive, more exalted or more holy, has ever been seen on earth than were his life, his whole conversation, and his death. In his every word there breathes the pure spirit of God. They are words, as St. Peter has expressed it, of eternal life. The records of humanity present nothing that can be compared, however remotely, with the life of Jesus.

If the earlier forms of belief had ever contained an element of true religion, this was now entirely obscured; they no longer, as we have said, could pretend to the slightest significance. In Him who united the nature of man with that of God, there shone forth, in contrast with these shadows, the universal and eternal relation of God to the world, and of man to God.

Jesus Christ was born among a people broadly separated and distinguished from all others by ritual laws of rigid and exclusive severity, but which also possessed the inappreciable merit of holding steadfastly to that worship of the one true God in which they had persisted from their earliest existence, and from which no power could sever them. It is true that they considered this monotheism as a national worship only, but it was now to receive a much wider significance. Christ abolished the law by fulfilling it; the Son of Man declared himself Lord also of the Sabbath, and rendered manifest the eternal import of those forms, which a narrow understanding had as yet but imperfectly comprehended. Thus, from the bosom of a people hitherto separated by insurmountable barriers of opinion and customs from every other, there arose, with all the force of truth, a faith which invited and received all men. The Universal Father was now proclaimed—that God, who, as St. Paul declared to the Athenians, "hath made of one blood all nations of men for to dwell on all the face of the earth." For this sublime doctrine, the moment, as we have seen, had now arrived—a race of men existed who could appreciate its value. "Like a sunbeam," says Eusebius, "it streamed over the face of the earth."[1] Its beneficent influence was quickly seen extending from the Euphrates to the Ebro, and overflowing the wide limits of the empire even to the Rhine and the Danube.

But however pure and blameless the religion of Christ, it was not in the nature of things that it should escape opposition from the creeds already established. These had entwined themselves with the habits and wants of daily life; they were bound up with all the old memories of the world; and had, be-

[1] "Hist. Eccl." ii. 3.

side, now received a certain modification which had brought them into harmony with the constitution of the empire.

The political spirit of the ancient religions displayed itself once again under a new aspect. All those self-governing powers that had once filled the world had become absorbed into one concentrated whole. There remained but one sole power that could be called self-dependent; religion acknowledged this when she decreed divine worship to the Emperor. To him temples were built and sacrifices offered, vows were made in his name, and festivals were solemnized in his honor, his statues gave the sacredness of a sanctuary to the place where they stood. The worship men paid to the genius of the Emperor was perhaps the only one common to the whole empire;[2] all idolatries accommodated themselves to this, for to all it offered countenance and support.

This worship of the Cæsar and the doctrines taught by Christ had a certain resemblance when viewed with relation to the various local religions, but they nevertheless presented the strongest possible contrast with each other.

The Emperor conceived religion in its most worldly aspect only, as bound to earth and the things of earth. "To him be these surrendered," says Celsus; "whatever each man possesses, let it come from him." Christianity regarded religion in the fulness of the spirit, and of superhuman truth.

The Emperor united Church and State: Christianity separated, before all things, that which is Cæsar's from that which belongs to God.

The offering of sacrifice to the Emperor was an acknowledgment of the most abject thraldom. In that very union of Church and State wherein consisted the perfection of independence under the self-governing powers, might now be found the seal and completion of man's subjection: thus the prohibition of this worship by Christianity was an act of emancipation. Finally, the adoration paid to the Emperor was restricted by the limits of the empire—then believed to comprise the whole earth—while the true faith was destined to reach to the world's real limits, and to embrace the whole human family. Christianity sought to reawaken the primitive consciousness of religious

[2] Eckkel, "Doctrina Nummorum Veterum," pt. ii. vol. viii. p. 456; he quotes a passage from Tertullian, whence it would appear that the worship of the emperor was sometimes more earnest than any other.

ruth (if it be granted that such consciousness preceded all idol-tries), or, at least, to infuse a belief complete in its purity, obscured by no inevitable connection with the state, and opposed to the exactions of that all-grasping power which, not content with earthly dominion, was seeking to extend its influence over things divine also. It was from Christianity that man derived the spiritual element wherein he could once again become self-sustaining, free, and personally invincible; a new vitality awoke in the bosom of the freshened earth, she became ructified for the development of new productions.

At this moment was exhibited the contrast between the earthly and the spiritual, between freedom and servitude—a gradual decay and a life-breathing and vigorous renovation.

It is not here that we can describe the long struggle between these opposing principles: all the elements of life throughout the Roman Empire became involved in the movement—all were gradually penetrated and influenced by the essential truth of Christianity, and were borne forward by this great effort of the spirit. "By its own act," says Chrysostom, "has the error of idolatry been extinguished;" already did Paganism appear to him as a conquered city, whose walls were beaten down, whose walls, theatres, and public buildings had been destroyed by fire, whose defenders had fallen by the sword, and among whose ruins remained only old men or helpless children. These, too, were soon dispersed, and a change without example ensued.

From the depths of the catacombs uprose the adoration of the martyrs. On those sites where the gods of Olympus had been worshipped—on the very columns that had supported their temples, were shrines erected to the memory of those who had rejected their divinity, and died for refusing to yield them worship. The religion of Christ, coming forth from the desert and the dungeon, took possession of the world. We sometimes feel astonished that precisely a secular building of the heathen, the basilica, should have been converted to the purposes of Christian worship: but in this fact there is a remarkable significance—the apsis of the basilica contained an Augusteum,[3] the assembled statues of such emperors as had received divine worship. These were replaced by the images of Christ and his apostles, as they are seen in many basilicas to the present day.

[3] I take this fact from E. Q. Visconti, "Museo Pio Clementino."

The rulers of the world, themselves considered as deities, gave place to the Son of God arrayed in the nature of man. The local deities passed away, and were seen no more. In every highway, on the steep summits of the hills, in the deep ravines and remote valleys, on the roofs of houses, and in the mosaic of the floors was seen the cross: the victory was complete and decisive. As, on the coins of Constantine, the labarum, with the monogram of Christ, is seen to rise above the conquered dragon, so did the worship and name of Jesus exalt themselves over the vanquished gods of heathenism.

Considered in this aspect also, how all-embracing is the influence—how immense the importance of the Roman Empire! In the ages of its elevation all nations were subjugated, all independence destroyed by its power; the feeling of self-reliance, resulting from the division of interests, was annihilated: but, on the other hand, its later years beheld the true religion awake in its bosom—the purest expression of a common consciousness extending far beyond its limits—the consciousness of a community in the one true God. May we not venture to say, that by this development the empire had fulfilled her destiny—that she had rendered her own existence no longer necessary? The human race had acquired the knowledge of its true nature; religion had revealed the common brotherhood of mankind.

This religion now received from the Roman Empire its external forms also.

Among the heathens, sacerdotal offices were conferred in like manner with those of civil life: the Jews set apart a particular tribe for the duties of the priesthood; but Christianity was distinguished from both these by the fact that a certain class of men, freely choosing the sacred profession, consecrated by the imposition of hands, and withdrawn from worldly cares and pursuits, is solemnly devoted " to things spiritual and divine." The Church was at first governed in accordance with republican forms; but these disappeared as the new belief rose to preeminence, and the clergy gradually assumed a position entirely distinct from that of the laity.

This did not take place, as I think, without a certain innate necessity. The advance of Christianity involved an emancipation of religion from all political elements, and this was inevitably followed by the establishment of a distinct ecclesiastical body, with a constitution peculiar to itself. In this separation of the Church from the State consists, perhaps, the most important and most effectually influential peculiarity of Christian times. The spiritual and temporal powers may come into close contact—they may remain in the most intimate communion; but a perfect coalition can only take place occasionally, and for short periods of time. In their reciprocal relations and position with regard to each other, has since then been involved one of the most important questions presented by all history.

It was nevertheless imperative on the ecclesiastical body to form their constitution on the model of that of the empire; and accordingly, the hierarchy of the bishops—metropolitan patriarchs—was formed in close correspondence with the gradations of the civil power. No long time had elapsed before the bishops of Rome acquired the supremacy. It is, indeed, a vain pretence to assert that this supremacy was universally acknowledged by East and West, even in the first century, or, indeed, at any time; but it is equally certain that they quickly gained a pre-eminence, raising them far above all other ecclesiastical dignitaries. Many causes concurred to secure them this position; for, if the relative importance of each provincial capital secured to its bishop a corresponding weight and dignity, how much more certainly would this result take place as regarded the ancient capital of the empire—that city whence the whole had derived its name?[4] Rome was, besides, one of the most illustrious seats of the apostles: here had the greater number of the martyrs shed their blood. The bishops of Rome had displayed the most undaunted firmness throughout the different persecutions, and had sometimes been scarcely installed into their sacred office before they followed their predecessor in the path of that martyrdom by which his seat had been vacated. In addition to all this, the emperors now found it advisable to favor the advancement of a great patriarchal authority. In a law that became decisive for the predominance of Rome as well as of Christianity, Theodosius the Great commands that all nations claiming the protection of his grace should receive the faith as propounded by St. Peter to the Romans.[5] Valentinian

[4] " Casauboni Exercitationes ad Annales Ecclesiasticos Baronii," p. 260.
[5] Codex Theodos. xvi. 1, 2: " All nations governed by our gentle clemency shall remain in that religion which the divine apostle Peter declares himself to have delivered to the Romans." Planck also mentions the edict of Valentinian III.

also forbade the bishops, whether of Gaul or of other provinces, to depart from the received customs of the Church without the sanction of that venerable man, the Pope of the Holy City. Thenceforth the power of the Roman bishops advanced beneath the protection of the Emperor himself; but in this political connection lay also a restrictive force: had there been but one emperor, a universal primacy might also have established itself; but this was prevented by the partition of the empire. The emperors of the East were too eagerly tenacious of their ecclesiastical rights to make it possible that they should promote that extension of power desired by the western patriarchs in their dominions. In this respect also the constitution of the Church presents the closest resemblance to that of the empire.

Section II.—The Papacy in Connection with the Frankish Empire

Scarcely was this great change completed, the Christian religion established, and the Church founded, when new events of great importance took place; the Roman Empire, so long conquering and paramount, was now to see itself assailed by its neighbors: in its turn it was invaded and overcome.

Amidst the general convulsion that ensued, Christianity itself received a violent shock. In their terror, the Romans bethought themselves once more of the Etruscan mysteries, the Athenians hoped to be saved by Achilles and Minerva, the Carthaginians offered prayers to the genius Cœlestis; but these were only temporary waverings, for even whilst the empire was shattered in the Western provinces, the Church remained firm and undisturbed throughout all.

But she fell, as was inevitable, into many embarrassments, and found herself in an entirely altered condition. A pagan people took possession of Britain; Arian kings seized the greater part of the remaining West; while the Lombards, long attached to Arianism, and, as neighbors, most dangerous and hostile, established a powerful sovereignty before the very gates of Rome.

The Roman bishops meanwhile, beset on all sides, exerted themselves, with all the prudence and pertinacity which have

remained their peculiar attributes, to regain the mastery—at
least in their ancient patriarchal diocese; but a new and still
heavier calamity now assailed them. The Arabs—not conquerors merely, as were the Germans; but men inspired even
to fanaticism by an arrogant and dogmatizing creed, in direct
opposition to the Christian faith—now poured themselves over
the West as they had previously done over the East. After
repeated attacks, they gained possession of Africa: one battle
made them masters of Spain, their general, Musa, boasting that
he would march into Italy by the passes of the Pyrenees and
across the Alps, and cause the name of Mahomet to be proclaimed from the Vatican.

This position was all the more perilous for the western portion
of Roman Christendom, from the fact that the iconoclastic dissensions were at that moment raging with the most deadly animosity on both sides. The Emperor of Constantinople had
adopted the opposite party to that favored by the Pope of
Rome; nay, the life of the latter was more than once in danger
from the Emperor's machinations. The Lombards did not fail
to perceive the advantages derivable to themselves from these
dissensions; their King, Astolphus, took possession of provinces
that till then had always acknowledged the dominion of the
Emperor, and again advancing toward Rome, he summoned
that city also to surrender, demanding payment of tribute with
vehement threats.[1]

The Roman See was at this moment in no condition to help
itself, even against the Lombards; still less could it hope to
contend with the Arabs, who were beginning to extend their
sovereignty over the Mediterranean, and were threatening all
Christendom with a war of extermination.

Happily, the true faith was no longer confined within the
limits of the Roman Empire.

Christianity, in accordance with its original destiny, had long
overpassed these limits—more especially had it taken deep root
among the German tribes of the West; nay, a Christian power
had already arisen among these tribes, and toward this the
Pope had but to stretch forth his hands, when he was sure to

[1] Anastasius Bibliothecarius: "Vitæ Pontificum. Vita Stephani III." ed. Paris, p. 83. Furious as a lion, he desisted not from pouring forth deadly threats against the Romans, affirming that all should be destroyed by the sword unless they submitted themselves to his rule.

find the most effectual succor and earnest allies against all his
enemies.

Among all the Germanic nations, the Franks alone had become Catholic from their first rise in the provinces of the Roman
Empire. This acknowledgment of the Roman See had secured
important advantages to the Frankish nation. In the Catholic
subjects of their Arian enemies, the western Goths and Bur-
gundians, the Franks found natural allies. We read so much of
the miracles by which Clovis was favored; how St. Martin
showed him the ford over the Vienne by means of a hind; how
St. Hilary preceded his armies in a column of fire, that we shall
not greatly err if we conclude these legends to shadow forth
the material succors afforded by the natives to those who shared
their creed, and for whom, according to Gregory of Tours, they
desired victory " with eager inclination." But this attachment
to Catholicism, thus confirmed from the beginning by consequences so important, was afterward renewed and powerfully
strengthened by a very peculiar influence arising from a totally
different quarter.

It chanced that certain Anglo-Saxons, being exposed for sale
in the slave-market of Rome, attracted the attention of Pope
Gregory the Great; he at once resolved that Christianity should
be preached to the nation whence these beautiful captives had
been taken. Never, perhaps, was resolution adopted by any
pope whence results more important ensued: together with the
doctrines of Christianity, a veneration for Rome and for the
Holy See, such as had never before existed in any nation, found
place among the Germanic Britons. The Anglo-Saxons began
to make pilgrimages to Rome, they sent their youth thither to
be educated, and King Offa established the tax called " St.
Peter's penny " for the relief of pilgrims and the education of
the clergy. The higher orders proceeded to Rome, in the hope
that, dying there, a more ready acceptance would be accorded
to them by the saints in heaven. The Anglo-Saxons appear to
have transferred to Rome and the Christian saints the old Teu-
tonic superstition, by which the gods were described as nearer
to some spots of earth than to others, and more readily to be
propitiated in places thus favored.

But beside all this, results of higher importance still ensued
when the Anglo-Saxons transplanted their modes of thought to

the mainland, and imbued the whole empire of the Franks with their own opinions. Boniface, the apostle of the Germans, was an Anglo-Saxon; this missionary, largely sharing in the veneration professed by his nation for St. Peter and his successors, had from the beginning voluntarily pledged himself to abide faithfully by all the regulations of the Roman See: to this promise he most religiously adhered. On all the German churches founded by him was imposed an extraordinary obligation to obedience. Every bishop was required expressly to promise that his whole life should be passed in unlimited obedience to the Romish Church, to St. Peter, and his representative. Nor did he confine this rule to the Germans only. The Gallican bishops had hitherto maintained a certain independence of Rome; Boniface, who had more than once presided in their synods, availed himself of these occasions to impress his own views on this western portion of the Frankish Church; thenceforward the Gallic archbishops received their pallium from Rome, and thus did the devoted submission of the Anglo-Saxons extend itself over the whole realm of the Franks.

This empire had now become the central point for all the German tribes of the West. The fact that the reigning family, the Merovingian race, had brought about its own destruction by its murderous atrocities, had not affected the strength of the empire. Another family, that of Pepin of Heristal, had risen to supreme power—men of great energy, exalted force of character, and indomitable vigor. While other realms were sinking together in one common ruin, and the world seemed about to become the prey of the Moslem, it was this race, the house of Pepin of Heristal, afterward called the Carlovingian, by which the first and effectual resistance was offered to the Mahometan conquerors.

The religious development then in progress was also equally favored by the house of Pepin: we find it early maintaining the best understanding with Rome, and it was under the special protection of Charles Martel and Pepin le Bref that Boniface proceeded in his apostolic labors.[2] Let us consider the temporal condition of the papal power. On the one side the East Roman

---

[2] "Bonifacii Epistolæ," ep. 12, "ad Danielem episc.": "Without the patronage of the Frankish ruler, I can neither govern the people nor defend the presbyters, deacons, monks, or handmaidens of God nor even could I forbid the pagan rites and sacrilegious idolatries in Germany without his mandate and the fear of his name."

Empire, weakened, falling into ruin, incapable of supporting Christendom against Islamism, or of defending its own domains in Italy against the Lombards, yet continuing to claim supremacy even in spiritual affairs; on the other hand, we have the German nations full of the most vigorous life, victorious over the Moslem, attached with all the fresh ardor and trusting enthusiasm of youth to that authority, of whose protecting and restrictive influences they still felt the need, and filled with an unlimited and most freely rendered devotion.

Already Gregory II perceived the advantages he had gained; full of a proud self-consciousness, he writes thus to that iconoclast Emperor, Leo the Isaurian: " All the lands of the West have their eyes directed toward our humility; by them we are considered as a God upon earth." His successors became even more and more impressed with the conviction that it was needful to separate themselves from a power (that of the Roman Empire) by which many duties were imposed on them, but which could offer them no protection in return. They could not safely permit a succession to the mere name and empire to fetter them, but turned themselves rather toward those from whom help and aid might also be expected. Thus they entered into strict alliance with those great captains of the West, the Frankish monarchs; this became closer and closer from year to year, procured important advantages to both parties, and eventually exercised the most active influence on the destinies of the world.

When Pepin the younger, not content with the reality of kingly power, desired also to possess himself of the name, he felt that a higher sanction was needful. This the Pope afforded him. In return, the new monarch undertook to defend " the Holy Church and the Republic of God " against the Lombards. Nor did he content himself with merely defending them. On the contrary, he compelled the Lombards to evacuate that portion of territory called the Exarchate, and which they had wrenched from the Roman Empire. In strict justice this should have been restored to the Emperor, from whom it had been taken; but when the proposal for such restoration was made to Pepin, his reply was, " That for no favor of man had he entered the strife, but from veneration to St. Peter alone, and in the hope of obtaining forgiveness for his sins." He caused

the keys of the conquered towns to be placed on the altar of St.
Peter, and in this act he laid the foundation of the whole temporal power of the popes.

In this reciprocity of services, the alliance between the Pope
and the Emperor continued to extend and strengthen its bonds.
At length the Holy See was delivered from its long oppressive
and dangerous neighbors, the Lombard chiefs, by the Emperor
Charlemagne. In his own person this monarch evinced the
most profound deference for the holy father: visiting Rome,
he kissed the steps of St. Peter, as he entered the vestibule
where the pontiff awaited him; here he confirmed all the possessions awarded by Pepin to the Church. The Pope on his
part always proved himself to be Charlemagne's most steady
friend, and the influence of the spiritual chief with the Italian
bishops rendered it an easy matter for the Emperor to make himself master of the Lombards and gain possession of their
dominions.

This tendency of events was soon to be followed by results
of still higher importance.

The strife of contending factions was now raging so violently
in Rome that the Pope could no longer maintain himself in his
own city without foreign aid. In this conjuncture Charlemagne once more visited Rome to afford the assistance needed.
The aged monarch was now full of fame and victory; after
long struggles he had gradually subdued all his neighbors, and
had united under his own banner the greater part of the Ro-
mano-Germanic nations of Christendom. These he had repeatedly led to victory against their common enemy, and it was
matter of remark that he possessed all the seats of the western
emperors, whether in Italy, Germany, or Gaul;[3] and had, besides, inherited all their power. It is true that these countries
had since become a totally different world, but should this
diminish the dignity of their leader? It was thus that Pepin
had gained the royal diadem, for to him who has secured the
power does the dignity also belong. It was in this sense that
the Pope again decided; impelled by gratitude, and well know-

[3] Thus it is that I understand the "Annales Laureshamenses, ad annum 801": "It seemed good to the apostolic Leo himself, that Charles himself, king of the Franks, should be named emperor, seeing he held that Rome where the Cæsars were ever accustomed to reside, also the other seats which they held in Italy and Gaul, as well as Germany; because God Almighty has put these in his power, wherefore it seemed to them right that by God's assistance he should have the name also."

ing his own need of a permanent protector, he placed the crown of the Western Empire on Charlemagne's head on Christmas eve of the year 800.

With this act, the series of events which had commenced with the first incursions of the German tribes into the Roman Empire was fully completed.

A Frank sovereign now filled the place of the western emperors, and exercised all their prerogatives. In the dominions conferred on St. Peter, we see Charlemagne performing unequivocal acts of sovereign authority. His grandson Lothaire nominated his own judges in Rome, and annulled confiscations made by the Pope. The pontiff, on the other hand, remaining head of the hierarchy in the Roman West, became, nevertheless, a member of the Frankish Empire. He separated himself from the East, and gradually ceased to command any influence there. Of his patriarchal diocese in the East the Greek emperors had long since bereft him.[4] But he received a degree of observance from the western churches (not excepting the Lombard, which had also been subjected to the Frankish laws and institutions) exceeding all that he had previously enjoyed. Permitting the introduction of schools for Frieslanders, Saxons, and Franks into Rome, by which that city itself began to be Germanized, he thus induced that intimate connection of German and Latin elements which has since so actively influenced the general character of the West. In his utmost adversity the power of the Pope struck new roots in a fresh soil; threatened by the most imminent ruin, it was at this moment that a firm and lengthened endurance was secured to it: the hierarchy, taking its rise in the Roman Empire, now diffused itself over the German nations; these presented a boundless field for ever-extending activity, and here it was that the germ of its being was first fully developed.

---

[4] Nicholas I laments the loss of the patriarchal power of the Roman See, "throughout old and new Epirus, Illyricum, Macedonia, Thessaly, Achaia, Dacia on the Danube, and Dacia on the Mediterranean, Mœsia, Dardania, and Prævalis; also the loss of the patrimony in Calabria and Sicily." Pagi (Critica in "Annales Baronii," iii. p. 216) compares this letter with one from Adrian I to Charlemagne, whence it is obvious that these losses were among the results of the iconoclastic disputes.

Section III.—Relation of the Popes to the German Emperors —Internal Progress of the Hierarchy

We now pass over some centuries, in order to arrive at that point of view whence the various events they produced may most profitably be considered.

The Empire of the Franks has fallen; that of the Germans has arisen into full and vigorous life.

Never was the German name more powerful in Europe than during the tenth and eleventh centuries, under the Saxon and first Salique emperors. We see Conrad II marching from the eastern frontier, where he had compelled the King of Poland to personal subjection and to a division of his territory, and condemned the Duke of Bohemia to imprisonment, and pouring down on the West to support Burgundy against the pretensions of the French nobles. These nobles he defeated on the plains of Champagne, his Italian vassals crossing the St. Bernard to his assistance. He caused himself to be crowned at Geneva, and held his diet at Soleure. Immediately after this, we find him in Lower Italy. "By the force of his word," says his historian, Wipps, " he extinguished all discords on the borders of his empire at Capua and Beneventum." Nor was Henry III less powerful: at one moment we find him on the Scheldt and the Lys, victorious over the counts of Flanders; no long time has elapsed, and we meet him in Hungary, which country he also compelled, at least for some time, to do him feudal service. He pressed beyond the Raab, where his conquests were limited by the power of the elements alone. The King of Denmark hastened to await his arrival at Merseberg: the Count of Tours, one of the most powerful princes of France, submitted to become his vassal; and the Spanish historians inform us that he demanded from the mighty and victorious Ferdinand I of Castile an acknowledgment of his own supremacy as sovereign liege of all Christian kings.

If we now ask on what basis a power so extended in its influence, and claiming supremacy throughout Europe, essentially reposed, we find in it a most active and important ecclesiastical element. The Germans also made their conquests and conversions go hand in hand with the Church, their marches, too, extended over the Elbe toward the Oder on the one hand, and the Danube on the other. Monks and priests prepared the way for German influence in Bohemia and Hungary; thus did a great increase of importance everywhere accrue to the ecclesiastical power. Baronial and even ducal rights were held in Germany by the bishops and abbots of the empire, not within their own possessions only, but even beyond them. Ecclesiastical estates were no longer described as situated in certain counties, but these counties were described as situated in the bishoprics. In Upper Italy nearly all the cities were governed by the viscounts of their bishops. We are not authorized to infer from this, that an entire independence was already conceded to the clerical body. The appointment to all ecclesiastical offices still resting with the sovereign (the chapters returned the ring and crosier of their deceased superior to his court, whence it was that they were conferred anew), it was generally advantageous to the prince that the man of his choice, one on whose devotion to himself he could rely, should be invested with temporal authority. It was in defiance of his refractory nobles that Henry III exalted a plebeian, on whom he could depend, to the seat of St. Ambrose in Milan: to this mode of action he was principally indebted for the obedience he subsequently met with in Upper Italy. No Emperor displayed greater munificence toward the Church than did Henry II; yet none was more tenacious of his claim to the nomination of bishops:[1] but these two facts are illustrative of each other. Nor was the endowment of bishops permitted to diminish the resources of the State. Church property was neither exempted from civil imposts nor from feudal service, and bishops were frequently found taking the field at the head of their vassals. How advantageous to the prince, therefore, was the right of nominating bishops, who, like the archbishop of Bremen, held the highest ecclesiastical authority in the kingdoms of Scandinavia, and over numerous Wendish tribes!

If, then, the ecclesiastical element was of such paramount importance to the institutions of the German Empire, it is manifest that much would depend on the relations existing between the Emperor and the head of the whole clerical body, the Pope of Rome.

---

[1] For instances of this, see Planck's "History of the Social Constitution of the Christian Church," iii. 407.

The papacy was not less closely allied with the German emperors than it had been with the Roman, and with the successors of Charlemagne. The political subordination of the Pope was unquestionable. It is true, that while the empire remained in weak and incapable hands, and before it passed definitively to the Germans, certain acts of sovereign authority had been exercised by popes over the imperial sceptre; but no sooner did the vigorous German princes attain to that dignity, than they became, if not without dispute, yet, in fact, as completely liege lords of the popedom as the Carlovingian monarchs had been. With a powerful hand Otho the Great maintained the Pope whom he had raised to the throne;[2] his sons followed the example. The circumstance of the Roman factions once more rising into activity, seizing the papal chair, and again resigning it, or making it an article of traffic and barter, as their family interests required, shows but more clearly the necessity for some higher intervention. The vigor with which this was exercised by Henry III is well known; his synod at Sutri deposed such popes as he considered irregularly chosen; and scarcely had the patrician ring been placed on his finger, and the crown of the empire on his brow, than he nominated the individual who should ascend the papal throne by his unrestricted will. Four German popes were successively appointed by him; and when the supreme ecclesiastical dignity became vacant, the ambassadors from Rome presented themselves at the imperial court to receive the announcement of a successor, as did the envoys of other bishoprics.

In this position of things, it was a matter of personal interest to the Emperor that the Pope should hold an important place in the eyes of the world. Henry III was an active promoter of all reforms undertaken by the popes whom he had nominated; nor did the growth of their power awaken his jealousy. That Leo IX should hold a synod at Rheims, in despite of the King of France—should exalt and depose French bishops, receiving the solemn acknowledgment that the Pope was sole primate of the universal church—this could in no way offend the Emperor, while his own supremacy over the pope-

[2] In Goldast. "Constitutt. Imperiales," p. 221, we find an instrument (with the Scholia of Dietrich von Niem) by which the right of Charlemagne to choose his own successor, and in future that of the popes, is transferred to Otho and the German emperors. This, however, is without doubt a fabrication.

dom remained undisputed; it gave, on the contrary, a more imposing weight to the authority he claimed to exercise over all
Europe. As by the Archbishop of Bremen he was placed in immediate relation with the North, so was he placed by the Pope
with the remaining powers of Christendom.

But this state of affairs involved a great danger to the empire. The ecclesiastical body was very differently constituted
under the Germanic and Germanized states, from what it had
been under the Roman Empire. The clergy now possessed a
large share of political influence; they had risen to princely
power. The Church still depended on the Emperor, the supreme temporal authority. But suppose this authority again
fallen into weak and incapable hands; suppose, then, that the
head of the Church, wielding the triple force arising from his
dignity—the object of universal reverence, from the devotion of
his own subjects, and from his influence over other states—
should seize the favorable moment and place himself in opposition to the imperial power.

The nature of things offered more than one inducement to
such a course. There was a principle inherent in the ecclesiastical constitution which opposed itself to a secular influence so
widely extended, and this would inevitably make itself felt,
should the Church become strong enough to bring it into effectual action. There is also, as it appears to me, an inconsistency in the fact that the Pope should exercise on all sides the
supreme spiritual power, and yet remain himself subjected to
the Emperor. The case would have been different had Henry
III really brought about his purpose of exalting himself to be
the head of all Christendom; but as he failed in this, there
needed but a certain complication of political affairs, and the
Pope might have been prevented, by his subordination to the
Emperor, from performing the duties imposed on him by his
office as common father of the faithful.

It was under these circumstances Gregory VII ascended the
papal throne. Gregory was a man of bold, prejudiced, and
aspiring mind, obstinate in his adherence to logical consequences, immovable in his purposes, yet skilful and pliant when
the object was to parry any well-founded objection. He perceived the end to which things were tending, and amidst the
trifling occurrences of every-day life, took note of the vast con-

tingencies preparing for the future. He resolved to free the pontificate from the authority of the empire. Having fixed his thoughts on this object, he soon seized the decisive means for attaining it. The resolution that he caused to be adopted by one of his councils, namely that no clerical office should in future be conferred by a layman, was equivalent to altering the constitution of the empire in its very essence. This reposed, as we have already said, on the connection between the spiritual and temporal institutions: the bond that held these together was the investiture; to deprive the Emperor of this his ancient right, was to declare a revolution.

It is obvious that Gregory could not have ventured to think of this measure, much less to put it in practice, had he not been favored by the convulsions that shook the empire during the minority of Henry IV, and by the frequent insurrections of the German princes and people against that monarch. Among the great vassals he found natural allies. They also felt oppressed by the overwhelming power of the Emperor; they also desired to become free. In a certain point of view, the Pope might be considered one of the magnates of the empire. It is not then surprising, that when the pontiff declared Germany an electoral monarchy—a doctrine tending greatly to augment the power of the princes—these last should offer no opposition to the efforts he made for his own emancipation from the imperial power.

Even in the contention for the investiture, their interests went hand in hand: the Pope was still far from claiming the direct nomination of the bishops; he referred the choice to the chapters, and over these the higher German nobility exercised the most commanding influence: in one word, the Pope had the aristocratic interests on his side.

But even with these allies, how long and sanguinary were the conflicts maintained by the popes before they could bring their enterprise to a fortunate issue! "From Denmark even to Apulia," says the hymn in praise of St. Anno—" from Carlingen to Hungary, have the arms of the empire been turned against its own vitals." The contention between the spiritual and temporal principles, which had hitherto acted in concert, spread fatal discord through the breadth of Europe. Frequently were the pontiffs driven from their capital, and compelled to witness the ascent of antipopes to the apostolic throne!

At length, however, the task was accomplished. After long centuries of confusion—after other centuries of often doubtful strife, the independence of the Roman See and that of its essential principle was finally attained. In effect, the position of the popes was at this moment most exalted; the clergy were wholly in their hands. It is worthy of remark that the most firm-minded pontiffs of this period—Gregory VII for example—were Benedictines. By the introduction of celibacy they converted the whole body of the secular clergy into a kind of monastic order. The universal bishopric now claimed by the popes bears a certain resemblance to the power of an abbot of Cluny, who was the only abbot of his order; in like manner these pontiffs aspired to be the only bishops of the assembled church. They interfered without scruple in the administration of every diocese,[3] and even compared their legates with the proconsuls of ancient Rome! While this closely knit body, so compact in itself, yet so widely extended through all lands— influencing all by its large possessions, and controlling every relation of life by its ministry—was concentrating its mighty force under the obedience of one chief, the temporal powers were crumbling into ruin. Already in the beginning of the twelfth century the provost Gerohus ventured to say: "It will at last come to this, that the golden image of the empire shall be shaken to dust—every great monarchy shall be divided into tetrarchates, and then only will the Church stand free and untrammelled beneath the protection of her crowned high-priest."[4] And this bold prophecy had well-nigh received a literal fulfilment; for in fact which was the more powerful in England during the thirteenth century—was it Henry III or those four-and-twenty to whom the government was for a certain period confided? In Castile, who were the effective rulers—the King or the altoshomes? The power of the Emperor seems to have

---

[3] One of the principal points in reference to which may be cited the following passage from a letter of Henry IV to Gregory VII: "rectores sanctæ ecclesiæ, videl archiepiscopos, presbyteros, sicut cervos pedibus tuis calcasti." [The rulers of the holy church —archbishops, bishops, and priests, to wit—these thou hast trodden beneath thy feet as were they slaves.] But we perceive that in this case public opinion was on the side of the Pope, since Henry thus continues his reproaches: "In quorum conculcatione tibi favorem ab ore vulgi comparasti." [In trampling on whom, thou hast gained applause from the mouths of the populace.]

[4] Schröckh quotes this passage, "Kirchengeschichte," vol. xxvii. p. 117.

become superfluous from the moment when Frederick conceded
the essential attributes of sovereignty to the princes of the empire. Italy, as well as Germany, was occupied by numerous independent powers; the only self-centred and comprehensive
sovereignty was that of the Pope. Thus it came to pass that the
independence of the ecclesiastical principle resolved itself into a
new kind of monarchy; the politico-religious character that
life had everywhere assumed, and the general course of circumstances, all tended to this result. When countries, long lost to
the Church, as Spain had been, were regained from Mahome-
tanism—when provinces, like Prussia, hitherto buried in the
darkness of paganism, were brought over to the faith and filled
with a Christian population—when even the capitals of the
Greek Church conformed to the Latin ritual, and when hundreds of thousands poured forth to plant the banner of the
cross on the holy sepulchre—is it not here manifest, that the
crowned priest, whose hand was in all these enterprises, and
at whose feet was offered the fealty of the subdued, must have
enjoyed unbounded influence and honor? In his name, and
under his guidance, the western nations poured themselves
forth as one people and sought to gain possession of the whole
world. It cannot awaken surprise that the Pope should exercise unlimited authority in his internal administration, when
we remember that a king of England consented to hold his
kingdom as a fief from the pontiff's hand, that a king of Aragon
resigned his realms to the apostle Peter, and that Naples beheld her throne conferred by the same all-commanding power
on a family wholly foreign to her soil. Extraordinary aspect of
those times—which yet no one has hitherto placed before us in
all its completeness and truth! The most wonderful combination of internal discord with the most brilliant external
progress of independence and subjection, of spiritual and temporal existences! Even piety herself adopted a twofold
character. At one time we see her withdrawn amidst rugged
mountains, or retiring to the lonely forest, where her harmless
days are devoted to divine contemplation. Awaiting death, she
denies herself every enjoyment that life presents her; or, appearing in the homes of man, she proceeds with youthful enthusiasm to exhibit, under forms profoundly suggestive, the
mysteries that float around her, and the ideas in which she has

her being. But a moment after and we find another piety—it is she who has invented the inquisition and who fulminates the terrible judgment of the glaive against all who reject her creed. "Neither sex, nor age, nor rank, have we spared," says the leader of the war against the Albigenses; "we have put all alike to the sword." Sometimes she presents these widely differing aspects at the same moment of time. At sight of Jerusalem the crusaders descended from their horses—they bare their feet, to the end that they may approach the holy walls in the guise befitting pilgrims. In the midst of carnage they believe themselves aided by the visible presence of saints and angels. Yet, scarcely have they passed the walls, than they rush into the wildest excesses of pillage and bloodshed. On the site of Solomon's temple thousands of Saracens were cruelly put to death, the Jews were burnt in their synagogues, and the holy threshold, on which they had come so far to kneel in adoration, they first profaned with blood. In this contradiction may be found a picture eloquently illustrative of those times, and of that politico-religious government. It is an inconsistency that will be seen to pervade their whole being.

Section IV.—Contrasts between the Fourteenth and Fifteenth Centuries

There are certain periods of history that tempt us to anxiously scrutinize, if we dare thus to express ourselves, the plans of God in his government of the world, and earnestly to examine the forces that are in action for the education of the human race.

However defective may have been the development that we have sought to describe, it was indispensable to the complete naturalization of Christianity in the West. The task of bending the refractory spirits of the northern tribes to the pure laws of Christian truth was no light one: wedded, as these nations were, to their long-cherished superstitions, the religious element required a long predominance before it could gain entire possession of the German character; but by this predominance, that close union of Latin and German elements was effected on which is based the character of Europe in later times. There is a spirit of community in the modern world which has always been regarded as the basis of its progressive improvement, whether in religion, politics, manners, social life, or literature. To bring about this community, it was necessary that the western nations should, at one period, constitute what may be called a single politico-ecclesiastical state.

But this, also, was to be no more than the phenomenon of a moment in the grand march of events; the necessary conversion once effected, new necessities supervened.

The advent of another epoch already announced itself in the simultaneous and almost universal impulse received by the languages of nations. Slowly, but with unceasing effort, they pressed themselves into the manifold branches of intellectual activity. Step by step the idiom of the church gave way before them; universality retired, and in its place appeared a new species of partition, founded on a higher principle. The ecclesiastical element had up to this time overborne every distinguishing nationality; now, modified and transformed, but again asserting individual existence, these nationalities displayed themselves in a new light.

We are forced irresistibly to the conviction that all the purposes and efforts of humanity are subjected to the silent and often imperceptible, but invincible and ceaseless march of events. The existence of the papal authority was demanded by the earlier phases of the world's progress; those immediately following were directly adverse to that authority. The impulse given by the ecclesiastical power was no longer necessary to the well-being of nations; it was consequently at once opposed. All had awakened to a sense of their own independence.

We shall do well if we recall to mind the more important events in which this fact becomes revealed.

It was the French, as is well known, by whom the first effectual resistance was opposed to the pretensions of the popes. The whole nation declared itself as one man against the excommunications of Boniface VIII. All the public authorities expressed their adhesion to Philip the Fair, and their cordial approbation of the steps taken by him in his contest with the pontiff, in documents amounting to several hundreds.

Next followed the Germans. When the popes once more assailed the empire with all their old animosity, although the latter no more possessed its ancient importance, yet, perceiving the dangers of foreign influence, the electoral princes assembled on the banks of the Rhine; seated on their stone chairs, in the field of Rense, they proceeded to adopt measures for maintaining " the honor and dignity of the empire." Their object was to secure its independence against the future aggressions of the papacy by a solemn resolution. This was instantly afterward promulgated with all due form, and by all the potentates united. Emperors, princes, and electors, all joined in a common opposition to the principles of the papal policy.[1]

England did not long remain behind. In no country had the popes possessed higher influence—nowhere had they dealt in a more arbitrary manner with the benefices of the Church; but when Edward III refused to continue the tribute, to the payment of which former kings had pledged themselves, his parliament united with him, and promised him their support. The King then took measures to prevent any further encroachments by the Pope.

We thus see one nation after another acquiring the sense of its own unity and independence. The civil power would no longer endure the presence of any higher authority. The popes no more found allies among the middle classes, while princes and legislative bodies were resolutely bent on withstanding their influence.

In addition to all this, the popedom itself had at this period fallen into a state of debility and confusion, by which the secular princes, who had hitherto sought only to defend themselves, were enabled to become in their turn aggressors.

Schism made its appearance. Let us observe the consequences that ensued. It was long at the option of each prince to attach himself to one pope or the other, as might best suit his political interests. The Church possessed no means within herself by which this division could be remedied; by the secular power alone could this be done. When a council was held in Constance for that purpose, the members no longer voted individually, as had formerly been the practice, but by the four nations, each nation exercising the right of deliberating in preliminary assemblies on the vote to be given. Unanimously they decided the deposition of a pope, and the newly elected pontiff

[1] Licet juris utriusque. See Ohlenschläger, " Staatsgeschichte des Röm. Kaiserthums in der ersten Hälfte des 14ten Jahrhunderts," No. 63.

was called on to accede to concordats with each separate nation. These concordats were of great importance, only from the precedent they afforded. During the council of Basle, many states remained neutral; it was by the immediate intervention of the princes alone, that this second breach in the Church could be closed.[2] There could arise no state of things better calculated to promote the preponderance of the temporal power and the independence of the several states.

And now the Pope was again in a position of great splendor. He was obeyed universally; the Emperor still led his palfrey on occasions of ceremony. There were bishops—not in Hungary only, but in Germany also, who styled themselves bishops " by the grace of the Apostolic See."[3] St. Peter's penny was still collected in the north; innumerable pilgrims from all countries came flocking to the "threshold of the apostles"—an eye-witness compares them to swarms of bees, or flights of migratory birds; but, spite of these appearances, the old relations of things were no longer in force.

If we desire proof of this, we need only recall the enthusiasm with which all ranks rushed toward the holy sepulchre in earlier times, and compare this with the coldness evinced in the fifteenth century toward every appeal in favor of a combined resistance to the Turks. How much more pressing was the necessity of protecting the native territory against the danger that unquestionably threatened it at all times, than that of maintaining the custody of the holy sepulchre in the hands of believers. Eneas Sylvius and the Minorite Capistrano employed their best eloquence—the first in the diet, the second before the people in the market-places of towns; and historians tell us many things of the impression they produced, but we do not find that anyone was moved to the taking up of arms. What efforts were made by the popes in this cause! One fitted out a fleet; another, Pius II, who was that same Eneas Sylvius just alluded to, betook himself, though weak and suffering from illness, to the port where those princes whose domains were most immediately endangered, if none others, were expected to assemble. He desired to be present, in order, as he said, to lift up, like Moses,

---

[2] Erklärrung des Papetes Felix in Georgius, " Life of Nicholas V," p. 65.
[3] Constance, Schwerin, Fünfkirchen.

—Schröckh. " Kirchengeschichte," vol. xxxiii. p. 60.

his hands to God during the battle, as he alone was empowered to do. Neither exhortations, nor entreaties, nor example could avail to move the people of his times. The youthful enthusiasm of chivalrous Christendom had passed away; no pope might ever awaken it more.

Other interests occupied the world. It was now the moment when the European kingdoms were finally consolidating their forces after long internal struggles. The central authorities having succeeded in suppressing the factions that had endangered the security of the throne, were gathering their subjects around them in renewed allegiance. The papacy, interfering in all things and seeking to dominate all, came very soon to be regarded in a political point of view; the temporal princes now began to put forth higher claims than they had hitherto done.

It is commonly believed that the papal authority was almost unrestricted up to the time of the Reformation; but the truth is that no inconsiderable portion of the rights and privileges of the clergy had been appropriated by the civil power, during the fifteenth and in the early part of the sixteenth centuries.

The encroachments of the Roman See were materially restricted in France by the pragmatic sanction, which for more than half a century was regarded as the palladium of the kingdom. It is true that Louis XI was hurried into certain concessions by that false devotion, to the forms of which he adhered the more rigidly, because altogether destitute of true religious feeling; but his successors insisted all the more pertinaciously on a return to this their fundamental law. It has indeed been asserted that when Francis I concluded his concordat with Leo X, the Roman Court thereby recovered its ancient preponderance, and it is very true that the Pope did regain the first-fruits (Annates); but he was compelled to sacrifice valuable sources of revenue in exchange, and above all the right of nomination to the bishoprics and other important benefices. The rights of the Gallican Church were unquestionably lost, but this was rather in favor of the King than the Pope: the principle, for which Gregory VII had moved the whole world, was resigned with little difficulty by Leo X.

Matters were by no means carried so far in Germany: the decrees of Basle, which in France had received the form of a pragmatic sanction,[4] were rendered much less effectual in Germany, where also they had at first been accepted, by the concordat of Vienna; but this change was not effected without large concessions on the part of Rome.

In Germany it was not enough to come to terms with the high chief of the empire; the subordinate states must also be separately won. The archbishops of Mayence and Treves obtained the privilege of naming to the vacant bishoprics, even during those months hitherto reserved for the Pope; the electoral prince of Brandenburg extorted the right of nomination to the three bishoprics of his dominions, while less important states, as Strasburg, Salzburg, and Metz, were also propitiated by concessions.[5] But not even by these was the general opposition extinguished. In the year 1487 the whole empire opposed itself to a tithe that the Pope desired to impose and effectually defeated his purpose.[6] In 1500 the imperial government accorded one-third only of the sum produced by indulgences to the papal legates, appropriating the remaining two, and applying them in aid of the war against the Turks.

In England, without any new concordat, without any pragmatic sanction, affairs were carried far beyond the concessions of Constance. Henry VII possessed the undisputed right of nomination to the bishoprics, and, not content with retaining the promotion of the clergy in his own hands, he appropriated the half of the first-fruits also. The ecclesiastical and secular powers were, to a certain extent, united in the person of Wolsey, when, in the early part of Henry VIII's reign, he added the title of legate to his many other offices, and, before Protestantism had even been thought of by the English sovereign, he had already proceeded to a merciless confiscation of the numerous monasteries.

Nor did the countries and kingdoms of southern Europe remain in the background. By the King of Spain also the nomination to episcopal sees was assumed as of right; that crown, with which were united the grand masterships of the

[4] "We perceive the connection from the following words of Æneas Sylvius: 'Concerning the decrees of the council of Basle, a dissension began, you declaring that they were to be implicitly observed; but the apostolic seat rejected them all, so at last a composition was made by which some of the decrees of the said council appear to have been received, others rejected.'"—Müller's "Reichstagstheatrum unter Friedrich III," Vorst iii. p. 604.

[5] Schröckh's "Kirchengeschichte," vol. xxxii. p. 173. Eichhorn's "Staats- und Rechts-geschichte," vol. iii. § 472, n. c.

[6] Müller's "Reichstagstheatrum," Vorst vi. p. 130.

religious orders, which had instituted and still directed the inquisition, made no scruple of appropriating various attributes
and immunities, formerly held sacred to the clergy; nor did
Ferdinand the Catholic shrink from opposing himself to the
papal legates whenever it suited his purpose to do so.

In like manner with the religious orders of Spain, those of
Portugal—namely, St. James, Avis, and the order of Christ,
which had inherited the wealth of the Templars, were also in the
patronage of the crown.[7] King Emanuel obtained a third of the
cruciata from Leo X, and not content with this he demanded
and received a tenth part of the church property in his dominions, with the express right of distributing it according to
his unrestricted will, and the merit of the recipient.

These things sufficiently show that a universal tendency to
the circumscription of papal power was at this time manifested
throughout Christendom, in the south as in the north. A participation in ecclesiastical revenues, and the right of promotion
to church benefices and offices, was that which the civil power
more especially desired. Nor did the popes attempt any strenuous opposition. Of their privileges and possessions they
maintained what they could; the rest they resigned. It was
remarked of Ferdinand of Naples by Lorenzo de' Medici in
relation to a dispute of the former with the Roman See—" He
will make no difficulty of promising, but when it comes to the
fulfilment his deficiencies will be overlooked, as those of kings
always are by the popes; "[8] for this spirit of opposition had penetrated even into Italy. Of Lorenzo de' Medici himself we are
told that he followed the example of more powerful sovereigns
in this respect, obeying just so much of the papal commands as
suited him, and no more.[9] We shall be mistaken if we consider
these movements as but so many acts of self-will: the life of the
European nations was no longer pervaded and impressed as it
had formerly been by ecclesiastical influence. The development
of national character, and the separate organization of the

[7] " Instruttione piena della cose di
Portogallo al Coadjutor di Bergamo:
nuntio destinato in Portogallo." MS.
among the Informazioni politiche in the
Royal Library of Berlin, vol. xii. Leo
X conferred this patronage of the orders, " the King agreeing to pay a very
large sum for the said patronage."
[8] Lorenzo to Johannes de Lanfre-
dinis, " Fabroni Vita Laurentii Medici,"
ii. p. 362.
[9] Antonius Gallus derebus Genuensi-
bus, " Muratori Scriptt. R. It." xxiii. p.
281, says of Lorenzo: " He followed
the contumacious license of the greater
kings and princes against the Roman
Church, allowing nothing of the pontifical rights but as he saw good."

various monarchies, were making important advances. It thus became indispensable that the relation of the ecclesiastical to the secular powers should be thoroughly remodified. A very remarkable change had become obvious, even in the popes themselves.

CHAPTER SECOND

THE CHURCH AND HER TERRITORIES IN THE BEGINNING OF THE SIXTEENTH CENTURY

Section I.—Extension of the Ecclesiastical States

WHATEVER judgment may be formed as to the popes of the earlier ages, it is certain that they had always important interests in view—the duty of upholding an oppressed religion, that of contending with paganism, of diffusing Christianity among the nations of the North, and of establishing an independent hierarchical government. To will, and to achieve some great object, is proper to the dignity of human nature; and while such was their tendency, the popes were sustained in their lofty efforts; but this spirit had passed away with the times by which it had been awakened. Schism had been suppressed, but it had become obvious that no hope remained of effecting a combined action against the enemy of the Church. Men would no longer give their lives to defend her from the Turks. It thus followed that her spiritual head now devoted himself to the interests of his temporal sovereignty, and pursued these with an avidity hitherto unknown. And this was in accordance with the temper and direction of the age: " I had once thought," remarks one of the speakers in the Council of Basle, " that the secular power should be wholly separate from that of the Church; but I have now learned that virtue without force is but slightly respected, and that the pope, without patrimony of the Church, would be merely the servant of kings and princes." This speaker, who had yet sufficient influence in the assembly to determine the election of Pope Felix, declares it not so very objectionable that a pope should have sons, who might defend him against the aggressions of tyrants.[1]

---

[1] See an extract from this speech in Schröckh.

This question was afterward considered from a different point of view among the Italians. It was held to be a thing of course that a pope should provide for his own family and promote its interests; nay, a pontiff neglecting to do this would have exposed himself to injurious remarks. "Others," writes Lorenzo de' Medici to Innocent VIII, "have not so long postponed their efforts to attain the papal chair, and have concerned themselves little to maintain the retiring delicacy so long evinced by your holiness. Now is your holiness not only exonerated before God and man, but this honorable conduct may cause you to incur blame, and your reserve may be attributed to less worthy motives. Zeal and duty lay it on my conscience to remind your holiness that no man is immortal. Be the pontiff as important as he may in his own person, he cannot make his dignity and that importance hereditary; he cannot be said absolutely to possess anything but the honors and emoluments he has secured to his kindred."[2] Such were the counsels offered by him who was considered the wisest man of Italy. It is true that he had himself a direct interest in the matter, having given his daughter in marriage to a son of the Pope, but he would never have dared to express himself thus boldly and without reserve, had not the views he was propounding been admitted without question among the higher classes of his country.

There is a certain internal connection between the fact that at this period the temporal princes were regularly seeking possession of the papal privileges, and the circumstance that enterprises partly secular now began to occupy the most earnest attention of the Pope. He felt himself above all an Italian prince.

No long time had elapsed since the Florentines had overcome their neighbors the Pisans, and the house of Medici had established its authority over both. The power of the Sforza family in Milan, that of the house of Aragon in Naples, and of the Venetians in Lombardy had all been achieved and consolidated within the memory of man. What was to prevent the Pope from establishing a yet more exalted sovereignty for himself in those domains which were regarded as the patrimony of the Church, but which were now under the rule of various independent chiefs?

---

[2] A letter of Lorenzo's without date, but apparently of the year 1489—since the fifth year of Innocent VIII is therein alluded to.—Fabroni, "Vita Laurentii," ii. 390.

Pope Sixtus IV was the first pontiff by whom this purpose was undertaken with a fixed will and effectual results. He was strenuously, and most successfully, followed by Alexander VI. From Julius II this plan received a direction wholly unexpected, and of which the effect was permanent.

Sixtus IV (1471–1484) conceived the idea of founding a principality for his nephew, Girolamo Riario, in the fertile and beautiful plains of Romagna. The other Italian powers were already disputing the possession of, or the preponderance in, this fair district; and, if the question had been one of right, the Pope had manifestly a better title than any one of these princes; but he was greatly their inferior in political force and the materials of war. He did not scruple to employ his spiritual influence—exalted by its nature and objects above all earthly purposes—for the furtherance of his worldly interests; nor did he shrink from debasing it by contact with the temporary intrigues in which these involved him. The Medici were especially obnoxious to the Pope, and mingling himself in the disputes of the Florentines, he gave rise to the suspicion that he had taken part in the conspiracy of the Pazzi, and is believed, as is well known, to have been privy to that assassination, committed by them before the very altar of a cathedral. He—the father of the faithful! When the Venetians ceased to favor the undertakings of his nephew, as for some time they had done, the Pope was not content with leaving them to their fate, in the midst of a war to which he had himself impelled them; he even went so far as to excommunicate them for persisting in it.[3]

He acted with equal violence in Rome. The Colonna family, opponents of Riario, was persecuted by him with the most savage ferocity. He seized on their domain of Marino, and causing the prothonotary Colonna to be attacked in his own house, took him prisoner, and put him to death. The mother of Colonna came to St. Celso, in Banchi, where the corpse lay, and lifting the severed head by its hair, she exclaimed: " Behold the head of my son. Such is the truth of the Pope. He promised that my son should be set at liberty if Marino were delivered into

[3] The " Commentarii di Marino Sanuto " on the war of Ferrara were printed at Venice in 1829; at page 56 he alludes to the defection of the Pope, quoting the words of the Venetian ambassador: " All men will see that we began this war by desire of the Pope; he, however, took measures for the breaking of the league."

his hands. He is possessed of Marino, and behold we have my son—but dead. Thus does the Pope keep his word." [4]

At such cost was it that Sixtus IV secured victory over his enemies, domestic and foreign. He did, in effect, exalt his nephew to be lord of Imola and Forli; but if his temporal influence gained extension by these means, there can be no doubt that his spiritual authority and character lost infinitely more. There was even an attempt made to assemble a council against him.

Meanwhile Sixtus was soon to be far surpassed. No long time after him (1492) Alexander VI took possession of the papal throne.

The great object of Alexander, through his whole life, was to gratify his inclination for pleasure, his ambition, and his love of ease. When at length he had attained to the supreme spiritual dignity, he seemed also to have reached the summit of happiness. Spite of his advanced years, the exultation he felt seemed daily to impart to him a new life. No painful thought was permitted to disturb his repose for a single night. His only care was to seize on all means that might aid him to increase his power, and advance the wealth and dignity of his sons: on no other subject did he ever seriously bestow a thought.[5]

This one consideration was at the base of all his political alliances, and of those relations by which the events of the world were at that time so powerfully influenced. How the Pope would proceed, in regard to the marriages, endowments, and advances of his children, became a question affecting the politics of all Europe.

The son of Alexander, Cæsar Borgia, followed close on the footsteps of Riario. He began from the same point, and his first undertaking was to drive the widow of Riario from Imola and Forli. He pressed forward to the completion of his designs with the most daring contempt of consequences; what Riario had only approached, or attempted, Cæsar Borgia carried forward to its utmost results. Let us take a rapid glance at the means by which his purposes were accomplished.

The ecclesiastical states had hitherto been divided by the

[4] " Alegretto Alegretti, Diari Sanesi," p. 817.   [5] " Relazione di Polo Capello," 1500, MS. (App. No. 3.)

factions of the Guelfs and the Ghibelines, the first represented
in Rome by the family of Orsini, the second by the house of
Colonna. The popes had usually taken part with one or the
other of these factions. Sixtus IV had done so, and his example was followed by Alexander and his son, who at first attached themselves to the Guelf, or Orsini party. This alliance
enabled them very soon to gain the mastery of all their enemies.
They drove the house of Sforza from Pesaro, that of Malatesta
from Rimini, and the family of Manfredi from Faenza. They
seized on those powerful, well-fortified cities, and thus commenced the foundation of an extensive lordship. But no sooner
had they attained this point, no sooner had they freed themselves from their enemies, than they turned every effort against
their friends. And it was in this that the practice of the Borgias
differed from that of their predecessors, who had ever remained
firmly attached to the party they had chosen; Cæsar, on the
contrary, attacked his own confederates, without hesitation or
scruple. The Duke of Urbino, from whom he had frequently
received important aid, was involved, as in a network, by the
machinations of Cæsar, and, with difficulty, saved his life, a
persecuted fugitive in his own dominions.[6] Vitelli, Baglioni,
and other chiefs of the Orsini faction, resolved to show him
that at least they were capable of resistance. But Cæsar Borgia,
declaring that "it is permitted to betray those who are the
masters of all treasons," decoyed them into his snares, with profoundly calculated cruelty, and mercilessly deprived them of
life. Having thus destroyed both parties, he stepped into their
place, gathered the inferior nobility, who had been their adherents, around him, and took them into his pay; the territories
he had seized on were held in subjection by force of terror and
cruelty.

The brightest hopes of Alexander were thus realized—the
nobles of the land were annihilated, and his house about to
found a great hereditary dominion in Italy. But he had already
begun to acquire practical experience of the evil which passions,
aroused and unbridled, are capable of producing. With no
relative or favorite would Cæsar Borgia endure the partici-

---

[6] Many interesting particulars regarding Cæsar Borgia are to be found
throughout the fourth volume of Sanuto's great MS. chronicles—as also certain of his letters; in one of these,
written to the Pope, he subscribes himself "Your holiness's humblest servant
and most devoted creature."

ation of his power. His own brother stood in his way: Cæsar caused him to be murdered and thrown into the Tiber. His brother-in-law was assailed and stabbed, by his orders, on the steps of his palace.[7] The wounded man was nursed by his wife and sister, the latter preparing his food with her own hands, to secure him from poison; the Pope set a guard upon the house to protect his son-in-law from his son. Cæsar laughed these precautions to scorn. "What cannot be done at noonday," said he, "may be brought about in the evening." When the prince was on the point of recovery, he burst into his chamber, drove out the wife and sister, called in the common executioner, and caused his unfortunate brother-in-law to be strangled. Toward his father, whose life and station he valued only as means to his own aggrandizement, he displayed not the slightest respect or feeling. He slew Peroto, Alexander's favorite, while the unhappy man clung to his patron for protection, and was wrapped within the pontifical mantle. The blood of the favorite flowed over the face of the Pope.

For a certain time the city of the apostles, and the whole state of the Church, were in the hands of Cæsar Borgia. He is described as possessing great personal beauty, and was so strong that in a bull-fight he would strike off the head of the animal at a single blow; of liberal spirit, and not without certain features of greatness, but given up to his passions and deeply stained with blood. How did Rome tremble at his name! Cæsar required gold, and possessed enemies: every night were the corpses of murdered men found in the streets, yet none dared move; for who but might fear that his own turn would be next? Those whom violence could not reach were taken off by poison.[8]

There was but one place on earth where such deeds were possible—that, namely, where unlimited temporal power was

[7] "Diario de Sebastiano di Branca de Telini," MS. Bibl. Barb. N. 1103, speaks of Cæsar's atrocities in the manner following: "First, he caused his brother, called Duke of Gandia, to be thrown into the river; he ordered his brother-in-law, who was son of the Duke of Calabria, and the handsomest man ever seen in Rome, to be assassinated: again, he contrived the murder of Vitellozzo, the bravest man of that time." He calls the Lord of Faenza "the handsomest lad in the world."

[8] To the manifold notices extant on this head, I have added something from Polo Capello (App. No. 3). On the death of distinguished men, people instantly suspected poisoning by the Pope. With regard to the death of the Cardinal of Verona, Sanuto has the following: "He was supposed to be poisoned that the Pope might take his riches, because Alexander placed guards around his house before he died."

united to the highest spiritual authority, where the laws, civil
and ecclesiastical, were held in one and the same hand. This
place was occupied by Cæsar Borgia. Even depravity may
have its perfection. The kindred of the popes have often distinguished themselves in the career of evil, but none attained to
the eminence of Cæsar Borgia. He may be called a virtuoso in
crime.

Was it not in the first and most essential tendencies of
Christianity to render such a power impossible? And yet,
Christianity itself, and the very position of the supreme head
of the Church, were made subservient to its existence.

There needed, then, no advent of a Luther, to prove to the
world that these things were in direct opposition to the spirit
of Christianity. Even at that time men complained that the
Pope was preparing the way for antichrist, and laboring for the
interest of Satan rather than the kingdom of God.[9]

We do not follow the history of Alexander in its minute
details. He once purposed, as is but too well authenticated,
to destroy one of the richest cardinals by poison: but the
latter contrived to win over the Pope's chief cook by means
of promises, entreaties, and gifts. The confection prepared
for the cardinal was set before the pontiff himself; and Alexander expired from the effects of that poison which he had
destined for another.[10] The consequences resulting from his
various enterprises after his death were entirely different from
those he had anticipated.

The papal families had always hoped to acquire hereditary
sovereignty; but, for the most part, their authority came to an
end with the life of the Pope, and his kindred returned to the
rank whence they had risen. If the Venetians beheld the career
of Cæsar Borgia with indifference, it was principally because
they had no doubt but that matters would in this respect take
their usual course: there were, perhaps, other motives in action,
but this was the principal; they " judged all this to be merely
a fire of straw, and believed that things would return to their
former position, if Alexander were once dead.[1]

On this occasion, they were nevertheless disappointed in

[9] A loose sheet, MS. from Sanuto's
chronicle.
[10] " Successo di la Morte di Papa
Alessandro," MS. (See App. No. 4.)
[1] " Priuli Cronaca di Venezia," MS.:

" Del resto poco stimavano, conoscendo, che questo acquisto che all'
hora faceva il duca Valentinois sarebbe
foco di paglia, che poco dura."

CHOICE EXAMPLES OF PALEOGRAPHY.

Fac-similes from Rare and Curious Manuscripts of the Middle Ages.

THE FOUR BOOKS OF KINGS.

French manuscript written about 1160.

Although this plate offers another excellent example of Gothic writing, one can trace here and there the Roman roundness and elegance which were lost in the angularity of the newer style. The *i*'s are still accented, but the *h*'s are terribly deformed, and the *u*'s, it will be noticed, are accented similarly to the *i*'s, in order to distinguish them from the *n*'s, which in the text assume the same form as the *u*. The small capitals which begin some of the sentences in the text are in the best Gothic style, and there are other characteristics in the text which enable us to fix the date of the manuscript. The title " Li Quarz Livres " is a mixture of small capitals, uncials, and minuscules, the *e* especially denoting the Gothic tendency. The page is taken from the Four Books of Kings (Kings I and II and the two Books of the Maccabees), and the signature at the foot is that of Blanche, fourth daughter of Philip the Long of France, who was a sister (*suer*) in a nunnery at Longchamps.

Left margin notes:
Cume li reis ocozias chaid e maheignez

Cum li reis enueiad mes sages p enqrere de deable si il poust guarir

Right margin note:
Cume les messages parlerent

es de moab mespriftrent
uers cei de israel áprés la
mort lú rei acab. E li reis
ócozias chaid as aliures á
munt de une sue mai-
sun qnl óue en samá-
rie. si en fud maláde é
mahaignez. Pur có cu-
mandat as suens que il
enalassent á belsebub le
deable de ácharón. pur en-
querre se il poust gua-
rir de sa enfermete cé-on as-
li angeles nre seignur ure
é parlad á helue de thesbi-
te si li dist. Va encuntre les
messages le rei de samá-
rie si lur di. Dune nest li
uers deu en israel. éś qua

dune alez prendre cunsel
del deable de acharon.
E pur có que fait lauez.
có dire nostre sires. Li reis
del lit uil gist ne leuerad
mais tut murrad. Helia-
le fist tut issi. E li messáge
le rei ócozie retornerent
é uindrent deuant lui.
E li rei enqst chalt pas p qi
tút tost fussent repairée
al respundirent Vns buen
nus encuntrad. si nus
dist. Returnez errant-
ment á nostre seignur
le rei. si li dites. Dun nest
den en israel. que uus eftes
cedalar é cunsel prendre
del deable de acharón. p
có del ltr inl seft aculché-
él ne leuerat. mais si li mú-
rad. Respundi li reis. De
quel semblant fud é
quele uestiure oue cil lu
uus encuntrad. é si par-
lad. Respundrent al.
Có sud uns buen huire-
pez. si out ún puitceint
de pels entur les reins.

madame pur *blanche* fille de *Roy* de france

Blanche

their expectations: a pope followed, who did indeed make it
his object to assume a position in direct contrast with that of
the Borgias; but who pursued the same end, though he took
different, and from that very circumstance, successful, means
for his purpose. Julius II (A. D. 1503–1513) enjoyed the incalculable advantage of finding opportunity for promoting the
interests of his family by peaceable means: he obtained for his
kindred the inheritance of Urbino. This done, he could devote
himself, undisturbed by the importunities of his kindred, to
the gratification of that innate love for war and conquest which
was indeed the ruling passion of his life. To this he was invited by the circumstances of the times, and the consciousness
of his eminent position: but his efforts were all for the Church
—for the benefit of the papal see. Other popes had labored to
procure principalities for their sons or their nephews: it was
the ambition of Julius to extend the dominions of the Church.
He must, therefore, be regarded as the founder of the Papal
States.

He found the whole territory in extreme confusion; all who
had escaped by flight from the hand of Cæsar had returned—
the Orsini, the Colonna, the Vitelli and Baglioni, Varani, Malatesta, and Montefeltri—everywhere throughout the whole land,
were the different parties in movement; murderous contests
took place in the very Borgo of Rome. Pope Julius has been
compared with the Neptune of Virgil, when rising from the
waves, with peace-inspiring countenance he hushes their storms
to repose.[2] By prudence and good management, he disembar-
rassed himself even of Cæsar Borgia, whose castles he seized
and of whose dukedom he also gained possession. The lesser
barons he kept in order with the more facility from the measures
to this effect that had been taken by Cæsar, but he was careful
not to give them such cardinals for leaders as might awaken the
ancient spirit of insubordination by ambitious enterprise. The
more powerful nobles, who refused him obedience, he attacked
without further ceremony. His accession to the papal throne
sufficed to reduce Baglioni (who had again made himself master of Perugia) within the limits of due subordination. Nor
could Bentivoglio offer effectual resistance when required to

[2] Tommaso Inghirami, in " Fea, Notizie intorno Rafaele Sanzio da Urbino,"
p. 57.

resign that sumptuous palace which he had erected in Bologna,
and whereon he had too hastily inscribed the well-known eulogy
of his own good fortune: of this he saw himself deprived in
his old age. The two powerful cities of Perugia and Bologna
were thus subjected to the immediate authority of the pontifical
throne.

But with all this Julius was yet far from having accomplished the end he had proposed to himself. The coasts of
the Papal States were in great part occupied by the Venetians;
they were by no means disposed to yield possession of them
freely, and the Pope was greatly their inferior in military power.
He could not conceal from himself that his attacking them
would be the signal for a commotion throughout Europe.
Should he venture to risk this?

Old as Julius now was, worn by the many vicissitudes of
good and evil fortune experienced through a long life, by the
fatigues of war and exile, and most of all by the consequences of
intemperance and licentious excess, he yet knew not what fear
or irresolution meant; in the extremity of age, he still retained
that grand characteristic of manhood, an indomitable spirit.
He felt little respect for the princes of his time, and believed
himself capable of mastering them all. It was precisely from
the tumults of a general war that he hoped to extract the fulfilment of his purposes; his only care was to be always in command of money, to the end that he might seize the favorable moment with his utmost power. He desired, as a Venetian of that
day felicitously remarks, "to be lord and master of the game
of the world." [3] Awaiting the fruition of his desires with an
excess of impatience, he yet kept them confined to his own
breast. If we inquire what enabled him to assume so commanding an attitude, we find it principally attributable to the fact that
the state of public opinion in his day permitted the frank avowal
of his natural tendencies; he was free to profess them openly;
nay, to make them his boast. The re-establishment of the States
of the Church was in that day considered not only a glorious,
but even a religious enterprise; every effort of the Pope was

[3] Sommario di la relatione di Dolne-
nego Trivixan," MS.: "Il papa vol
esser il dominus et maistro del jocho
del mundo." (App. No. 6.) There
exists also a second relation by Polo
Capello, of the year 1510, whence a few
notices are inserted in the App. No. 5.

Francesco Vettori, "Sommario dell' istoria d' Italia," MS., says of him: "Julius was more fortunate that prudent,
and had more courage than strength,
but was ambitious and desirous of
grandeur to an immoderate degree."

directed toward this end; by this one idea were all his thoughts animated; they were, if I may so express myself, steeled and moulded into this one unvarying form. In furtherance of this, his grand aim, he engaged in the boldest operations, risking all to obtain all. He took the field in person, and having stormed Mirandola, he pressed into the city across the frozen ditches and through the breach; the most disastrous reverses could not shake his purpose, but rather seemed to waken new resources within him. He was accordingly successful; not only were his own baronies rescued from the Venetians, but in the fierce contest that ensued, he at length made himself master of Parma, Placentia, and even Reggio, thus laying the foundation of a power such as no pope had ever possessed before him. From Placentia to Terracina the whole fair region admitted his authority. He had ever sought to present himself in the character of a liberator; governing his new subjects with a wise benignity, he secured their attachment and even devotion; the temporal princes were not without alarm at sight of so many warlike populations in allegiance to a pope. " Time was," says Machiavel, " when no baron was so insignificant but that he might venture to brave the papal power; now, it is regarded with respect even by a king of France."

Section II.—Prevalence of Secular Views and Interests in the Church

It was an inevitable consequence that the whole body of the hierarchy should be influenced by the character and tendencies of its chief, that all should lend their best aid to the promotion of his purposes, and be themselves carried forward by the impulse thus given.

Not only the supreme dignity of the pontiff, but all the offices of the Church, were regarded as mere secular property. The Pope nominated cardinals from no better motive than personal favor, the gratification of some potentate, or even (and this was no infrequent occurrence) for actual payment of money! Could there be any rational expectation that men so appointed would fulfil their spiritual duties? One of the most important offices of the Church, the Penitenziaria, was bestowed by Sixtus IV on one of his nephews. This office held a large portion of

the power of granting dispensations; its privileges were still
further extended by the Pope, and in a bull issued for the express purpose of confirming them, he declared all who shall
presume to doubt the rectitude of such measures, to be " a stiff-
necked people and children of malice." [1] It followed as a matter of course that the nephew considered his office as a benefice,
the proceeds of which he was entitled to increase to the utmost
extent possible.

A large amount of worldly power was at this time conferred
in most instances, together with the bishoprics; they were held
more or less as sinecures according to the degree of influence
or court favor possessed by the recipient or his family. The
Roman Curia thought only of how it might best derive advantage from the vacancies and presentations; Alexander extorted double annates or first-fruits, and levied double, nay
triple tithes: there remained few things that had not become
matter of purchase. The taxes of the papal chancery rose
higher from day to day, and the comptroller, whose duty it
was to prevent all abuses in that department, most commonly
referred the revision of the imposts to those very men who
had fixed their amount.[2] For every indulgence obtained from
the datary's office, a stipulated sum was paid; nearly all the
disputes occurring at this period between the several states of
Europe and the Roman Court arose out of these exactions,
which the Curia sought by every possible means to increase,
while the people of all countries as zealously strove to restrain
them.

Principles such as these necessarily acted on all ranks affected by the system based on them, from the highest to the lowest.
Many ecclesiastics were found ready to renounce their bishoprics; but they retained the greater part of the revenues, and not
unfrequently the presentation to the benefices dependent on
them also. Even the laws forbidding the son of a clergyman
to procure induction to the living of his father, and enacting
that no ecclesiastic should dispose of his office by will, were

[1] Bull of the 9th of May, 1484: " Quoniam nonnulli iniquitatis filii, elationis
et pertinaciæ suæ spiritu assumpto po-
testatem majori pœnitentiarii nostri in
dubium revocare præsumunt, decet nos
adversus tales adhibere remedia," etc.—
Bullarium Romanum, ed. Cocquelines,
iii. p. 187.
[2] " Reformationes cancellariæ aposto-

licæ Smi. Dni. Nri. Pauli III.," 1540,
MS., in the Barberini library in Rome,
enumerates all the abuses that have
crept in since the days of Sixtus and
Alexander. The grievances of the German nation relate especially to these
" new devices " and the officers of the
Roman chancery.

ontinually evaded; for as all could obtain permission to ap-
oint whomsoever he might choose as his coadjutor, provided
e were liberal of his money, so the benefices of the Church be-
ame in a manner hereditary.

It followed of necessity that the performance of ecclesias-
ical duties was grievously neglected. In this rapid sketch, I
onfine myself to remarks made by conscientious prelates of the
Roman Court itself. " What a spectacle," they exclaim, " for
. Christian who shall take his way through the Christian world,
s this desolation of the churches! All the flocks are abandoned
y their shepherds, they are given over to the care of hire-
ings."[3]

In all places incompetent persons were intrusted with the
erformance of clerical duties; they were appointed without
crutiny or selection. The incumbents of benefices were prin-
ipally interested in finding substitutes at the lowest possible
ost, thus the mendicant friars were frequently chosen as par-
icularly suitable in this respect. These men occupied the
ishoprics under the title (previously unheard of in that sense)
f suffragans; the cures they held in the capacity of vicars.

Already were the mendicant orders in possession of extraor-
linary privileges, and these had been yet further extended by
Sixtus IV, who was himself a Franciscan. They had the right
f confessing penitents, administering the Lord's Supper, and
estowing extreme unction, as also that of burying within the
recincts, and even in the habit of the order. All these privi-
eges conferred importance as well as profit, and the mendicant
riars enjoyed them in their utmost plenitude; the Pope even
hreatened the disobedient secular clergy, or others, who should
nolest the orders, more particularly as regarded bequests, with
he loss of their respective offices.[4]

The administration of parishes as well as that of bishoprics
eing now in the hands of the mendicant orders, it is manifest

[3] The counsel of the select cardinals
nd other prelates, respecting the amel-
oration of the church, written by
pecial command of our most holy lord
aul III, in the year 1538, printed more
han once even at the time, and im-
ortant as pointing out the evil, so far
s it lay in the administration, precisely
nd without reserve. Long after it had
een printed, this MS. still remained
ncorporated with the MSS. of the Cu-
ia.

[4] Most ample privileges of the minorite friars of the order of St. Francis,
which are called on that account a
great sea.—Bullarium Rom. iii. 3, 139.
A similar bull was issued in favor of
the Dominicans; this " Mare-Mag-
num " attracted much attention in the
Lateran council of 1512; but privileges,
so at least was then the case, are more
readily conferred than revoked.

that they must have possessed enormous influence. The higher offices and more important dignities were monopolized, together with their revenues, by the great families and their dependents, shared only with the favorites of courts and of the Curia; the actual discharge of the various duties was confided to the mendicant friars who were upheld by the popes. They took active part also in the sale of indulgences, to which so unusual an extension was given at that time, Alexander VI being the first to declare officially that they were capable of releasing souls from purgatory. But the orders also had fallen into the extreme of worldliness. What intrigues were set on foot among them for securing the higher appointments! What eagerness was displayed at elections to be rid of a rival or of a voter believed unfavorable! The latter were sent out of the way as preachers or as inspectors of remote parishes; against the former, they did not scruple to employ the sword, or the dagger, and many were destroyed by poison.[5] Meanwhile the comforts men seek from religion became mere matter of sale; the mendicant friars, employed at miserably low wages, caught eagerly at all contingent means of making profit.

"Woe is me!" exclaims one of the prelates before alluded to, "Who are they that have turned my eyes to fountains of tears? Even those set apart and elect have fallen off; the vineyard of the Lord is laid waste. Were they to perish alone, this were an evil, yet one that might be endured: but since they are diffused through all Christendom as are the veins through the body, so must their corruption and downfall bring on the ruin of the world!"

Section III.—Intellectual Tendency

Could we unfold the book of history, and lay its facts before our eyes in their connected reality; were the fleeting events of time to display their most concealed mechanism before us, as do the eternal forms of nature, how often should we not be comforted by perceiving in the first as in the last, that the fresh germ

[5] In a voluminous report from Caraffa to Clement, which is given by Bromato, " Vita di Paolo IV.," in a mutilated form only, the passage following occurs in the manuscript of the monasteries: "They proceed to commit murders, not only by poison, but openly with the dagger and the sword, to say nothing of firearms."

is hidden beneath the decay we deplore, and that new life is proceeding from death!

Deeply as we may lament the earthward tendency of spiritual things, and the corruption we have just described as existing in religious institutions; yet, but for these evils, the mind of man could with difficulty have entered on that peculiar path, which, more directly than any other, has led to his essential progress, moral and intellectual.

We cannot deny the fact, that, ingenious, diversified, and profound as are the productions of the middle ages, they are yet based on views of the world, visionary in character and but little in accordance with the reality of things. Had the Church remained in full and conscious power, she would have adhered firmly to these views, narrowing and restricting as they were; but as she now was, the human intellect was left at liberty to seek a new development in a totally altered direction.

We may safely assert that, during those ages, the mind of man was necessarily held within the limits of a closely bounded horizon. The renewed acquaintance with antiquity removed this barrier, and opened a loftier, a more comprehensive, and a grander prospect.

Not that the classic authors were altogether unknown to the middle ages. The avidity with which the Arabs, to whom we are indebted for the introduction of so many branches of science into the West, collected and appropriated the works of the ancients, was but little inferior to the zeal with which the Italians of the fifteenth century pursued the same object. Caliph Mamoun does not lose by comparison in this respect with Cosmo de' Medici. There was nevertheless a difference, which, though at first sight it may seem of no great moment, is in my opinion all-important. The Arabs translated, but they often destroyed the originals. Their translations being pervaded, and thus transmuted, by their own peculiar ideas, the end was, that in their hands, Aristotle was wrested, so to speak, into a system of theosophy. Astronomy was perverted to astrology, and this last applied to medicine. They may thus be said to have aided in producing those visionary views of things to which we have before alluded. The Italians, on the contrary, extracted true profit from all they read. They proceeded from the Romans to the Greeks. The art of printing disseminated the originals throughout the world in copies innumerable: the true Aristotle superseded that falsified by the Arabs. Men studied science from the unaltered works of the ancients: geography directly from Ptolemy, botany from Dioscorides, medicine from Galen and Hippocrates. How rapidly was the mind of man then delivered from the fantasies that had hitherto peopled the world—from the prejudices that had held his spirit in thrall.

We should, however, say too much, were we to assert for these times an immediate evidence of originality in the cultivation of literature and science, the discovery of new truths, or the production of grand ideas; as yet men sought only to comprehend the ancients, none thought of going beyond them. The efficacy of the classic writers lay not so much in the impulse given to production and the growth of a creative spirit in literature, as in the habit of imitation that their works called forth.

But in this imitation will be found one of the causes most immediately contributing to the mental progress of that period.

Men sought to emulate the ancients in their own language. Leo X was an especial patron of this pursuit: he read the well-written introduction to the history of Jovius aloud in the circle of his intimates, declaring that since the works of Livy nothing so good had been produced. A patron of the Latin improvisators, we may readily conceive the charm he would find in the talents of Vida, who could set forth a subject like the game of chess, in the full tones of well-cadenced Latin hexameters. A mathematician, celebrated for expounding his science in elegant Latin, was invited from Portugal; in this manner he would have had theology and jurisprudence taught, and church history written.

Meanwhile it was not possible that things could remain stationary. Once arrived at this point, to whatever extent the direct imitation of the ancients in their own tongues might be carried, it was utterly insufficient to occupy the whole field of intellect; there was something in it incomplete, unsatisfactory, and it was so widely practised that this defect could not long escape the general notice. The new idea gradually arose of imitating the ancients in the mother tongue. The men of that day felt themselves to stand in the same position with regard to the classic authors, as did the Romans with regard to the Greeks: they determined no longer to confine themselves within the bounds of a contest in mere details; on the broad fields of literature were they now resolved to vie with their masters, and with youthful enthusiasm did they rush forward on this new career.

The language of nations was fortunately receiving at this precise moment an improved and regulated form. The merit of Bembo does not consist so much in the finished style of his Latin, nor in those essays in Italian poetry still remaining to us, as in his well-devised and happily successful efforts to give correctness and dignity to his mother tongue, and to establish its construction according to fixed rules. This it is for which he has been praised by Ariosto; he appeared precisely at the right moment, his own literary attempts serving to exemplify his doctrines.

If we examine the circle of works, formed on antique models, but of which the medium was that Italian so incomparable for harmony and flexibility, and which had been so skilfully adapted to the purposes of the writer, the following observations are forced on our attention.

But little success resulted from the efforts of those who sought too close an adherence to the classic model. Tragedies, like the " Rosmunda " of Rucellai, constructed, as the editors assure us, entirely after the antique: didactic poems, like " The Bees " of the same author (wherein we are from the very first referred to Virgil, who is turned to account in a thousand ways throughout the poem), were by no means favorably received, nor did they produce any real effect on the progress of literature. Comedies were from the first less restrained. It was in their very nature to assume the color and impression of the time; but the groundwork was almost invariably some fable of antiquity, or a plot borrowed from Plautus.[1] Men, even of such talent as was possessed by Bibbiena and Machiavelli, have failed to secure for their attempts

[1] Marco Minio, among many other remarkable things, describes to the Signory the circumstances attending the first production of a comedy in Rome. His date is the 13th of March, 1519. (See App. No. 8.) " The festival being finished, they went to a comedy given by Monsignore Cibo, where was a fine sight, with decoration more superb than I can tell. In the comedy there was feigned to be a Ferrara, and in the said hall was made Ferrara, exactly as it is. They say that Monsignor Cibo, passing through Ferrara, and wishing to have a comedy, that one was given him; it was taken from the ' Suppositi ' of Plautus and the ' Eunuchus ' of Terence—very beautiful." He doubtless means the " Suppositi " of Ariosto, but we may remark that he mentions neither the name of the author nor the title of the piece, only whence it was taken.

in comedy the entire approbation of later times. In works of a different description, we occasionally perceive a species of conflict between their component parts, ancient and modern. Thus, in the "Arcadia" of Sanazzaro, how peculiarly do the prolix periods and stilted Latinity of the prose contrast with the simplicity, the earnest feeling, and rare melody of the verse!

If the success obtained, considerable as it was, did not arrive at perfection, that should by no means excite astonishment: a great example was at all events given—an attempt made that has proved infinitely productive; still, the modern elements of literature neither did nor could move with perfect freedom in the classic forms: the spirit was mastered by rules imposed on it from without, and in flagrant discord with its own nature.

But how could anything really great be produced by mere imitation? The master-works of antiquity do assuredly possess their own influence as models, but this is the influence of mind on mind. It is the firm conviction of our own times that the beautiful type is to educate, to form, to excite, but never to enslave.

The most felicitous creation might, on the other hand, be reasonably hoped for, when the genius of those times should arouse itself to the production of a work, departing in form and matter from the writers of antiquity, and affected by their internal influence only.

The romantic epos owes its peculiar charm to the fact that it fulfils these conditions. A Christian fable, combining the religious influence with heroic interests, supplied the groundwork: the most prominent figures were depicted by a few bold broad general traits; efficient situations, but slightly developed, were ready to the hand of the poet, as was the poetic expression which was presented to him immediately from the common colloquy of the people. In aid of all this came the tendency of the age to adapt itself to the antique, of which the humanizing influences colored and informed the whole. How different is the Rinaldo of Bojardo—noble, modest, replete with a joyous love of action and adventure—from the desperate son of Aimon of the old legend! How does the extravagant, the violent, the gigantic of the earlier representation, become transformed into the intelligible, the graceful, and the charming! There is doubtless something attractive and agreeable in the simplicity of the unadorned old stories; but how greatly is our enjoyment increased, when the melody of Ariosto's verse floats along with us, and we pass from one bright picture to another in companionship with a cultivated mind and frank, cheerful spirit! The unlovely and formless has wrought itself into beauty, symmetry, and music.[2]

A keen susceptibility to pure beauty of form, with the power of expressing it, is manifested at a few favored periods only; the end of the fifteenth and beginning of the sixteenth centuries was one of them. How can I hope to indicate, were it but in outline, the wealth of art, whether in conception or practice, that filled those times—the fervid devotion that gave life to every effort? We may boldly affirm, that whatever of most beautiful the later ages have produced in architecture, sculpture, or painting is all due to this short period. The tendency of the time was not toward abstract reasonings, but rather toward a vivid life and active practice: in this earnest medium did men live and move. I may even say that the fortress erected by the prince against his enemy, and the note written by the philologist on the margin of his author, have a certain something in common: a severe and chaste beauty forms the groundwork of all the productions of the period.

We cannot, however, refuse to acknowledge that when art and poetry took possession of religious materials, they did not leave the import of them unchanged. The romantic epos, presenting us with a legend of the Church, is usually in direct opposition to the spirit of that legend. Ariosto found it needful to dismiss from his fable the background containing its original signification.

In earlier times the share of religion was equal with that of art, in every work of the painter or sculptor; but no sooner had the breath of antiquity been felt on the bosom of art than the bonds that had chained her to subjects exclusively religious were cast from her spirit. We see this change manifest itself more decidedly from year to year even in the works of Raphael. People may blame this, if they please; but it would seem to be certain that the co-operation of the profane element was necessary to the full development and bloom of art.

---

[2] I have endeavored to work out this subject in a special treatise read before the Royal Academy of Sciences.

And was it not profoundly significant that a pope should himself resolve to demolish the ancient basilica of St. Peter, the metropolitan church of Christendom, every part of which was hallowed, every portion crowded with monuments that had received the veneration of ages, and determine to erect a temple, planned after those of antiquity, on its site? This was a purpose exclusively artistic. The two factions then dividing the jealous and contentious world of art, united in urging Julius II to this enterprise. Michael Angelo desired a fitting receptacle for that monument to the pope which he proposed to complete on a vast scale, and with that lofty grandeur which he has exhibited in his Moses. Yet more pressing was Bramante. It was his ambition to have space for the execution of that bold project, long before conceived, of raising high in air, on colossal pillars, an exact copy of the Pantheon, in all the majesty of its proportions. Many cardinals remonstrated, and it would even appear that there was a general opposition to the plan; so much of personal affection attaches itself to every old church, how much more then to this, the chief sanctuary of Christendom![3] But Julius was not accustomed to regard contradiction; without further consideration he caused one-half of the old church to be demolished, and himself laid the foundation-stone of the new one.

Thus rose again, in the heart and centre of the Christian worship, those forms in which the spirit of the antique rites had found so eloquent an expression. At San Pietro in Montorio, and over the blood of the martyr, Bramante erected a chapel in the light and cheerful form of a peripteros.

If this involve a contradiction, it was one that pervaded the whole existence and affected all the habits of the times.

Men frequented the Vatican, less to kneel in devotion on the threshold of the apostles than to admire those great works of ancient art that enriched the dwelling of the pontiff—the Belvedere Apollo and the Laocoon.

It is true that the Pope was exhorted as earnestly as ever

---

[3] The following passage is given by Fea, from the unprinted work of Panvinius (" De rebus antiquis memorabilibus et de præstantia basilicæ S. Petri Apostolorum Principis," etc.): "In which matter he had men of almost all clsses against him, and especially the cardinals; not because they did not wish to have a new basilica erected with all possible magnificence, but because they grieved that the old one should be pulled down, revered as it was by the whole world, ennobled by the sepulchres of so many saints, and illustrious for so many great things that had been done in it."

o make war against infidels. I find this, for example, in a preface of Navagero,[4] but the writer was not concerning himself for the interests of Christianity; his hope was that the pontiff would thus recover the lost writings of the Greeks and perhaps of the Romans.

In this exuberance of effort and production, of intellect and art, and in the enjoyment of increasing temporal power attached to the highest spiritual dignity, lived Leo X. Men have questioned his title to the honor of giving his name to the period, and he had not perhaps any great merit in doing so, but he was indubitably favored by circumstances. His character had been formed in the midst of those elements that fashioned the world of his day, and he had liberality of mind and susceptibility of feeling that fitted him for the furtherance of its progress and the enjoyment of its advantages. If he found pleasure in the efforts of those who were but imitators of the Latin, still more would the works of his contemporaries delight him. It was in his presence that the first tragedy was performed, and (spite of the objections liable to be found in a play imitating Plautus) the first comedy also that was produced in the Italian language; there is, indeed, scarcely one that was not first seen by him. Ariosto was among the acquaintance of his youth. Machiavelli composed more than one of his works expressly for him. His halls, galleries, and chapels were filled by Raphael with the rich ideal of human beauty, and with the purest expression of life in its most varied forms. He was a passionate lover of music, a more scientific practice of which was just then becoming diffused throughout Italy; the sounds of music were daily heard floating through the palace, Leo himself humming the airs that were performed. This may all be considered a sort of intellectual sensuality, but it is at least the only one that does not degrade the man. Leo X was full of kindness and ready sympathies; rarely did he refuse a request, and when compelled to do so evinced his reluctance by the gentlest expressions. " He is a good man," says an observant ambassador, " very bounteous and kindly; he would avoid all disorders, if it were not that his kinsmen incite him to them."[5]
' He is learned," says another, " and the friend of the learned;

[4] Naugerii Præfatio in " Ciceronis Orationes," t. i.
[5] Zorzi: " As to the Pope, he desires neither wars nor troubles, but his kindred embroil him in both." (See App. 7.)

religious too, but he will enjoy his life."[6] It is true that he did
not always attend to the pontifical proprieties. He would sometimes leave Rome—to the despair of his master of the ceremonies—not only without a surplice, but, as that officer ruefully
bemoans in his journal, "what is worst of all, even with boots
on his feet!" It was his custom to pass the autumn in rural
pleasures. At Viterbo he amused himself with hawking, and
at Corneto with hunting the stag. The Lake of Bolsena afforded him the pleasure of fishing, or he would pass a certain
time at his favorite residence of Malliana, whither he was accompanied by improvisatori and other men of light and agreeable talents, capable of making every hour pass pleasantly.
Toward winter he returned with his company to Rome, which
was now in great prosperity, the number of its inhabitants
having increased full one-third in a very few years. Here the
mechanic found employment, the artist honor, and safety was
assured to all. Never had the court been more animated, more
graceful, more intellectual. In the matter of festivities, whether
spiritual or temporal, no cost was spared, nor was any expenditure found too lavish when the question was of amuse-
ments, theatres, presents, or marks of favor. There was high
jubilee when it was known that Giuliano de' Medici meant to
settle with his young wife in Rome. "God be praised," writes
Cardinal Bibbiena to him, "for here we lack nothing but a court
with ladies."

The debasing sensuality of Alexander VI cannot fail to
be regarded with horror and loathing; in the court of Leo X
there were few things deserving absolute blame, although we
cannot but perceive that his pursuits might have been more
strictly in accordance with his position as supreme head of the
Church.

Easily does life veil its own incongruities as they pass, but
no sooner do men set themselves to ponder, examine, and compare, than at once they become fully apparent to all.

Of true Christian sentiment and conviction there could be
no question in such a state of things; they were, on the contrary, directly opposed.

The schools of philosophy disputed as to whether the reasonable soul were really immaterial and immortal—but one

[6] Marco Minio, "Relazione." He calls him "bona persona." (See App. No. 8.)

single spirit only and common to all mankind—or whether it were absolutely mortal.

Pietro Pomponazzo, the most distinguished philosopher of the day, did not scruple to uphold the latter opinion. He compared himself to Prometheus, whose heart was devoured by the vulture, because he had sought to steal fire from Jupiter; but with all the painful efforts Pomponazzo could make, with all his subtlety, he could arrive at no other result than this: ' If the lawgiver declared the soul immortal, he had done so without troubling himself about the truth." [7]

Nor are we to believe that these opinions were confined to a few, or held only in secret. Erasmus declares himself astonished at the blasphemies that met his ears; attempts were made to prove to him—a foreigner—by passages from Pliny, that the souls of men are absolutely identical with those of beasts. [8]

While the populace had sunk into almost heathen superstition, and expected their salvation from mere ceremonial observances, but half understood, the higher classes were manifesting opinions of a tendency altogether anti-religious.

How profoundly astonished must Luther have been, on visiting Italy in his youth! At the very moment when the sacrifice of the mass was completed, did the priests utter blasphemous words in denial of its reality!

It was even considered characteristic of good society in Rome to call the principles of Christianity in question. "One passes," says P. Ant. Bandino,[9] "no longer for a man of cultivation, unless one put forth heterodox opinions regarding the Christian faith." At court, the ordinances of the Catholic Church, and of passages from holy Scripture, were made subjects of jest—the mysteries of the faith had become matter of derision.

[7] Pomponazzo was very seriously assailed on this subject, as appears from extracts of papal letters by Contelori, and from other proofs. " Peter of Mantua has asserted that, according to the principles of philosophy and the opinion of Aristotle, the reasoning soul is or appears to be mortal, contrary to the determination of the Lateran council; the Pope commands that the said Peter shall retract, otherwise that he be proceeded against."

[8] Burigny, " Life of Erasmus," i. 139. Here may also be quoted the following passage from Paul Canensius in the ' Vita Pauli II ":—" With no less diligence he banished from the Roman Court a nefarious sect, and the abominable opinion of some youths who, depraved of morals, maintained that our orthodox faith was founded rather on certain subtleties of the saints than on the true testimonies of things." A very decided materialism is evinced by " The Triumph of Charlemagne," a poem by Ludovici, as may be seen from the quotations of Daru in the 40th book of his " Histoire de Venise."

[9] In Caracciolo's MS. life of Paul IV: " At that time he seemed neither a gentleman nor a good courtier who did not hold some false and heretical opinion as to the doctrines of the Church."

We thus see how all is enchained and connected—how one event calls forth another. The pretensions of temporal princes to ecclesiastical power awaken a secular ambition in the popes, the corruption and decline of religious institutions elicit the development of a new intellectual tendency, till at length the very foundations of the faith become shaken in the public opinion.

Section IV.—Opposition to the Papacy in Germany

There appears to me something especially remarkable in the dispositions of Germany, as exhibited at this moment. In the intellectual development we have just been considering, her part was a decided and influential one, but conducted in a manner peculiar to herself.

In Italy, the promoters of classical study, and those from whom the age received its impulse toward it, were poets; as, for example, Boccaccio and Petrarch. In Germany, the same effect was due to a religious fraternity, the Hieronymites—a community united by a life of labor, passed in sequestration from the world. It was one of this brotherhood, the profound and blameless mystic, Thomas à Kempis, from whose school proceeded all those earnest and venerable men who, first drawn to Italy by the light of ancient learning, newly kindled there, afterward returned to pour its beneficent influence over the breadth of Germany.[1]

The difference thus observable in the beginning was equally apparent in the subsequent progress.

In Italy the works of the ancients were studied for the sciences they contained; in Germany, for the aids they offered to the study of philosophy. The Italians sought a solution of the highest problems that can occupy the human intellect, if not by independent thought, at least with the help of the ancients; the Germans collected all that was best throughout antiquity for the education of their youth. The Italians were attracted toward the ancients by the beauty of form; this they sought to imitate, and thence proceeded to the formation of a national literature: among the Germans, these same

[1] Meiners has the merit of having first brought to light this genealogy from the " Daventria Illustrata of Revius." Lives of celebrated men belonging to the period of the revival of letters.

studies took a more spiritual direction. The fame of Erasmus and Reuchlin is familiar to all; if we inquire what constitutes the principal merit of the latter, we find it to be his
having written the first Hebrew grammar—a monument of
which he hoped, as did the Italian poets of their works, that
" it would be more durable than brass "; as by him the study
of the Old Testament was first facilitated, so was that of the
New Testament indebted to Erasmus. To this it was that his
attention was devoted; it was he who first caused it to be
printed in Greek, and his paraphrases and commentaries on
it have produced an effect far surpassing the end he had proposed to himself.

While the public mind of Italy had become alienated from,
and even opposed to, the Church, an effect in some respects
similar had taken place in Germany. There, that freedom
of thought which can never be wholly suppressed, gained
admission into the literary world, and occasionally displayed
itself in decided scepticism. A more profound theology, also,
had arisen, from sources but imperfectly known, and though
discountenanced by the Church, had never been put down;
this now formed an essential part of the literary movement in
Germany. In this point of view, I consider it worthy of remark, that, even as early as the year 1513, the Bohemian
brethren made advances to Erasmus, whose modes of thought
were, nevertheless, entirely different from their own.[2]

Thus, on either side the Alps, the progress of the age was
in direct opposition to ecclesiastical ascendancy. In Italy this
tendency was associated with science and literature; in Germany it arose from biblical studies, and a more profound theology. There it was negative and incredulous; here it was
positive, and full of an earnest faith. There it destroyed the very
foundations of the Church; here the desire was to construct the
edifice anew. In Italy it was mocking and sarcastic, but ever
pliant and deferential to power; in Germany, full of a serious
indignation, and deeply determined on a stubbornness of assault
such as the Roman Church had never before experienced.

The fact that this was first directed against the abuses arising
from the sale of indulgences, has sometimes been regarded as
mere matter of accident; but as the alienation of that which

[2] Füsslin, " Kirchen- und Ketzer-geschichte," ii. 82.

is most essentially spiritual, involved in the doctrine of indulgences laid open and gave to view the weakest point in the whole system—that worldliness of spirit now prevalent in the Church—so was it, of all things, best calculated to shock and offend the convictions of those earnest and profound thinkers, the German theologians. A man like Luther, whose religion was sincere and deeply felt, whose opinions of sin and justification were those propounded by the early German theologists, and confirmed in his mind by the study of Scripture, which he had drunk in with a thirsting heart, could not fail to be revolted and shocked by the sale of indulgences. Forgiveness of sins to be purchased for money! this must of necessity be deeply offensive to him, whose conclusions were drawn from profound contemplation of the eternal relation subsisting between God and man, and who had learned to interpret Scripture for himself.

It is true that he did, by all means, oppose the sale of indulgences; but, the ill-founded and prejudiced opposition he encountered, leading him on from step to step, he was presently made aware of the connection subsisting between this monstrous abuse and the general disorders of the Church. His was not a nature to shrink from, or tremble at, the most extreme measures. With unhesitating boldness, he attacked the head of the Church himself. From the midst of an order, hitherto the most submissive adherents and devoted defenders of the papacy, that of the Friars-Mendicant, now rose the most determined and most vigorous opponent the pontificate had yet known. And as Luther, with the utmost precision and acuteness, held up its own declared principles in the face of that power which had so widely departed from them—as he did but express truths of which all men had long been convinced—as his opposition, the full import of which had not yet become apparent, was acceptable to those who rejected the faith, and yet, because it was undertaken in defence of those principles, was consonant to the mind of the earnest believer—so had his writings an incalculable effect, and were rapidly disseminated, not in Germany alone, but through the whole world.

CHAPTER THIRD

POLITICAL COMPLICATIONS.—CONNECTION BE-
TWEEN THESE AND THE REFORMATION

THE secular spirit that had now taken possession of the papacy had occasioned a twofold movement in the world. The one was religious; a falling off from the Church had begun, whence it was manifest that the future would behold results of immeasurable consequence. The second movement was of a political nature; the conflicting elements so long in action were still fermenting violently, and could not fail to produce new combinations. These two movements, their effect on each other, and the contests to which they gave rise, imposed their influence on the history of the popedom during a period of ages.

Well would it be for states and princes, would all be convinced that no essential good can result to them except from their own exertions—that no benefit is real unless acquired by their own native strength and effort!

While the Italian powers were laboring to conquer each other by foreign aid, they were in effect destroying that independence which they had enjoyed during the fifteenth century, and exposing their common country to be the prize of a foreign victor. A large share in this result must be imputed to the popes. It is certain that they had now acquired a sovereignty such as had never before been possessed by the Papal See; but this was by no means attributable to themselves —it was to the French, the Spaniards, the Germans, and Swiss, that they were indebted for the whole. Very little would Cæsar Borgia have accomplished, had it not been for his alliance with Louis XII; nor could Julius II have escaped destruction, enlarged as were his views, and heroic his achievements, had he not been upheld by the Spaniards and Swiss.

How could those who had gained the victory fail to seek their utmost profit in the preponderance it procured them? Julius did not neglect to ask himself this question, and sought to maintain a kind of equipoise by employing only the least formidable—the Swiss, namely: believing he might lead them as he pleased.

But the event failed to justify this expectation: two great powers arose, and these contended, if not for the sovereignty of the world, at least for supremacy in Europe; with neither of them could the pontiff hope to compete, and it was in Italy that they sought their battle-ground.

The French were the first to show themselves: soon after the accession of Leo X they appeared, in greater force than any with which they had ever before crossed the Alps, to regain possession of Milan. Francis I, in all the ardor of his chivalrous youth, was their leader. Everything depended on the question of whether the Swiss could resist him or not; therefore it was that the battle of Marignano had so paramount an importance; for here this question was resolved. The Swiss were totally routed, and since that defeat they have exercised no independent influence in Italy.

The battle had remained undecided on the first day, and a report of victory to the Swiss having reached Rome, bonfires had been lighted throughout the city. The earliest intelligence of the second day's battle and its result was received by the envoy of the Venetians, who were in alliance with Francis, and had in no small degree contributed to decide the fortune of the day. At a very early hour of the morning he hastened to the Vatican to communicate his intelligence to the Pope, who came forth when but half-dressed to give him audience. " Your holiness," said the envoy, " gave me bad news last night, and they were false beside; to-day I bring you good news, and they are true: the Swiss are beaten." He then read the letters he had received, and which, being written by men known to the Pope, left no doubt remaining.[1] Leo did not conceal his profound alarm. " What then will become of us? What will become even of yourselves?" he inquired. "We hope the best

---

[1] " Summario de la relatione di Zorzi:" " E cussi dismissiato venne fuori non compito di vestir. L' orator disse: Pater sante eri vra santa mi dette una cattiva nuova e falsa, io le daro ozi una bona e vera, zoe Sguizari è rotti." The letters were from Pasqualigo, Dandolo, and others. (App. No. 7.)

for both." " Sir Envoy," replied the Pope, " we must throw ourselves into the King's arms and cry misericordia." [2]

In effect, the French acquired a decided preponderance in Italy by this victory. Had it been vigorously followed up, neither Tuscany near the States of the Church, both so easily incited to revolt, could have offered them resistance, and the Spaniards would have found it sufficiently difficult to maintain themselves in Naples. " The King," says Francesco Vettori, explicitly, " might become lord of Italy." How much was at this moment depending on Leo !

Lorenzo de' Medici said of his three sons, Julian, Peter and John, that the first was good, the second a fool, but that for the third, John, he was prudent. This third was Pope Leo X; and he now showed himself equal to the difficult position into which he had fallen.

Contrary to the advice of his cardinals, he betook himself to Bologna to have a conference with the King: [3] then it was that they concluded the concordat (before alluded to), in which they divided between them the rights of the Gallican Church; Leo was compelled to give up Parma and Placentia, but he succeeded in dispersing the storm that had threatened him, persuaded the King to return, and himself remained secure in the possession of his dominions.

How fortunate this was for the pontiff, may be seen from the effects immediately produced by the mere approach of the French. It is highly deserving of remark that Leo, after his allies had been defeated and himself obliged to yield up a portion of his territory, was yet able to retain his hold on two provinces, but lately conquered, accustomed to independence, and replete with every element of revolt.

Leo X has been constantly censured for his attack on Urbino. a princely house, which had afforded refuge and hospitality to his own family when driven into exile. The provocation to this attack, and Leo's motive for resolving on it, were as follows:—
The Duke of Urbino, being in the Pope's pay, had deserted him at a very critical moment; the pontiff then said that " if he did

[2] " Domine orator, vederemo quel fara il re Christmo se metteremo in lo so man dimandando misericordia, Lui orator disse: Pater sante, vostra santità non avrà mal alcuno."
[3] Zorzi: " This Pope is learned and practised in matters of state, and he took counsel with his advisers about going to Bologna to hold conference, with the modesty proper to the Apostolic See; many cardinals, among whom was Cardinal Hadrian, sought to dissuade him, but for all that he would go."

not visit him with punishment for this, there would be no baron
in the States of the Church so powerless as not to venture opposing him. He had found the pontificate respected; nor
should it cease to be while in his hands."[4] As, however, the
duke was upheld by the French, at least in secret—as he had
partisans throughout the States, and even in the college of cardinals, a contest with him was likely to prove dangerous: it
was no easy matter to expel so warlike a prince. Leo was occasionally seen to tremble at the receipt of unfavorable news,
and was often reduced to extreme perplexity. It is said, too,
that a plan was formed for poisoning him in the course of treatment for a malady under which he labored. The Pope did at
length succeed in defending himself from this enemy, but we
have seen that it was not without great difficulty. The defeat
of his party by the French affected him, not only in his capital,
but even in his very palace.[5]

The second great power had meanwhile become consolidated. How extraordinary does it seem that one and the same
prince should hold the sceptre in Vienna, Brussels, Valladolid,
Saragossa, and Naples! Nor was this all—his rule extended
even to another continent; yet this was brought about almost
imperceptibly by a series of family alliances. This aggrandizement of the house of Austria, which linked together so many
different countries, was one of the most important and eventful changes that Europe had yet witnessed. At that moment
when the nations were diverging from the point that had hitherto been their common centre, they were again gathered, by their
political circumstances, into new combinations and formed into
a new system. The power of Austria instantly placed itself in
opposition to the preponderance of France. With his imperial
dignity, Charles V acquired legal claims to supremacy, at least
in Lombardy. This being the state of things in Italy, war was
kindled with but slight delay.

The popes, as we have before remarked, had hoped to secure
entire independence by the extension of their states; they now
found themselves hemmed in between two greatly superior

[4] Franc. Vettori ("Sommario della
Storia d' Italia"), intimately connected
with the Medici, gives this explanation
(see App. 16). The defender of Francesco Maria, Giovo. Batt. Leoni, relates
facts tending very nearly to the same
import.

[5] Fea, in the "Notizie intorno Rafaele," p. 35, has given the sentence
against the three cardinals from the
Acts of the Consistory, and this refers
distinctly to their understanding with
Francesco Maria.

powers. A pope was not so insignificant as that he could remain neutral in a strife between them, neither was he sufficiently powerful to secure preponderance for that scale into which he should cast his weight; his safety could only be found in the dexterous use of passing events. Leo is reported to have said, that when a man has formed a compact with one party, he must none the less take care to negotiate with the other;[6] this double-tongued policy was forced on him by the position in which he was placed.

But the pontiff could not seriously entertain a doubt as to the party which it was his interest to adopt; for had he not felt it of infinite importance to regain Parma and Placentia—had the promise of Charles V, that an Italian should hold possession of Milan, a thing so much to his advantage, been insufficient to determine his choice, there was still another consideration, and one that appears to me entirely conclusive—this was a motive connected with religion.

Throughout the whole period of time that we are contemplating, there was no assistance so much desired by the temporal sovereigns in their disputes with the popes as that of a spiritual opposition to their decrees. Charles VIII of France had no more efficient ally against Alexander VI than the Dominican Giralamo Savonarola of Florence. When Louis XII had resigned all hope of a reconciliation with Julius II, he summoned a council to meet at Pisa, and this, though producing no great effect, yet excited much alarm in Rome. But when had the Pope so bold or so prosperous an opponent as Luther? The mere fact that so fearless a foe to the popedom had made his appearance, the very existence of such a phenomenon, was highly significant, and imparted to the person of the reformer a decided political importance. It was thus that Maximilian considered it, nor would he permit injury of any kind to be offered to this monk; he caused him to be specially recommended to the elector of Saxony—"there might come a time when he would be needed"—and from that moment the influence of Luther increased day by day. The Pope could neither convince nor alarm this impracticable opponent, neither could he get him into his hands. It must not be supposed that Leo

[6] Suriano, "Relatione di 1533": "Dicesi del Papa Leone, che quando il aveva fatto lega con alcuno prima, soleva dir che però non si dovea restar de tratar cum e altro principe opposto."

failed to perceive the danger; more than once did he urge the
many theologians and men of talent by whom he was surrounded in Rome, to engage themselves in contest with this
formidable controversialist. One resource yet remained to him.
Might he not hope that by an alliance with the Emperor, he
should secure the aid of that sovereign for the repression of
these religious innovations? as it is certain that they would be
protected and even promoted by the Emperor, should Leo declare
against him.

The affairs of Europe, religious and political, were the subject of discussion in the Diet of Worms (1521). Here the
Pope entered into a league with the Emperor for the recovery
of Milan. On the day when the alliance was concluded, the
edict of outlawry proclaimed against Luther is said to have
been also dated. There may have been other motives operating
to produce this act of proscription; but no one will persuade
himself that there was not an immediate connection between
the outlawry and the political treaty.

And no long time elapsed before the twofold effect of this
league became manifest.

Luther was seized on the Wartburg and kept in concealment.[7] The Italians at once refused to believe that Charles had
allowed him to escape, from a conscientious regard to the safe-
conduct he had granted. "Since he perceived," said they,
"that the Pope greatly feared of Luther's doctrine, he designed
to hold him in check with that rein."[8]

However this may be, Luther certainly disappeared for some
time from the stage of the world; he was to a certain extent
without the pale of the law, and the Pope had in any case procured the adoption of decisive measures against him.

The combined forces of the Pope and Emperor were meanwhile successful in Italy; one of Leo's nearest relations, Cardinal Giulio de' Medici, the son of his father's brother, was
himself in the field, and entered with the conquering army into
Milan. It was asserted in Rome that the Pope had designs of
conferring on him the duchy; but I find no distinct proof of

[7] Luther was believed to be dead; it was said that he had been murdered by the partisans of the Pope. Palavicini ("Istoria del Concilio di Trento," i. c. 28) infers from the letters of Alexander, that the nuncios were in danger of their lives on that account.

[8] Vettori: "Carlo si excusò di non poter procedere più oltre rispetto al salvocondotto, ma la verità fu, che conoscendo che il papa temeva molto di questa doctrina di Luthero, lo volle tenere con questo freno." (See text.)

this, nor do I think the Emperor would readily have acceded to it: even without this, however, the advantages gained by Rome were enormous. Parma and Placentia were recovered, the French were compelled to withdraw, and the Pope might safely calculate on exercising great influence over the new sovereign of Milan.

It was a crisis of infinite moment: a new state of things had arisen in politics—a great movement had commenced in the Church. The aspect of affairs permitted Leo to flatter himself that he should retain the power of directing the first, and he had succeeded in repressing the second. He was still young enough to indulge the anticipation of fully profiting by the results of this auspicious moment.

Strange and delusive destiny of man! The Pope was at his villa of Malliana, when he received intelligence that his party had triumphantly entered Milan; he abandoned himself to the exultation arising naturally from the successful completion of an important enterprise, and looked cheerfully on at the festivities his people were preparing on the occasion.

He paced backward and forward till deep in the night, between the window and a blazing hearth[9] —it was the month of November. Somewhat exhausted, but still in high spirits, he arrived in Rome, and the rejoicings there celebrated for his triumph were not yet concluded, when he was attacked by a mortal disease. " Pray for me," said he to his servants, " that I may yet make you all happy." We see that he loved life, but his hour was come, he had not time to receive the sacrament nor extreme unction. So suddenly, so prematurely, and surrounded by hopes so bright!—he died—" as the poppy fadeth."[10]

The Roman populace could not forgive their pontiff for dying without the sacraments — for having spent so much money, and yet leaving large debts. They pursued his corpse to its grave with insult and reproach. " Thou hast crept in like a fox," they exclaimed; " like a lion hast thou ruled us, and

[9] " Copia di una lettera di Roma alli Signori Bolognesi, a di 3 Dec. 1521, scritta per Bartholomeo Argilelli." See vol. xxxii. of Sanuto. The intelligence reached the Pope on the 24th of November, during the Benedicite. This also he accepted as a particularly good omen—" Questa e una buona nuova che havete portato," he remarked. The Swiss immediately began to fire feux-de-joie. Leo requested them to desist, but in vain.

[10] There was instant suspicion of poison. " Lettera di Hieronymo Bon a suo barba, a di 5 Dec.," in Sanuto: " It is not certainly known whether the Pope died of poison or not. He was opened. Master Fernando judged that he was poisoned, others thought not. Of this last opinion is Master Severino, who saw him opened, and says he was not poisoned."

like a dog hast thou died." [1] Aftertimes, on the contrary, have designated a century and a great epoch in the progress of mankind, by his name.

We have called him fortunate. Once he had overcome the first calamity, that after all affected other members of his house rather than himself, his destiny bore him onward from enjoyment to enjoyment, and from success to success; the most adverse circumstances were turned to his elevation and prosperity. In a species of intellectual intoxication, and in the ceaseless gratification of all his wishes, did his life flow on. This was in a great measure the result of his own better qualities—of that liberal kindness, that activity of intellect, and ready perception of good in others, which were among his distinguishing characteristics. These qualities are the fairest gifts of nature—felicitous peculiarities, rarely acquired, but when possessed how greatly do they enhance all life's enjoyments! His state affairs did but slightly disturb the current of his pleasures: he did not concern himself with the details, looking only to leading facts; thus he was not oppressed by labor, since it called into exercise the noblest faculties of his intellect only. It was perhaps precisely because he did not chain his thoughts to business, through every day and hour, that his management of affairs was so comprehensive. Whatever the perplexity of the moment, never did he lose sight of the one guiding thought that was to light his way; invariably did the essential and moving impulse emanate directly from himself. At the moment of his death, the purposes he had proposed to himself in the policy he had pursued were all tending toward the happiest results. It may be considered a further proof of his good fortune that his life was not prolonged. Times of a different character succeeded, and it is difficult to believe that he could have opposed a successful resistance to their unfavorable influences. The whole weight of them was experienced by his successors.

.   .   .   .

The conclave lasted long:—"Sirs," said the Cardinal de' Medici, whom the return of the enemies of his house to Urbino and Perugia filled with alarm, and who feared for Florence itself—"sirs, I perceive that of us who are here assembled, no one can become pope. I have proposed to you

[1] "Capitoli di una lettera scritta a Roma, 21 Dec. 1521:" "I judge there never died a pope in worse repute since the Church of God had existence."

three or four, but you have rejected them all. Neither can I accept those whom you propose; we must seek a pope among those who are not present." Assenting to this, the cardinals asked who it was that he had in view: "Take," said he, "the Cardinal of Tortosa, an aged venerable man, who is universally esteemed a saint."[2] This was Adrian of Utrecht, formerly a professor of Louvain;[3] he had been tutor to Charles V who from personal attachment had given him the office of a governor, and promoted his elevation to the dignity of cardinal. Cardinal Cajetan, although not of the Medicean party, rose to speak in praise of the candidate proposed. Who could have believed that the cardinals, ever accustomed to consult their personal interests in the choice of a pope, would agree to select an absent Netherlander, with whom no one could make conditions for his own private advantage? They suffered themselves to be surprised into this determination, and when the affair was concluded, they could not themselves account for the decision they had arrived at. "They were well-nigh dead with fright," quoth one of our authorities. They are also said to have persuaded themselves that Adrian would not accept the dignity. Pasquin amused himself at their expense, representing the pope elect as a schoolmaster, and the cardinals as schoolboys whom he was chastising.

On a worthier man, however, the choice of the conclave could scarcely have fallen. The reputation of Adrian was without a blemish; laborious, upright, and pious, he was of so earnest a gravity, that a faint smile was his nearest approach to mirth, yet benevolent withal, full of pure intentions, a true servant of religion.[4] What a contrast when he entered that city

[2] "Lettera di Roma a di 19 Zener.," in Sanuto. "Medici doubting how his affairs might go if things were too much protracted, resolved to put an end; and having in his mind that cardinal of Tortosa, as being closely attached to the Emperor, said, etc."

[3] It is thus that he calls himself in a letter of 1514, to be found in Casper Buniannus: "Adrianus VI sive analecta historica de Adriano VI." In documents belonging to his native country he is called "Master Aryan Florisse of Utrecht." Modern writers sometimes call him Boyens, because his father signs himself Floris Boyens; but this means no other than Bodewin's son, and is not a family name. See Bourmann, in the notes to "Moringi Vita Adriani," p. 2.

[4] "Litteræ ex Victorial directivæ ad Cardinalem de Flisco," in the 33d volume of Sanuto, describe him in the terms following: "A man tenacious of his own; very cautious in conceding; and never, or very rarely, accepting. He performs early mass daily. Whom he loves, or whether he love any, none hath discovered; he is not affected by anger, nor moved by jests, nor has he seemed to exult at obtaining the pontificate; on the contrary, it is said that on receiving the news of it he uttered a groan." In the collection of Burmann, will be found an "Itenerarium Adriani," by Ortiz, who accompanied the pope and knew him intimately. He declares (p. 223) that he never observed anything in him deserving censure; he was a mirror of all the virtues.

wherein Leo had held his court with so lavish a splendor! There
is a letter of his extant in which he declares that he would
rather serve God in his priory at Louvain, than be pope.[5] And
his life in the Vatican was in fact the counterpart of what he
had led as professor at Louvain. It is characteristic of the man,
and we may be permitted to relate the circumstance, that he
brought his old housekeeper from his priory to his palace,
where she continued to provide for his domestic wants as before. Nor did he make any alteration in his personal habits.
He rose with the earliest dawn, said mass, and then proceeded
in the usual order to his business and studies, which were
interrupted only by the most frugal meal. He cannot be said
to have remained a stranger to the general culture or acquirements of his age: he loved Flemish art, and prized the learning that was adorned with a tinge of eloquence. Erasmus ac-
knowledges that he was especially protected by the Pope from
the attacks of bigoted schoolmen.[6] But he disapproved the almost heathenish character which modes of thought had assumed at Rome in his day; and as to poets, he would not even
hear them named. No one could be more earnest than was
Adrian VI (he chose to retain his original designation) in his
desire to ameliorate the grievous condition into which Christendom had fallen at his accession.

The progress of the Turkish arms, with the fall of Belgrade
and of Rhodes, furnished a new impulse to his anxiety for
the re-establishment of peace among the Christian powers.
Although he had been preceptor to the Emperor, he yet assumed
an entirely neutral position. The imperial ambassador who
had hoped, on the new outbreak of war, that he should move
the pontiff to declare for his late pupil, was compelled to leave
Rome without accomplishing his purpose.[7] When the news
of the conquest of Rhodes was read to the Pope, he bent his
eyes to the ground, said not a word, and sighed deeply.[8] The

[5] Florenz. Oem Wyngaerden: "Vittoria," 15 Feb. 1522. See Burmann, p.
398.
[6] Erasmus says of him in one of his
letters: "Although he favored the
scholastic teaching, he is very fair
toward polite learning." Burm. p. 15.
Jovius relates with complacency the
progress that his reputation as a
"scriptor annalium valde elegans" (a
most elegant annalist) had caused him
to make with Adrian, especially as he
was no poet.
[7] Gradenigo Relatione, as quotes the
viceroy of Naples, Girolamo Negro
(some interesting letters from whom respecting this period we find in the
"Lettere di Principi," t. i.), says, p.
109, of John Manuel: "He went away
half despairing."
[8] Negro, from the narration of the
Venetian secretary, p. 110.

anger of Hungary was manifest; nor was he altogether free from apprehension respecting Italy or Rome itself. His utmost efforts were directed to the procuring, if not peace, at least a suspension of hostilities for three years; during which time preparations might be made for a general expedition against the Turks.

Equally was he determined to anticipate the demands of the Germans, with regard to the abuses that had made their way into the Church. His avowal that such existed was most explicit. "We know," he observes in the instructions for the Nuncio Chieregato, whom he sent to the diet, "We know that for a considerable period many abominable things have found place beside the holy chair—abuses in spiritual matters—exorbitant straining of prerogatives—evil everywhere. From the head the malady has proceeded to the limbs; from the Pope it has extended to the prelates; we are all gone astray, there is none that hath done rightly, no not one." On his part he proceeds to promise all that may be expected from a good pope: he will promote the learned and upright, repress abuses, and, if not all at once, yet gradually, bring about a reformation both in the head and members, such as men have so long desired and demanded.[9]

But to reform the world is not so light a task; the good intentions of an individual, however high his station, can do but little toward such a consummation. Too deeply do abuses strike their roots; with life itself they grow up and become entwined; so that it is at length difficult to eradicate the one without endangering the other.

The fall of Rhodes was far from inclining the French to make peace. On the contrary, perceiving that this loss would give the Emperor new occupation, they resolved on more vigorous measures against him. They established a connection in Sicily (not without the privity of the very cardinal in whom Adrian most confided), and made a descent on that island. The Pope was at length constrained to form an alliance with the Emperor, which was, in fact, directed against France.

The Germans, again, were not now to be conciliated by what would once have been hailed as a reformation of head and mem-

[9] "Instructio pro te Francisco Chieregato," etc., to be found, amongst other writers, in Rainaldus, tom. xi. p. 363.

bers; and even had they been, how difficult, how almost impracticable, would such reform have been found!

If the Pope attempted to reduce those revenues of the Curia in which he detected an appearance of simony, he could not do so without alienating the legitimate rights of those persons whose offices were founded on these revenues; offices that, for the most part, had been purchased by the men who held them.

If he contemplated a change in the dispensations of marriage, or some relaxation of existing prohibitions, it was instantly represented to him, that such a step would infringe upon and weaken the discipline of the Church.

To abate the crying abuse of indulgences, he would gladly have revived the ancient penances; but the Penitenziaria at once called his attention to the danger he would thus incur; for, while he sought to secure Germany, Italy would be lost![10]

Enough is said to show that the Pope could make no step toward reform, without seeing himself assailed by a thousand difficulties.

In addition to all this came the fact that in Rome Adrian was a stranger, by birth, nation, and the habits of his life, to the element in which he was called on to act; this he could not master, because it was not familiar to him; he did not comprehend the concealed impulses of its existence. He had been welcomed joyfully, for people told each other that he had some 5,000 vacant benefices to bestow, and all were willing to hope for a share. But never did a pope show himself more reserved in this particular. Adrian would insist on knowing to whom it was that he gave appointments and intrusted with offices. He proceeded with scrupulous conscientiousness,[1] and disappointed innumerable expectations. By the first decree of his pontificate he abolished the reversionary rights formerly annexed to ecclesiastical dignities; even those which had already been conceded, he revoked. The publication of this edict in Rome could not fail to bring a crowd of enemies against him. Up to his time a certain freedom of speech and of writing had been suffered to prevail in the Roman Court; this he would no longer tolerate. The exhausted state of the papal exchequer,

[10] In the first book of the "Historia de Concilio Tridentino," by P. Sarpi, ed. of 1629, there is a good exposition of this state of things, extracted from a diary of Chieregato.

[1] Ortiz, "Itinerarium," c. 28, c. 39, particularly worthy of credit, because he says: "When with my own eyes I looked over provisions and things of that kind."

and the numerous demands on it, obliged him to impose new taxes. This was considered intolerable on the part of one who expended so sparingly. Whatever he did was unpopular and disapproved.[2] He felt this deeply, and it reacted on his character. He confided less than ever in the Italians. The two Netherlanders, Enkefort, his datary, and the secretary, Hezius, to whom a certain authority was intrusted, were conversant neither with business nor the court: he found it impossible to direct them himself, neither would he resign his habits of study; not contenting himself with reading only, but choosing to write also. He was by no means easy of access; business was procrastinated, tediously prolonged, and unskilfully handled.

Thus it came to pass that in affairs of vital importance to the general interest, nothing effectual was accomplished. Hostilities were renewed in Upper Italy; Luther was more than ever active in Germany; and in Rome, which was, besides, afflicted with the plague, a general discontent prevailed.

Adrian once said: "How much depends on the times in which even the best of men are cast!" The painful sense he entertained of his difficult position is eloquently expressed in this sorrowing outburst. Most appropriately was it engraven on his monument in the German church at Rome.

And here it becomes obvious, that not to Adrian personally must it be solely attributed, if his times were so unproductive in results. The papacy was encompassed by a host of conflicting claimants—urgent and overwhelming difficulties that would have furnished infinite occupation, even to a man more familiar with the medium of action, better versed in men and more fertile in expedients than Adrian VI.

Among all the cardinals, there was no one who seemed so peculiarly fitted to administer the government successfully—no one who appeared so well prepared to support the weight of the popedom, as Giulio de' Medici. He had already managed a large share of the public business under Leo—the whole of the details were in his hands; and, even under Adrian, he had maintained a certain degree of influence.[3] This time he did

[2] "Lettere di Negro," Capitolo del Berni: "And when anyone follows the free custom of indulging his feelings in writing or in song, he threatens to have him tossed into the river."
[3] The "Relatione di Marco Foscari" reports of him, with reference to those times: "He lived in excellent repute; it was he who governed the papacy, and he had more people at his audiences than the Pope himself."

not permit the supreme dignity to escape him, and ascended the papal throne under the name of Clement VII.

The faults and mistakes of his immediate predecessors were carefully avoided by the new pope. The instability, prodigality, and pleasure-seeking habits of Leo, and that ceaseless conflict with the tastes and opinions of his court into which Adrian had suffered himself to be drawn, were all eschewed by Clement VII. Everything was arranged with the utmost discretion, and his own conduct was remarkable for the blameless rectitude and moderation of its tenor.[4] The pontifical ceremonies were performed with due care. Audience was given from early morning to night, with untiring assiduity. Science and the arts were encouraged in that direction toward which they had now become decidedly bent. Clement was himself a man of extensive information. He spoke with equal knowledge of his subject, whether that were philosophy and theology, or mechanics and hydraulic architecture. In all affairs he displayed extraordinary acuteness; the most perplexing questions were unravelled, the most difficult circumstances penetrated to the very bottom by his extreme sagacity. No man could debate a point with more address: under Leo, he had already manifested a prudence in counsel, and a circumspect ability in practice that none could surpass.

But it is in the storm that the pilot proves his skill. Clement entered on the duties of the pontificate—if we consider it merely as an Italian sovereignty—at a moment of most critical import.

The Spaniards had contributed more than any other power to extend and uphold the States of the Church; they had reestablished the Medici in Florence. Thus leagued with the popes, their own advancement in Italy had kept pace with that of the house of Medici. Alexander VI had made a way for them into Lower Italy, Julius had given them access to the central regions, and their attack on Milan, undertaken in alliance with Leo X, had made them masters of Upper Italy. Clement himself had frequently afforded them powerful aid. There is still extant an instruction from him to one of his ambassadors at the Court of Spain, wherein he enumerates the

[4]Vettori says, for the last hundred years there has not been so good a man pope: "Not proud, no trafficker in church property, not avaricious, not given to pleasure, moderate in food, frugal in dress, religious and devout."

services he had rendered to Charles V and his house. It was principally attributable to his efforts that Francis I did not press forward to Naples at his first arrival in Italy. He had prevented Leo from throwing impediments in the way of Charles's election to the imperial crown, and had induced him to repeal the old constitution by which it was enacted that no king of Naples could at the same time be emperor. Unmoved by the promises of the French, he had given his best support to the alliance of Leo with Charles for the recovery of Milan; and to favor this undertaking, he spared neither his own person nor the resources of his country and adherents. It was he who procured the election of Adrian; and at the time when this was done, it seemed nearly equivalent to making Charles himself pope.[5] I will not inquire how much of Leo's policy was due to the counsellor and how much to the pontiff himself; but thus much is certain, that Cardinal Medici was always on the side of the Emperor. Even after he had become pope, the imperial troops were furnished by him with money, provisions, and grants of ecclesiastical revenues. Once again they were partially indebted to his support for their victory.

Thus intimately was Clement connected with the Spaniards, but, as not unfrequently happens, this alliance was the cause of extraordinary evils.

The popes had contributed to the rise of the Spanish powers; but that rise had never been the result they had sought. They had wrested Milan from the French, but not with the purpose of transferring it to Spain. There had even been more than one war carried on to prevent Milan and Naples from falling into the hands of one and the same possessor.[6] The fact that the Spaniards, so long masters of Lower Italy, should be now daily obtaining firmer footing in Lombardy, and that of their delaying the investiture of Sforza, were regarded in Rome with the utmost impatience and displeasure.

Clement was also personally dissatisfied. It may be perceived from the instructions before cited, that even as cardinal he had not always thought himself treated with the considera-

[5] Instruction to Cardinal Farnese, afterward Paul III, when he went as legate to Charles V, after the sack of Rome. (App. No. 15.)
[6] It is expressly stated in the before-mentioned instructions that the Pope had displayed a readiness to acquiesce even in what displeased him; "to the effect that the state of Milan should remain in possession of the Duke, a thing which had been the object of all the Italian wars."

tion due to his merits and services. He did not even now
meet with the deference that he felt to be his right; and the
expedition against Marseilles in the year 1524 was undertaken in direct opposition to his advice. His ministers, as they
declared themselves, expected still further marks of disrespect
toward the apostolic see, perceiving nothing in the Spaniards
but imperious insolence.[7]

How closely had the by-gone course of events, and his personal position, bound Clement both by necessity and inclination
to the Spanish cause, yet how many were the reasons that now
presented themselves, all tending to make him execrate the
power he had so largely contributed to establish, and place
himself in opposition to the cause for which he had hitherto so
zealously labored!

There is, perhaps, no effort in politics so difficult to make
as that of retracing the path we have hitherto trodden—of
recalling that chain of sequences which we ourselves have
elicited.

And how much was now depending on such an effort!
The Italians were profoundly sensible to the fact, that the acts
of the present moment would decide their fate for centuries.
A powerful community of feeling had taken rise and prevailed throughout the nation. I am fully persuaded that this
may be in great part ascribed to the literary and artistic progress of Italy—a progress in which it left other nations so far
behind. The arrogance and rapacity of the Spaniards, alike
leaders as soldiers, were, besides, intolerable to all; and it
was with contempt and rage combined that the Italians beheld
this horde of half-barbarous foreigners masters in their country. Matters were still in such a position that they might yet
free themselves from these intruders: but the truth must not
be disguised. If the attempt were not made with the whole
force of the nation's power, if they were now defeated, they
were lost forever.

I could have desired to set forth the complicated events of
this period in their fullest development—to exhibit the whole
contest of the excited powers in its minutest detail; but I can
here follow a few of the more important movements only.

[7] M. Giberto, "datario a Don Michele di Silva," "Lettere di Principi," i.
197, b.

The first attempt made, and one that seemed particularly well devised, was that of gaining over the best general of the Emperor to the Roman side. It was known that he was greatly dissatisfied, and if, together with him, that army by means of which Charles mastered Italy could also be won, as was confidently hoped, what more could be required? There was no dearth of promises, by way of inducement—even that of a crown was included amongst them; but how grievously had they miscalculated, how instantly were the delicate complications of their astute prudence shivered to atoms against the rugged materials to which it was applied! This General Pescara was an Italian born, but of Spanish race; he spoke only Spanish, he would be nothing but a Spaniard; for the elegant cultivation of the Italians he had neither taste nor aptitude; the best furniture of his mind had been drawn from Spanish romances, and these breathe, above all, of loyalty and fidelity. His very nature was opposed to a national enterprise in favor of Italy.[8] No sooner had he received the Italian overtures than they were communicated, not to his comrades alone, but even to the Emperor; he used them only to discover the purposes of the Italians, and to frustrate all their plans.

But these very overtures made a deadly strife with the Emperor unavoidable; for how was it possible that the mutual confidence of the parties should fail to be utterly destroyed?

In the summer of 1526, we at length see the Italians putting their own hands to the work, and that with all their might. The Milanese are already in arms against the imperialists, a combined Venetian and papal force advance to their support, assistance is promised from Switzerland, and treaties have been concluded with France and England. "This time," says Giberto, the most trusted minister of Clement VII, "the question is not of some petty vengeance, some point of honor, or a single town; this war is to decide whether Italy shall be free, or is doomed to perpetual thraldom." He had no doubt

---

[8] Vettori has pronounced over him the least enviable eulogy imaginable; here it is: "He was proud beyond all measure, envious, ungrateful, greedy, virulent, and cruel; without religion, without humanity; he was born for the very destruction of Italy." Morone also declares to Guicciardini that there was no man more faithless and malicious than Pescara ("Hist. d 'Italia," xvl. 476); and yet the proposal above described was made to him! I do not cite these opinions as believing them true, but simply because they prove that Pescara had shown no feeling as regarded the Italians but those of hatred and enmity.

of the result—he was persuaded that it would be a fortunate
one. " Posterity will envy us," he declares, " for having lived
at such a moment; for having witnessed and had our share in
so much happiness." His hope is, that no foreign aid will be
required. " The glory will be all our own; and so much the
sweeter will be the fruit."[9]

It was with thoughts and hopes such as these, that Clement
undertook his war with Spain;[10] it was his boldest and most
magnanimous project, but also his most unfortunate and ruin-
ous one.

The affairs of the Church were inextricably interwoven
with those of the state, yet Clement would seem to have left
the commotions of Germany entirely out of consideration; it
was, nevertheless, in these that the first reaction became
manifest.

In July, 1526, that moment when the papal forces were
advancing toward Northern Italy, the diet had assembled
at Spires, with the purpose of arriving at some definitive resolution in regard to the disorders of the Church. It was not
in the nature of things that the imperial party, or Ferdinand
of Austria, who represented the Emperor, and who had himself the hope of possessing Milan, should be very earnest in
the maintenance of the papal influence north of the Alps,
when they were themselves attacked by the Pope, with so much
determination, on their southern side. Whatever intentions
might have been earlier formed or announced by the imperial
court,[1] the open war now entered on by the Pope against the
Emperor would assuredly put an end to all considerations in
favor of the former. Never had the towns expressed themselves more freely, never had the princes pressed more urgently
for the removal of their burdens. It was proposed that the
books containing the new regulations should be burnt forthwith, and that the holy scriptures should be taken as the sole
rule of faith. Although some opposition was made, yet never
was a more independent or more decisive resolution adopted.
Ferdinand signed a decree of the empire, whereby the states

[9] G. M. Giberto al vescovo di Veruli,
" Lettere di Principi," i. p. 192, a.
[10] Foscari also says: " His present
wish to ally himself with France is for
his own good and that of Italy, not because he has any love for the French."

[1] The instructions of the Emperor,
which had occasioned some alarm to
the Protestants, bear the date of March,
1526, when the Pope had not yet concluded his alliance with France.

were declared free to comport themselves in matters of religion as each should best answer it to God and the Emperor, that is, according to its own judgment. In this resolution, no reference whatever was made to the Pope, and it may fairly be regarded as the commencement of the true reformation, and the establishment of a new church in Germany. In Saxony, Hesse, and the neighboring countries, it was practically adopted without delay. The legal existence of the Protestant party in the empire is based on the decree of Spires, of 1526.

It may be easily asserted that this expression of opinion in Germany was decisive for Italy also. The Italians were far from being zealous, as a nation, for their great enterprise, and even among those who desired its success, unanimity did not prevail. Able as he was, and thoroughly Italian in spirit, the Pope was yet not one of those men who calmly control the current of circumstances, and seem to hold fortune enchained. His keen perception of realities seemed injurious rather than serviceable to him: his conviction that he was the weaker party was stronger than was expedient; all possible contingencies, every form of danger, presented themselves too clearly before him; they bewildered his mind and confused his decisions. There is a practical and inventive faculty by which some men intuitively perceive the simple and practicable in affairs, and, guided by this, they rapidly seize on the best expedient. This he did not possess;[2] in the most critical moments he was seen to hesitate, waver, and waste his thoughts in attempts to spare money. His allies having failed in their promises, the results he had hoped for were far from being obtained, and the imperialists still maintained their hold in Lombardy, when, in November, 1526, George Frundsberg crossed the Alps with a formidable body of lanzknechts, to bring the contest to an end. This army was altogether Lutheran—leader and followers. They came resolved to avenge the Emperor on the Pope, whose secession from the alliance had been represented to them as the cause of all the evils so generally felt and complained of. The wars so long continued through Christendom, and the successes of the Ottomans, who were pouring their troops over Hungary,

[2] Suriano, " Rel. di 1533," finds in him " a very cold heart, which causes his holiness to be endowed with no common timidity—for I will not say cowardice—but I think I have noticed that frequently in the Florentine character. This timidity makes his holiness very irresolute."

all were attributed to the faithlessness of Clement. "When once I make my way to Rome," said Frundsberg, "I will hang the Pope."

With anxious thought is the storm seen to gather in the narrowing and lowering horizon. Rome, loaded perhaps with vices, yet not the less teeming with the noblest effort, the most exalted intellect, the richest culture; powerfully creative, adorned with matchless works of art, such as the world has never since produced; replete with riches, ennobled by the impress of genius, and exercising a vital and imperishable influence on the whole world, this Rome is now threatened with destruction. As the masses of the imperial force drew together, the Italian troops dispersed before them, the only army that yet remained followed them from afar; the Emperor had been long unable to pay his troops, and could not alter their direction even did he desire to do so. They marched beneath the imperial banner, guided only by their own stormy will and impulse. Clement still hoped, negotiated, offered concessions, retracted them; but the sole expedient that could have saved him—the contenting these hordes, namely, with all the money they may find the boldness to demand—this, he either could not, or would not adopt. Will he then at least make a stand against the enemy with such weapons as he has? Four thousand men would have sufficed to secure the passes of Tuscany, but the attempt was not even thought of. Rome contained within her walls some thirty thousand inhabitants capable of bearing arms; many of these men had seen service, they wore swords by their sides, which they used freely in their broils among each other, and then boasted of their exploits. But to oppose the enemy, who brought with him certain destruction, five hundred men were the utmost that could ever be mustered without the city. At the first onset the Pope and his forces were overthrown. On the sixth of May, 1527, two hours before sunset, the imperialists poured their unbridled numbers into Rome. Their former general, Frundsberg, was no longer at their head; in a disturbance among his troops he had been unable to repress them as was his wont, and, being struck by apoplexy, remained behind in a state of dangerous illness. Bourbon, who had led the army so far, was killed at the first fixing of the scaling-ladders. Thus, restrained by no leader, the bloodthirsty soldiery, hardened by long privations and rendered savage by their trade, burst over the devoted city. Never fell richer booty into more violent hands, never was plunder more continuous or more destructive.[3] How vivid a lustre was cast over the beginning of the sixteenth century by the splendor of Rome! It designates a period most influential on the development of the human mind. This day saw the light of that splendor extinguished forever.

And thus did the pontiff, who had hoped to effect the liberation of Italy, find himself besieged, as it were a prisoner, in the castle of St. Angelo; by this great reverse the preponderance of the Spaniards in Italy was irrevocably established.

A new expedition undertaken by the French, and promising great results in its commencement, was a total failure. They were compelled to give up all their claims upon Italy.

No less important was another occurrence: before Rome was yet captured, when it was merely seen that the march of Bourbon was in that direction, the enemies of the Medici in Florence had availed themselves of the confusion of the moment, and once more expelled the family of the Pope. The revolt of his native city was more painful to Clement than even the downfall of Rome. With astonishment did men behold him, after so many indignities, again connect himself with the imperialists. He did so because he saw that with the help of the Spaniards alone could his kindred and party be reinstated in Florence; this he would secure at all hazards; the domination of the Emperor was at least more endurable to Clement than the disobedience of his rebels. In proportion as the fortunes of the French were seen to decline, did the Pope make approaches to the Spaniards; and when the first were at length entirely defeated, he concluded the treaty of Barcelona with the last. He so completely changed his policy, that the very army by which Rome had been sacked before his eyes, and himself so long held captive, was now called to his assistance; recruited and strengthened, it was led to the reduction of his native city.

[3] Vettori: "The slaughter was not great, because men rarely kill those who will not defend themselves; but the booty was of inestimable value—money, jewels, vessels of gold and silver, garments, tapestry, household furniture, merchandise of all sorts, and ransoms." He does not blame the pope, but the inhabitants, for this misfortune; he describes them as proud, avaricious, murderous, envious, luxurious, and hypocritical. Such a population could not sustain itself.

Thenceforth Charles was more powerful in Italy than any emperor had been for many centuries. The crown that he had received at Bologna had now regained its full significance; Milan gradually became as entirely subjected to his authority as was Naples. His restoration of the Medici to their seat in Florence secured him a direct and permanent influence in Tuscany. The remaining states of Italy either sought his alliance or submitted to his power. With the strength of Germany and Spain, united by the force of his victorious arms, and in right of his imperial dignity, did he hold all Italy in subjection, from the Alps to the sea.

To this point it was then that the Italian wars conducted the country; from that period never has she been freed from the rule of the stranger. Let us now examine the progress of the religious dissensions that were so intimately entwined with the political events.

If the Pope acquiesced in the establishment of Spanish supremacy in all directions, he had at least the hope that this powerful Emperor, who was described to him as so devoted to Catholicism, would in all cases assist to re-establish the papal dominion in Germany. There is even a stipulation to that effect in the treaty of Barcelona. The Emperor promised to lend his utmost efforts for the reduction of Protestantism, and did indeed seem bent on accomplishing that purpose. To the Protestant delegates who waited on him in Italy he returned a most discouraging reply, and on his progress into Germany (1530) certain members of the Curia, and more especially Cardinal Campeggi, who accompanied him as legate, proposed extreme measures, infinitely dangerous to the peace of Germany.

There is still extant a memorial, from the cardinal to the Emperor, presented during the sitting of the diet at Augsburg, in which these projects are set forth. I allude to this with extreme reluctance, but in deference to the truth, I must say a few words respecting it.

Cardinal Campeggi does not content himself with deploring the disorders in religion, but insists more particularly on the political evils resulting from them; he points to the decadence of power among the nobles in all the cities of the empire, as one of the consequences of the Reformation. He declares that neither ecclesiastical nor secular princes can any longer obtain he obedience due to them, so that even the majesty of the Cæsar has come to be no longer regarded! He then proceeds to show how this evil may be remedied.

The mystery of his curative system was not very profound. There required only, according to him, that the Emperor should form a compact with the well-affected princes, whereupon attempts should be made to convert the disaffected, either by promises or threats. But suppose these last to be recusant—what was next to be done? The right would then exist of "rooting out these pestilential weeds by fire and sword."[4]

"The first step in this process would be to confiscate property, civil or ecclesiastical, in Germany as well as in Hungary and Bohemia. For, with regard to heretics, this is lawful and right. Is the mastery over them thus obtained, then must holy inquisitors be appointed, who shall trace out every remnant of them, proceeding against them as the Spaniards did against the Moors in Spain." The university of Wittenberg was furthermore to be placed under ban, all who studied there being declared unworthy of favor, whether from pope or emperor. The books of the heretics were also to be burnt, the monks who had abandoned their convents were to be sent back to them, and no heretic was to be tolerated at any court. But first of all, unsparing confiscation was necessary. "And even though your majesty," says the legate, "should deal only with the heads of the party, you may derive a large sum of money from them, and this is indispensable, in any case, for proceeding against the Turks."

Such are the main propositions, and such is the tone of this project:[5] how does every word breathe of oppression, carnage, and rapine! We cannot wonder that the very worst should be apprehended by the Germans from an emperor who came among them surrounded by such counsellors, nor that the Protestants should take counsel together as to the degree of resistance they might lawfully oppose to such measures in their own self-defence.

[4] "If there be any, which God forbid, who will obstinately persist in this diabolical path, his majesty may put hand to fire and sword, and radically tear out his cursed and venomous plant."
[5] Such a project did they venture to call an instruction. "Instructio data Cæsari a reverendmo. Campeggio in dieta Augustana, 1530." I found it in a Roman library, in the handwriting of the time, and beyond all doubt authentic.

Happily, however, as affairs stood, an attempt at such proceedings as those recommended by the legate was not greatly to be feared.

The Emperor was by no means sufficiently powerful to carry out this proposal: a fact that Erasmus demonstrated very clearly at the time.

But even had he possessed the power, he would scarcely have found the will to do it.

Charles was by nature rather kind, considerate, thoughtful, and averse to precipitation, than the contrary: the more closely he examined these heresies, the more did he find in them a certain accordance with thoughts that had arisen in his own mind. The tone of his proclamation for a diet gives evidence of a desire to hear the different opinions, to judge of them, and seek to bring all to the standard of Christian truth. Very far removed was this disposition from the violence of purpose intimated by the legate.

Even those whose system it is to doubt the purity of human intentions, will find one reason unanswerable: it was not for the interest of Charles to adopt coercive measures.

Was he, the Emperor, to make himself the executor of the papal decrees? Should he set himself to subdue those enemies of the Pope—and not his only, but those of all succeeding pontiffs—who furnished them with so much occupation? The friendly dispositions of the Papal See were by no means so well assured as to awaken a confidence that could induce him to this.

Rather it was his obvious interest that things should remain as they were for the moment, since they offered him an advantage, unsought on his part, but which he had only to seize in order to attain a higher supremacy than he even now enjoyed.

It was generally believed, whether justly or not I will not inquire, that a general council of the Church alone could avail for the settlement of differences so important, the removal of errors so fatal. Church councils had maintained their credit precisely because a very natural repugnance to them had been evinced by the popes, and all opposition to them by the papal chair had tended to raise them in public estimation. In the year 1530, Charles applied his thoughts seriously to this matter, and promised to call a council within a brief specified period.

In the different complications of their interests with those of the pontificate, the princes had ever desired to find some spiritual restraint for the Church. Charles might thus assure himself of most zealous allies in a council assembled under existing circumstances. Convened at his instigation, it would be held under his influence; and to him also would revert the execution of its edicts. These decrees would have to bear upon two important questions—they would affect the Pope equally with his opponents, the old idea of a reformation in head and members would be realized, and how decided a predominance would all this secure to the temporal power— above all, to that of Charles himself!

This mode of proceeding was most judicious; it was, if you will have it so, inevitable, but it was, at the same time, for the best interest of the Emperor.

On the other hand, no event could be better calculated to awaken anxiety in the pontiff and his court. I find that at the first serious mention of a council, the price of all the salable offices of the court declined considerably.[6] The danger threatened by a council to the existing state of things is obvious from this fact.

In addition to this, Clement VII had personal motives for objecting to the measure: he was not of legitimate birth, neither had he risen to the supreme dignity by means that were altogether blameless: again, he had been determined by considerations entirely personal, to employ the resources of the Church in a contest with his native city; and for all these things a pope might fairly expect heavy reckoning with a council. Thus it inspired him with a deadly terror, and Soriano tells us that he would not willingly utter its very name.

He did not reject the proposal in terms; this he could not do with any regard to the honor of the papal see, but we can easily conceive the reluctance of heart with which he would receive it.

He submitted, without doubt—he was entirely compliant; but he did not fail to set forth the objections existing to the measure, and that in the most persuasive forms. He represented all the dangers and difficulties inseparable from a council,

[6] "Lettera anonima all' arcivescovo Pimpinello" ("Lettere di Principi," iii. 5). "The mere rumor of a council has so depreciated all offices that no money can be got for them." I see that Pallavicini also quotes this letter, lii. 7, 1. I do not know on what authority he ascribes it to Sanga.

declaring its consequences to be of a very doubtful nature.[7]
Next he stipulated for the concurrence of all other princes, as
well as for a previous subjection of the Protestants—demands
that were perfectly in accordance with the papal system and
doctrine, but utterly impracticable in the existing state of things.
But how could it be expected from him that, within the limit
of time assigned by the Emperor, he should proceed, not apparently only, but in earnest, and with resolution to promote a
work so likely to injure himself? Charles often reproached
him with his backwardness, ascribing to it all the mischief that
afterward ensued. He doubtless still hoped to evade the necessity that hung over him.

But it clung to him fast and firmly: when Charles returned
to Italy in 1533, still impressed with what he had seen and
heard in Germany, he pressed the Pope in person during a
conference held at Bologna, and with increased earnestness,
on the subject of the council, which he had so frequently
demanded in writing. Their opinions were thus brought into
direct collision—the Pope held fast by his conditions, the Emperor declared their fulfilment impossible—they could come
to no agreement. In the documents respecting these matters
that remain to us, a sort of discrepancy is perceptible—the Pope
appearing less averse from the Emperor's wishes in some than
in others; however this may be, he had no alternative—a fresh
proclamation[8] must be issued. He could not so effectually
blind himself as not to perceive that when the Emperor, who
was gone to Spain, should return, mere words would be
insufficient to content him—that the danger he dreaded, and
with which a council summoned under such circumstances
certainly did menace the Roman See, could then be no longer
averted.

[7] For example, "All' imperatore: di
man propria di papa Clemente," "Lettere di Principi," ii. 197: "On the
contrary, no remedy can be more dangerous, or produce greater evils (than
the council), if the proper circumstances do not concur."

[8] Respecting the negotiations at Bologna, valuable information, derived
from the archives of the Vatican, may
be found in one of the best chapters of
Pallavicini, lib. iii. c. 12. He names
the variation alluded to in the text, and
says, it rested on explicit discussion;
and, in effect, we find in the despatches
to the Catholic States in Rainaldus,
xx. 659, Hortleder, i. xv., the stipulation for a general concurrence repeated;
the Pope promises to communicate the
results of his efforts. Among the points
proposed for the consideration of the
Protestants, it is said expressly in the
7th article: "But if it happen that any
prince refuse to co-operate in so pious
a work, our supreme lord shall nevertheless proceed with the consent of the
more sanely disposed part." This
would seem to be the discrepancy that
Pallavicini had in view, although he
mentions another point of difference.

The situation was one in which the possessor of a power, of whatever kind, might well be excused for resorting even to extreme measures, if these were the only means that could insure his own safety. The political preponderance of the Emperor was already excessive, and if the Pope had resigned himself to this state of things, he could not but feel his own depressed condition. In arranging the long-standing disputes of the Church with Ferrara, Charles V had decided for the latter; this mortified the pontiff deeply, and though he acquiesced in the decision, he complained of it among those of his own circle. How much more afflicting was it now, then, when this monarch, from whom he had hoped the immediate subjugation of the Protestants, was preferring his claim, under pretext of religious dissension, to an amount of predominance in ecclesiastical affairs, such as no emperor had enjoyed for centuries. Nay, that he was proceeding without scruple to acts that must compromise the spiritual authority and dignity of the holy see. Must Clement indeed endure to see himself sink utterly into the Emperor's hands, and he wholly given up to his tender mercies?

His resolution was taken even whilst in Bologna. More than once Francis had proposed to cement his political alliances with Clement by means of a family connection. This the pontiff had hitherto declined—in the desperate position of his present affairs, he recurred to it as a ground of hope. It is expressly affirmed that the real cause of Clement's once again lending an ear to the French King was the demand of Charles for a council.[9]

The Pope would most probably never more have attempted to establish an equilibrium of power between these two great monarchs, and to divide his favor equally between them, from motives purely political; but it was on this course that he now determined, in consideration of the dangers threatening the Church.

[9] Soriano, "Relatione," 1535. "The Pope went to Bologna against his will, and, as it were, by compulsion, as I have heard from good authority; and an evident sign of this was that his holiness consumed a hundred days in that journey which he might have made in six. Clement then, considering this state of his affairs, and the servitude, so to speak, in which he was placed by the affair of the council, which the Emperor would not cease to urge, began to be more compliant toward the most Christian king, and then was concluded the conference at Marseilles, and also the marriage, the niece (Clement's) being now marriageable." At a previous period the Pope would have alleged her birth and age as a pretext for evading the agreement.

Another meeting between Francis and the Pope was arranged, and which took place in Marseilles, where the closest alliance was agreed upon. Precisely as Clement had confirmed his friendship with the Emperor, during the Florentine difficulties, by accepting a natural daughter of Charles as wife to one of his nephews, so did he now cement the bond which the embarrassments of the Church compelled him to form with Francis, by the betrothal of his young niece, Catherine de' Medici, to the King's second son: in the first instance, it was against the French, and their indirect influence on Florence, that he sought to defend himself; on this occasion, the Emperor and his intentions with regard to a council, were the cause of fear.

He now took no further pains to conceal his purpose. We have a letter addressed by him to Ferdinand I, wherein he declares that his efforts to procure the concurrence of the Christian princes to the assembling of a council had been without effect. King Francis I, to whom he had spoken, thought the present moment unfavorable for such a purpose, and refused to adopt the suggestion, but he (Clement) still hoped at some other opportunity to obtain a more favorable decision from the Christian sovereigns.[10] I cannot comprehend the doubt that has existed in regard to the real intentions of the Pope. It was but in his last communication with the Catholic princes of Germany, that he had repeated his demand for universal concurrence as a condition to the proposed council. Is not his present declaration, that he cannot bring about this general agreement, equivalent to the positive assertion that he recalls his announcement of the council?[1] In his alliance with France, he had found alike the courage to pursue this line of conduct, and the pretext for it. I can by no means convince myself that the council ever would have been held in his pontificate.

This was not, however, the only consequence of the new league; another and a most unexpected one presently developed itself, one, too, of the most extensive and permanent importance, more especially as regards the Germans.

Most extraordinary was the combination that resulted from this alliance, in consequence of the peculiar complications of

[10] March 20, 1534.—Pallavicini, iii. xvi. 3.
[1] " For the matter of the council, your serenity may then be most certain, that it was eschewed by Clement in all possible ways and by every sort of means."

ecclesiastical and secular interests.   Francis I was on the most
friendly terms with the Protestants, and now, becoming so
closely connected with the Pope, he may be said, in a certain
sort, to have combined the Protestants and the pontiff in one
and the same system.

And here we perceive what it was that constituted the
strength of that position, to which the Protestants had now
attained.   The Emperor could have no intention of again subjecting them unconditionally to the Pope, because the agitations
they occasioned were absolutely needful to him for the purpose
of keeping the pontiff in check.   Clement, on the other hand,
as it gradually became manifest, was not disposed, even on his
part, to see their existence entirely dependent on the favor or
disfavor of the Emperor; it was not altogether unconsciously
that the Pope had become in a measure leagued with the Protestants; his hope was that he might avail himself of their opposition to Charles, and supply that monarch with occupation by
their means.

It was remarked at the time that the French King had
made Clement believe the principal Protestant princes dependent on himself, and that he had both the will and power to induce them to renounce the project of a council;[2] but if we do
not greatly mistake, these engagements went much further.
Soon after the meeting of Francis with the Pope, another took
place between the French King and the landgrave, Philip of
Hesse; these sovereigns united for the restoration of the Duke
of Würtemberg, who had at that time been dispossessed of his
states by the house of Austria.   Francis agreed to furnish supplies of money, and the landgrave effected the undertaking with
astonishing rapidity in one short campaign.   We have full
proof that the landgrave had been instructed to make an advance on the hereditary dominions of Austria;[3] the universal
opinion being that Francis was meditating again to attack
Milan, and this time from the side of Germany.[4]   A still clearer

[2] Sarpi, " Historia del Concilio Tridentino," lib. i. p. 68.   An important
part of what Sarpi has asserted, though
not the whole, is confirmed by Soriano.
This ambassador says: " Having made
Clement believe that those princes and
chiefs of the Lutheran faction depended
on his most Christian majesty, so that
at least he (the Pope) should escape the
council."   This is all that I have ventured to assert.

[3] In the instructions to his ambassador to France, August, 1532 (Rommel,
" Urkundenbuch,"   61), he   excuses
himself " that he did not go on to attack the king in his hereditary possessions."
[4] Jovius, " Historiæ sui temporis,"
lib. xxxii. p. 129. Paruta, " Storia Venez," p. 389.

insight is afforded to us of this matter by Marino Giustiniano, at that time Venetian ambassador in France; he expressly declares that these German operations had been determined on by Clement and Francis at Marseilles: he adds further, that a descent of these troops upon Italy was by no means foreign to the plan of operations, and that secret aid was to be afforded by Clement to the enterprise.[5] It would be somewhat rash to accept these assertions, however confidently made, as fully authentic; still further proof would be required: but even though we do not accord them entire belief, there does unquestionably remain a very extraordinary phenomenon for our consideration —it is one that could never have been looked for—that the Pope and the Protestants, at the very moment when each was pursuing the other with implacable hatred, when both were engaged in a religious warfare that filled the world with discord, should yet on the other hand be strictly bound together by the ties of a similar political interest!

On earlier occasions of difficulty and complication in the temporal affairs of Italy, the crooked, ambiguous, and over-subtle policy of Clement had been more injurious to his interests than all his enemies, and the same dubious measures produced him yet more bitter fruits in his ecclesiastical jurisdiction.

Threatened in his hereditary provinces, King Ferdinand hastened to conclude the peace of Kadan; by this he abandoned Würtemberg, and even formed a close league with the landgrave himself. These were the brightest days of Philip of Hesse; he had restored an exiled German prince to his rights by the strong hand, and this rendered him one of the most influential

[5] "Relatione del clarissimo M. Marino Giustinian el Kr. venuto d' ambasciator al Christianissimo re di Francia, del 1535" ("Archivio Venez."): "Francis had a meeting with Clement at Marseilles, where, seeing the Emperor remain firm, they decided on that movement in Germany, under the pretext of restoring the Duke of Wurtemburg to his own; in consequence of which, if God had not intervened by means of the Emperor, all those troops would have poured into Italy by secret favor of Clement." I am of opinion that more minute information will yet be obtained on this point. Soriano has also the following: "Di tutti li desiderii (del re) s'accommodò Clemente, con parole tali che lo facevano credere S.S. esser disposta in tutto alle sue voglie, senza però far provisione alcuna in scrittura." That an Italian expedition was talked of cannot be denied, the Pope maintained that he had rejected the proposal—"Non avere bisogno di moto in Italia." The King had told him that he must remain quiet, "with his hands drawn back into his sleeves." It seems probable that the French were affirming what the Italians had denied, the ambassador in France being more positive than the ambassador in Rome; but, supposing the Pope to say that he desired no movement in Italy, it is obvious how little that expression would exclude the idea of a movement in Germany.

chiefs of the empire. But he had secured another important result by his victory: the treaty of peace concluded in consequence, contained a momentous decision in regard to the religious dissensions—the imperial chamber of justice was directed to take cognizance of no more suits relating to confiscated church property.

I do not know that any other single event was of equal importance with this expedition of the landgrave Philip's, in the promotion of Protestant ascendancy among the Germans. In that direction to the imperial chamber is involved a judicial security of most extensive significance. Nor were its effects slow to follow. The peace of Kadan may be regarded, as it appears to me, as the second great epoch in the rise of a Protestant power in Germany. For a certain period the progress of Protestantism had declined in rapidity; it now began anew to extend itself, and most triumphantly: Würtemberg was reformed without delay; the German provinces of Denmark, Pomerania, and the March of Brandenburg; the second branch of Saxony, one branch of Brunswick and the Palatinate followed. Within a few years the reformation of the Church extended through the whole of Lower Germany, and permanently established its seat in Upper Germany.

And the enterprise that had conducted to all this, the undertaking by which this enormous increase of desertion from the ranks of the Church had been brought about, was entered on with the knowledge, perhaps even with the approbation, of Pope Clement himself!

The papacy was in a position utterly false and untenable; its worldly tendencies had produced a degeneracy that had in its turn called forth opponents and adversaries innumerable. These tendencies being persisted in, the increasing complications and antagonism of temporal and ecclesiastical interests, promoted its decadence, and at length bore it wholly to the ground.

Among other misfortunes the schism of England must be attributed chiefly to this state of things.

The fact that Henry VIII, however inimical to Luther, however closely bound to the Papal See, was yet disposed to threaten the popedom with ecclesiastical innovation on the first political difference, is one that well deserves remark. This occurred in

relation to matters purely political, so early as the year 1525. [6]
It is true that all differences were then arranged, the King made
common cause with the Pope against the Emperor; and when
Clement, shut up in the castle of St. Angelo, was abandoned by
all, Henry VIII found means to send him assistance; from this
cause the Pope was perhaps more kindly disposed toward Henry
personally, than toward any other sovereign. [7] But since that
time the question of the King's divorce had arisen; it is not to
be denied that, even in the year 1528, the Pope had allowed
Henry to believe a favorable decision probable, even though he
did not promise it, " once the Germans and Spaniards should be
driven out of Italy." [8] But so far were the imperialists from being " driven out," that they now first established themselves,
as we know, in permanent possession of the land. We have
seen in how strict an alliance Clement connected himself with
them. Under circumstances so essentially changed, he could
by no means fulfil those expectations, which, be it observed, he
had warranted by a passing hint only. [9] Scarcely was the peace
of Barcelona concluded, than he summoned the suit for the divorce before the tribunals of Rome. The wife whom Henry
desired to put away, was aunt to the Emperor; the validity of
the marriage had been expressly affirmed by a former pope; it
was now to be tried before the tribunals of the Curia, and these
were under the immediate and perpetual influence of the Emperor; was there a possibility of doubt as to the decision?
Hereupon, Henry at once adopted the course that had for some
time been in contemplation. In essentials, in all that regarded
the dogmas of the Church he was doubtless a Catholic, and

[6] Wolsey had written threats to the effect, " che ogni provincia doventarà Lutherana"; an expression in which may perhaps be perceived the first symptoms of secession from Rome shown by the English Government.— " S. Giberto ai nuntii d' Inghilterra," " Lettere di Principi," i. p. 147.
[7] Contarini, " Relatione di 1530," expressly affirms this. Soriano too says, 1533: " His holiness loves the English King, and was at first strictly united with him." The design of Henry as to his divorce, he declares without ceremony to be a " piece of folly."
[8] From the despatches of Doctor Knight of Orvieto, January 1 and 9, 1528. Herbert's " Life of Henry VIII," p. 219.
[9] The whole situation of affairs is explained by the following passages from a letter by the papal secretary, Sanga, to Campeggi, dated Viterbo, September 2, 1528, at the moment when the Neapolitan enterprise had failed (a fact alluded to in the letter), and Campeggi was preparing for his journey to England: " Lettere di diversi Autori," Venetia, 1556, p. 39. " Your reverend lordship knows, that our lord the pope, considering himself most deeply obliged to that most serene king, would think nothing too great to do for his gratification; but his beatitude the pope must still avoid giving the Emperor cause for a new rupture, seeing that he is now victorious, and probably not indisposed to peace; for not only would all hope of peace be destroyed by new dissensions with the Emperor, but he would also put our lord to fire and slaughter through all his states."

so did he remain; but this question of the divorce, which was so unreservedly treated in Rome according to political views, and with no other consideration, exasperated him to an ever-increasing opposition of the Pope's temporal ascendancy. To every step that was taken in Rome to his disadvantage, he replied by some measure directed against the Curia; and by giving more formal expression to his determined purpose of emancipating himself from its influence. When at last then, in the year 1534, the definitive sentence was pronounced, he no longer demurred, but declared the entire separation of his kingdom from the Pope. So weak had those bonds already become, by which the Roman See was united to the several national churches, that it required only the determination of a sovereign to wrest his kingdom altogether from their influence.

These events filled the last year of Clement's life; they were rendered all the more bitter by the consciousness that he was not altogether blameless as regarded them, and that his misfortunes stood in afflictive relationship to his personal qualities. Day by day the course of things became more threatening and dark. Already was Francis preparing to make a new descent on Italy; and for this design he declared himself to have had the oral, if not the written, sanction of Clement's approval. The Emperor would no longer be put off with pretences, and urged the assembling of the council more pressingly than ever. Family discords added their bitterness to these sufferings; after his labors and sacrifices for the reduction of Florence, the Pope was doomed to see his two nephews enter into dispute for the sovereignty of that city, and proceed to the most savage hostilities against each other. His anxious reflections on all these calamities, with the fear of coming events, " sorrow and secret anguish," says Soriano, brought him to the grave.[10]

We have pronounced Leo fortunate. Clement was perhaps a better man, certainly he had fewer faults, was more active, and, as regarded details, even more acute than Leo; but in

[10] Soriano: " The Emperor did not cease to press for a council; his most Christian majesty demanded that his holiness should fulfil the promises made to him; and of which the conditions had been stipulated between them; whereupon his holiness gave himself up to heavy thoughts; and this grief and anxiety it was that conducted him to his death. His sorrow was increased by the follies of Cardinal de' Medici, who was more than ever resolved at that time to renounce the cardinal's hat, for the purpose of entering into competition with the political parties then agitating Florence."

all his concerns, whether active or passive, he was the very sport of misfortune; without doubt the most ill-fated pontiff that ever sat on the papal throne was Clement VII. To the superiority of the hostile powers pressing on him from all sides, he opposed only the most uncertain policy, ever depending on the probabilities of the moment; this it was that wrought his utter downfall. Those efforts for the establishment of an independent temporal power, to which his more celebrated predecessors had devoted their best energies, he was doomed in his own case to find resulting in perfect subjugation; it was his lot to see those from whom he had hoped to rescue his native Italy, establish their dominion over her soil forever. The great secession of the Protestants proceeded unremittingly before his eyes; and the measures he adopted in the hope of arresting its progress, did but serve to give it wider and more rapid extension. He left the papal see, immeasurably lowered in reputation, and deprived of all effectual influence, whether spiritual or temporal. That northern Germany, from of old so important to the papacy, to whose conversion in remote times the power of the popes was principally indebted for its establishment in the West; and whose revolt against Henry IV had so largely aided them in the completion of their hierachy, had now risen against them. To Germany belongs the undying merit of having restored Christianity to a purer form than it had presented since the first ages of the Church — of having rediscovered the true religion. Armed with this weapon, Germany was unconquerable. Its convictions made themselves a path through all the neighboring countries. Scandinavia had been among the first to receive them; they had diffused themselves over England contrary to the purposes of the King, but under the protection of the measures he had pursued. In Switzerland they had struggled for, and, with certain modifications, had attained to, a secure and immovable existence; they penetrated into France; we find traces of them in Italy, and even in Spain, while Clement yet lived. These waves roll ever onward. In these opinions there is a force that convinces and satisfies all minds; and that struggle between the spiritual and temporal interests, in which the papacy suffered itself to become involved, would seem to have been engaged in for the furtherance of their progress and the establishment of their universal dominion.

JULIUS THE SECOND.

Photogravure from the original painting by Raphael.

BOOK II

CHAPTER FIRST

BEGINNING OF A REGENERATION OF CATHOLICISM

WE are not to believe that the influence of public opinion on the world has begun to make itself felt for the first time in our own day; through every age of modern Europe, it has constituted an important element of social life. Who shall say whence it arises or how it is formed? It may be regarded as the most peculiar product of that identification of interests which holds society in compact forms, as the most intelligible expression of those internal movements and evolutions, by which life, shared in common, is agitated. The sources whence it takes its rise are equally remote from observation with those whence its aliment is derived; requiring little support from evidence or reason, it obtains the mastery over men's minds by the force of involuntary convictions. But only in its most general outline is it in harmony with itself; within these it is reproduced in greater or smaller circles innumerable, and with modifications varied to infinity. And since new observations and experiences are perpetually flowing in upon it, since original minds are ever rising, that, though affected by its course, are not borne along by its current, but rather themselves impress on it a powerful reaction; it is thus involved in an endless series of metamorphoses; transient and multiform, it is sometimes more, sometimes less, in harmony with truth and right, being rather a tendency of the moment than a fixed system. It is sometimes the attendant only of the occurrence that it has contributed to produce, and from which it derives form and extension. There are times nevertheless, when, encountering a rugged will that refuses to be overcome, it bursts forth into exorbitant demands. That its perception of defects and deficiencies is frequently the just one, must needs be confessed; but the modes of proceeding required as the remedy—these, its very nature forbids it to conceive with force of perception, or employ with effect. Thence it is, that in long lapses of time, it is sometimes to be found in directly opposite extremes; as it aided to found the papacy, so was its help equally given to the overthrow of that power. In the times under consideration, it was at one period utterly profane, at another as entirely spiritual; we have seen it inclining toward Protestantism throughout the whole of Europe; we shall also see, that in a great portion of the same quarter of the world, it will assume an entirely different coloring.

Let us begin by examining, first of all, in what manner the doctrines of the Protestants made progress even in Italy.

Section I.—Opinions analogous to those of the Protestants entertained in Italy

Throughout the Italian peninsula, as elsewhere, an incalculable influence has been exercised on the development of science and art, by literary associations. They formed themselves, now around some prince, some distinguished scholar, or even some private individual of literary tastes and easy fortune; or occasionally they grew up in the free companionship of equals. These societies are usually most valuable when they arise, naturally and without formal plan, from the immediate exigencies of the moment. It is with pleasure that we shall follow the traces they have left.

At the same time with the Protestant movements in Germany, there appeared certain literary societies, assuming a religious complexion, in Italy.

When, under Leo X, it become the tone of society to doubt or deny the truth of Christianity, a reaction displayed itself in the minds of many able men; men who had acquired the high culture of the day, and took part in its refinements, while avoiding its depravities. It was natural that such persons should seek the society of each other; the human mind requires, or at least it clings to, the support of kindred opinion: this support is indispensable, as regards its religious convictions, for these have their basis in the most profound community of sentiment.

As early as the time of Leo X we find mention of an "Oratory of Divine Love," which had been founded by some distinguished men in Rome, for their mutual edification; they met for the worship of God, for preaching, and the practice of spiritual exercises, at the church of St. Silvestro and Dorothea, in the Trastevere, near the place where the apostle Peter is believed to have dwelt, and where he presided over the first assemblies of the Christians. The members were from fifty to sixty in number; among them were Sadolet, Giberto, and Caraffa, all of whom afterward became cardinals. Gaetano di Thiene, who was canonized and Lippomano, a theological writer of high reputation and great influence, were also of the number; Giuliano Bathi, the incumbent of the church where they met, was the central point around which they grouped themselves.[1]

That this association was by no means opposed to the doctrines of Protestantism, will be readily inferred from their place of assemblage; on the contrary, its views were to a certain extent in harmony with them; as for example, in the hope entertained of arresting the general decadence of the Church, by the revived force of religious convictions; a point whence Luther and Melancthon had also departed. This society consisted of men actuated at that moment by community of feeling, but great diversity of opinion was afterward displayed among them; and eventually this made itself manifest in tendencies altogether distinct and heterogeneous.

After the lapse of some years, we again meet with a certain portion of this Roman society in Venice.

Rome had been pillaged, Florence subdued, Milan was the mere haunt of factions, and battle-ground of contending armies; in this general ruin, Venice had remained undisturbed by foreigners or armies, and was considered to be the universal refuge. Here were assembled the dispersed literati of Rome, and those Florentine patriots against whom their native land was closed forever; among these last more particularly, as may be seen

[1] I take this notice from Caracciolo, Vita di Paolo IV," MS.: "Those few upright men and learned prelates, who were in Rome in that time of Leo ., seeing that in the city of Rome, and throughout all Italy, where, from vicinity to the apostolic see, the observance of the rites should most flourish, divine worship was very ill performed, united themselves, in number about sixty, in an oratory called of Divine Love, there to make, as in a strong tower, every effort to maintain the divine laws." In the "Vita Cajetani Thienæi" (A.A. SS. August II.), c. i. 7-10, Caracciolo repeats this with more minute details, but enumerates only fifty members. The "Historia Clericorum regularium vulgo Theatinorum," by Joseph Silos, confirms it in many passages, which are printed in the "Commentarius prævius" to the "Vita Cajetani."

in the historian Nardi, and in Bruccioli, the translator of the
Bible, a very decided spirit of devotion, not unmarked by the
influence of Savonarola, became manifest. This was shared by
other refugees, and among them by Reginald Pole, who had
quitted England to withdraw himself from the innovations of
Henry VIII. From their Venetian hosts, these distinguished
men found a cordial welcome. In the circle of Peter Bembo
of Padua, who kept open house, the point of discussion was
more frequently mere letters, as Ciceronian Latin; but among
the guests of Gregorio Corteri, the learned and sagacious abbot
of San Georgio in Venice, subjects of much more profound
interest were agitated. Bruccioli makes the bowers and groves
of San Georgio the scene of some of his dialogues. Near
Treviso was the villa of Luigi Priuli, called Treville.[2] He was
one of those upright and accomplished Venetians, of whom
we occasionally meet specimens in the present day, full of
a calm susceptibility to true and noble sentiments, and formed
for disinterested friendship. Here the inmates employed themselves chiefly in spiritual studies and conversation. Hither
came that Benedictine, Marco of Padua, from whom it would
appear to be that Pole declares himself to have drawn his
spiritual nurture. Here also was the eminent Venetian Gaspar
Contarini, who must be considered as the head of the assembly.
Of him Pole says, that nothing which the human mind can
discover by its own powers of investigation, was unknown to
him; and nothing wanting to him that the grace of God has
imparted to the human soul. To this eminence of wisdom he
further says, that Contarini added the crown of virtue.

If we now inquire what were the leading convictions of these
men, we find that foremost among them was the doctrine of
justification, which, as taught by Luther, had originated the
whole Protestant movement. Contarini wrote a special treatise
concerning this, which Pole cannot find words strong enough
to praise. "Thou," he exclaims to his friend, "thou hast
brought forth that jewel which the Church was keeping half-
concealed." Pole himself finds that Scripture, in its more profound and intimate revelations, is entirely in accordance with
this doctrine. He congratulates Contarini on having been the
first to bring to light " that holy, fruitful, indispensable truth." [3]

[2] " Epistolæ Reginaldi Poli," ed. Quirini, tom. ii. "Diatriba ad epis-
tolas Schelbornii," clxxxiii.   [3] Epistolæ Poli," tom. iii. p. 57.

o this circle of friends belonged M. A. Flaminio, who resided
or some time with Pole, and whom Contarini desired to take
ith him into Germany. Let us observe how distinctly he
rofesses this doctrine. "The Gospel," says he, in one of his
tters,[4] "is no other than the glad tidings, that the only-begotten
on of God, clothed in our flesh, has satisfied for us the justice
f the Eternal Father. Whoever believes this, enters the
ngdom of God; he enjoys the universal forgiveness; from
carnal creature, he becomes spiritual; from being a child of
rath, he becomes a child of grace, and lives in a sweet peace
f conscience." It would be difficult to announce the Lutheran
octrines in language more orthodox.

These convictions extended themselves, as a literary opinion
r tendency might have done, over a great part of Italy.[5]

It is, however, highly worthy of remark, that an opinion
o lately alluded to from time to time only in the schools, should
ow suddenly seize on the minds of men, and employ their in-
ellectual activity throughout an entire century; for it is
ndisputable, that this doctrine of justification was the parent
f wild commotions, dissensions, and even revolutions, through-
ut the greater part of the sixteenth century. One might
lmost declare, that this disposition of men's minds to occupy
nemselves with so transcendental a question, had arisen by
ay of counterpoise to the worldliness of the Church, which
ad now nearly lost all consciousness of the relation of God to
nan; that the examination of this, the most profound mystery
f that relation, had been entered on, by the world generally,
s a contrast to the blind indifference then affecting the
ierarchy of Rome.

Even in the pleasure-loving Naples, these doctrines were
romulgated, and that by a Spaniard, Juan Valdez, secretary
o the viceroy. Unfortunately the writings of Valdez have
vholly disappeared; but we may gather very explicit inti-
nations of their character from the objections of his opponents.

---

[4] To Theodorina Sauli, February 12, 542. "Lettere Volgari" (" Raccolta el Manuzio "), Vinegia, 1553, ii. 43.
[5] Among other documents, the letter f Sadolet to Contarini (" Epistola Sadolati," lib. ix. p. 365), in regard to his Commentary on the Epistle to the Romans," is very remarkable. "In uibus commentariis," says Sadolet: In which commentary I have en-

deavored to illustrate the whole mystery of Christ's death and passion." He had not, however, quite satisfied Contarini, in whose opinion he did not entirely concur; he promises meanwhile to give, in his new edition, a clear explanation of original sin and grace. "About this disease of our nature, and the reparation of our will brought about by the Holy Spirit."

About the year 1540, a little book, " On the Benefits bestowed
by Christ," was put into circulation ; it " treated," as a report of
the inquisition expresses it, " in an insidious manner of justification, undervalued works and merits, ascribing all to faith ;
and as this was the very point at which so many prelates and
monks were stumbling, the book had been circulated to a great
extent." Inquiries have frequently been made as to the author
of this work ; we learn his name with certainty from the report
just quoted. " It was," says this document, " a monk of San
Severino, a disciple of Valdez, and the book was revised by
Flaminio."[6] From this extract we find, then, that the author-
ship of the treatise, " On the Benefits of Christ," is due to a
friend and pupil of Valdez. It had incredible success, and
made the study of those doctrines of justification, for some time,
popular in Italy. The pursuits of Valdez were, however, not
exclusively theological, his attention being occupied in part by
the duties of an important civil office. He founded no sect ;
this book resulted from a liberal study of Christian truth. His
friends looked back with delight on the happy days they had
enjoyed with him on the Chiaja, and at Posilippo, in that fair
vicinity of Naples, " where nature rejoices in her splendor, and
smiles at her own beauty." Valdez was mild, agreeable, and
not without expansion of mind. " A part only of his soul," as
his friends declare, " sufficed to animate his slight and feeble
frame ; the greater part, the clear, unclouded intellect, was
ever uplifted in the contemplation of truth."

An extraordinary influence was exercised by Valdez over
the nobility and learned men of Naples ; a lively interest was
also taken by the women of that day in this movement, at
once religious and intellectual. Among these was Vittoria
Colonna. After the death of her husband, Pescara, she had
devoted herself entirely to study ; in her poems, as well as

[6] Schelhorn, Gerdesius, and others
have ascribed this book to Aonius Palearius, who says, in a certain discourse : " This year I wrote in the
Italian tongue, showing what advantages were brought to mankind by the
death of Christ." The compendium of
the inquisitors, which I found in Caracciolo, " Vita di Paolo IV," MS., expresses itself, on the contrary, as follows : " The author of that book on the
benefits of Christ, was a monk of San
Severino in Naples, a disciple of Valdez
—Flaminio was the reviser ; it was
often printed, but particularly at Modena : it deceived many, because it
treated of justification in an attractive
manner, but heretically." But since
that passage from Palearius does not so
clearly point out this book as to make
it certain that no other is meant, since
Palearius says he was called to account
for it in the same year, while the compendium of the inquisition expressly
declares : " That book was approved
by many in Verona alone, but being
known and reprobated, was placed in
the index many years after " ; so I conclude that the opinions of the above
named scholars are erroneous.

her letters, will be found evidence of a deeply felt morality, and unaffected sense of religious truth. How beautifully does she console a friend for the death of her brother, "whose peaceful spirit had entered into everlasting rest; she ought not to complain, since she could now speak with him, unimpeded by those absences formerly so frequent, which prevented her from being understood by him."[7] Pole and Contarini were among her most confidential friends. I do not believe that she devoted herself to spiritual exercises of a monastic character; I think, at least, that so much may be inferred from Aretino, who writes to her, with much naïveté, that he is sure she does not take the silence of the tongue, casting down of the eyes, and assuming coarse raiment, to be essential, but purity of soul alone.

The house of Colonna generally was favorable to this religious movement, and more especially so were Vespasiano, Duke of Palliano, and his wife, Julia Gonzaga, the same who is reputed to have been the most beautiful woman in Italy. Valdez dedicated one of his books to Julia.

These opinions had moreover made active progress among the middle classes. The report of the inquisition would seem to exaggerate, when it reckons 3,000 schoolmasters as attached to them; but admitting the number to be smaller, how deep an effect must have been produced on the minds of youth, and of the people!

With almost equal cordiality were these doctrines received in Modena. The bishop himself, Morone, an intimate friend of Pole and Contarini, received them favorably; at his express command it was that the book, "On the Benefits of Christ," was printed, and extensively distributed. Don Girolamo da Modena was president of a society in which the same principle prevailed.[8]

. There has from time to time been mention made of the Protestants in Italy, and we have already adduced several names recorded in their lists. There is no doubt that many of the convictions predominant in Germany had taken root in the minds of these men; they sought to establish the articles

---

[7] "Lettere Volgari," i. 92; "Lettere di diversi Autori," p. 604. The first of these is a particularly useful collection.
[8] In Schelhorn's "Amoenitatt. Literar." tom. xii. p. 564, we find the

"Articuli contra Moronum," published by Vergerio in 1558, reprinted; these accusations do not fail to appear there; I took the more exact notices from the Compendium of the Inquisitors.

of their faith on the testimony of Scripture; in the particular
of justification they did certainly approach very near to the
doctrines of Luther. But, that they adopted these on all other
points must not be asserted; the conviction that the Church
is one and indivisible, and reverence for the pope, were too
deeply impressed on their minds to admit this; there were besides many Catholic usages too closely interwoven with the
national character to have been easily departed from.

Flaminio composed an exposition of the Psalms, of which
the dogmatic tenor has been approved by Protestant writers,
but even to this he prefixed a dedication, wherein he calls the
pope, "the warder and prince of all holiness, the vicegerent of
God upon earth."

Giovan. Battista Folengo ascribes justification to grace alone,
he even speaks of the uses of sin, which is not far removed from
the injury that may arise from good works. He remonstrates
zealously against trusting in fasts, frequent prayers, masses,
and confessions; nay, even in the priesthood itself, the tonsure
or the mitre.[9] Yet, in the same convent of Benedictines, where
he had taken his vows at sixteen, did he peaceably close his life
at the age of sixty.[10]

It was for some time not far otherwise with Bernardino
Ochino. If we may believe his own words, it was at the first
a deep longing, as he expresses it, "for the heavenly paradise to be achieved through God's grace," that led him to
become a Franciscan. His zeal was so fervid that he soon
passed over to the severer discipline and penances of the
Capuchins. Of this order he was elected general in its third
chapter, and again in the fourth, an office that he filled to
the satisfaction of all. But however rigorous his life (he
went always on foot, had no other bed than his cloak, drank no
wine, and strictly enforced the rule of poverty on others also,
as the most effectual means for attaining evangelical perfection), yet did he gradually become convinced and penetrated
by the doctrine of justification by grace alone, earnestly then
did he preach it from the pulpit, and urge it in the confessional. "I opened my heart to him," says Bembo, "as I

[9] "Ad Psalm. 67," f. 246. An extract
from these explanations will be found
in Gerdesius, "Italia Reformata," p.
257-261.

[10] "Thuani Historiæ, ad. a. 1559," i.
473.

ould have done to Christ himself. I felt as I looked at
im that I had never beheld a holier man." Cities poured
orth their multitudes to his teachings, the churches were too
mall for his hearers, all were alike edified, old and young,
men and women, the profound scholar and the untaught peasant.
His coarse raiment, his gray hair, and beard that swept his
breast, his pale emaciated countenance, and the feebleness
brought on by his persistence in fasting, gave him the aspect
of a saint.[1]

There was thus a line within Catholicism which the opinions
analogous to Lutheranism did not overpass. Priesthood and
the monastic orders encountered no opposition in Italy, nor
was there any thought of questioning the supremacy of the
pope. How indeed could such a man as Pole, for example,
be otherwise than strongly attached to this last principle, he
who had fled his native land in preference to acknowledging
his own king as head of the Church? They thought, as
Ottonel Vida, a disciple of Vergerio, expresses himself to
his master, " in the Christian Church has each man his appointed office: on the bishop is laid the care of the souls
in his diocese; these he is to guard from the world and the evil
spirit. It is the duty of the metropolitan to secure the residence
of the bishop, and he is himself again subjected to the pope, to
whom has been confided the general government of the Church,
which it is his duty to guard and guide with holiness of mind.
Every man should be vigilant and upright in his vocation."[2]
Separation from the Church was regarded by these men as the
extremity of evil. Isidoro Clario, who corrected the Vulgate,
with the assistance of the Protestant writers, and prefixed an
introduction which was subjected to expurgation, warns the
Protestants against any such intention in a treatise written for
that especial purpose. " No corruption," he declares, " can be
so great as to justify a defection from the hallowed communion of the Church." " Is it not better," he demands, " to
repair what we have, than to endanger all by dubious attempts
to produce something new? Our sole thought should be, how
the old institution could be ameliorated and freed from its
defects."

[1] Boverio, " Annali di Frati Minori Capuccini," i. 375. Gratiani, " Vie de Commendone," p. 143.　[2] Ottonello Vida Dot. al Vescovo Vergerio, " Lettere Volgari," i. 80.

With these modifications, the new doctrines had a large
number of adherents in Italy, among them Antonio dei Pagliarici of Siena, to whom had even been attributed the author-
ship of the work, " On the Benefits bestowed by Christ ";
Carnesecchi of Florence, who is mentioned as a disseminator of
this work, and as upholding its tenets; Giovan. Battista Rotto
of Bologna, who was protected by Morone, Pole and Vittoria
Colonna, and who found means to aid the poorest of his followers with money and other succors; Fra Antonio of Volterra,
and indeed some man of eminence in nearly every town of Italy,
connected themselves with the professors of these doctrines. [3]
It was a system of feelings and opinions, decidedly religious,
but tempered by attachment to the Church and its forms, which
moved the whole land from one end to the other, and in every
phase of society.

Section II.—Attempts at Internal Reform, and a Reconcilia-
tion with the Protestants

An expression has been attributed to Pole, to the effect that
a man should content himself with his own inward convictions,
without greatly encumbering his thoughts as to whether there
were errors and abuses in the Church.[1] Yet it was precisely
from a party to which he himself belonged that the first attempt
at a reformation proceeded.

The most honorable act of Paul III, and that by which he
signalized his accession to the papal throne, was the elevation
of many distinguished men to the college of cardinals without
any consideration but that of their personal merits. The first
of these was the Venetian Contarini, by whom the others
were afterward proposed. They were men of irreproachable
character, in high repute for learning and piety, and well acquainted with the requirements of different countries. Caraffa,
for example, who had long resided in Spain and the Nether-

---

[3] Our authority on this subject is the extract from the Compendium of the Inquisitors, " Compendio," fol. 9, c. 94: Bologna was in great peril, because heretics of great note were there, among them one Gio. Ba. Rotto, who had the friendship and support of very powerful persons, as Morone, Pole, and the Marchesa di Pescara; he collected money with all his strength, and di-

vided it among the poor and concealed heretics who were in Bologna. He afterward recanted before Father Salmerone, by order of the legate of Bologna. The same course was pursued in all the towns.
[1] Passages from Atanagi in McCrie's " Reformation in Italy," German translation, p. 172.

ands; Sadolet, bishop of Carpentras in France; Pole, a refugee
from England; Giberto, who, after having long taken active
part in administering the affairs of the state, was then ruling
his bishopric of Verona with exemplary wisdom; Federigo
Fregoso, archbishop of Salerno, almost all, be it observed, members of the Oratory of Divine Love, before mentioned, and
many of them holding opinions inclining to Protestantism.[2]

It was these same cardinals who now prepared a plan for
the reform of the Church by command of the Pope himself.
This became known to the Protestants, who rejected it with
derision. They had indeed meanwhile advanced far beyond
its most liberal provisions. But we are not on that account
permitted to deny the extreme significance of such an act on
the part of the Catholic Church. Here we have the evil
grappled with in Rome itself. In the presence of the Pope it
was that former popes were accused of misgovernment, and,
in the introduction to the document now laid before him, his
predecessors were accused of having " frequently chosen servants, not as desiring to learn from them what their duties demanded, but rather to procure the declaration that those things
were lawful toward which their desires led them." This abuse
of the supreme power was declared to be the most prolific source
of corruption.[3]

Nor did matters rest there. Certain short pieces are extant,
written by Gaspar Contarini, in which he makes unsparing
war on those abuses most especially, from which the Curia
derived profit. The practice of compositions or the acceptance
of money in payment for spiritual favors, he denounces as
simony that may be considered a kind of heresy. It was taken
very ill that he should inculpate former popes. " How! " he
exclaims, " shall we concern ourselves about the fame of three
or four popes, and not amend what has been suffered to decay,
and win a good reputation for ourselves? In good truth it
would be asking very much, to require that we should defend
all the acts of all the popes! " The abuse of dispensations also
he attacks most earnestly and effectively; he considers it

[2] " Vita Reginaldi Poli," in the edition of his letters by Quirini, tom. i.
p. 12. " Florebelli de vita Jacobi Sadoleti Commentarius," prefixed to the
" Epp. Sadoleti," col. 1590, vol. iii.
[3] This is the council of select cardinals and other prelates for the improvement of the church before alluded to.
It is signed by Contarini, Caraffa, Sadolet, Pole, Fregoso, Giberto, Cortese,
and Aleander.

idolatrous to say, as many did, that the pope was restrained by
no other rule than his absolute will from the suspension or confirmation of the positive law and right. What he says on this
subject is well worth repeating: " The law of Christ," he declares, " is a law of freedom, and forbids a servitude so abject
that the Lutherans were entirely justified in comparing it with
the Babylonish captivity. But furthermore, can that be called
a government of which the rule is the will of one man, by
nature prone to evil, and liable to the influence of caprices and
affections innumerable? No; all true dominion is a dominion
of reason, whose aim is to lead all whom it governs to the proposed end—happiness. The authority of the pope is equally
with others a dominion of reason, God has conferred this rule
on St. Peter and his successors, that they might lead the flocks
confided to their care into everlasting blessedness. A pope
should know that those over whom he exercises this rule are
free men; not according to his own pleasure must he command,
or forbid, or dispense, but in obedience to the rule of reason,
of God's commands, and to the law of love, referring everything to God, and doing all in consideration of the common
good only. For positive laws are not to be imposed by mere
will, they must be ever in unison with natural rights, with
the commandments of God, and with the requirements of circumstances. Nor can they be altered or abrogated, except in
conformity with this guidance and with the imperative demands of things." " Be it the care of your holiness," he
exclaims to Paul III, " never to depart from this rule; be not
guided by the impotence of the will which makes choice of evil;
submit not to the servitude which ministers to sin. Then wilt
thou be mighty, then wilt thou be free, then will the life of the
Christian commonwealth be sustained in thee."[4]

It will be seen that this was an attempt to found a papacy
guided by reasonable laws, and is the more remarkable as proceeding from that same doctrine regarding justification and
free-will which had served as the groundwork of the Protestant
secession. We do not merely conjecture this from our
knowledge that Contarini held these opinions, he declares it in

[4] G. Contarini, " Cardinalis ad Paulum
III. P. M. de potestate Pontificis in
compositionibus," printed by Rocca-
berti, " Bibliotheca, Pontificia Maxima,
tom. xiii. I have also in my possession
a " Tractatus de compositionibus datarii
Revmi. D. Gasparis Contarini," 1536,
of which I cannot find that any copy
has been printed.

xpress terms. He asserts that man is prone to evil, that this
proceeds from the impotence of the will, which, when it turns to
vil, becomes rather passive than active; only through the grace
of Christ is it made free. He afterward utters a distinct recognition of the papal authority, but demands that it be exercised
n obedience to the will of God and for the common good.

Contarini laid his writings before the pope. In a bright
and cheerful day of November, in the year 1538, he journeyed
with him to Ostia: "On the way thither," he writes to Pole,
"this our good old man made me sit beside him, and talked
with me alone about the reform of the compositions. He told
me that he had by him the little treatise I had written on the
subject, and that he had read it in his morning hours. I had
already given up all hope, but he now spoke to me with so much
Christian feeling, that my hopes have been wakened anew; I
now believe that God will do some great thing, and not permit
the gates of hell to prevail against his Holy Spirit."[5]

It may be readily comprehended, that a complete reformation of abuses, in which were involved so many personal rights
and conflicting claims, and which had become so closely interwoven with all the habits of life, was of all things the most difficult that could be undertaken. Nevertheless, Pope Paul did
gradually seem disposed to enter earnestly on the task.

He appointed commissions, accordingly, for carrying reform
into effect,[6] as regarded the Apostolic Chamber, the Ruota,
Chancery, and Penitentiaria: he also recalled Giberti to his
councils. Bulls, enacting reform, appeared, and preparations
were made for that council so dreaded and shunned by Pope
Clement, and which Paul also might have found many reasons
of a private nature for desiring to avoid.

And now, supposing ameliorations really to have been made,
the Roman Court reformed, and the abuses of the constitution
done away with: if then, that same tenet from which Luther
had started, had been taken as the principle of renovation in
life and doctrine, might not a reconciliation have been possible?
For even the Protestants did not tear themselves hastily or without reluctance from the communion of the Church.

[5] "Gaspar C. Contarinus Reginaldo C. Polo," "Ex ostiis Tiberinis," November 11, 1538. ("Epp. Poli," ii. 142.)

[6] "Acta consistorialia" (August 6, 1540) in Rainaldus, "Annales Ecclesiastici," tom. xxi. p. 146.

To many minds this seemed possible, and earnest hopes were founded on the results of the religious conference.

According to theory the Pope should not have permitted this conference, since its object was to determine religious differences (as to which he claimed the supreme right of judging) by the intervention of the secular power. Paul was, in fact, extremely reserved on the occasion of this council, though he suffered it to proceed, and even sent his deputies to be present at the sittings.

The affair was proceeded in with great circumspection; carefully selecting men of moderate character—persons, indeed, who fell afterward under the suspicion of Protestantism: he, moreover, gave them judicious rules for the direction of their political conduct, and even for the government of their lives.

Thus, for example, when he sent Morone, who was yet young, to Germany in the year 1536, he strictly enjoined him to "contract no debts, but pay all things regularly in the lodgings assigned him": further, Morone was recommended "to clothe himself without luxury, but also without meanness; to frequent the churches, certainly, but to avoid all appearance of hypocrisy." He was, in fact, to represent in his own person that Roman reform of which so much had been said, and was advised to maintain a "dignity tempered by cheerfulness."[7] In the year 1540, the bishop of Vienna had recommended a very decisive course. He was of opinion that those articles of Luther and Melancthon's creed, which had been declared heretical, should be laid before the adherents of the new doctrines, and that they should be directly and shortly asked whether they would renounce them or not. To such a measure, however, the Pope would by no means instruct his nuncio. "We fear they would rather die," said he, "than make such a recantation."[8] His best hope was to see only the prospect of a reconciliation. On the first gleam of this, he would send a formula, in terms free from all offence, which had been already prepared by wise and venerable men. "Would it were come to that! Scarcely do we dare to expect it!"

[7] "Instructio pro causa fidei et concilii data episcopo Mutinæ." October 24, 1536, MS.
[8] "Instructiones pro Revmo. D. Ep. Mutinensi, apostolico nuncio interfuturo conventui Germanorum Spiræ, 12 Maij, 1540, celebrando:" "It is to be feared, it is even certain, that not only such as trust to a safe conduct, will reject what things are piously and prudently contained in these articles, but even where instant death threatens, that would rather be chosen."

But never were parties in a better position to warrant this
ope of the pontiff than at the conference of Ratisbon in the
ear 1541: political relations looked extremely favorable; the
Emperor, who desired to employ all the forces of the empire in
war with the Turks or with France, wished for nothing more
earnestly than a reconciliation.   He chose the most sagacious
nd temperate men he could find among the Catholic theologians,
amely Gropper and Julius Pflug, to proceed to the conference.
On the other side, the landgrave Philip was again on good
erms with Austria, and hoped to obtain the chief command in
he war for which men were preparing themselves.   With admiration and delight the Emperor beheld this warlike chief ride
nto Ratisbon on his stately charger, the rider no less vigorous
han his steed.   The yielding Bucer and gentle Melancthon ap-
eared on the Protestant side.

The earnest desire of Paul for an amicable result from this
onference, was made manifest by his choice of the legate
whom he sent to it—no other than that Gaspar Contarini,
whom we have seen so profoundly attached to the new modes
f thought that were prevalent in Italy; so active in devising
measures of general reform.   He now assumed a position of
till higher importance: placed midway between two systems
f belief—between two parties that were then dividing the
world—commissioned, at a moment of peculiarly advantageous
spect, to reconcile these parties, and earnestly desiring to effect
hat purpose.   It is a position which, if it do not impose on us
he duty of considering his personal character more clearly, yet
enders it allowable that we should do so.

Messire Gaspar Contarini, the eldest son of a noble house in
Venice, that traded to the Levant, had especially devoted him-
elf to philosophical pursuits: his mode of proceeding in regard
o them is not unworthy of remark: he set apart three hours
daily for his closer studies, never devoting to them more, and
never less; he began each time with exact repetition.   Adher-
ng to this method, he proceeded to the conclusion of each sub-
ect, never allowing himself to do anything lightly or with half
measures.[9]   He would not permit the subtleties of Aristotle's
ommentators to lead him into a similar subtleties, perceiving

---

[9] "Joannis Casæ Vita Gasparis Contarini," in "Jo. Casæ Monumentis La-
nis," ed. Hal. 1708, p. 88.

that nothing is more astute than falsehood. He displayed the most remarkable talent, with a steadiness still more remarkable; he did not seek to acquire the graces of language, but expressed himself with simplicity and directly to the purpose—as in nature the growing plant is unfolded in regular succession, yearly producing its due results, so did his faculties develop themselves.

When, at an early age, he was elected into the council of the Pregadi, the senate of his native city, he did not for some time venture to speak; he wished to do so, and felt no want of matter, but he could not find courage for the effort: when at length he did prevail on himself to overcome this reluctance, his speech, though not remarkable for grace or wit, and neither very animated nor very energetic, was yet so simple and so much to the purpose, that he at once acquired the highest consideration.

His lot was cast in a most agitated period. He beheld his native city stripped of her territory, and himself aided in the recovery. On the first arrival of Charles V in Germany, Contarini was sent to him as ambassador, and he there became aware of the dissensions then beginning to arise in the Church. They entered Spain at the moment when the ship Vittoria had returned from the first circumnavigation of the globe,[10] and Contarini was the first, so far as I can discover, to solve the problem of her entering the port one day later than she should have done according to the reckoning in her log-book. The Pope, to whom he was sent after the sack of Rome, was reconciled to the Emperor, partly by his intervention. His sagacious and penetrating views of men and things, together with his enlightened patriotism, are clearly evinced by his short essay on the Venetian constitution, a most instructive and well-arranged little work, as also by the different reports of his embassies, which are still occasionally to be found in manuscript.[1]

On a Sunday, in the year 1535, at the moment when the imperial council had assembled, and Contarini, who had meanwhile risen to the highest offices, was seated by the balloting urn,

[10] Boccatello, "Vita del C. Contarini" ("Epp. Poli," iii.), p. 103. There is also another edition, but it is taken from the volume of letters, and has the same number of pages.
[1] The first is of 1525, the other of 1530. The first is particularly important for the earlier times of Charles V. I have found no trace of it either in Vienna or Venice; in Rome I discovered one copy, but have never been able to get sight of another.

he intelligence came, that Pope Paul, whom he did not know,
and with whom he had no sort of connection, had appointed
him cardinal. All hastened to congratulate the astonished man,
who could scarcely believe the report. Aluise Mocenigo, who
had hitherto been his opponent in affairs of state, exclaimed that
the republic had lost her best citizen.[2]

For the Venetian noble there was nevertheless one painful
consideration attached to this honorable event. Should he
abandon his free native city, which offered him its highest dignities, or in any case a sphere of action where he might act
in perfect equality with the first in the state, for the service of
a pope, often the mere slave of passion and restricted by no
effectual law? Should he depart from the republic of his fore-
fathers, whose manners were in harmony with his own, to
measure himself against others in the luxury and display of
the Roman court? We are assured that he accepted the cardinalate, principally because it was represented to him, that in
times so difficult, the refusal of this high dignity (having the
appearance of despising it) might produce an injurious effect.[3]

And now, the zeal that he had formerly devoted with exclusive affection to his native country, was applied to the affairs
of the Church generally. He was frequently opposed by the
cardinals, who considered it extraordinary that one but just
called to the sacred college, and a Venetian, should attempt
reform in the court of Rome. Sometimes the Pope himself was
against him; as when Contarini opposed the nomination of a
certain cardinal, " We know," said the pontiff, " how men sail
in these waters, the cardinals have no mind to see another made
equal to them in honor." Offended by this remark, the Venetian replied, " I do not consider the cardinal's hat to constitute
my highest honor."

In this new position he maintained all his usual gravity,
simplicity, and activity of life, all his dignity and gentleness
of demeanor; nature leaves not the simply-formed plant without the ornament of its blossom, in which its being exhales and
communicates itself. In man, it is the disposition, the
character, which, being the collective product of all his higher
faculties, stamps its impress on his moral bearing, nay, even on

[2] Daniel Barbaro to Domenico Veniero, " Lettere Volgari," i. p. 73.
[3] Casa, p. 102.

his aspect and manner; in Contarini this was evinced in the
suavity, the inherent truthfulness and pure moral sense, by
which he was distinguished; but above all in that deep religious conviction which renders man happy in proportion as
it enlightens him.

Adorned with such qualities, moderate, nearly approaching
the Protestant tenets in their most important characteristics,
Contarini appeared in Germany; by a regeneration of Church
doctrines, commencing from this point, and by the abolition of
abuses, he hoped to reconcile the existing differences.

But had not these already gone too far? Was not the breach
too widely extended? Had not the dissentient opinions struck
root too deeply? These questions I should be reluctant to
decide.

There was also another Venetian, Marino Giustiniano, who
left Germany shortly before this diet, and who would seem to
have examined the aspect of things with great care. To him
the reconciliation appears very possible.[4] But he declares
that certain concessions are indispensable. The following he
particularizes:—" The pope must no longer claim to be the
vicegerent of Christ in temporal as well as spiritual things.
He must depose the profligate and ignorant bishops and priests,
appointing men of blameless lives, and capable of guiding and
instructing the people, in their places; the sale of masses, the
plurality of benefices, and the abuse of compositions must no
longer be suffered; a violation of the rule as regards fasting
must be visited by very light punishment at the most." If in
addition to these things, the marriage of priests be permitted,
and the communion in both kinds be allowed, Giustiniano believes that the Germans would at once abjure their dissent,
would yield obedience to the pope in spiritual affairs, resign
their opposition to the mass, submit to auricular confession, and
even allow the necessity of good works as fruits of faith—in so
far, that is, as they are the consequence of faith. The existing
discord having arisen because of abuses, so there is no doubt
that by the abolition of these it may be done away with.

And on this subject we shall do well to remember what the
landgrave, Philip of Hesse, had declared the year before;

[4] " Relazione del Clarmo. M. Marino
Giustinian Kavr. (ritornato) dalla lega-
zione di Germania sotto Ferdinando,
re di Romani."—Bibl. Corsini in Rome,
No. 481.

namely, that the temporal power of the bishops might be tolerated, whenever means should be found for securing the suitable exercise of their spiritual authority. That, as regarded the mass, an agreement might be made, provided the communion in both kinds were conceded.[5] Joachim of Brandenburg declared himself ready to acknowledge the pope's supremacy. Meanwhile advances were made from the other side also. The imperial ambassador declared repeatedly that concessions should be agreed to by both parties, so far as was consistent with the honor of God. Even the non-protesting party would have willingly seen the spiritual power withdrawn from the bishops throughout Germany; they being now to all intents secular princes: this power they would then have had placed in the hands of superintendents, when means might have been adopted for a general change in the administration of church property. There was already some talk of things neutral and indifferent, that might either be retained or omitted, and even in the ecclesiastical electorates, prayers were appointed to be offered up for a prosperous issue to the work of reconciliation.

In what degree this reconciliation was either possible or probable need not be made the subject of dispute; it would in all cases have been extremely difficult; but if only the most remote probability existed, it was worth the attempt. Thus much is obvious, that a great wish for reunion had certainly arisen, and that many hopes and expectations were built on it.

And now came the question as to how far the Pope, without whom nothing could be done, was disposed to depart from the rigor of his demands. On this point a certain part of the instructions given to Contarini at his departure is worthy of attention.[6]

The unlimited power with which the Emperor had pressed Paul to invest the legate had not been accorded, the Pope suspecting that demands might be made in Germany, which not only the legate, but even he, the pontiff, might find it dangerous to concede without first consulting the other nations, yet he did

[5] Letters from the landgrave in Rommel's "Urkundenbuch," p. 85. Compare this with the letter of the bishop of Lunden in Seckendorf, p. 299. "Contarini al Cardinal Farnese, 1541, 28 April" ("Epp. Poli," iii. p. 255.) The landgrave and the elector both demanded the marriage of priests and communion in both kinds; the former made more difficulty with respect to the pope's supremacy, the latter with regard to the doctrine whether the mass be a sacrifice."

[6] "Instructio data Revmo. Cli. Contarino in Germaniam legato, d. 28 mensis Januarii, 1541," to be seen in MS. in various libraries, and printed in Quirini, "Epp. Poli," iii. 286.

not decline all negotiations. "We must first see," he remarks,
"whether the Protestants are in accord with us as to essential
principles; for example, the supremacy of the Holy See, the
sacraments, and some others." If we ask what these "others"
were, we find that on this point the Pope does not clearly express
himself concerning them. He describes them generally, as
"whatever is sanctioned by the Holy Scriptures, as well as by
the perpetual usage of the Church, with which the legate is well
acquainted." "On this basis," he further observes, "attempts
may be made for the arrangement of all differences."[7]

This vague mode of expression was beyond all question
adopted with design. Paul III may have been willing to see
how far Contarini could proceed toward a settlement of affairs, and reluctant to bind himself beforehand to a ratification
of all his legate's acts; he chose beside to give Contarini a
certain latitude. It would without doubt have cost the legate
new efforts and infinite labor, to have made those conditions
pleasing to the intractable Roman Curia, which he, with all his
cares, had only wrung out by great effort at Ratisbon, but which
yet were certain of being unsatisfactory at Rome. In the first
instance everything depended on a reconciliation and union
among the assembled theologians; the conciliatory and mediate
tendency was still too weak and undefined to possess any great
efficacy, as yet it could scarcely receive a name, nor, until it
had gained some fixed station, could any available influence be
hoped from it.

The discussions were opened on the fifth of April, 1541, and
a plan of proceeding, proposed by the Emperor, and admitted
after some slight alterations by Contarini, was adopted; but
even here, at the first step, the legate found it requisite to dissent
in a certain measure from his instructions. The Pope had required in the first place, a recognition of his supremacy, but
Contarini perceived clearly that on this point, so well calculated to arouse the passions of the assembly, the whole affair

---

[7] Videndum imprimis est, an Protes-
tantes et ii qui ab ecclesiæ gremio de-
fecerunt, in principiis nobiscum con-
veniant, cujusmodi est hujus sanctæ
sedis primatus, tanquam a Deo et Salvatore nostro insititutus, sacrosanctæ
ecclesiæ sacrament et alia quædam,
quæ tum sacrarum litterarum auctoritate,
tum universalis ecclesiæ perpetua obser-
vatione, hactenus observata et compro-
bata fuere et tibi nota esse bene scimus,
quibus statim initio admissis omnis
super aliis controversiis concordia ten-
taretur." (See the text.) We must not
fail to keep in view the position of the
Pope, which was in the highest degree
orthodox, and, from its very nature,
inflexible, in order to comprehend how
much lay in such a turn of affairs.

ight be wrecked at the very outset; he therefore permitted
he question of papal supremacy to be placed last, rather than
rst on the list for discussion. He thought it safer to begin
ith subjects on which his friends and himself approached the
'rotestant opinions, which were besides questions of the highest
nportance, and touching the very foundations of the faith. In
he discussions concerning these, he himself took most active
art. His secretary assures us, that nothing was determined by
he Catholic divines, until he had been previously consulted,
ot the slightest variation made without his consent.[8] Morone,
ishop of Modena, Tomaso da Modena, master of the sacred
alace, both holding the same opinions with himself as to
ustification, assisted him with their advice.[9] The principal
ifficulty proceeded from a German theologian, Doctor Eck,
n old antagonist of Luther; but when forced to a close dis-
ussion, point by point, he also was at length brought to a
atisfactory explanation. In effect, the parties did actually
gree (who could have dared to hope so much) as to the four
rimary articles, of human nature, original sin, redemption,
nd even justification. Contarini assented to the principal point
a the Lutheran doctrine, namely, that justification is obtained
y faith alone, and without any merit on the part of man; add-
ng only, that this faith must be living and active. Melancthon
cknowledged that this was in fact a statement of the Prot-
stant belief itself;[10] and Bucer boldly declared, that in the arti-
les mutually admitted, " everything requisite to a godly, right-
ous, and holy life before God, and in the sight of man, was
omprehended."[1]

Equally satisfied were those of the opposite party. The
ishop of Aquila calls this conference holy, and did not doubt
hat the reconciliation of all Christendom would result from its
abors. The friends of Contarini, those who shared his opinions
nd sympathized with his feelings, were delighted with the
rogress he was making. " When I perceived this unanimity
f opinion," remarks Pole in a letter of this period to Contarini,

[8] Boccatelli, " Vita del Cardinal Con-
rini," p. 117.
[9] Pallavicini, iv. xiv. p. 433, from
ontarini's " Letters."
[10] Melancthon to Camerar, May 10th
" Epp." p. 360): " They admit that men
e justified by faith, and that even in
he sense in which we teach." Compare

Planck, " Geschichte des protestantisch-
em Lehrbegriffs," iii. ii. 93.
[1] All the negotiations and documents,
for the reconciliation of the religious
parties, executed by his Imperial Majesty, A.D. 1541, by Martin Bucer, in
Hortleder, bk. i. chap. 37, p. 280.

" I was sensible to such pleasure as no harmony of sounds could
have afforded me, not only because I foresee the coming of
peace and union, but because these articles are in very truth the
foundation of the Christian faith. They seem, indeed, to treat
of various matters, faith, works, and justification; upon this
last, however, on justification, do all the rest repose. I wish
thee joy, my friend, and I thank God, that on this point the
divines of both parties have agreed. He who hath so mercifully
begun this work, will also complete it.[2]

This, if I do not mistake, was a moment of most eventful
import, not for Germany only, but for the whole world. With
regard to the former, the points we have intimated tended in
their consequences to change the whole ecclesiastical constitution of the land; to secure a position of increased liberty as
regarded the Pope, and a freedom from temporal encroachment
on his part. The unity of the Church would have been maintained, and with it that of the nation. But infinitely farther
than even this, would the consequences have extended. If the
moderate party, from whom these attempts proceeded, and by
whom they were conducted, had been able to maintain the predominance in Rome and in Italy, how entirely different an
aspect must the Catholic world necessarily have assumed!

A result so extraordinary was, however, not to be obtained
without a vehement struggle.

Whatever was resolved on at Ratisbon, must be confirmed
by the sanction of the Pope, on the one hand, and the assent
of Luther on the other: to these latter a special embassy was
sent.

But already many difficulties here presented themselves.
Luther could not be convinced that the doctrine of justification
had really taken root among Catholics; his old antagonist, Doctor Eck, he regarded with some reason as incorrigible, and
he knew that this man had taken active part on the occasion in
the articles agreed upon. Luther could see nothing but a piece-
meal arrangement, made up from both systems. He, who

---

[2] Polus Contareno, " Capranicæ," May
17, 1541, " Epp. Poli," tom. i. iii. p. 25.
The letters of the bishop of Aquila, in
Rainaldus, 1541, Nos. 11, 12, also deserve
attention. It was believed that if the
point of the Lord's Supper could be settled, every other difficulty might be
readily arranged. What above all gives
the highest hope to everyone is the
declaration of the Emperor that he will
in no case depart until affairs are amica-
bly arranged, and also that our theologians conduct the disputations in all
respects with the knowledge and according to the advice of the most reverend prelate."

onsidered himself to be continually engaged in a conflict
etween heaven and hell, imagined that here also he discerned
ie labors of Satan. He most earnestly dissuaded his master,
ie elector, from proceeding to the diet in person, declaring that
he was the very man for whom the devil was in search; "[3]
nd certainly the appearance of the elector, and his assent to
ie resolutions adopted, would have had an important effect.

These articles meanwhile had arrived in Rome, where they
wakened universal interest. The cardinals Caraffa and San
Iarcello found extreme offence in the declaration respecting
ustification; and it was not without great difficulty that Priuli
iade its real import obvious to them.[4] The Pope did not ex-
ress himself so decidedly as Luther had done; it was signified
⊃ the legate by Cardinal Farnese, that his holiness neither
ccepted nor declined the conclusions arrived at; but that all
thers who had seen the articles thought they might have been
xpressed in words much clearer and more precise, if the mean-
ig of them were in accordance with the Catholic faith.

But however strenuous this theological opposition, it was
.either the only, nor perhaps the most effectual one; there was
et another, proceeding from causes partly political.

A reconciliation, such as that contemplated, would have given
n unaccustomed unity to all Germany, and would have greatly
xtended the power of the Emperor, who would have been at
10 loss to avail himself of this advantage.[5] As chief of the
noderate party, he would inevitably have obtained predominant
ifluence throughout Europe, more especially in the event of
. general council. All the accustomed hostilities were neces-
arily awakened at the mere prospect of such a result.

Francis I considered himself as more particularly threatened,
nd neglected no means that might serve to impede the pro-
ected union; he remonstrated earnestly against the concessions
nade by the legate at Ratisbon,[6] declaring that "his conduct

---

[3] Luther to John Frederick, in De
Vette's collection, v. 353.
[4] I cannot pardon Quirini for having
ailed to give unmutilated the letter of
'riuli touching these affairs, and which
ie had in his hands.
[5] There was always an imperial party,
which promoted this tendency; and
ere, among other things, will be found
he whole secret of those negotiations
indertaken by the archbishop of Lun-
len. He had represented to the Em-

peror ("Instruzione di Paolo III.,"
Montepalciano, 1539), if his majesty
would endure that the Lutherans should
remain in their errors, he might dispose of all Germany at his will and
pleasure. The Emperor himself also
then desired toleration.
[6] He spoke of it to the papal ambassadors at his court. "Il Cl. di Man-
tova al Cl. Contarini," in Quirini, iii.
278. "Loces, 17 Maggio, 1541." "S.
Ma. Chma. diveniva ogni dì più ardente

discouraged the good, and emboldened the wicked; that from extreme compliance to the Emperor, he was permitting things to get to such extremities, as would soon be irremediable; the advice of other princes also, ought surely to have been taken." Affecting to consider the Pope and Church in danger, he promised to defend them with his life, and with all the resources of his kingdom.

Other scruples besides those of a theological description before mentioned, had already arisen in Rome. It was remarked that the Emperor, on opening the diet and announcing a general council, did not add that the Pope alone had power to convene it: symptoms it was thought appeared of an inclination on his part to arrogate that right to himself. It was even said that in the old articles agreed on with Clement VII at Barcelona, there was a passage that might intimate such a purpose. Did not the Protestants continually declare that it rested with the Emperor to summon a council? And might not he be supposed to receive favorably an opinion so manifestly in harmony with his own interests?[7] Herein was involved the most imminent danger of further divisions.

Meanwhile Germany also was in movement. We are assured by Giustiniani, that the importance accruing to the landgrave from his position as head of the Protestant party, had already tempted others to secure themselves equal influence by assuming the lead of the Catholics. A member of this diet assures us, that the dukes of Bavaria were adverse to all proposals for agreement, and that the elector of Mayence displayed hostility equally decided. He cautioned the Pope, in a letter written specially to that effect, against a national council, and indeed against any council to be held in Germany; " where the concessions demanded would be exorbitant."[8] Other documents also are extant, in which certain German Catholics complain directly to the Pope of the progress made by Protestantism

nelle cose della chiesa, le quali era risoluto di voler difendere e sostenere con tutt le forze sue e con la vita sua e de' figliuoli, giurandomi che da questo si moveva principalmente a far questo officio." (See the text.) Granvella had, on the other hand, different instructions. "He declared to me," says Contarini, in a letter to Farnese, ibid. 255, "on oath, that he had letters in hand written by the most Christian king to the Protestant princes, exhorting them by no means to make agreement with the Catholics, and avowing himself desirous to learn their opinions, which were not displeasing to him." According to this, Francis impeded the reconciliation by efforts with both sides.

[7] Ardinghello, " al nome del Cl. Farnese al Cl. Contarini, 29 Maggio, 1541."

[8] Literæ Cardinalis Moguntini," in Rainaldus, 1541, No. 27.

at the diet, the pliability of Gropper and Pflug, and the absence of Catholic princes from the discussions.[9]

Suffice it to say, that in Rome, France, and Germany, there arose among the enemies of Charles V, among those who either were or appeared to be the most zealous for Catholicism, a determined opposition to his efforts for the conciliation of differences. An unusual degree of intimacy was remarked in Rome as existing between the pontiff and the French ambassador. It was thought the former meant to propose a marriage between Vittoria Farnese, his relative, and one of the house of Guise.

A powerful effect was inevitably produced by these agitations on the different divines. Eck remained in Bavaria. "The enemies of the Emperor, whether in or out of Germany," says the secretary of Contarini, "dreading the power he would obtain in the union of all Germany, began to sow the tares of discord among these divines. Carnal envy hath interrupted the conference."[10] If we consider how many difficulties were involved in the very nature of such an attempt, it cannot surprise us that agreement as to any one article was no longer possible.

Those who attribute the whole, or indeed the greater share of the blame attached to his failure to the Protestants, pass beyond the limits of justice. After a certain time, the Pope announced his positive will to the legate, that neither in his official capacity, nor as a private person, should he tolerate any resolution in which the Catholic faith and opinions were expressed in words admitting the possibility of ambiguous acceptation. The formula in which Contarini had thought to reconcile the conflicting opinions as to the supremacy of the pope and the power of councils, was rejected at Rome unconditionally.[1] The legate was compelled to offer explanations that seemed in flagrant contradiction to his own previous words.

But, to the effect that the conference might not be altogether

[9] Anonymous also in Rainaldus, No. 25. The side from which they came is obvious, from the fact that Eck is thus spoken of: "One able theologian was at least brought forward." "Nihil," they say, "Nothing will be done to strengthen the Church, from fear of offending him (the Emperor)."
[10] Beccatelli, "Vita," p. 119: "Hora il diavolo, che sempre alle buone opere s' attraversa, fece si che sparsa questa fama della concordia che tra Catholici e Protestanti si preparava, gli invidi dell' imperatore in Germania e fuori, che la sua grandezza temevano, quando tutti gli Alemani fussero stati uniti, cominciavono a seminare zizania tra quelli theologi collocutori."
[1] Ardinghello a Contarini, ibid. p. 224.

without result, the Emperor desired that both parties would, for the present at least, abide by the articles mutually assented to, and that with regard to those still in dispute, each should tolerate the differences of the other; but neither Luther nor the pope could be moved to hear of this, and the cardinal was given to understand that the sacred college had resolved unanimously not to extend tolerance under any conditions whatever in regard to articles so vitally essential.

After hopes so inspiriting, after a commencement so propitious, Contarini saw himself compelled to return without effecting any part of his purpose. He had wished to accompany the Emperor to the Netherlands, but neither was this permitted to him. Returning to Italy, it was his lot to endure all the slanders touching his conduct, and the concessions he was charged with making to Protestantism, that from Rome had been circulated over the whole country. This was sufficiently vexatious, but he had a loftiness of mind that rendered the failure of plans so comprehensive, and so replete with good for all, still more grievous and more permanently painful to him.

How noble and impressive was the position that moderate Catholicism had assumed in his person! But, having failed in securing its benevolent and world-embracing designs, it now became a question whether it would even maintain its own existence. In every great tendency should reside the power of vindicating its own existence, of rendering itself effectual and respected; if it be not strong enough to secure this, if it cannot achieve the mastery, its doom is inevitable; it must sink into irremediable ruin.

Section III.—New Ecclesiastical Orders

The minds of men had meanwhile become affected in another direction, in its origin not remote from that already indicated, but soon diverging from it; and though likewise seeking reform as its end, yet in a manner directly opposed to that adopted by Protestantism.

If the priesthood as heretofore existing had been repudiated by Luther in its very conception, and in every principle of its being, so was it as zealously upheld in its utmost extent by

others, and a movement was at once made in Italy for its renovation and re-establishment in all its original force; in the
hope that a more rigid observance of its tenor would restore it
to the respect of the Church. Both parties were sensible to the
decadency of ecclesiastical institutions; but while the Germans
were content with nothing less than the abolition of monas-
ticism, the Italians sought to restore and regenerate it. Whilst
in Germany the churchman was throwing off so many of the
restraints that had bound him, men were seeking in Italy to
make these fetters yet more stringent. On this side the Alps a
new path had been entered on; byond them, attempts were
repeated that had already been made from time to time throughout the lapse of ages.

There is no period in church history unprovided with
examples of a decline toward worldly corruption in the monastic bodies, but, arrived at a certain point of decadence,
they had appeared to recall their origin, and had returned to
habits of a more blameless purity. The Carlovingians even
in their early day had found it needful to enforce the rule of
Chrodegang on the clergy, compelling them to community of
life, and to voluntary subordination. Nor did the simple rule
of Benedict of Nursia long suffice to maintain order even
among religious houses. During the tenth and eleventh centuries, small secluded congregations, with special rules after
the model of Cluny, were found to be requisite. This produced
an instant effect on the secular clergy; by the enforcement of
celibacy, they also, as before remarked, became in a manner
subjected to the forms of monastic life. None the less, however, did corruption prevail; and. spite of the powerful religious
impulse given by the crusades to all Europe, an impulse so
extensively influential, that even the knights and nobles submitted their profession of war to the forms of monastic law,
these institutions had sunk into the utmost decay, when the
mendicant orders arose. On their first appearance, they doubtless did much to restore things to their primitive simplicity and
severity; but we have seen how they too became gradually
degenerate and tainted by the world's disorders, until at length
the most glaring evidence of decadence in the Church might
be found among these friars-mendicant.

From the year 1520, a conviction had been gaining ground

through all those countries into which Protestantism had not yet penetrated, that reformation was deeply needed by the institutions of the hierarchy; this conviction became ever more and more confirmed as the new tenets made progress in Germany and elsewhere. It found place even amongst the orders themselves; sometimes appearing in one order, sometimes in another.

The extreme seclusion to which the order of Camaldoli was subjected, had not been able to preserve even this one; it was found by Paolo Giustiniani to partake largely of the general disorder. In the year 1522, he formed a new congregation of the same order, which received the name of Monte Corona, from the mountain on which its chief establishment was afterward placed.[1] For the attainment of spiritual perfection, Giustiniani held three things to be essential: solitude, vows, and the separation of the monks into distinct cells. He alludes with special satisfaction in one of his letters to these little cells and oratories,[2] of which many may yet be found on the loftiest mountains, and niched amidst the beautiful wilds of nature; inviting the spirit at once to the most sublime aspirations and the deepest repose. The reforms effected by these hermits made themselves felt through the whole world.

Among the Franciscans, who were perhaps more deeply tainted than any, a new experiment of reform was made in addition to all that had been attempted before. The Capuchins determined on reviving the regulations of their founder —the midnight service, the prayer at stated hours, the discipline and silence—the life imposed by their original institute, that is to say, in all the extremes of its austerity. We may be tempted to smile at the undue importance attached to mere trifles, but it cannot be questioned that these monks comported themselves on many occasions in compliance with all the rigor of their duties, as, for example, during the plague of 1528, when their courage and devotion were most exemplary.

Nothing of real value could, however, be effected by a reform of the monastic orders only, while the secular clergy were

[1] We may reasonably date the foundation from the drawing up of the rules, after Masacio was granted to the new congregation in the year 1522. Basciano, the successor of Giustiniani, was the founder of Monte Corona. Helyot, "Histoire des Ordres Monastiques," v p. 271.
[2] "Lettera del b. Giustiniano al Vescovo Teatino," in Bromato, "Storia di Paolo IV." lib. iii. § 19.

so utterly estranged from their vocation; a reformation, to be
efficient, must affect them likewise.

And here we again encounter members of that Roman
oratory before mentioned: two of these, men, as it would
seem, of characters totally dissimilar in other respects, undertook to prepare the way for this needful reformation—the one,
Gaetano da Thiene, peaceful and retiring, of gentle manner
and few words, disposed to the reveries of religious enthusiasm, and of whom it was said that he desired to reform the
world without permitting it to be known that he was in the
world;[3] the other, John Peter Caraffa, of whom we shall have
further occasion to speak, turbulent, impetuous, and fiercely
bigoted. But Caraffa also perceived, as he says himself, that
his heart was only the more heavily oppressed the more it
followed its own desires—that peace could be found only by
the resignation of the whole being to God, and in converse
with heavenly things. Thus, these two men agreed in their
desire for seclusion; the one from an instinct of his nature;
the other impelled by yearnings after an ideal perfection; both
were disposed to religious activity, and convinced that reform
was needed, they combined to found an institution (since called
the Order of Theatines), having for its objects at once the
reformation of the clergy and a life of contemplation.[4]

Gaetano belonged to the " protonotari participanti "; he at
once resigned all emolument. Caraffa held the bishopric of
Chieti and the archbishopric of Brindisi, but he renounced
them both.[5] In company with two intimate friends, also members of the oratory, they solemnly assumed the three vows on
the fourteenth of September, 1524.[6] To the vow of poverty
they made the special addition that not only would they possess
nothing, but would even abstain from begging, and await the

[3] Caracciolus, " Vita S. Cajetani Thienæi," c. ix. 101: " In conversation humble, gentle, and of few words, and in
prayer I remember to have often seen
him weeping." He is very well described in the testimony of a pious
society at Vicenza, which may be
found in the same work, c. i. No. 12.
[4] Caracciolus, c. 2, § 19, declares their
intention to be: " To make up what is
wanting in the clergy, who are cor-
rupted by vice and ignorance to the
ruin of the people, so that the mischief
done by evil example might be remedied."

[5] From a letter by the papal datary of
September 22, 1524, we have authentic
proof that the Pope long hesitated to
accept the resignation (" non volendo
privare quelle chiese di cosi buon pas-
tore ") [not wishing to deprive those
churches of so good a pastor]. He
yielded only to Caraffa's urgent entreaties.
[6] The documents relating to this ceremony are to be found in the " Commentarius prœvius, AA. SS. Aug." ii,
p. 249.

alms that might be brought to their dwelling. After a short
abode in the city, they withdrew to a small house on the Monte
Pincio, near the Vigna Capisucchi, which afterward became
the Villa Medici. Here, though within the walls of Rome,
there prevailed at that time a deep solitude, and in this place they
lived amidst the privations of their self-imposed poverty, in
spiritual exercises and in study of the gospels. Of this the
plan had been previously arranged, and it was repeated with
great exactitude every month. They afterward descended into
the city to preach.

They did not call themselves monks, but regular clergy—
they were priests with the vows of monks. Their intention
was to establish a kind of seminary for the priesthood. By
the charter of their foundation, they were expressly allowed
to receive secular clergy. They did not originally adopt any
prescribed color or form of dress, leaving these to be determined by the local customs of their inmates; they suffered
even the services of the Church to be performed everywhere
according to the national usages; they were thus freed from
many restraints under which monks labored, expressly declaring that neither in the habits of life, nor in the service of the
Church, should any mere custom be permitted to become binding on the conscience;[7] but on the other hand, they devoted
themselves rigidly to their clerical duties—to preaching, the
administration of the sacraments, and the care of the sick.

And now a custom that had long fallen into disuse among
Italians, was again seen to prevail; priests appeared in the
pulpit wearing the cross, the clerical cap and gown: at first
this occurred principally in the oratory, but afterward, when
the wearers were proceeding on missions, in the streets also.
Caraffa himself preached with all that exuberance of eloquence
which remained his characteristic up to the last hour of his
life. Together with his associates, for the most part men of
noble birth, who might have possessed all the enjoyments of
the world, he now began to visit the sick, whether in hospitals
or private houses, and to wait by the pillow of the dying.

[7] Rule of the Theatines in Bromato,
" Vita di Paolo IV." lib. iii. § 25: " No
custom, and no mode of living or ritual
whatsoever, whether of those things
that belong to divine worship, and are
in any way practised in churches, or of
matters that relate to the living in
community with us, or without in the
accustomed dwelling, shall be ever permitted to acquire the force of prescrip-
tion."

The best effects were produced by this return to the performance of clerical duties. The order of the Theatines did not indeed become a seminary for priests precisely, its numbers were never sufficient for that; but it grew to be a seminary for bishops, coming at length to be considered the order of priests peculiar to the nobility; and, as from the first the rule that all new members should be noble was sedulously observed, so demands for a proof of noble birth were afterward occasionally made as a condition to acceptance by this order. It will be readily understood that the original intention of living on alms, and yet refusing to beg, could not have been fulfilled except on these conditions.

The great point gained by all these efforts, meanwhile, was this, that the useful purpose of conjoining the clerical duties and consecration of the secular clergy with the vows of monks, gained extensive approval and imitation.

The North of Italy had been scourged by continual wars since the year 1521: these were followed of necessity by desolation, famine, and disease. How many children were here made orphans, and menaced by ruin both of body and soul! Happy is it for man that pity stands ever by the dwelling of misfortune. A Venetian senator, Girolamo Miani, collected such of these children as had come wanderers and fugitives to Venice, and sheltered them in his house; he sought them among the islands neighboring to the city, and, giving slight heed to the clamors of his reluctant sister-in-law, he sold the plate and richest tapestries of his palace to procure shelter, food, clothing, and instruction for these destitute children. After a time his whole existence was devoted to this occupation. His success was very great, more especially in Bergamo: the hospital that he had founded there was so effectually supported that he was encouraged to make similar experiments in other towns. In Verona, Brescia, Ferrara, Como, Milan, Pavia, and Genoa, hospitals of the same kind were by degrees established. Eventually, Miani associated himself with certain friends of like character, and formed a congregation of regular clergy, modelled on that of the Theatines, and called "di Somasca." Their principal occupation was to educate the poor: their hospitals received a constitution which was common to all.[8]

[8] " Approbation of a society, consisting of persons ecclesiastical and others, lately formed for the support of poor orphans and converted women," this last

Few cities have been so heavily visited by the horrors of war as Milan, exposed to repeated sieges, and captured now by one party, now by another. To mitigate the effect of these misfortunes by acts of mercy, to remedy the disorders and correct the barbarism consequent on these evils, by instruction, preaching, and example, was now the object proposed to themselves by Zaccaria, Ferrari, and Morigia, the three founders of the order of Barnabites. We learn from a Milanese chronicle, the surprise with which these new priests were at first regarded, as they passed through the streets in their homely garbs and round cap—all still young, but with heads already bent in the earnestness of thought. Their dwelling-place was near the church of St. Ambrosio, where they lived in community. The countess Lodovica Torella, who had sold her paternal inheritance of Guastalla, and devoted the money thus obtained to good works, was the chief support of this society.[9] The Barnabites had also the form of regular clergy.

The effect produced by these congregations, each in its separate circle, was doubtless very considerable; but, either from the exclusive end that they had proposed to themselves, as in the case of the Barnabites, or from the restriction of their means, as, by the very nature of their constitution was inevitable in that of the poverty-vowed Theatines, they were incompetent to the carrying out of a deep-searching reform, and inadequate to the exercise of any widely extensive influence. Their existence is remarkable, because the voluntary character of their efforts betokens a tendency that largely contributed to the regeneration of Catholicism, but the force that was to stand against the bold advance of Protestantism, required to be of a totally different character.

This power was, however, approaching, and had already entered on a similar path, but the modes of its development were altogether unexpected, and in the highest degree peculiar.

object was, in some hospitals, joined with the first-named. (Bull of Paul III. June 5, 1540.) Bullarium Cocquelines, iv. 173. It would appear, nevertheless, from the bull of Pius V, "Injunctum Nobis," December 6, 1568, that the members of this congregation did not take their first vows till that date.

[9] "Chronicle of Burigazzo," in Custode. Continuation by Verri, "Storia di Milano," vol. iv. p. 88.

Section IV.—Ignatius Loyola

The chivalry of Spain was the only one that had preserved a certain remnant of its religious character, down to the period before us. The war with the Moors, but just arriving at its conclusion in the Peninsula, and still proceeding in Africa; the vicinity of the subjugated Moriscoes still remaining, and with whom the intercourse held by the victors was marked by the rancor characteristic of religious hatred; with the adventurous expeditions yet undertaken against infidels beyond the seas; all combined to perpetuate this spirit. In such books as the "Amadis de Gaul," full of a simple, enthusiastic loyalty and bravery, that spirit was idealized.

Don Iñigo Lopez de Recalde,[1] the youngest son of the house of Loyola, was born in a castle of that name, between Azpeitia and Azcoitia, in Guipuscoa. He was of a race that belonged to the noblest in the land—" de parientes mayores "—and its head claimed the right of being summoned to do homage by special writ. Educated at the court of Ferdinand the Catholic, and in the train of the Duke of Najara, Iñigo was deeply imbued with the spirit of his nation and class. He aspired to knightly renown, and for none of his compatriots had the glitter of arms, the fame of valor, the adventures of single combat and of love, more attractive charms than for him; but he also displayed an extraordinary fervor of religious enthusiasm, and had already celebrated the first of the apostles, in a romance of chivalry, at his early period of his life.[2]

It is, nevertheless, probable, that his name would have be- come known to us, only as one of those many brave and noble Spanish leaders, to whom the wars of Charles V gave oppor- tunities so numerous for distinguishing themselves, had he not been wounded in both legs, at the defence of Pampeluna, against the French, in 1521. Of these wounds he was never com- pletely cured; twice were they reopened, and such was his fortitude, that, in these severe operations, the only sign of pain he permitted to escape him was the firm clenching of his hands.

[1] He is so called in judicial acts. how he became possessed of the name Recalde " is not known, but this does not impugn its authenticity. " Acta Sanctorum, 31 Julii, Commentarius prævius," p. 410.

[2] Maffei, " Vita Ignatii."

His sufferings were, unhappily, unavailing; the cure remained deplorably incomplete.

He was much versed in, and equally attached to, the romances of chivalry, more especially to the Amadis. During his long confinement, he also read the life of Christ, and of some of the saints.

Visionary by nature, and excluded from a career that seemed to promise him the most brilliant fortunes, condemned to inaction, and at the same time rendered sensitive and excitable by his sufferings, he fell into the most extraordinary state of mind that can well be conceived. The deeds of St. Francis and St. Dominic, set forth by his favorite books in all the lustre of their saintly renown, not only seemed to him worthy of imitation, but, as he read, he believed himself possessed of the courage and strength required to follow in their footsteps, and to vie with them in austerity and self-denial.[3] It is true that these exalted purposes were sometimes chased by projects of a much more wordly character. Then would he picture himself repairing to the city where dwelt the lady to whose service he had devoted himself. " She was no countess," he said, " and no duchess, but of yet higher degree." The gay and graceful discourses with which he would address her, how he would prove his devotion, the knightly exploits he would perform in her honor ; such were the fantasies between which his mind alternated.

The more his recovery was protracted, and his hope of ultimate cure was deferred, the more also did the spiritual revery gain ascendancy over the worldly vision. Shall we do him wrong, if we impute this result to the increased conviction that his former vigor could not be restored, that he could not hope again to shine in military service or the knightly career?

Not that the transition was so abrupt, or to so opposite an extreme, as it might, on the first view, appear to be. In his spiritual exercises, the origin of which was coincident with the first ecstatic meditations of his awakened spirit, he imagines two camps, one at Jerusalem, the other at Babylon; the one belonging to Christ, the other to Satan; in the one is every

[3] The " Acta antiquissima, a Ludovico Consalvo ex ore Sancti excepta, AA. SS. LL." p. 634, gives very authentic information on the subject. The thought occurred to him once: "Quid, si ego hoc agerem, quod fecit b. Franciscus, quid si hoc, quod b. Dominicus? " Again: " Of many vain things that offered themselves to his mind, one he retained." The honor that he meant to pay his lady [" non era condesa ni duquesa mas era su estado mas alto que ninguno destas "], a singularly frank and simple acknowledgment.

ing good—in the other, whatever is most depraved and
icious. These are prepared for combat. Christ is a king
who has signified his resolve to subjugate all unbelievers;
whoever would fight beneath his banners must be fed with
the same food, and clad in like garments with him; he must
endure the same hardships and vigils; according to the measure
of his deeds, shall he be admitted to share in the victory and
rewards. Before Christ, the Virgin, and the whole court of
heaven, shall each man then declare that he will truly follow
his Lord, will share with him in all adversities, and abide by
him in true poverty of body and of spirit.[4]

By these fanciful imaginations, it probably was that his
transition from the chivalry of arms to that of religion was
facilitated; for it was indeed to a sort of spiritual knighthood
that his aspirations now tended, the ideal perfection of which
was to consist in emulation of the achievements performed,
and privations endured, by the saints. Tearing himself from
home and kindred, he now sought the heights of Montserrat,
not driven to this by remorse for his sins, nor impelled by any
reality of religious feeling, but, as he has himself declared,
merely by the desire of achieving deeds equally great with
those to which the saints are indebted for their renown. His
weapons and armor he hung up before an image of the Virgin;
kneeling or standing in prayer, with his pilgrim's staff in his
hand, he here passed the night, holding a vigil somewhat
different from that of knighthood, but expressly suggested by
the Amadis,[5] where all the rites proper to it are minutely
described. The knightly dress in which he had arrived at
Montserrat he gave away, assuming the coarse garb of the
hermits, whose lonely dwellings are scooped among those
naked rocks. After having made a general confession, he set
off toward Jerusalem, not going direct to Barcelona, lest he
should be recognized on the highways, but making a round by
Manresa, whence, after new penances, he meant to gain his port
of embarkation for the holy city.

But in Manresa he was met by other trials; the fantasies

[4] "Exercitia spirituali: Secunda
Iebdomada." "Contemplatio regni
esu Christi ex similitudine regis ter-
eni subditos suos evocantis ad bel-
im;" and in other places.
[5] "Acta antiquissima." A strange
mistake of the compiler, for certainly
Amadis is not an author. "When his
mind was filled with things from Amadis of Gaul, and other writers of that
sort, many of which he met with."

to which he had yielded himself, not so much from conviction as caprice, began here to assume the positive mastery. He devoted himself to the severest penances in the cell of a convent of Dominicans; he scourged himself thrice a day, he rose to prayer at midnight, and passed seven hours of each day on his knees.

He found these severities so difficult of practice that he greatly doubted his own ability to persevere in them for his whole life, but, what was still more serious, he felt that they did not bring him peace. He had spent three days on Montserrat in confessing the sins of all his past life; but, not satisfied with this he repeated it in Manresa, recalling many faults before forgotten, nor permitting the most trifling errors to escape him; but the more laborious his exploration, so much the more painful became the doubts that assailed him. He did not believe that he should be either accepted by or justified before God. Having read in the works of the fathers that a total abstinence from food had once moved the compassion and obtained the mercy of the Almighty, he kept rigid fast from one Sunday to another, but his confessor forbad him to continue this attempt, and Iñigo, who placed the virtue of obedience above all others, desisted immediately; occasionally it appeared to him that his melancholy had been removed, falling away as does a heavy garment from the shoulders, but his former sufferings soon returned. His whole life seemed to him but one continuous series of sin, and he not unfrequently felt tempted to throw himself from the window.[6]

This relation cannot fail to remind us of the nearly similar sufferings endured by Luther some twenty years before, when he also was assailed by similar doubts. The great demand of religion, a perfect reconciliation with God, and its full assurance, could never be obtained in the ordinary manner prescribed by the Church, with such certainty as to satisfy the unfathomable longings of a soul at enemity with itself. But out of this labryrinth Ignatius and Luther escaped by very different paths, the latter attained to the doctrine of recon-

[6] Maffei, Ribadeneira, Orlandino, and all his other biographers describe these struggles; but more authentic than all are the writings of Ignatius himself on this subject; the following passage, for example, clearly depicts his condition: "When agitated by these thoughts he was often sorely tempted to throw himself from a large window in his cell, near the place where he prayed; but when he saw that it was a sin to destroy himself, he cried out again, ' Lord, I will not do aught that may offend thee.' "

ciliation through Christ without works; this it was that laid open to him the meaning of the Scriptures which then became his strong support; but of Loyola we do not find that he examined the Scriptures or became impressed by any particular dogma. Living in a world of internal emotion, and amid thoughts arising for ever within him, he believed himself subjected to the influence now of the good, and now of the evil spirit. He arrived finally at the power of distinguishing the inspirations of the one from that of the other, perceiving that the soul was cheered and comforted by the first, but harassed and exhausted by the latter.[7] One day he seemed to have awakened from a dream, and thought he had tangible evidence that all his torments were assaults of Satan. He resolved to resign all examination of his past life from that hour, to open those wounds no more, never again to touch them. This was not so much the restoration of his peace as a resolution, it was an engagement entered into by the will rather than a conviction to which the submission of the will is inevitable. It required no aid from Scripture, it was based on the belief he entertained of an immediate connection between himself and the world of spirits. This would never have satisfied Luther. No inspirations—no visions would Luther admit; all were in his opinion alike injurious. He would have the simple, written, indubitable word of God alone. Loyola, on the contrary, lived wholly in fantasies and inward apparitions; the person best acquainted with Christianity was, as he thought, an old woman, who had told him, in the worst of his mental anguish, that Christ would yet appear to him in person. For some time this was not clear to him; but at length he believed not only to have the Saviour in person before his eyes, but the Virgin Mother also. One day he stood weeping aloud on the step of the church of St. Dominick, at Manresa, because he believed himself to see the mystery of the Trinity at that moment standing before his sight.[8] He spoke of nothing else through the whole day, and was inexhaustible in similes and comparisons respecting it. Suddenly also the mystery of the creation

[7] One of his most peculiar and most original perceptions, the beginning of which is referred by himself to the fancies of his illness. In Manresa it became a certainty, and it is described with great expansion in the "Spiritual Exercises," wherein are found especial rules: "For discovering whether the movements of the soul proceed from good spirits or evil, so that the first be admitted and the last repelled."

[8] Figured by three keys of a musical instrument.

was made visible to him in mystic symbols. In the host he
beheld the God and the man. Proceeding once along the banks
of the Llobregat to a distant church, he sat down and bent his
eyes earnestly on the deep stream before him, when he was
suddenly raised into an ecstasy wherein the mysteries of the
faith were visibly revealed to him. He believed himself to rise
up a new man. Thenceforth neither testimony nor Scripture
was needful to him; had none such existed he would have gone
without hesitation to death for the faith which he had before
believed, but which he now saw with his eyes.[9]

If we have clearly comprehended the origin and development of this most peculiar state of mind, of this chivalry of
abstinence, this pertinacity of enthusiasm, and fantastic asceticism, we shall not need to follow Iñigo Loyola through
every step of his progress. He did, in fact, proceed to Jerusalem, in the hope of confirming the faith of the believer as
well as that of converting the infidel. But how was this last
purpose to be accomplished, uninstructed as he was, without
associates, without authority? Even his intention of remaining in the Holy Land was frustrated by an express prohibition
from the heads of the Church at Jerusalem, who had received
from the Pope the privilege of granting or refusing permissions
of residence there. Returning to Spain he had further trials
to encounter, being accused of heresy on attempting to teach
and inviting others to participate in those spiritual exercises on
which he had now entered. It would have been an extraordinary
sport of destiny, if Loyola, whose Society, centuries later, ended
in Illuminati, had himself been associated with a sect of that
name; [10] and it is not to be denied that the Spanish Illuminati of
that day—the Alumbrados—did hold opinions bearing some an-
alogy to his fantasies. They had rejected the doctrine then
taught in Christendom, of salvation by works, like him they gave
themselves up to ecstasies, and believed, as he did, that they beheld religious mysteries, above all that of the Trinity, in immediate and visible revelation. They made general confession
a condition to absolution, and insisted earnestly on the neces-

[9] " Acta antiquissima:" " his visis
haud mediocriter tun confirmatus est "
(the original has " y le dieron tanta
confirmacione siempre de la fe ") " ut
sæpe etiam id cogitârit, quod etsi nulla
scriptura mysteria illa fidei doceret,
tamen ipse ob ea ipsa quæ viderat, sta-
tueret sibi pro is esse moriendum."
(See the text.)
[10] This charge was made against Lainez and Borgia also.—Llorente, " Hist.
de l'Inquisition," iii. 83. Melchior Cano
calls them plainly illuminati, the gnos-
tics of the age.

ity for inward prayer, as did Loyola and his followers of later
imes. I would not venture to affirm that Loyola was entirely
untouched by these opinions, but neither would I assert that he
belonged to the sect of Alumbrados. The most striking distinc-
ion between them and him is, that whereas they believed them-
elves to be exalted by the claims of the spirit above all the common duties of life, he, on the contrary, still impressed by his early
habits, placed the soldier's virtue, obedience, before all others;
his every conviction and whole enthusiasm of feeling he compelled himself to place in subjection to the Church and to all who
were invested with her authority.

These troubles and obstacles had meanwhile a decisive influence on his future life; in his then circumstances, without learning or profound theological knowledge, and without political
support, his existence must have passed and left no trace. The
utmost effect he would have produced would have been the conversion of some two or three Spaniards, but being enjoined, by
the universities of Alcala and Salamanca, to study theology for
four years before attempting to expound or teach the more obscure points of doctrine, he was compelled to enter on a path
which gradually led him forward to an unexpected field for the
exertion of his religious activity.

He proceeded then to Paris, which at that time was the most
celebrated university of the world.

His studies were at first surrounded by unusual difficulties, he
had to begin with the class of grammar (on which he had entered
in Spain), and with those of philosophy, before he could be admitted to that of theology; [1] but his grammatical inflections and
the analysis of logical forms were alike interrupted by, and inter-
mingled with the ecstasies of those religious significations with
which he had been accustomed to connect them; there was something of magnanimity in his at once declaring these aberrations
to be occasioned by the evil spirit, who was seeking to lure him
from the right way; he subjected himself to the most rigorous
discipline in the hope of combating them.

But though his studies now opened a new world to his gaze
—the world of reality—he did not for a moment depart from his

[1] From the oldest chronicle of the
Jesuits, "Chronicon Breve, AA. SS.
L." p. 525, we learn that Ignatius was
in Paris from 1528 to 1535: "Ibi vero
non sine magnis molestiis et persecu-
tionibus prima grammaticæ de integro,
tum philosophiæ ac demum theologico
studio sedulam operam navavit." (See
the text.)

religious intentions, nor fail to share them with others. It was indeed at this time that he effected those first conversions, by which the future world was destined to be so powerfully and permanently influenced.

Of the two companions who shared the rooms of Loyola in the college of St. Barbara, one, Peter Faber, a Savoyard, proved an easy conquest; growing up among his father's flocks, he had one night devoted himself solemnly, beneath the canopy of heaven, to study and to God. He went through the course of philosophy with Ignatius (the name that Loyola received among foreigners), and the latter communicated to him his own ascetic principles. Ignatius taught his young friend to combat his faults, prudently taking them not altogether, but one by one, since there was always some virtue to the possession of which he should more especially aspire. He kept him strictly to confession and to frequent participation of the Lord's Supper. They lived in the closest intimacy. Ignatius received alms in tolerable abundance from Spain and Flanders, these he constantly divided with Faber. His second companion, Francis Xavier of Pampeluna, in Navarre, was by no means so easily won; his most earnest ambition was to ennoble still further the long series of his ancestors, renowned in war during five hundred years, by adding to their names his own, rendered illustrious by learning. He was handsome and rich, possessed high talent, and had already gained a footing at court. Ignatius was careful to show him all the respect to which he laid claim, and to see that others paid it also, he procured him a large audience for his first lectures, and, having begun by these personal services, his influence was soon established by the natural effect of his pure example and imposing austerity of life. He at length prevailed on Xavier, as he had done on Faber, to join him in the spiritual exercises. He was by no means indulgent; three days and three nights did he compel them to fast. During the severest winters, when carriages might be seen to traverse the frozen Seine, he would not permit Faber the slightest relaxation of discipline. He finished by making these two young men entirely his own, and shared with them his most intimate thoughts and feelings.[2]

[2] Orlandinus, who likewise wrote a life of Faber, which I have not seen, is more circumstantial on this point also (in his great work, " Historiæ Societatis Jesu," pars i. p. 17) than is Ribadeneira.

How full of mighty import was that little cell of St. Barbara, uniting as it did these three men, who there formed plans and devised enterprises, inspired by their visionary and enthusiastic ideas of religion, and that were to lead, they themselves could have no conception whither.

Let us examine the more important features in the development of this association. After having gained over certain other Spaniards, to whom Ignatius had rendered himself indispensable either by good counsels or other aid, as Salmeron, Lainez, and Bobodilla, they proceeded one day to the church of Montmartre. Faber, who was already in orders, read the mass. They took the vow of chastity, and swore to proceed to Jerusalem, after the completion of their studies, there to live in poverty, and dedicate their days to the conversion of the Saracens. Or, should they find it impossible to reach that place, or to remain there, they were next to offer their services to the Pope, agreeing to go whithersoever he might assign them their labors, without condition and without reward. Having taken this oath, each received the host, which Faber also instantly took himself. This completed, they proceeded in company to a repast at the fountain of St. Denis.

Here we see a league formed between enthusiastic young men, and of which the purposes were absolutely unattainable, still in accordance with the original ideas of Ignatius, or departing from them only so far as, on a calculation of probabilities, they might find themselves unable to carry them into effect.

In the beginning of the year 1537, we find them in effect assembled in Venice, with three other companions, prepared for the commencement of their pilgrimage. We have already observed many changes in the fortunes of Loyola: from a military knighthood we have seen him pass to a religious chivalry; we have marked his subjection to the most violent mental conflicts, and have seen him force his way through them by the aid of a visionary asceticism; formed by heavy labors, he became a theologian and the founder of a fanatical society, and now at length his purposes assumed their final and permanent character. His departure for Jerusalem was deferred by the war just then commencing between Venice and the Turks, and the prospect of his intended pilgrimage was rendered more remote; but the institution of the Theatines, with which he became acquainted

in Venice, may be said to have first opened his eyes to his true
vocation.   For some time Ignatius lived in the closest intimacy
with Caraffa, taking up his abode in the convent of Theatines,
which had been established in Venice.   He served in the hospitals which Caraffa superintended, and wherein he exercised his
novices, but, not entirely content with the institution of the
Theatines, he proposed to Caraffa certain changes in its mode
of action, and this is said to have caused the dissolution of their
intimacy.[3]   But even these facts make it obvious that a deep
impression had been produced on him by that society; he there
saw an order of priests devoting themselves zealously and
strictly to their true clerical duties.   Should he, as seemed ever
more probable, remain on this side the Mediterranean, and find
the scene of his activity in Western Christendom, he perceived
clearly that this must be his course also, if he would turn his
labors to the best advantage.

In pursuit of this conviction, he took priest's orders in Venice,
with all his companions; and, after forty days of prayer, he began to preach in Vicenza, together with three others of his
society.   On the same day and at the same hour, they appeared
in different streets, mounted on stones, waved their hats, and
with loud cries exhorted the people to repentance.

Preachers of a very unwonted aspect were these; their clothing in rags, their looks emaciated, and their language a mixture
of Spanish and Italian well-nigh unintelligible; they remained
in this neighborhood until the year had expired during which
they had resolved to delay their journey to Rome; they then
proceeded thither.

Having determined to make this journey by different roads,
they were now about to separate; but first they established certain rules by means of which they might observe a fixed uniformity of life, even when apart: next came the question what
reply should be made to those who might inquire their profession.   They pleased themselves with the thought of making
war as soldiers against Satan, and in accordance with the old
military propensities of Loyola, they assumed the name of the
Company of Jesus, exactly as a company of soldiers takes the
name of its captain.[4]

---

[3] Sacchinus, "cujus sit autotoritatis, quod in B. Cajetani Thienæi vita de beato Ignatio traditur," discusses all the particulars of this intimacy.

[4] Ribadeneira, Vita brevior, c. 12, declares that Ignatius chose this title, "lest it (the company) should be called by his own name." Nigroni ex-

Their situation in Rome was in the first instance by no means free from difficulty. Ignatius thought he saw every door closed against them, and they had also once more to defend themselves from suspicions of heresy; but no long time had elapsed before the mode of their lives, with their zeal in preaching, instructing youth, and tending the sick, attracted numerous adherents, and so many showed a disposition to join them, that they felt themselves in a condition to prepare for a formal institution of their society.

They had already taken two vows, they now assumed the third, that of obedience; but as this had been ever held by Loyola to be the first of virtues, so they desired to surpass all other orders in that particular. It was already going very far to elect as they resolved to do, their general for life; but even this did not suffice to their enthusiasm; they superadded the special obligation " to perform whatsoever the reigning pontiff should command them, to go forth into all lands, among Turks, heathens, or heretics, wherever he might please to send them, without hesitation or delay, as without question, condition, or reward."

How entirely is all this in contrast to the tendency hitherto manifested by that period! Whilst from every other side the Pope met only opposition or defection, and had only continued desertions to expect; here was a body of men, earnest, enthusiastic, and zealous, uniting to devote themselves exclusively to his service; there could be no hesitation in such a case for the pontiff. In the year 1540, he gave his sanction to their institute, at first with certain restrictions, but afterward, in 1543, the Society of Jesus was absolutely and unconditionally established.

And now its members also made their final arrangements; six of the oldest associates met to choose their president, who, according to the first sketch of their plan presented to the Pope, ' should dispense offices and grades at his own pleasure, should form the rules of their constitution, with the advice and aid of the members, but should alone have the power of commanding in every instance, and should be honored by all as though Christ

---

ounds the word "societas," "As who should say a cohort or centruy called n to do battle against spiritual enemies." "After we had offered ourselves and our life to Christ our Lord, and to his true and lawful vicar on earth." In the " Deliberatio Primorum Patrum, AA. SS. LL." p. 463.

himself were present in his person." The choice fell unanimously on Ignatius, " to whom," as Salmeron expressed it in the letter declaring his assent, " they were all indebted for their birth in Christ and for the milk of the word." [5]

At length, then, the Society of Jesus had acquired its form. This association also was a company of clerks regular, its duties were likewise a combination of the clerical and monastic, but the members were nevertheless broadly distinguished from those of other congregations.

The Theatines had freed themselves from many of the less important obligations of conventual life, but the Jesuits went much further,[6] they dispensed entirely with the monastic habit, exempted themselves from all those devotional exercises in common, by which so much time is occupied in convents, and abstained from singing in the choir.

Exempted from these less important practices, they devoted all their energies and every hour of their lives to the essential duties of their office; not to one only, as did the Barnabites, although they attended sedulously to the sick as one measure toward acquiring a good name; nor with the restrictions that fettered the Theatines, but to all the greater duties equally, and with whatever force they could command. First to preaching; before separating in Vicenza, they had mutually agreed to preach chiefly for the common people, to think more of making an impression on their hearers, than of shining themselves by display of eloquence, and to this system they adhered. Secondly to confession: for by this they were to hold the immediate guidance and government of consciences. The spiritual exercises by which they had themselves become united with Ignatius afforded them important aid. Finally, they devoted themselves to the education of youth: they had intended to bind themselves to this last by a special clause in their vows, and although they had not done so, yet the practice of this duty was made imperative by the most stringent rules; to gain the rising generation was among the purposes most earnestly pursued. They laid aside, in short, all secondary matters, devoting themselves

[5] Suffragium Salmeronis.
[6] This they consider the difference between themselves and the Theatines. Didacus Payba Andradius: " Orthodoxarum Explicatt." lib. i. fol. 14: " They (the Theatines) devote themselves principally to meditating on things sacred and eternal, and to psalmody; but the Jesuits add to continual contemplation of divine mysteries, the exposition of the Gospel, instruction of the people, administration of the sacraments, and all other apostolic duties."

wholly to such labors as were essential, of immediate result, and calculated for the extension of their influence.

Thus was a system pre-eminently practical evolved from the visionary aspirations of Ignatius; and from the ascetic conversions he had made, there resulted an institution, framed with all that skilful adaptation of means to their end which the most consummate worldly prudence could suggest.

His most sanguine hopes were now more than fulfilled—he held the uncontrolled direction of a society, among whose members his own peculiar views found cordial acceptance, and wherein the religious convictions at which he had arrived by accident or the force of his genius, were made the object of profound study, and the venerated basis and guide of belief. His plan relating to Jerusalem was not, indeed, to be carried out, for nothing useful could now be obtained by it; but in other directions the company he ruled went forth on the most remote, and above all, most successful missions. The care of souls, which he had so earnestly enforced, was entered on with a zeal that he could not have hoped for, and to an extent surpassing his highest anticipations. And lastly, he was himself the object of an implicit obedience, combining that of the soldier to his captain with that of the priest to his spiritual chief.

But before we further describe the practical efficiency and widely spread influence attained by the Company of Jesus, let us investigate one of the most important causes contributing to their successful progress.

Section V.—First Sittings of the Council of Trent

The interests by which the Emperor was moved to the demand of a council are already before us, together with those inclining the Pope to avoid and refuse it. There was, however, one point of view in which an assembly of the Church might be considered desirable even by the pontiff—that the doctrines of the Catholic Church might be inculcated with unwavering zeal, and successfully extended, it was essential to remove the doubts existing in the bosom of the Church itself, touching more than one of its tenets. The authority to do this effectually was exclusively vested in a council; an important consideration for the Pope, therefore, was the choice of a time when it might be held in favorable circumstances and under his own influence.

The eventful moment in which the two religious parties had become more nearly approximate than at any other period, on the ground of a moderate opinion, taking a medium between both creeds, was also decisive of this question. We have remarked that the Pope believed he saw symptoms of an intention on the part of the Emperor himself to call a council. At this moment, then, assured from all sides of adherence from the Catholic princes, he lost no time in anticipating the imperial purpose. The movements we have before described were still proceeding when the pontiff resolved to interpose no further delay, but at once take steps for the œcumenic assembling of the Church.[1] He made known his intention at first to Contarini, and through him to the Emperor: the negotiations proceeded with earnest purpose; the Pope's letters of convocation were issued, and in the following year we find his legates already in Trent.[2]

Again, however, new obstacles presented themselves; the number of bishops who appeared was not sufficient. The times were too deeply involved in war; nor was the state of things generally altogether favorable. It was not until December, 1545, that the opening of the council actually took place: then, indeed, the old loiterer, Time, did at length bring the wished-for moment.

For when could one occur more propitious than that when the Emperor was at variance with both the chiefs of the Protestant party, and preparing to make war on them? Since he would require the aid of the Pope, he could not venture now to assert those claims which he was believed to intend bringing forward in a council. By the war he would be kept entirely occupied; the power of the Protestants made it impossible to foresee the extent of embarrassments in which he might become involved; he would thus be in no condition to press too earnestly for those reforms with which he had so long been threatening the papal throne. The Pope had, besides, another

[1] Ardinghello al Cl. Contarini, 15 Giugno, 1541, in Quirini, iii. ccxlvi.: "It being considered that no agreement has been made among Christians, that toleration is most illicit and hurtful, and war very dangerous and difficult, his holiness has determined to resort to the remedy of a council; he will therefore now have the suspension removed, and will declare and assemble such council at the first moment possible."

[2] They arrived on November 22, 1542.

method of baffling his purposes: the Emperor demanded that the council should begin with the subject of reform, but the papal legates carried a resolution that the question of reform and the questions of the Church should be treated together;[3] in effect, however, the discussion of the dogmas was that first entered on.

Again, the Pope not only succeeded in averting whatever might have been injurious to his interests, but contrived to secure all that could be turned to his advantage; the establishment of the disputed doctrines was to him of the very first importance, as we have shown: it was now to be decided whether any of those opinions, tending toward the creed of the Protestants, could hold a place within the limits of the Catholic faith.

Contarini was no more, but Pole survived: he was present; and there were in the assembly many others warmly attached to these opinions. The question now was, would they be able to make their tenets prevail?

In the first instance (for proceedings were very systematically arranged) revelation itself was discussed, with the sources whence our knowledge of it is to be derived; and even at this early stage, voices were raised in favor of opinions tending toward Protestantism: the Bishop Nachianti of Chiozza would hear of nothing but Scripture; he maintained that in the Gospel was written whatever was needful, but he had an overwhelming majority against him, and the resolution was adopted, that the unwritten traditions, received from the mouth of Christ, and transmitted to the latest ages under the guardianship of the Holy Spirit, were to be regarded with reverence equal to that paid to the Scriptures. In respect to these last, no reference was made to the original text, the Vulgate was declared an authentic translation, but a promise was given that for the future it should be printed with the most scrupulous care.[4]

The foundation of their work thus laid (and it was said with good reason that half the business was thereby accomplished), the speakers proceeded to the great and decisive article of justi-

[3] An expedient suggested by Thomas Campeggi, Pallavicini, vi. vii. 5; for the rest, a bull concerning reform had been prepared in the beginning, but it was never published. Bulla Reformationis Pauli Papæ III., concepta, non vulgata: primum edidit H. N. Clausen. Havn. 1829.

[4] Conc. Tridentii, sessio IV.: "For public readings, disputations, and proceedings, let it be held authentic." It was to be printed in an amended form, posthac [hereafter], not exactly as Pallavicini says, "as soon as possible."

fication and the doctrines connected with it.   To this portion of
the controversy the principal interest was attached.

Among the members of this council there were many who
held opinions on this point entirely similar to those of the Protestants.   The archbishop of Sienna, the bishop della Cava,
Giulio Contarini, bishop of Belluno, and with them five theologians, ascribed justification to the merits of Christ and to
faith alone and wholly; charity and hope they declared to be the
attendants, and works the proof of faith, but nothing more—
the basis of justification must be faith alone.

But was it to be expected, at a moment when pope and emperor were attacking the Protestants with force of arms, that
their primal doctrine—that on which the whole existence of
their creed was founded—should be received as valid by a council assembled under the auspices of these two powers?   It was
in vain that Pole exhorted them not to reject an opinion simply
because it was held by Luther; too much of bitter and personal
animosity was connected with this tenet; the bishop della Cava
and a Greek monk proceeded to actual violence against each
other.   It was seen that the council could not even debate to
any purpose, on so unequivocal an expression of Protestant
opinion: the discussions were confined—and even this was a
great point gained—to that intermediate system propounded by
Gaspar Contarini and his friends.

Seripando, the general of the Augustines, advanced this doctrine, but not without the express declaration that he was upholding no tenet of Luther, but rather those of his most renowned opponents, as Pflug and Gropper: justification, he
contended, was twofold[5]—the one inherent in us, indwelling,
and that through which, from children of sin, we become children of God.   But this also is of free grace, and unmerited; it
becomes manifest in virtues, and is active in works, but not of
itself capable of conducting us to the glory of God.   The other
is the righteousness and merits of Christ imparted and attributed to us; this atones for all our sins—it is perfect and equal
to our salvation.   Thus was it that Contarini had taught: " If
we make question," he remarks, " as to which of these justifica-
tions we must rely on—that indwelling or that imparted through
Christ—the devout man will reply, that we must confide in the

[5] Parere dato a 13 di Luglio, 1544. See Pallavicini, viii, xi. 4.

latter only. Our own righteousness is incomplete and ineffective, marred by its deficiencies—that of Christ alone is true and sufficient; this only is entirely pleasing in the sight of God, and in virtue of this alone may we trust to be justified before God."[6]

But even thus modified, leaving as they did the essentials of Protestant doctrine unharmed, so that its adherents might have sanctioned the change, these tenets encountered the most violent opposition.

Caraffa, who had already opposed the Protestant tendency when it appeared at Ratisbon, had now his place among those cardinals to whom the control of the council of Trent was intrusted. He brought forward a treatise of his own on the subject of justification, and in this he contended eagerly against all such opinions as those upheld by the moderate party.[7] Already had the Jesuits assumed a position by his side; Salmeron and Lainez had secured the advantageous privilege of addressing the assembly; the one at the commencement, the other at the close of its sittings: each possessed learning and ability, was fired with zeal, and in the bloom of life. Enjoined by Ignatius to commit themselves to no opinion approaching to innovation on the doctrines of the Church,[8] they combated the tenets of Seripando with their utmost force. Lainez appeared on the field of controversy with an entire volume, rather than a mere reply; he had the majority of the theologians on his side.

The distinction drawn between the two kinds of justification was left unquestioned by these disputants, but they affirmed that the imputed righteousness became involved in the inherent, or that Christ's merits were immediately ascribed and imparted to man through faith; that we must by all means place our reliance on the merits of Christ, not because these merits complete, but because they produce our own. This was precisely the point on which all turned, for as according to Contarini and

[6] Contarini "Tractatus de Justificatione." But the reader must not consult the Venice edition of 1589, which was that I first saw, where this passage will be sought in vain. In 1571 the Sorbonne had approved the treatise as it stood; in the Paris edition of that year it is given unmutilated. In 1589, on the contrary, the inquisitor-general of Venice, Fra Marco Medici, refused to permit its appearance; and, not satisfied by the omission of condemned passages, he so altered them as to bring them into harmony with the Catholic tenets. We are amazed on finding the collection in Quirini. These instances of unjustifiable violence must be remembered, if we wish to explain so bitter a hatred as that cherished by Paul Sarpi.
[7] Bromato, "Vita di Paolo IV." tom. ii. p. 131.
[8] Orlandinus, vi. p. 127.

Seripando, the merits of works could avail nothing, so by this
view of the case was their efficacy restored. The old doctrine
of the schoolmen taught, that the soul, clothed with grace,
merits for itself eternal life.[9] The archbishop of Bitonto, one
of the most learned and eloquent of these fathers, distinguished
between a previous justification, dependent on the merits of
Christ, by which the sinner is rescued from the state of repro-
bation; and a subsequent justification, worked out by our own
righteousness, dependent on the grace imputed to, and dwelling
in us: in this sense, the bishop of Fano declares faith to be but
the gate of justification, where we must not stand still, but must
traverse the whole course.

However closely these opinions may appear to approximate,
they are in fact diametrically opposed to each other; the Lutheran doctrine does indeed assert the necessity of inward regeneration, points out the way to salvation, and declares that good
works must follow; but it maintains that the divine grace proceeds from the merits of Christ. The council of Trent, on the
contrary, admits the merits of Christ, it is true, but attributes
justification to these merits only so far as they promote regeneration, and thereby good works, on which, as a final result, this
council makes all depend. " The sinner," it declares,[10] " is
justified, when, through the merits of the most holy passion,
and through the operation of the sacred Spirit, the love of God
is implanted in his heart and abides in it; thus become the friend
of God, man goes forward from virtue to virtue, and becomes
renewed from day to day; whilst he walks by the commandments of God and the Church, he grows with the help of faith
through good works, in the righteousness obtained through the
grace of Christ, and becomes more and more justified."

And thus were the Protestant opinions altogether excluded
from Catholicism, all mediation was utterly rejected. This
occurred precisely at the moment when the Emperor was victorious in Germany, the Lutherans were submitting in almost
every direction, and preparations were making to subdue those
who still hoped to hold out. The advocates of moderate views,
Cardinal Pole and the archbishop of Sienna, had already quitted
the council, but as might be expected, under different pretexts;[1]

[9] Chemnitius, " Examen Concilii Tridentini," i. 355.
[10] Sessio VI. c. vii. 10.

[1] It was at least a strange coincidence,
if both were prevented, as is said, by
the accident of sudden illness, from re-

instead of guiding and moderating the faith of others, they had cause to fear, lest their own should be assailed and condemned.

The most important difficulty was thus overcome. Since justification is progressive in the heart of man, and undergoes continual development, the sacraments are manifestly indispensable; for by these it is begun, or if begun, is continued; or when lost, is recovered. The whole seven might then all be retained without difficulty as heretofore, and their origin referred to the Author of Faith, since the institutions of Christ's Church were communicated, not by Scripture only, but also by tradition. Now these sacraments embrace the whole life of man as we know well; in every stage of its progress, they represent the true power of the hierarchy; by these does she rule every day and hour of the layman's existence, since they are not the types of grace only, they impart grace, completing thus the mystical relation in which man is believed to stand with God.[2]

Therefore it is that tradition was received, for the Holy Ghost is perpetually abiding in the Church; and the Vulgate, because the Romish Church has by special grace been kept wholly free from error. It is in harmony with this indwelling of the divine element, that the justifying principle should also have its abode in man; that the grace bound up in the visible sacrament should be imparted to him step by step, embracing his whole life, and holding full possession to, and of, the hour of his death. The visible Church is at the same time the true Church, which has been called the invisible. Beyond her own pale can no religious existence be acknowledged.[3]

Section VI.—The Inquisition

Time had not been lost in the meanwhile, measures having already been adopted for the suppression of the Protestant doctrines, and for the careful dissemination of those they had sought to subvert.

And here we must once more look back to the time of the Ratisbon conference. When it became obvious that no con-

---

turning to Trent. "Polo ai Cli. Monte e Cervini, 15 Sept., 1546," "Epp." tom. iv. p. 189. The opinions maintained by Pole were greatly injurious to that prelate—"Mendoza al Emperador Carlos, 13 July, 1547." "The cardinal of England has done himself much harm by what he has said of justification."

[2] Sessio VII., Proœmium.

[3] Sarpi gives the discussions on this point: "Historia del Concilio Tridentino," p. 241. (See the edition of 1629.) Pallavicini's account is very insufficient.

clusion could be arrived at with the professors of the new
tenets; and that even in Italy disputes had arisen concerning the
sacraments, while doubts as regarded purgatory and other
points of great moment in the Roman ritual were awakening
among the people, the Pope one day inquired of Cardinal
Caraffa, " what remedy could be devised for these evils?" The
Cardinal replied, that a thoroughly searching inquisition was
the only one sure to be efficient, and his opinion was supported
by that of John Alvarez de Toledo, cardinal of Burgos.

The old Dominican Inquisition had long fallen to decay, the
choice of inquisitors was committed to the monastic orders,
and it sometimes happened that these men partook of the very
opinions that they were appointed to suppress. The primitive
form had been so far departed from in Spain, that a supreme
tribunal of the Inquisition had been established for that country.
Caraffa and Burgos were both old Dominicans, zealots for the
purity of Catholicism, holding stern and gloomy views of moral
rectitude, in their own lives rigidly austere, and immovable in
their opinions; these men advised the Pope to establish a supreme tribunal of inquisition in Rome, universal in its jurisdiction, and on which all others should depend. " As St. Peter,"
exclaimed Caraffa, " subdued the first heresiarchs in no other
place than Rome, so must the successors of Peter destroy all
the heresies of the whole world in Rome."[1] The Jesuits account it among the glories of their order, that their founder,
Loyola, supported this proposition by a special memorial. The
bull was published on the twenty-first of July, 1542.

By this edict six cardinals were appointed commissioners of
the Apostolic See, and inquisitors general and universal in matters of faith on both sides the Alps, Caraffa and Toledo being
the first among them. These cardinals were invested with the
right of delegating similar power to ecclesiastics, in all such
places as should seem good to them, as also of determining all
appeals against the acts of these delegates, even without the
intervention of the ordinary ecclesiastical courts. All were subjected to their authority without distinction of rank or person—
no station or dignity was to be exempt. The suspected were
at once to be thrown into prison, the guilty to be punished by
loss of life and confiscation of property. One restriction only

[1] Bromato, " Vita di Paolo IV.," lib. vii. § 3.

was imposed on the power of these men; they were at liberty
to inflict punishment, but the right of pardon was reserved by
the Pope to himself; they might condemn heretics without restraint, but to absolve those once condemned was in the power
of the Pope only. Thus were they to proceed, enforcing and
executing whatever might most effectually "suppress and up-
root the errors that have found place in the Christian community, and permitting no vestige of them to remain."[2]

Caraffa lost not a moment in carrying this edict into execution; he would have thought it waste of time to wait for the
usual issue of means from the apostolic treasury, and though
by no means rich, he hired a house for immediate proceedings
at his own expense; this he fitted up with rooms for the officers,
and prisons for the accused, supplying the prisons with strong
bolts and locks, with dungeons, chains, blocks, and every other
fearful appurtenance of his office. He appointed commissioners general for the different countries. Teofilo di Tropea,
his own chaplain, was the first of those named for Rome, so far
as I have been able to discover, and of this man's severity, many
cardinals, among whom was Pole, had afterward grievous experience.

The manuscript life of Caraffa gives the following rules[3] as
drawn up by Caraffa himself; and as being "the best he could
devise for promoting the end in view:—

"First. When the faith is in question, there must be no delay;
but at the slightest suspicion, rigorous measures must be resort-
ed to with all speed.

"Secondly. No consideration to be shown to any prince or
prelate, however high his station.

"Thirdly. Extreme severity is rather to be exercised against
those who attempt to shield themselves under the protection of
any potentate: only he who makes plenary confession shall be
treated with gentleness and fatherly compassion.

"Fourthly. No man must debase himself by showing toleration toward heretics of any kind, above all toward Calvinists."

It will be remarked that all is severity, inflexible and remorse-

[2] "Licet ab initio. Deputatio non-
nullorum S. R. E. Cardinalium Gener-
alium Inquisitorum hæreticæ pravitatis,
21 Julii, 1542." Cocquelines, iv. 211.
[3] Caracciolo. "Vita di Paolo IV.,"
MS., c. 8: "He held as a positive axiom
this rule, that in matters of faith one
must in no way pause at all, but in the
first suspicion or intimation of this
plague of heresy, proceed by all force
and violence to its utter extirpation."

less; till confession has been wrung out no mercy may be hoped
for. A fearful state of things; and then more especially so
when opinions were not well fixed or fully developed, and many
were seeking to conciliate the more profound doctrines of
Christianity with the institutions of the existing Church. The
weaker resigned themselves and submitted; those of firmer
character, on the contrary, now first decidedly attached themselves to the proscribed opinions, and sought to withdraw from
the violence threatening them.

One of the first among these was Bernardino Ochino. It had
for some time been remarked that his conventual duties were
performed with less zeal than he had formerly displayed. In
the year 1542, his hearers became dissatisfied with the mode of
preaching he had adopted. He distinctly asserted the doctrine
of justification by faith alone. Following St. Augustine, he
says, "He who hath made thee without help of thine, shall he
not also save thee without asking thine aid?" On the doctrine
of purgatory also, his comments were not entirely orthodox.
Already had the nunico of Venice interdicted his preaching for
some days; this caused his citation to Rome, and he had proceeded to Bologna, and even reached Florence on his way
thither, when, fearing most probably the Inquisition just then
established, he determined to escape. Not inaptly does the historian of his order [4] describe his melancholy pause on reaching
the summit of Mount Bernard; when, looking once more back
on his beautiful Italy, he recalls the honors he had received
there; the countless multitudes by whom he had been eagerly
received, and respectfully listened to, and who afterward conducted him with reverential admiration to his abode: certainly
no man loses so much as an orator in losing his country: yet
was he leaving it, and that when far advanced in years. Up to
this moment he had retained the seal of his order; this he now
resigned to his companion, and then turned his steps toward
Geneva. His opinions, however, were not yet well settled, and
he afterward fell into very extraordinary errors.

Peter Martyr Vermigli left Italy about the same time. "I
tore myself," he exclaims, "from all those false pretensions,
and saved my life from the danger impending." He was subsequently followed by many of the scholars whom he had taught
in Lucca. [5]

[4] Boverio, "Annali," i. p. 438.   [5] From a letter of Peter Martyr to the

More nearly did Celio Secundo Curione permit the danger
to approach him. He waited until the bargello appeared to
arrest him, then, being a large and powerful man, he cut his
way through the sbirri with the knife he wore, threw himself
on his horse, and rode off. He also reached Switzerland in
safety.

Disturbances had before taken place in Modena; they now
reappeared, many being denounced to the Inquisition. Filippo
Valentini withdrew to Trent, and Castelvetri thought it advisable, at least for a time, to secure himself by a retreat into Germany.

For persecution and dismay were now proceeding throughout all Italy; the rancor of contending factions came in aid of
the inquisitors. How often did he who had long vainly waited
for an opportunity of destroying his enemy, now compass his
designs by an accusation of heresy! Now had the old bigoted
monks again become possessed of weapons, wherewith to combat that band of cultivated men whose literary labors had led
them toward religious speculations, and whose intelligent reasonings had made them an object of hatred to the monks, who
were in their turn despised and disliked by the literati. " Scarcely is it possible," exclaims Antonio dei Pagliarici, "to be a
Christian, and die quietly in one's bed."[6] The academy of
Modena was not the only one whose members separated. The
Neapolitan also, founded by the Seggi, and originally intended
for the study of literature only, but which had proceeded to theological disputations, in accordance with the spirit of the age,
broke up by command of the viceroy.[7] The whole body of men
of letters was subjected to the most rigorous supervision. In
the year 1543, Caraffa decreed that no book, whether new or
old, and whatever its contents, should for the future be printed
without permission from the inquisitors. Booksellers were
enjoined to send in a catalogue of their stock, and to sell nothing without their assent. The officers of customs also received
orders to deliver no package, whether of printed books or MS.

community he had left, wherein he expresses regret for having occasionally
veiled the truth, in Schlosser. "Lives
of Beza and Peter Martyr," p. 400. Gerdesius and McCrie have collected
many detached notices in the works
already quoted.
[6] "Aonii Palearii Opera," ed. Wet-
sten. 1696, p. 91. "Il Cl. di Ravenna al

Cl. Contarini," "Epp. Poli," iii. 208,
already alludes to this: "This city (Ravenna) being filled with factions, no
man being free from the stain, they take
all occasions that offer of loading each
other with accusations."
[7] Giannone, "Storia di Napoli,"
xxxii. c. v.

to its address, without first laying them before the Inquisition.[8]
This gradually gave rise to an Index of prohibited books; the
first examples were set in Louvain and Paris.   In Italy, Giovanni della Casa, who was on terms of the closest intimacy with
the house of Caraffa, caused the first catalogue to be printed
at Venice; this included about seventy works.   Lists more
carefully arranged and longer, appeared at Florence in 1552, in
Milan, in 1554; and the first published in the form afterward
used, was put forth at Rome in 1559.   Writings by cardinals
were included in this last, together wtih the poems of Della
Casa himself.

Nor were printers and booksellers the only persons subjected
to these stringent regulations; even on private persons it was
enforced as a duty of conscience to denounce all forbidden
books, and contribute their utmost toward the destruction of all
that should come to their knowledge.   These laws were carried
into execution with incredible success.   Though many thousands of the work " On the Benefits Bestowed by Christ " were
disseminated, not one was suffered to escape; the book entirely
disappeared, and is no longer to be found.   Whole piles of confiscated copies were burnt in Rome.

The secular arm was called in aid of the clergy for all these
rules and restrictions.[9]   The purposes of the Papal See were in
this instance largely assisted by the extent of its own dominions, since they could here set the example they desired to see
followed, and offer a model for the imitation of other lands.
The Governments of Milan and Naples could present but slight
opposition, because they had themselves intended to establish
the Spanish Inquisition in their own territories, with this difference only; that in Naples the confiscation of property was not
permitted.   In Tuscany the Inquisition was rendered accessible
to the influence of the civil power by the agency of the legate
whom the duke, Cosmo de' Medici, found means to get appointed to his court.   Notwithstanding this, however, the fra-
ternities founded by it gave great offence.   In Sienna and Pisa,

---

[8] Bromato, vii. 9.
[9] Many laymen offered their assistance.   Says the Compendium of the
Inquisitors, " this evil was opportunely
remedied by the holy office in Rome,
who placed able and zealous inquisitors in every city, employing also zealous and learned laymen in aid of the
faith, as, for example, Godescalco in
Como, Count Albano in Bergamo, and
Mutio in Milan.   These secular persons
were employed, because many bishops,
vicars, monks, and priests, nay, members of the Inquisition itself, were also
heretics."

the most oppressive severities were put in force against the universities. The Inquisitor for the Venetian States was in some measure subjected to the control of the civil power. In the capital, three Venetian nobles were appointed to sit in his tribunals from April, 1547; while, throughout the provinces, the rector of each town took part in the proceedings, seeking counsel occasionally from learned doctors, or, if persons of great eminence were accused, applying for his guidance to the Council of Ten. With all this, however, the ordinances of Rome were for the most part, and on all essential matters, fully carried into effect.

And in this manner were all the agitations of dissentient opinion subdued by main force, and annihilated throughout Italy. Almost the whole order of the Franciscans were compelled to recantation, and the disciples of Valdez had for the most part to retract their opinions. In Venice a certain degree of freedom was allowed to the foreigners, principally Germans, who resided there for purposes of trade or study; but the natives, on the contrary, were compelled to abjuration, and their meetings were broken up. Many took to flight, and these fugitives were to be found in every town of Germany and Switzerland. Those who would not abjure their faith and could not escape, were subjected to the penalty. In Venice, they were taken beyond the lagoons by two boats: arrived in the open sea, a plank was laid between these, on which was placed the condemned; at the same moment the rowers pulled in opposite directions; the plank fell: once more did the unhappy victim invoke the name of Christ, and then the waves closed over him, he sank to rise no more. In Rome, the auto-da-fe was held formally at certain intervals before the Church of Santa Maria alla Minerva. Many sought escape by flying from place to place with their wives and children; we trace their wanderings for a time, then they disappear; they had most probably fallen into the toils of their merciless hunters. Others remained quiet. The Duchess of Ferrara, who, but for the Salic law, would have sat on the French throne, was not protected by her birth and high rank. Her husband was himself her accuser. "She sees no one," says Marot, "the mountains rise between herself and her friends; she mingles her wine with her tears."

Section VII.—Further Progress of the Jesuit Institution

Such was the position of things in the Catholic hierarchy. All opponents set aside by force, the tenets of the Church firmly reinstated in the mind of the age, and the ecclesiastical power enforcing their observance with weapons against which no resistance could avail. Then it was that, in closest alliance with this all-mastering power, the Order of the Jesuits arose.

Not in Rome only, but throughout all Italy, the most extraordinary success attended its efforts; designed, in the first instance for the common people, it was not slow to gain acceptance from the higher classes also.

It was highly favored in Parma by the Farnese;[1] princesses submitted themselves to the spiritual exercises it enjoined. In Venice, the Gospel of St. John was expounded by Lainez, expressly for the nobles; and in 1542, he succeeded, with the assistance of one of the Lippomano family, in laying the foundation of the Jesuits' college in that city. So extraordinary a degree of influence was gained by Francesco Strada over the citizens of Montepulciano, that many of them were induced to accompany him through the streets, begging; Strada knocking at the different doors, and his companions receiving the donations. They made themselves extremely popular in Faenza, although this city had previously been much under the influence of Bernardino Ochino. They formed schools there, succeeded in allaying enmities of a hundred years' standing, and in forming societies for the relief of the poor. I name these instances as examples only; suffice it to say, that they appeared everywhere, gained numerous adherents, and firmly established their ascendancy.

But as Ignatius Loyola was altogether a Spaniard, and entirely possessed by the ideas proper to his nation, as also he had thence received his most zealous disciples, so had it followed, that his society, wholly Spanish in spirit, made greater progress in Spain than even in Italy. A very important conquest was gained at Barcelona, in the person of Francesco

[1] Orlandinus expresses himself in singular terms. Says he: " Both the city and certain private persons, who were said to be in some degree related to the pontiff, presented a letter of supplication to the end they might retain Faber." As if all the world did not know that Paul III had a son. Moreover, the Inquisition was subsequently established in Parma, as a consequence of the opposition manifested toward the priests who favored Jesuitism.

Borgia, Duke of Candia. Such multitudes flocked to hear
Araoz, in Valencia, that no church could contain them, and a
pulpit was prepared for him in the open air. Equally successful
was Francesco Villanova, in Alcala, where he gained numerous
adherents of high consideration, notwithstanding his mean birth,
weakness of health, and total want of all learning. From this
city, and that of Salamanca, where, in 1548, the Jesuits commenced their establishment, in a small, wretched house, they
afterward extended themselves over all Spain.[2] Nor were
they less cordially received in Portugal. Of the two first who, at
his own request, were sent to him, the King retained one, Simon
Roderic, near his person; the other he despatched to the East
Indies, and this was that Xavier who there gained for himself
the name of an apostle and the glory of a saint. At both the
peninsular courts, the Jesuits obtained extraordinary popularity;
that of Portugal they reformed altogether, and in the Spanish
Court they were almost instantly selected as confessors by the
most distinguished nobles, as the president of the council of
Castile, and the cardinal of Toledo.

So early as the year 1540, certain young men had been sent
by Loyola to study in Paris; from that city the society extended
itself over the Netherlands. In Louvain the most decisive success attended the efforts of Faber. Eighteen young men, already masters of arts or bachelors in that university, attached
themselves to his steps, offering to abandon home and country,
for the purpose of following him to Portugal. Already were the
Jesuits seen in Germany; among the first who joined them was
Peter Canisius, afterward so effectual a promoter of their interests, and who entered their order on his twenty-third
birthday.

This rapid success was, of necessity, most powerfully influential in the development of the institution; the form assumed by it was as follows:—

Into the circle of his first companions, the class of the professed, Ignatius received but few; he found that men at once
highly educated, good, and pious, were very rare; even in the
first sketch of his purposes laid before the Pope, he declares the
intention of training young men according to his own views,
and in colleges, which he hopes to found in different universities.

[2] Ribadeneira, " Vita Ignati," c. xv. n. 244; c. xxxviii. n. 280.

Of these, a number surpassing his expectations presented themselves, as we have said; they constituted the class of scholastics, as distinguished from that of the members "professed."[3]

But in this arrangement a certain inconvenience was discovered. The professed, by their fourth and special vow, had bound themselves to perpetual travels in the service of the Pope; but it would be utterly inconsistent to assign to these men the government of the many colleges now required, since such institutions would demand their continual residence. Ignatius thus found it necessary to constitute a third class, standing between the two just described. These were called spiritual coadjutors; they were priests, possessing the classic learning and general science required for the instruction of youth, and devoting themselves expressly to that employment. No portion of the Jesuit institution was more important than this, and, so far as my researches have enabled me to discover, its character was peculiar to that body, which is indebted to it for a large part of its unexampled influence and success. These coadjutors were allowed to settle themselves in such places as they chose to select; they assumed the control of education, and silently established a wide-spreading ascendancy for the order. They also took three vows only, and these, be it remarked, were simple, and not solemn; that is to say, the society could absolve them from these vows, in certain cases, carefully defined, while any attempt on their part to leave the order, was followed by immediate excommunication.

But one thing more was now requisite. The studies and occupations to which these classes were destined must have suffered undue interruption, had they been also subjected to the care of providing for their own subsistence. This, then, they were spared. The professed lived on alms in their houses, and the colleges were permitted to possess revenues in common. For the administration of this income, so far as it did not devolve on the professed, who were excluded from all share in the enjoyment of it, Ignatius appointed secular coadjutors, to whom the management of other affairs, merely external, was also intrusted. These secular coadjutors were equally bound

[3] Pauli III, "Facultas coadjutores admittendi, d. 5 Junii, 1546": "So that they shall be held to keep their vows, for whatever time thou my son and those who shall preside for the time being over the society, shall think fit to employ their services, spiritual or temporal, and not longer."

by the three simple vows, but had to content themselves with the persuasion, that they were serving God, by aiding a society devoted to the salvation of souls; they were not suffered to seek for any other reward.

These arrangements were perfectly well calculated in themselves, and, at the same time, laid the foundation of a hierarchy, eminently proper, by its several gradations, to subjugate the minds of those on whom it acted.[4]

And now, if we examine the laws of which the code of the Jesuits came gradually to be formed, we shall perceive that an entire separation of its members from all the usual interests and relations of life was one of their principal objects. Love of kindred they denounced, as a carnal inclination.[5] The man who resigned his property to enter the order, was in no case to bestow it on his relations, but must distribute all to the poor.[6] He who had once become a Jesuit could neither receive nor write a letter that was not read by his superior. The society demands the whole being; all the faculties and inclinations of the man must be held in its fetters.

It claims to share in the most intimate of his secrets; all his faults, nay, even all his virtues, must be carefully enumerated: a confessor is appointed him by his superiors, the general reserving to himself the right of granting absolution in such cases as it may be deemed expedient that he should take cognizance of.[7] He insisted on this regulation as a means to his obtaining a perfect knowledge of his subordinates, that so he might the better use them at his pleasure.

For in the order of Jesuits, obedience takes the place of every motive or affection that usually awakens men to activity—obedience, absolute and unconditional, without one thought or question as to its object or consequences.[8] No man shall aspire to any rank above that he holds. The secular coadjutor may not even learn to read or write without permission, if it happen that

---

[4] The basis of the society was formed of "novices, guests, and indifferents"; from these arose the different classes.

[5] "Summarium Constitutionum," § 8, in the "Corpus Institutorum Societatis Jesu," Antwerp, 1709, tom i. In Ordinus, iii. 66, Faber is lauded for having once passed through his native town, after many years of absence, and proceeding on his journey without permitting himself even to make halt.

[6] "Examen generale," c. iv. § 2.

[7] Rules found separately in the "Summarium Constitutionum," §§ 32, 41; the "Examen generale," §§ 35, 36; and "Constitutionum Pauli III," c. i. n. 11. "Illi casus reservabuntur," it is remarked in the latter place, "those cases to be reserved which it shall seem needful or very expedient that the superior should know."

[8] The letter of Ignatius "to the Brethren of the Society of Jesus in Portugal."

he do not possess these attainments. With the most unlimited abjuration of all right of judgment, in total and blind subjection to the will of his superiors, must he resign himself to be led, like a thing without life, as the staff, for example, that the superior holds in his hand, to be turned to any purpose seeming good to him. The society is to him as the representative of the divine providence. [9]

What a power was that now committed to the general— vested in him for life was the faculty of wielding this un- questioning obedience of thousands; nor is there one to whom he is responsible for the use made of it. By that plan of the order submitted to the pontiff in 1543, every member of the society, who might chance to be at the same place with the general, was to be called to the discussion of even the most trifling affairs: but by Julius III he was freed from this re- striction in 1550, and is to take counsel only when he shall him- self desire it. For some material change in the constitution, or for the suppression of houses and colleges alone, was a consul- tation imperative; [10] in every other case, all power is committed to him of acting as may be most conducive to the good of the society. He has assistants in the different provinces, but these confine themselves strictly to such matters as he shall confide to them. All presidents of provinces, colleges, and houses, he names at his pleasure: he receives or dismisses, dispenses or furnishes, and may be said to exercise a sort of papal authority on a small scale. [1]

In all this there was one only danger to be feared, namely, that the general, possessing so great a power, might himself depart from the principles of the society: certain restrictions were therefore imposed on his habits of life. To us it will

[9] "Constitutiones," vi. 1. "And let each one be certain that they who live under obedience should suffer them- selves to be moved and governed by divine providence (through their supe- riors), as though they were dead bod- ies." Here is also the other Constitu- tion, vi. 5, according to which it would seem that even a sin might be en- joined. "It has seemed good to us in the Lord . . . that no constitutions, declarations, or order of living can in- duce an obligation to mortal or venial sin, unless the superior command them, in the name of the Lord Jesus Christ, or in virtue of obedience." A man can scarcely trust his eyes as he reads this; and, certainly, another meaning besides that suggested by the first perusal may be extracted. "Obligatio ad peccatum mortale vel veniale," may rather point to the binding force of the constitution, which he who violates is guilty of "mor- tal or venial sin"; but the words should be more precise, for no one could be blamed for seriously referring "ea" to "peccatum," and not to "constitu- tiones."

[10] Says Julius III. ("Confirmatio In- stituti"): "He shall have the right to himself to ordain those things which to him shall seem conducive to the glory of God, assisted, so far as he shall see fit, by his brethren."

[1] "Constitutiones," ix. 3.

certainly not seem so important as it may have appeared to
Ignatius, that the Society or its deputies were intrusted with
the arrangement of certain external observances, the hours of
meals and sleep, for example, the dress, and whatever concerned the daily habits.[2] It is, nevertheless, still something,
that the supreme power should be deprived of a freedom of
action enjoyed by the most insignificant individual. The assistants who were not named by himself, maintained a constant
supervision over him in these respects; and one officer, called
the admonitor, was specially appointed to warn him of any lapse.
In the event of any gross fault, the assistants could summon the
general congregation, who had the power of pronouncing a
sentence of deposition against the offending general.

This carries us a step further in our examination of the order.

We must not suffer ourselves to be dazzled by the hyperbolical
descriptions left us of their power by the Jesuits themselves;
rather let us consider what may have been practicable, the great
extent soon obtained by the society considered. We shall then
arrive at the following results: To the general remained the
supreme guidance of the whole order, more particularly the
control of the superiors, whose conscience he was to scrutinize
and direct—whose duties he alone could assign. These superiors, on the other hand, possessed a similar power within
their own jurisdiction, and frequently exercised it with a
severity exceeding that of the general himself.[3] The superiors
and general were to a certain extent counterpoised by each
other. The general was also to be informed as to the personal
characteristics of every subordinate, and although it is obvious
that he could interfere on important occasions only, yet the
supervision remained in his hands. A select number of the
professed, on the other hand, were authorized to exercise supervision over him.

Other institutions have existed, forming a world within the
world, and which, releasing their members from all exterior
obligations, have sought to absorb their whole being to themselves, and to inspire each individual with a new principle of
life and action. This was pre-eminently the purpose of the
Jesuits, and it was fully accomplished. But there was a further

[2] " Schedula Ignatii, AA. SS." "Com-
mentatio prævia," n. 872.   [3] Mariana, " Discurso de las enferme-
dadas de la Compania de Jesus," c. xi.

peculiarity in their proceedings; while the order was itself taking captive the mind, and holding it as a mere piece of property, it nevertheless demanded the full development of all the faculties in each individual. No Jesuit was in any sense his own property; he belonged fully and unreservedly to the order: thus all personal consideration was merged in a life of mutual supervision and subordination. But a firmly compacted and perfect unity was thus formed—a body endowed with nerve and vigorous power of action. It was to secure this last effect that the monarchical power was so earnestly enforced, to this did they subject themselves unreservedly; nor did they ever abandon it, unless the possessor himself departed from its vital principles.

There was perfect consistency in the refusal of the Jesuits to permit their members the acceptance of ecclesiastical dignities; for these might have involved the fulfilment of duties, or the forming of relations, over which the society could no longer exercise control. In the earlier days of Jesuitism this rule was most strictly observed: when the bishopric of Trieste was proposed to Jay, he neither would nor dared to accept it; and on the retraction of the proposal, in consequence of a letter from Ignatius, by Ferdinand I who had offered it, the general caused solemn masses to be said in thanksgiving and Te Deum to be sung.[4]

A second effectual distinction is, that the order of Jesuits emancipated itself from the more ascetic and cumbrous forms of monastic devotion. The members severally were also enjoined to avoid excess in their religious exercises: they were not to weaken themselves by fasting, vigils, or castigations, or to abstract more time than was strictly needful from the service of mankind. In labor, also, moderation was commanded, "the spirited steed must have the curb rather than the spur, and no man should load himself so heavily with his weapons that he cannot wield them to advantage." On no account was any member of the society to labor until the elasticity of his mind became endangered by his toils.[5]

Thus the society, regarding its members as its own exclu-

[4] Extract from the "Liber memorialis of Ludovicus Gonsalvus": "Quod desistente rege, S. Ignatius indixerit missas et 'Te Deum laudamus,' in gratiarum actionem."—"Commentarius prævius," in "AA. SS. Julii 7," n. 412.
[5] "Constitutiones," v. 3, 1. "Epistola Ignatii ad Fratres qui sunt in Hispania." "Corpus Institutorum," ii. 540.

sive property, was desirous of seeing them attain to tne nighest culture of their energies, physical and mental—but ever in accordance with its first great principle of obedience.

This careful development of the individual was, in fact, indispensable to the performance of the duties assigned him— those of the pulpit, that is, of the school and the confessional: to the two latter in particular the Jesuits devoted themselves with a zeal more peculiarly their own.

The instruction of youth had been hitherto left to those men, who after long study of profane literature, had turned their attention to theological subjects, which they treated in a manner never very acceptable to the court of Rome, and eventually altogether reprobated by it. The Jesuits took upon themselves to expel these men from their office, and to occupy it in their stead. They began by the closest observance of a carefully considered system, dividing the schools into classes, and pursuing in these a method strictly uniform, from the earnest principles of learning to the highest degree of science. They paid great attention to the moral culture, and formed their pupils to good character and correct manners; they were favored by the civil power, and finally their instructions were given gratis. Whenever a prince or city had founded one of their colleges, no private person needed further to incur expense for the education of his children. They were expressly forbidden to ask or accept remuneration or reward; as were their sermons and masses, so was their instruction altogether gratuitous. There was not even the usual box for offerings in their churches. As men are constituted, this of itself must have aided to make the Jesuits popular, the rather as they taught with great ability and equal zeal. " Not only were the poor assisted by this practice," says Orlandini, " it was a solace to the rich also."[6] He remarks further on the extraordinary success of their efforts, " many are now shining in the purple of the hierarchy," he declares, " whom we had but lately on the benches of our schools, others are engaged in the government of states and cities. We have trained up bishops and their counsellors, nay, other spiritual communities have been filled from our schools." The most re-

---

[6] Orlandinus, lib. vi. 70. A comparison might be made with the conventual schools of the Protestants, in which the religious tendency was also fully predominant. See Sturm, in Ruhkopf, " Geschichte des Schulwesens," p. 378. The points of difference must, of course, be also considered.

markable talents among these pupils were appropriated by the order whenever that was possible, as may well be supposed, and the society had in fact formed itself into a body of instructors of all ages, that, extending over every Catholic country, acquired an amount of influence altogether incalculable. From the Jesuits education received that tone of religion by which it has since been marked, and was impressed by a strict unity of character, whether as regards method, doctrine, or discipline.

But how predominant was the ascendancy assured to them by the address with which they gained possession of the confessional, and the direction of consciences! No age of the world has been more accessible than was the period of their commencement to such influence as they exercised; but perhaps none has more needed it. Their code of laws enjoins the Jesuits " to pursue one uniform method in their manner of giving absolution, to exercise themselves in cases of conscience, to adopt a short and rapid mode of interrogating their penitents, and to have the examples of the saints, their words and other helps, ever ready for every sort of sin ";[7] rules which are obviously well calculated to meet the wants of mankind. But the extraordinary success obtained by the society, and which involved a real diffusion of their peculiar modes of thinking, was further promoted by another essential adjunct.

This was the very remarkable little manual of spiritual exercises which Ignatius, I will not say originated, but which he certainly worked out in a most peculiar manner.[8] By this his first disciples were attracted, and it was equally efficacious with later ones; among his followers generally it ever maintained the highest authority, and served more than all else to make them his own; its utility was progressive and powerful, the more so perhaps because it was recommended for occasional study only; and as a resource in moments of inward distress and spiritual craving.

It is not a book of doctrine, but rather a guide to self-contemplation, " the longings of the soul," says Ignatius, " are not to be appeased by a cloud of acquirements; by intuitive perception of things sacred alone can it be satisfied."[9]

[7] " Regula Sacerdotum." §§ 8, 10, 11.
[8] For, after all that has been written on either side, it is manifest that Ignatius had a similar work, by Garcia de Cisneros, in view; the most peculiar part of it seems, nevertheless, to have been entirely his own. " Comm. præv." n. 64.
[9] " Non enim abundantia scientiæ, sed sensus et gustus rerum interior desiderium animæ replere solet." (See the text.)

It is the guidance of this perception that he proposes to himself; the spiritual adviser intimates the subjects to be reflected on; the neophite has only to follow them out. His thoughts are to be fixed on them before retiring to rest, and immediately on awaking; he must abstract himself with determination from all other objects of thought, windows and doors must be closed, kneeling or prostrate on the earth, he must continue his task of self-examination.

He begins by a deep consciousness of sin, he reflects that for one single crime the angels were cast into hell, while for him, who has committed so many, the saints are ever interceding. The heavens, with their stars, animals, and all plants of the earth, minister to his good. That he may now be freed from his guilt, and may not be condemned to eternal damnation, he calls on the crucified Redeemer, he receives his replies, there is between them a dialogue as of a friend with his friend, a servant with his master.

He next seeks edification from profound reflections on the events of sacred history: " I see," he exclaims, " how the three persons of the Godhead look down upon the whole earth, which they behold filled with men condemned to hell; they resolve that the second person shall, for their redemption, assume the nature of man. I survey the whole wide circuit of the globe, and in one corner I discern the hut of the Virgin Mary, whence proceeds salvation." He proceeds from step to step through the sacred histories, he represents to himself the different events in all the fulness of their details, and according to the categories of their import; the religious fancy, freed from the trammels of the letter, is allowed the utmost scope for expansion, the disciple imagines himself to touch the garments, to kiss the footsteps of the sacred personages; in this excitement of the imagination, in the full conviction how great is the blessedness of a soul replete with divine grace and virtues, he returns to the consideration of his own condition; if his position in life be still undecided, he must choose it now, in accordance with the wants and wishes of his heart, whilst he has one only aim in view, that of becoming consecrated to the glory of God, in whose presence, and in that of all the saints, he believes himself to stand. If his choice be already made, he then reviews his manner of life, his daily walk and conversation, the ordering of his household, his need-

ful expenditure, what he has to give to the poor, on all which he
reflects in the frame of mind that he will desire to have always
maintained, when arrived at the hour of his death; having no
other object before him than such as may tend to the glory of
God and his own salvation.

Thirty days are devoted to these exercises; reflections on
sacred history, on his own personal circumstances, prayers and
resolutions occupy the hours, and alternate with each other.
The soul is kept in ceaseless excitement and activity, occupied
with itself; finally, when the individual represents to himself the
provident care of God, "who in all his creatures effectually
works for the good of man," he once more believes himself to
be standing before the Lord and his saints, he beseeches the Almighty to permit the dedication of his service and adoration to
himself. He offers up his whole being, freedom, memory, understanding, will; thus does he conclude with him the covenant of
love. "Love consists in the community of all faculties and
possessions." In return for this its devotion, God imparts his
grace to the soul.

It will suffice for our purpose to have given a rapid glance
at this extraordinary book. In its general tenor, its various
propositions, and their manner of connection, there is a certain
persuasiveness that does certainly excite the spirit, but re-
strains it at the same time within most narrow limits. Admirably calculated for its peculiar aim, that of contemplation
guided by the fancy, it is all the more successful from its being
the result of Loyola's own experiences. He has here recorded
all the most remarkable phenomena of his religious awakening
and spiritual progress, from their first commencement to the year
1548, when he received the sanction of the Pope. It has been
said that the Jesuits profited by the experience of the Protestants, and in some few particulars this may have happened;
but on the whole, they present a very strong contrast to each
other. In this work at least, Ignatius has opposed to the dis-
cursive, logical, and very close method of the Protestants (a
method by its very nature polemical), one of his own which is
entirely different, being short, intuitive, calculated for awakening the imaginative faculties and prompting to instant resolve.

And in this manner did those visionary elements that had
characterized his commencement, condense themselves at length

to an extraordinary force of practical influence. Never wholly freed from the military habits of his early days, Loyola formed his society into a sort of religious standing army; selected carefully man by man, enrolled under the influence of the religious fantasy, each one trained for the especial service he was intended to perform, and commanded by himself: such were the cohorts that he dedicated to the service of the Pope. He lived to see their ascendancy over the greater portion of the earth's surface.

At the period of his death, the company of Ignatius numbered thirteen provinces, exclusive of the Roman.[1] A mere glance will serve to show where the strength of the order lay; the majority of these provinces, seven, namely, belonged to the western peninsula and its colonies. In Castile there were ten colleges. Aragon and Andalusia had each five. Portugal had gone beyond even this: houses were established there both for professed members and novices. Over the colonies of Portugal the Company of Jesus exercised almost absolute mastery. Twenty-eight members of the order were occupied in Brazil, while in East India, from Goa to Japan, not less than a hundred were employed. An attempt on Ethiopia was also made from this quarter, and a Provincial was sent thither, the success of the enterprise not being doubted. All these provinces of Spanish and Portuguese languages and manners were directed by one commissary general, Francesco Borgia. The nation that had given birth to the founder, was also that where his influence was most immediately and firmly established. But the effect produced in Italy was very little inferior. There were three provinces of the Italian tongue: first, the Roman, under the immediate direction of the general; this comprised Naples; it was furnished with houses for novices and professed; two colleges within the city, the " Collegium Romanum " and " Collegium Germanicum," namely: the last erected for Germans only, by the advice of Cardinal Morone, but not with any great effect. Second, the Sicilian, containing four colleges completed and two begun. The first Jesuits had been introduced into Sicily by the viceroy della Vega;[2] Messina and Palermo had vied with each other in establishing colleges, and from these it was

---

[1] In the year 1556. Sacchinus, " Historia Societatis Jesu," p. ii., sive Lainius, from the beginning.   [2] Ribadeneira, " Vita Ignatii," n. 293.

that the others afterward arose. The third Italian province comprehended all the north of Italy, and contained ten colleges. The order was not equally successful in other countries, where it was either opposed by Protestantism, or by a strong tendency to Protestant opinion. In France they had .but one college actually in operation; and though two provinces were counted in Germany, both were as yet in their infancy. The first was to comprise Vienna, Prague, and Ingolstadt, but its condition was extremely precarious; the second was intended to include the Netherlands, but Philip II had not yet assured a legal existence to the Jesuits in that part of his dominions.

This great and rapid success was a guarantee of the power to be attained by the order. The position it had secured in those purely Catholic countries, the two peninsulas, was a circumstance of the utmost importance.

Conclusion

Thus we perceive, that while the tenets of Protestantism were enlarging their influence over the minds of men on the one hand, a new impulse had on the other been received by Catholicism, and was acting vigorously in Rome, and the court of its pontiff more especially. This last, equally with its opponent, had taken rise from the spirit of worldliness pervading the Church; or rather from the necessity of a change that this corrupt spirit had forced on the general perception.

These impulses had at first displayed a tendency toward approximation. There was a certain period during which Germany had not entirely resolved on casting off the hierarchy; there was also a moment when Italy seemed approaching toward a national modification of that hierarchy. That moment passed away.

The Protestants, guided by Scripture, retraced their steps with ever-increasing firmness, toward the primitive forms of Christian faith and life. The Catholics, on the contrary, held fast by the ecclesiastical institutions, as these had been consolidated in the course of a century, and determined only on renovating all, and infusing increased energy, a more rigid severity, and deeper earnestness of purpose into each. On the one hand there rose up Calvinism, its spirit far more anti-

atholic than that of Lutheranism; on the other, whatever could
ut recall the idea of the Protestant doctrines was confronted
y unflinching opposition, and repelled with determined hos-
lity.

Thus rise two neighboring and kindred springs on the sum-
it of the mountain, but each seeks its path to the valleys in an
pposite direction, and their waters are separated forever.

Vol. I.—11

CHOICE EXAMPLES OF PALEOGRAPHY.

Fac-similes from Rare and Curious Manuscripts of the Middle Ages.

TITLE-PAGE OF ST. PAUL'S EPISTLE TO TITUS.

From a Greek manuscript, written about 550.

The page reproduced here is the superscription, or title, of St. Paul's Epistle to Titus, and reads, "Epistle of Paul, Apostle, to Titus, ordained first Bishop of the Cretans, written from Nicopolis in Macedonia." The manuscript itself is perhaps as perfect an example of uncial writing as can be found, as well as one of the most ancient. It was copied, we are told, from a manuscript executed by the hand of the "holy Pamphilus" (see foot of the fac-simile), and was deposited in the library of Cæsarea in Palestine (see *ibid.*), whence it found its way through many vicissitudes to France.

ΠΑΥΛΟΥΑΠΟϹΤΟΛΟΥ
ΕΠΙϹΤΟΛΗΠΡΟϹΤΙΤΟΝ
ΤΗϹΚΡΗΤΩΝΕΚΚΛΗϹΙΑϹ
ΠΡΩΤΟΝΕΠΙϹΚΟΠΟΝ
ΧΕΙΡΟΤΟΝΗΘΕΝΤΑ
ΕΓΡΑΦΗΑΠΟΝΙΚΟΠΟΛΕΩϹ
ΤΗϹΜΑΚΕΔΟΝΙΑϹ, ϹΤΙΧ ϚΖ

ΕΓΡΑΨΑΚΑΙΕΞΕΘΕΜΗΝ ..

ΠΡΟϹΤΟΕΝΚΑΙϹΑΡΙΑΑΝΤΙ
ΓΡΑΦΟΤΗϹΒΙΒΛΙΟΘΗΚΗϹ
ΤΟΥΑΓΙΟΥΠΑΜΦΙΛΟΥ.....

BOOK III

THE POPES ABOUT THE MIDDLE OF THE SIXTEENTH CENTURY.

THE sixteenth century is distinguished from all others by the number of religious systems produced in its course. Even to the present day are these affecting us; the various opinions taking their birth at that period have formed the medium in which we still "live, move, and have our being."

If we seek to ascertain the precise moment when the separation between Catholics and Protestants was completed, we shall find that it was not strictly coincident with the first appearance of the reformers, for opinions did not immediately assume a fixed character, and, for a certain time, there was rational ground of hope that a compromise between the conflicting doctrines might be effected. It was not until the year 1552 that all prospect of this kind was utterly destroyed, and that the three great forms of Christianity in the West were separated forever.

Now indeed did the wide divergence of all become apparent. Lutheranism assumed a severity, an exclusiveness, an asceticism hitherto unknown to its habits. The Calvinists departed from it in the most essential doctrines, though Calvin himself had in earlier times been considered a Lutheran; while, in hostile contrast to both, Catholicism invested herself with those forms that still distinguish her practice. Each of these theological systems sought eagerly to establish itself in the position it had assumed, each labored to displace its rivals and to subjugate the world.

On the first glance it might seem that Catholicism, seeking only to renew existing institutions, would have found less difficulty than its opponents in pressing forward and securing the ascendancy, but the advantage it possessed was in a manner rendered nugatory by many opposing influences. No less than its rivals had Catholicism to contend with the various impulses then affecting the world: eagerness for temporal advancement, profane learning, and heterodox opinions in religion. It was not unlike a principle of fermentation, of which it may still be questioned whether it can seize and assimilate the elements surrounding it, or must itself be overmastered by them.

The first important obstacle was presented by the popes themselves, their personal character and the policy they pursued.

It will have become obvious to the reader, that a temper of mind in direct contrast with their spiritual character had taken firm hold on the heads of the Church, and had elicited that opposition from which Protestantism had received so mighty an impetus.

The question now was, whether the zeal for ecclesiastical innovation just arisen in the Church would overcome and transform this temper, and to what extent.

To me it appears that the antagonism of these two principles, the conflict between the policy, whether active or passive, hitherto prevailing and now become inveterate, and the necessity acknowledged for a complete internal reform, is that which constitutes the paramount interest in the history of the popes next following.

Section I.—Paul III

It is an error prevalent in our times, that we attach undue importance to the purposes and influence of governments, princes, and other eminent persons; their memory is frequently loaded with the sins of the multitude, as frequently they have credit for performing what in fact proceeded from the general effort of the community.

The Catholic movement, considered in the preceding book, took its rise under Paul III; but we should mistake if we ascribed its origin to that pope. He perceived its importance to the Roman See, and not only permitted it to take its course, but in many ways promoted its success. Still we may declare without hesitation that his own feelings were at no time in sympathy with the earnest sincerity of its spirit.

Alexander Farnese (this was the name of Paul III) was

quite as worldly in character as any of his predecessors. Born
in the year 1468, his education was completed within the fifteenth century. He studied under Pomponius Lætus at Rome,
and in the gardens of Lorenzo de' Medici at Florence; thus
imbued with the love of art and elegant literature proper to his
period, he did not escape the contagion of its morals. His
mother found it needful on a certain occasion to permit his remaining for a time in the restraint of the castle Saint Angelo.
The future pontiff seized a moment when the attention of his
guard was attracted by the procession of the Corpus Christi,
and, lowering himself from the walls by a rope, he succeeded in
making his escape. He acknowledged a son and daughter, both
illegitimate; but no great offence was taken at such affairs in
that day, and they were not suffered to impede his fortunes;
we thus find him a cardinal while still very young. His hereditary estates were situated at Bolsena, and he there constructed a
villa so inviting to the elegant tastes of Pope Leo X that he
honored the cardinal by more than one visit to it. The Farnese
palace also, one of the finest in Rome, was commenced during
his cardinalate; but these occupations were by no means the
principal interests of his life, he had much higher ambitions,
and from the first had fixed his thoughts on the supreme
dignity.

It is entirely characteristic of Farnese that he sought to attain
this eminence by means of a complete neutrality. The French
and Imperial factions then divided Italy, Rome, and the college of cardinals. He conducted himself with so deliberate a
caution, with so fortunate a circumspection, that no one could
say to which of these parties he most inclined. He was on the
point of being elected pope, even at the death of Leo, and again
at that of Adrian, and he could not live in charity with the
memory of Clement VII, whom he accused of occupying the
papal chair for twelve years, during which it ought to have been
his own. At length, in October, 1534, the fortieth year of his
cardinalate and the sixty-seventh year of his life, he attained
the end so long desired, and ascended the papal throne.[1]

[1] Onuphrius Panvinius: "Vita Pauli III": In the year 1538, Marc Antonio Contarini made a report to the Venetian senate on the court of the pontiff. Unfortunately, I have not found this work either in the archives of Venice or elsewhere. In a MS. concerning the Turkish war, with the title, "Tre Libri delli Commentari della Guerra, 1537-8-9," now in my possession, I find a short extract therefrom, whence I have derived the notices given in the text. "Of the state of the court, he affirmed, that for a long time the prelates had not led

He was now to feel all the weight of those contentions so profoundly agitating the world, the strife of those two great parties between which he was himself to hold so important a place; the necessity for opposing the Protestants, at the same time that he was drawn into secret connection with them by their political position; the wish he could not but feel from the situation of his Italian principality to weaken the preponderance of Spain, and the great danger involved in every attempt to do so; the pressing need of reform, and the mortifying restrictions with which this seemed to threaten the papal power.

The mode in which his character develops itself in the turmoil of these contradictory demands is entirely worthy of notice.

The habits of Paul III were easy, magnificent and liberal; rarely has a pope been so much beloved in Rome as he was. There was an elevation of mind in his choice of the distinguished men we have before alluded to for the sacred college, and that even without their knowledge; how well does this contrast with the littleness of personal consideration by which such appointments had usually been made. Nor was he content with merely appointing them, he granted to all an unwonted degree of liberty; he endured contradiction in the consistory, and encouraged unrestricted discussion.

But thus leaving due liberty to others, and according to every man the advantages incident to his position, he would allow no one of his prerogatives to fall into disuse or be neglected. Certain remonstrances being addressed to him by the Emperor on his having advanced two of his grandsons to the cardinalate at too early an age, he replied that he would do as his predecessors had done, that examples might be cited of infants in the cradle becoming cardinals. The partiality he displayed for his family was beyond what had been customary even in the head of the Church,[2] and his resolution to raise his house to the

such reformed lives; that the cardinals had more liberty to give their opinions, than for many years past; the Pope was so far from complaining of this, that he did his best to promote it; from all which one might hope now to see greater reforms. He considered that among the cardinals were men of such high eminence, that by the common opinion the world had nothing to equal them."

[2] Soriano, 1535: "He is Roman of blood, and of very high spirit, sensitive to injuries done him, and greatly disposed to exalt his own people." Varchi ("Istorie Fiorentine," p. 636) declares of the Pope's principal secretary, Messer Ambrogio, "that he could have whatever he desired, and desired to have whatever he could." Among other gifts, he once received sixty washing-basins, with their ewers. "How comes it," asked some one about the court, "that with so many washing-basins, Messer Ambrogio cannot keep clean hands?"

princely dignity, as other popes had done, was early made manifest.

Not that he sacrificed every other consideration to this purpose, as did Alexander VI; this could not be alleged against him; he labored earnestly, on the contrary, for the promotion of peace between France and Spain, and for the suppression of the Protestants; he strove anxiously to subjugate the Turks, and to advance the reformation of the Church; but also, and together with all these cares, he had it much at heart to exalt his own house.

Proposing to himself so many conflicting purposes, whether for the public service or his own private affairs, this pontiff was necessarily forced on a policy in the utmost degree circumspect, watchful, and temporizing, so much always depending on the favorable moment, the happy combination of circumstances. These he was compelled to prepare and mature by degrees most cautiously calculated, and when the decisive moment had arrived, it was to be seized with the utmost promptitude, and made to yield the largest possible amount of profit.

The various ambassadors found it difficult to treat with him. They were surprised to see, that though betraying no want of courage, he was ever reluctant to decide. His object was to entangle others, and to gain some promise that should fetter them, some assurance that could not be recalled; but never would he utter a word that could pledge himself. This disposition was obvious, even in minor affairs; he was disinclined either to refuse or to promise anything, but seemed always anxious to keep his hands free up to the last moment. How much more, then, in circumstances of difficulty! It would occasionally happen, that he would himself suggest some means of escape from an evil, some expedient against a danger; but if anyone sought to act on this, the Pope at once drew back, he desired to remain always master of his own proceedings.[3]

[3] In the " Lettres et Mémoires d'Etat, par Guill. Ribier, Paris, 1666, are found numerous specimens of his negotiations and their character, from 1537 to 1540, and from 1547 to 1549 in the despatches of the French ambassadors. Matteo Dandolo describes them minutely in a MS. now in my possession. "Relatione di Roma, 1551, d. 20 Junii, in Senatu." "To negotiate with Pope Paul was ever thought difficult by all men, because he was very slow in speech, not wishing to utter a word that was not most select and elegant, whether in the vulgar tongue, or in Latin or Greek; for he professed them all three, and soon discovered in me what little I knew of them, and being very old; he spoke in low tones, and was very prolix; he would not refuse what was asked from him; but neither would he that the man who negotiated with him should be sure that he had had the 'yes,' rather than the 'no'

Paul III belonged, as we have said, to the classic school of which we have spoken before, and was studious of elegance in expression, as well in Latin as Italian. His words were selected and weighed, with reference to their form, as well as import; they were then delivered in low tones, and with the most cautious deliberation.

It was not easy for a man to be sure of the terms on which he stood with Pope Paul. Many people thought it safer to infer the very opposite from what his words would imply; but this was not, perhaps, always advisable. Those who observed him most nearly, remarked, that when his hopes of any project were at the highest, he usually abstained from all mention of the subject, or of any person or thing that could lead to it.[4] Thus much was manifest to all, that he never abandoned a purpose, when once he had fixed his mind on it; he trusted to carry all his undertakings to a prosperous issue, if not immediately, yet at some future time, by some change of measures, or under altered circumstances.

It was perfectly consistent with the habits of a mind so constituted, with forethought so closely calculating, with a disposition so warily to guard all points, and secretly to ponder on all purposes, that Paul should take the heavenly as well as the earthly influences into his reckoning. The influence of the stars on human actions was rarely questioned in those times, and this pontiff held no important sitting of his consistory, undertook no journey, without selecting that day when the aspect of the constellations was most favorable.[5] An alliance with France was impeded by the weighty fact, that no conformity could be discovered between the nativity of her monarch and that of the Pope. Paul would seem to have felt himself to be surrounded by mutually opposing agencies, not only of this world below, but also of that above, whose part in his affairs he sought to ascertain from the configurations of the stars. His hope was to propitiate both, to mitigate their evil influences, to derive profit from their favorable conjunctures, and dexterously

from his holiness: he would always be on the vantage ground of being able to grant or to refuse, wherefore he was always most slow to resolve when he chose to deny."

[4] Remarks of the Cardinals Carpi and Margareta, "who are the persons," says Mendoza, "most familiar with his disposition."

[5] Mendoza: "The matter has come to this, that very few cardinals will transact business, were it but to buy a load of wood, except through some astrologer or wizard." As regards the Pope also, we find the most unquestionable particulars related.

to steer his bark to port between the rocks that menaced from every side.

Let us see by what means he sought this end; whether he found them adequate to his purposes, or not; whether he did indeed raise himself above the conflicting forces of the world, or whether he were swallowed up in the vortex.

In the early part of his pontificate he did, in effect, succeed in forming an alliance with Charles V and the Venetians, against the Turks. With great earnestness did he exhort the Venetians to this enterprise, and hopes were again felt that the boundaries of Christendom might be extended to Constantinople.

There was nevertheless, a formidable obstacle to this undertaking in the war that had again been declared between Charles V and Francis I. The Pope made every possible effort to bring about a reconciliation; the conference held between these two sovereigns at Nice was entirely of his arrangement, he himself proceeding to join it, and the Venetian ambassador, who was present, can find no words sufficiently strong for the eulogy of his zeal, and of the patience he displayed on that occasion. It was not, however, without the utmost assiduity on his part that matters were brought to bear; the last moment was approaching—for he had threatened to depart[6]—when at length the princes came to an understanding, which seemed afterward to grow into a sort of intimacy.

Thus actively employed for the public welfare, the Pope did not forget those of his own family; men observed, that if possible, he always combined the two interests, and made the one advance the other. Thus, from the Turkish war he took occasion to appropriate Camerino. It was on the point of being incorporated with Urbino; the last Verana, heiress of Camerino, having married Guidobaldo II, who had entered on the government of Urbino, in the year 1538.[7] The Pope, however, declared that Camerino could not descend in the female line. The Venetians were in justice bound to support the duke, whose ancestors had constantly lived under their protection, and served in their armies, and they made an urgent and spirited appeal in his behalf, but were deterred from doing more by the

[6] " Relatione del C. M. Nicolo Tiepolo del Convento di Nizza." Informatt. Politiche, vi. (Library of Berlin). There exists also an old impression.
[7] Adriani, " Istorie," 58, H.

fear of war. They reflected, that if the Pope should call the Emperor to his aid, that monarch would have so much the less power to make head against the Turks; or if France came to his assistance, the peace of Italy would be endangered, and their own position become more isolated,[8] and less advantageous. These things all considered, they left the duke to his fate, and he was compelled to resign Camerino, which the Pope conferred on his grandson Ottavio. Already was the house of Farnese advancing in splendor and power. How useful to Paul had been the conference at Nice! even while it was yet in progress, his son, Pier Luigi, obtained Novara, with its territories, from the Emperor, who also gave his solemn promise to marry his natural daughter, Margaret, on the death of Alessandro de' Medici, to Ottavio Farnese. The Pope may be fully believed, when he affirms that he did not on that account ally himself exclusively with the imperial party. On the contrary, he desired to form an equally close connection with Francis I. Nor did the French King seem averse to this proposal, but promised him the hand of a prince of the blood—the Duke of Vêndome—for his grand-daughter Vittoria.[9]

In this relationship to the two most exalted houses of the world, Paul found extreme satisfaction; he was fully sensible to the honor he derived from it, and even alluded to it in the consistory. The position of peace-maker, too, that he now occupied between those great powers, was equally flattering to his ambition, as spiritual chief of the Church.

But the further progress of these affairs was not altogether so fortunate. No advantage whatever could be gained over the Ottomans; on the contrary, it was Venice who was compelled to accept a peace on very unfavorable terms. The promise given by Francis at Nice was afterward recalled; and though Paul did not abandon the hope of eventually effecting a family alliance with the house of Valois, the negotiations were tediously protracted. It is true, that the good understanding brought about by the Pope between the Emperor and King,

---

[8] The deliberations are to be found in the before-mentioned Commentary on the Turkish War, which thus acquires a peculiar interest.

[9] Grignan, ambassadeur du roi de France à Rome, au Connétable. Ribier, i. p. 251: "Monseigneur, his said holiness has a marvellous wish for the Vendome marriage, for he has declared himself entirely to me, saying, that because she is his only niece, and so greatly beloved by him, he desires nothing on earth, after the good of Christendom, more than to see his said niece married in France, of which the said King had talked to him at Nice, and you, Monseigneur, afterward spoke to him of it."

seemed, for some time, to become even more perfect, insomuch, indeed, that Paul had well-nigh felt his jealousy awakened, and complained that they neglected him who had been the cause of this concord.[10] But this state of things did not long endure; contests ensued, the war was recommenced, and the Pope then raised his thoughts to new designs.

In earlier times he had openly asserted among his friends, and even declared to the Emperor, that Milan belonged to the French, and ought of right to be restored to them.[1] Gradually, however, this opinion was abandoned; and we presently meet with a proposal from Cardinal Carpi (who was more in his confidence than any other member of the Sacred College) to Charles V, of which the purport was altogether of a different character, and pointed to opposite conclusions.[2]

"The Emperor," he now declares, "should not think of being either count, duke, or prince, he should be emperor only. He should not possess numerous provinces, but rather great vassals. His prosperity has decreased since he took possession of Milan—not that we counsel him to restore it to Francis, whose thirst for territorial acquisitions this would only serve to stimulate, but neither is it advisable that he should retain it."[3] "If the Emperor has enemies, it is because he is suspected of a desire to appropriate foreign dominions. Let him remove this suspicion; let him place Milan in the rule of some duke of its own, and Francis will then find no more adherents. The Emperor, on the contrary, will have all Germany and Italy on his part; he may carry his banners among the most remote nations, and will associate his name [this is the expression] with immortality."

But if Charles must neither keep the duchy nor resign it to the French, to whom then must he transfer it? Paul thought the dilemma might be well escaped by according it to his grandson and the son-in-law of the Emperor, Octavio Farnese. This

[10] Grignan, March 7, 1539. Ribier, i. 406. Le Cardinal de Boulogne au Roi, April 20, 1539. Ibid. 445. The Pope said to him—"qu'il estoit fort estonné, veu la peine et travail qu'il avoit pris pour vous appointer, vous et l'empereur, que vous le laissiez ainsi arrière."
[1] M. A. Contarini confirmed this in his report.
[2] Discurso del Revmo. Cle. di Carpi, del 1543 (perhaps rather a year earlier), a Carlo V. Cesare, del modo del dominare."—Bibl. Corsini. n. 443.

[3] "Se la M. V. dello stato di Milano le usasse cortesia, non tanto si spegnerebbe quanto si accenderebbe la sete sua; si che è meglio di armarsi di quel ducato contra di lui.—V. M. ha da esser certa, che, non per affettione che altri abbia a questo re, ma per interesse particolare, e la Germania e l'Italia, sinche da tal sospetto non saranno liberate, sono per sostentare ad ogni lor potere la potentia di Francia." (See the text.)

he had already hinted in earlier missions. At a new conference
held with Charles at Busseto, he proposed it in form. Negotiations on the subject proceeded to some extent, and the
pontiff entertained the most lively hopes. The Marchese di
Vasto, governor of Milan, whom Paul had gained to his wishes,
being somewhat credulous and fond of display, appeared one
day with well-prepared words to conduct Margaret, as his future
sovereign, to Milan. I find, however, that the negotiation was
broken off in consequence of certain exorbitant demands on the
part of the Emperor.[4]   It is nevertheless difficult to believe
that any consideration, however tempting, could induce Charles
to resign a principality so important and so well situated, to
any foreign influence.

The house of Farnese was indeed becoming sufficiently formidable to the Emperor, even without this addition to their
power and importance. Of the Italian provinces over which
Charles governed, or wherein he held the ascendancy, there was
not one in which the existing government had not been founded,
or at least maintained, by force. Throughout the land, from
Milan to Naples, in Florence, in Genoa, in Sienna, everywhere
in short, were to be found numbers of disaffected persons, belonging to different vanquished parties; Rome and Venice were
full of emigrants. The Farnese were not prevented by their
close connection with the Emperor from allying themselves
with these parties; subdued indeed, but still formidable from
the importance of their chiefs, their wealth and numbers. At
the head of the victors stood the Emperor; the vanquished
sought refuge with the Pope. These last were bound together
by ties innumerable, they were always closly connected with
France, either openly or secretly, and were incessantly occupied
with new plans and undertakings; these sometimes related to
Sienna, sometimes to Genoa, at other times to Lucca. How
eagerly did Paul seek to obtain footing in Florence! But in

---

[4] Pallavicini directly denies these
transactions. There is, indeed, room
to doubt their having occurred, from
what is said by Muratori (" Annali
d' Italia," x. 2, 51). His authority is
that of historians who may have written from hearsay; but a letter from
Girolamo Guicciardini to Cosmo de'
Medici, Cremona, June 26, 1543, in
the Archivio Mediceo at Florence, is
decisive. Granvella has also spoken of
it. " His majesty was not ill-disposed,
if, on his part, the Pope fulfilled

those large offers made by the Duke
of Castro at Genoa." I do not know
what these offers may have been, but,
in any case, they were too large for the
Pope.   According to Gosselini, secretary to Ferrante Gonzaga, the Emperor
feared, " that once his back was turned,
the Farnesi would bethink themselves
of seizing it." Very circumstantial and
amusing particulars on this head are to
be found in a Neapolitan biography of
Vasto, not yet printed, and now in the
Chigi library at Rome.

the young Duke Cosmo, he met the very man best fitted to oppose him. With a proud self-reliance does Cosmo express himself on the subject.[5] "The Pope," says he, "who has succeeded in so many undertakings, has now no wish more eager
than that of doing something in Florence as well; he would
fain estrange this city from the Emperor, but this is a hope that
he shall carry with him into his grave."

The Emperor and Pope still stood opposed to each other in
a certain point of view, as heads of rival factions; if Charles
had married his daughter into the family of the Pope, this
was only to keep the latter in check, and as he has said himself, to maintain the existing state of things in Italy. Paul on
his side, desired to avail himself of his alliance with the Emperor, to abstract if possible some portion of the imperial power
to himself; he would fain have derived advantage from the
protection of the Emperor, and at the same time have exalted
his house by aid of the Emperor's opponents. There was still
a Guelfic and a Ghibelline party, in fact if not in name; the
last as usual adhering to the Emperor, and the first to the Pope.

Notwithstanding these elements of discord, we find amicable
relations existing between the two leaders in the year 1545.
Margaret having the hope of soon presenting a descendant of
the Cæsar to the family of Paul, the feelings of the Farnesi were
again turned toward the Emperor. Cardinal Alessandro Farnese repaired to meet Charles at Worms, and this was one of the
most important embassies ever despatched by Paul III: the
cardinal once more succeeded in appeasing the displeasure of
Charles; in regard to some of the charges brought against his
brothers and himself he set up a sufficient justification; for
others, he begged forgiveness, and promised that all would
conduct themselves in future as became obedient servants and
sons of his majesty. To this Charles replied, that on their doing so, he would treat them as his own children. All which
being settled, they next proceeded to the discussion of important
matters. They talked of the war with the Protestants, and decided on the immediate convocation of the council. Should
the Emperor resolve to take up arms against the Protestants,
the Pope would engage to support him with all the power he

---

[5] A Letter of Cosmo, also of the year
1537, and found in Medicean Archives:
"Al papa non è restato altra voglia in
questo mondo se non disporre di questo
stato e levarlo dalla divotione dell' imperatore," etc.

could muster, bring all his treasures to aid, and even, " were it necessary, his very crown should be sold in the service."[6]

And in effect, the council was opened in that same year, a circumstance to which we first find a satisfactory explanation in the arrangements just described. In 1546, war also commenced; the Pope and the Emperor united their power to annul the league of Smalcald, which was equally hostile to the temporal claims of the one as to the spiritual authority of the other. Paul contributed on this occasion both troops and money.

It was the Emperor's purpose to carry on warlike measures at the same time that he employed peaceful negotiations; while he should punish and curb the disobedience of the Protestants by war, he desired that the council should determine ecclesiastical disputes, and should above all establish such reforms as might render submission in some degree possible on the part of the Protestants.

The success of the warlike operations exceeded all anticipation; the position of the Emperor seemed at first utterly desperate, but under the most perilous circumstances, he maintained his firmness; and the autumn of 1546 saw North Germany entirely at his mercy. Cities and princes now emulously proffered submission; the moment seemed to have come, when, the Protestant party in Germany being entirely subjugated, the whole north of Europe might again be made Catholic.

In this crisis what did the Pope?

He recalled his troops from the imperial army, and transferred the council, now on the point of completing its mission, and exercising its powers of pacification, from Trent, where, at the request of the Germans, it was established, to his own second capital, Bologna; alleging as the pretext for this step, that some contagious disease had broken out in the former city.

There is no doubt as to his motives for these proceedings. The ecclesiastical duties of the popedom were again in direct collision with its political interests. All Protestant Germany

[6] Respecting this embassy we have authentic information from Granvella himself: " Dispaccio di Monsignor di Cortona al Duca di Fiorenza Vormatia, 29 Maggio, 1545 " : (Granvella) " mi concluse in somma ch'el cardinale era venuto per giustificarsi d'alcune calumnie, e supplica S. M. che quando non potesse interamente discolpare l'attioni passate di Nro. Signore sue e di sua casa, ella si degnasse rimetterle e non ne tener conto.—Expose di più, in caso che S. M. si risolvesse di sbattere per via d'arme, perche ger giustitia non si vedeva quasi modo alcuno, li Luterani, S. Beatitudine concorrerà con ogni somma di denari."

eally subjugated by the Emperor, and entirely obedient to his
behests, seemed by no means desirable in the eyes of the Pope;
his astute calculations had taught him to look for something
wholly different—that Charles might gain certain successes,
whence advantage would accrue to the Catholic Church; this
he had hoped and expected; but he also believed, as he admits
himself,[7] that the Emperor would fall into difficulties innumerable, and be surrounded by such perplexities as would leave him,
Paul, at perfect liberty for the pursuance of his own projects.
Fortune mocked at all these deeply pondered plans: he had now
to fear, and France pointed out the fact to his notice, that the
imperial predominance would be extended to Italy also, and
make itself felt in his spiritual affairs as well as those temporal.

Nor was this all; the council also occasioned him increasing
anxiety: it had long oppressed him,[8] and he had more than once
bethought him of means by which to dissolve it.   The victories
of Charles were constantly adding to the boldness of the imperialist bishops, who now proposed measures of unusual au-
dacity.   Under the title of " censuræ," the Spanish prelates
brought forward certain articles tending in their collective form
to a circumscription of the papal dignity.   The Reformation,
by which Rome had so long been held in fear, seemed now indeed to have become inevitable.

Strangely do the words sound that relate the following facts,
yet are they perfectly true.   At the moment when all North
Germany was trembling at the prospect of restoration to the
papal authority, at that moment the Pope was, and felt himself,
an ally of the Protestants!   His joy at the progress made by
the elector John Frederic against Duke Maurice, was manifest;
he wished nothing more ardently, than that the former might
be equally able to hold out against the Emperor.   Francis I was
at this time using his utmost efforts to combine the whole world
in a league against Charles; and the Pope exhorted him earnestly " to succor those who were still holding out against the
Emperor, and were not yet overborne."[9]   Once more it seemed

---

[7] " Charles Cl. de Guise, au Roy, 31
Oct., 1547 " (Ribier, ii. p. 75); written
after an audience of the Pope, Paul declares the motives that led him to take
part in the German war: " Also, to
speak frankly, it would be better to put
impediments in the Emperor's way at
such points as that he shall not be able
to get through with success."

[8] " Du Mortier, au Roy, 26 Avril,
1547: " " I assure you, Sire, that when
the council was at Trent, it was a burden that oppressed him greatly."
[9] " Le même, au même," Ribier, i.
637: " His holiness hears that the
Duke of Saxony is very strong, whereat
he is greatly content, as thinking that
the common enemy will be thereby re-

probable to him that Charles might fall upon still greater difficulties, and have his hands occupied for a long time. "He
believes this," says the ambassador of France, "because he
wishes it."

But his hopes were again disappointed, the Emperor's good
fortune baffled all his calculations: Charles was victorious at
Mühlberg, and carried off the two Protestant leaders prisoners.
He could now direct his attention more closely than ever to his
Italian designs.

It will be readily understood that the Emperor was deeply
irritated by the proceedings of Paul—he saw through their motives most clearly. "The purpose of his holiness," writes he
to his ambassador, "has from the first been to entangle us in
this enterprise, and then to leave us in our embarrassment."[10]
That the Pope should recall his troops was a matter of no great
moment; irregularly paid, and therefore undisciplined and dis-
orderly, they were good for very little—but the transfer of the
council was indeed of importance.

And here we cannot but remark how wonderfully the Protestants were aided on this occasion, as before, by those dissensions between the papacy and the empire, arising from the
political position of the former. By this council the means
were presented of compelling the Protestants to submission, but
the council itself had divided (the imperialist prelates remaining at Trent): thus, no decrees of universally binding validity
being any longer possible, it was manifest that no recusant
could be forced to give in his adhesion. The Emperor had to
endure that the most essential part of his purpose should be
rendered nugatory by the defection of his ally. Not only did
he continue to insist on the recall of the council to Trent, but
even gave it to be understood that he would repair to Rome,
and hold the council there himself.

In this emergency Paul at once resolved on his path. "The
Emperor is mighty," he remarked; "but we also can effect

strained from his enterprises, and he
knows well that it would be useful to
aid those in secret who resist him, saying that you could not spend money to
better purpose."

[10] "Copia de la Carta que S. M.
scrivio a Don Diego de Mendoça, a 11
de Hebrero, 1547, aõs:" "Quanto mas
yva el dicho (prospero suceso) adelante,
mas nos confirmavamos en creher que
fuese verdad lo que antes se havia sa-
vido de la intention y inclinacion de
S. S. y lo que se dezia (es) que su fin
havia sido por embaraçar nos en lo que
estavamos y dexarnos en ello con sus
fines, desiños y platicas, pero que, aunque pesasse a S. S. y a otros, espe-
ravamos con la ayuda de N. S., aunque
sin la de S. S., guiar esta impresa a
buen camino." (See the text.)

omething, and still have some friends." The long talked of
onnection with France was now formed, by the affiancing of
Orazio Farnese to a natural daughter of Henry II. Great
fforts were made to include the Venetians in a general league:
he exiles of the different countries at once aroused themselves
o action. Disturbances broke out in Naples precisely at this
ritical moment, and a Neapolitan delegate presented himself
o implore the pontiff's protection for his vassals in that country,
while more than one of the cardinals recommended his acceding
o their prayer.

And now again the Italian factions stood face to face, and
with hostility all the more declared and decided from the fact
hat their respective leaders were openly at variance. On the
ne side were the governors of Milan and Naples, the Medici
n Florence, the house of Doria in Genoa: the centre of this
arty may be found in Don Diego Mendoza, imperial am-
assador to the Roman Court. On the other side were the Pope
nd the Farnesi, the exiles and the malcontents, with a newly
rganized Orsini party, the adherents of France. That portion
f the council remaining in Trent took part with the imperialists,
while the members who had withdrawn to Bologna held fast to
he pontiff.

The hatred borne by each of these parties toward the other
was suddenly manifested by a deed of violence.

The close intimacy at one time subsisting between the Pope
nd Emperor had emboldened Paul to invest his son Pier
Luigi with the cities of Parma and Placentia, to be held as a
dukedom in fief of the holy see;—not that he could proceed
o this step with the reckless boldness of an Alexander or a
Leo; he offered compensation to the Church by the cession of
Camerino and Nepi, seeking to prove that the "Camera
Apostolica" would suffer no loss by that transaction. To this
ffect he calculated the cost of defending those frontier towns,
he sums to be disbursed by Pier Luigi in this behalf, and the
evenue to be derived by the Church from her newly annexed
erritory. It was, however, only while in private conference
with each cardinal that he could bring any one of them to his
pinion—even then he totally failed with many: some remon-
trated openly, others purposely abstained from attending the
onsistory called to arrange the affair, and Caraffa, in par-

ticular, was seen on that day to make a solemn visit to the Seven Churches.[1] The Emperor, also, was dissatisfied with this project of exchange; or, if the dukedom was to be transferred, he would have preferred to see it in the hands of his son-in-law Ottavio,[2] to whom Camerino also belonged. He permitted the transfer to proceed, because the friendship of the Pope was at that moment needful to him; but he never concurred in it heartily; he knew Pier Luigi too well; all the cords of those secret associations which constituted the opposing power so formidable to the Emperor's ascendancy in Italy, were held by this son of the Pope. There was no doubt of his being aware of Fiesco's conspiracy; it was he who was believed to have saved Pietro Strozzi, the powerful chief of the Florentine exiles, by facilitating his escape across the Po, after an unsuccessful attack on Milan, and when the life of Strozzi hung on the turn of the moment; he was even suspected of a long-meditated intention of seizing the Milanese for himself.[3]

One day the Pope, who still believed that he was in the guardianship of favoring stars, and hoped to conjure whatever storms were threatening, repaired to the audience with feelings more than commonly cheerful, he enumerated the prosperous events of his life, and compared himself with the Emperor Tiberius. On that same day, his son, the possessor of his acquisitions, and the heir of his good-fortune, fell a victim to the violence of their common enemies. Pier Luigi was attacked by conspirators at Placentia, and assassinated.[4]

The duke, who ruled his people with all the depotism proper to those times, and who sought more particularly to keep the nobles in subjection, had rendered himself obnoxious to the Ghibellines of Placentia by various acts of violence; it was by them that his assassination was perpetrated; but there can be no doubt that the general belief of the day was well founded, and this accused Ferrante Gonzaga, governor of Milan, of participation in the deed.[5] Gonzaga's biographer, at that time his

[1] Bromato, "Vita di Paolo IV.," ii. 222.

[2] The negotiations for this affair are to be found in the Letter of Mendoza, dated November 29, 1547. The Pope says, "he had granted the fief to Pier Luigi, because the cardinals preferred this; and because he had himself but short time to live, as was clear from his failing health."

[3] Gosselini, "Vita di Ferr. Gonzaga," p. 20. Segni, "Storie Fiorentine," p. 292.

[4] "Mendoça, al Emperador," September 18, 1547: [He wasted the greater part of the time (on that day), in relating his felicities, and in comparing himself to the Emperor Tiberius.]

[5] "We have ascertained Ferrante to be the author," declares the Pope in the consistory. "Extrait du Consistoire

confidential secretary, and who seeks to exculpate him from the charge, declares that the intention was not to kill Pietro Luigi, but to take him prisoner.[6] I find in certain manuscripts intimations yet more significant of the Emperor himself having been in the secret of this design. I am reluctant to believe this without further evidence; but thus much is certain, the imperial troops at once took possession of Placentia, asserting the rights of the empire to that city as its fief. This was a kind of retaliation on the Pope for his defection at the war of Smalcald.

There is no parallel for the state of affairs that now ensued.

An expression was reported as proceeding from the cardinal Alessandro Farnese, to the effect that he could free himself from his difficulties only by the death of certain imperial ministers, that he could not bring this about by force, and must have recourse to stratagem. Thus warned, the persons threatened were seeking to secure themselves from poison, when two or three Corsican bravoes were arrested in Milan; and these men, whether with truth or falsely I do not determine, confessed that they were hired by the connections of Paul to assassinate Ferrante Gonzaga. Be this as it may, Gonzaga was exasperated anew; he declared that he must secure his own life as best he might, that nothing remained to him but to rid himself of some two or three of his enemies, either by his own hand or that of another.[7] Mendoza believes that there was a purpose entertained in Rome, of destroying all the Spaniards found here; the populace were to be secretly incited to this, and when the deed was done it was to be excused on the plea that their fury could not be controlled.

No means of reconciliation seemed to present themselves; there had been a wish to employ the daughter of the Emperor as mediatrix, but Margaret had never cordially attached herself to the Farnese family; her husband, who was much younger than herself, she utterly contemned, and exposed his evil qualities to the ambassadors without reserve; she declared herself ready, " rather to cut off her child's head, than to ask anything of her father that might be displeasing to him."

enu par N. S. Père," in a despatch from "Morvillier, Venise, 7 Sept. 542:" Ribier, ii. p. 61.
[6] Gosselini, p. 45: " Neither the Emperor nor Don Fernando, men of noble natures, ever would consent to the death of the Duke Pier Luigi Farnese, but did all in their power to save him, giving special orders to the conspirators, that they should keep him alive, but a prisoner."
[7] "Mendoça al Emperador:" " Don Hernando procurara de asegurar su vida come mejor pudiere, hechando a parte dos o tres estos o por su mano o por mano de otros." (See the text.)

The correspondence of Mendoza with his court lies before
me; it would be difficult to find anything that might be fairly
compared with these letters, for the deeply rooted hatred they
display, felt alike on both sides, each seeking to conceal his
feelings from the other, but neither succeeding; one perceives
in each, a sense of superiority that has steeped itself in bitterness,
a contempt that is yet on its guard, a mistrust such as men feel
toward some notoriously inveterate malefactor.

If the Pope sought aid or refuge in this state of things, there
was no country whence he could hope to find either, save France
alone.

We find him accordingly employed through long hours with
Cardinals Guise and Farnese, and the French ambassador,
discussing the relations of the papal see to France. He had
" read in old books," he said, " and heard from others during
his cardinalate, that the holy see was always pre-eminent in
might and prosperity while attached to France; but on the contrary, it ever sustained losses when this alliance had ceased; he
had made experience of that truth since his own accession to
the papal throne, and he could not forgive his predecessors Leo
and Clement; he could not forgive himself, for the favor that
had been shown to the Emperor; now, at all events, he was
fully determined to unite himself forever with France. He
hoped yet to live till he saw the papal court devotedly attached
to the French King, whom he would seek to make the greatest
prince in the world. His own house should be connected with
that of France by indissoluble ties." [8]

His intention was to form a league with France, Switzerland, and Venice, at first defensive only, but of which he remarked himself that it was " the door to an offen ve alliance." [9]
The French calculated that their friends, once united, would
secure to them as important a territory in Italy as that possessed by the Emperor. The whole Orsini party was again
ready to devote itself with life and property to the King of
France. The Farnesi thought that in the Milanese they could

[8] " Guise, au Roy, 31 Oct. 1547," Ribier, ii. 75.
[9] " Guise, au Roy, 11 Nov. 1547," Ribier, ii. 81: " Sire, il semble au pape,
à ce qu'il m'a dit, qu'il doit commencer
à vous faire déclaration de son amitié
par vous présenter luy et toute sa mai-
son: et pour ce qu'ils n'auroient puis-
sance de vous faire service, ny vous
aider à offenser, si vous premièrement
vous ne les aidez à défendre, il luy a
semblé devoir commencer par la ligne
défensive, laquelle il dit estre la vraye
porte de l'offensive." The whole correspondence relates to this topic.

at the least count on Cremona and Pavia; the Neapolitan exiles promised to bring 15,000 men into the field, and at once to deliver up Aversa and Naples. Into all these plans the Pope entered with great eagerness, he was the first to inform the French ambassador of a design upon Genoa. To make himself master of Naples, he would not have shrunk from a league with Algiers or the Grand Turk himself. Edward VI had just ascended the throne of England, and in that country the helm of state was directed by a government decidedly Protestant; none the less did Paul advise Henry II to make peace with England, "that he might be at liberty," says the Pope, "to accomplish other designs for the interests of Christendom." [10]

But violent as was the Pope's hostility to the Emperor, close as was his connection with France, and important as were the plans he proposed to adopt, yet the treaty was never completed, nor could he bring himself to resolve on taking the final step.

The Venetians were utterly astounded. "How," say they, "the Pope is assailed in his dignity, injured in his nearest kindred, the best possessions of his house are torn from his grasp! it should be his part to seize on every alliance and on all terms; yet, after so many offences and insults, we still see him irresolute and wavering."

Great personal injuries for the most part rouse men to extreme resolves; there are nevertheless certain natures, which still deliberate, however deeply offended, not because they are less prone to avenge themselves than others, but because, though the desire for vengeance is strong, the consciousness that their opponent is the more powerful is yet stronger. The prudence that weighs all consequence overpowers their resentment. Great reverses do not stimulate such men, on the contrary, they render them spiritless, feeble, and vacillating.

The Emperor was too powerful to feel any serious apprehension of the Farnesi; he went on his way without giving himself further trouble concerning them. He protested solemnly against the sittings of the council in Bologna, declaring beforehand that every act which might be passed there was null and void. In the year 1548, he published the " Interim "

[10] " François de Rohan, au Roy, 24 Feb. 1548 ": Ribier, ii. 117: " S. S. m'a commandé de vous faire entendre et conseiller de sa part, de regarder les moyens que vous pouvez tenir, pour vous mettre en paix pour quelque temps avec les Anglais, afin que n'estant en tant d'endroits empesché vous puissiez plus facilement exécuter vos desseins et enterprises pour le bien public de la Chrestienté." (See the text.)

in Germany. Paul found it intolerable, as was natural, that
the Emperor should prescribe a rule of faith; but however
earnestly he complained of this, or of church property being
left in the hands of its present (Protestant) possessors, the
Emperor remained utterly immovable, though Cardinal Farnese declared that in the "Interim" he could point out some
seven or eight heresies.[1] In the affair of Placentia, again,
Charles would abate no hair's breadth of his pretensions. The
Pope demanded immediate restitution of that city; the Emperor
maintained his claim to it in right of the empire. Paul ap-
pealed to the treaty of 1521, wherein Placentia was guaranteed
to the papal chair. The Emperor drew attention to the word
"Investiture," by which he declared that the empire had reserved its sovereign rights. Paul replied that the word was
not used in its feudal import on that occasion. The Emperor
did not continue the discussion of rights, but declared that his
conscience would not permit him to resign the city.[2] Very
willingly would the Pope have taken up arms at that moment.
Gladly would he have united himself with France, and called
his adherents into action. The intrigues of these last did indeed
make themselves felt at Naples, Genoa, Sienna, Placentia, and
even in Orbitello. Fain would Paul have revenged himself
by some unexpected onslaught; but on the other hand, there ever
rose before him the formidable power of the Emperor, whose
influence he dreaded, more especially in ecclesiastical affairs.
He was even beset by apprehensions lest a council should be
called, not only inimical to his interests, but that might even
proceed to his deposition. We are assured by Mendoza, that
the attempted assassination of Ferrante Gonzaga by those Corsican bravoes before named, had alarmed him to excess.

Whatever may have been the truth as regards these things,
it is certain that he remained inactive, and concealed his rage.
The Farnesi were not altogether dissatisfied at seeing Charles
take possession of Sienna; they hoped to have it ceded to them-

[1] "Hazer intendere a V. M. como en
el Interim ay 7 o 8 heregias:" "Mendoça, 10 Juni, 1548." In the letters of
the Commendator Annibal Caro, scritte
al nome del Cl. Farnese, which are also
composed with great reserve, will be
found, i. 65, another letter respecting
the Interim, to Cardinal Sfondrato,
wherein it is said—"The Emperor has
caused a scandal in Christendom, and
might have been better employed."
[2] "Lettere del Cardinal Farnese
scritte al Vescovo di Fano, Nuntio all'
Imperatore Carlo:" Informationi Politiche, xix., together with certain instructions from the Pope and Farnese,
throw light on these transactions, of
which I can only intimate the most
striking features.

selves in compensation for their losses. The most singular proposals were made respecting this city. "If the Emperor agrees to this," said they to Mendoza, "the Pope must re-establish the council in Trent, and not only proceed in other respects according to the Emperor's desires (as for example by acknowledging his right to Burgundy), but also declare Charles his successor on the papal throne. For," say they, "the climate of Germany is cold, that of Italy is warm; and, for a man who suffers from the gout as the Emperor does, warm countries are more healthful."[3] I will not maintain that these absurdities were uttered in earnest, for the old Pope was firmly persuaded that he should outlive the Emperor; but all this serves to show on how doubtful a path the policy of the Farnesi was conducting them, how widely they were departing from the established order of things.

The French meanwhile did not fail to perceive these movements, and the papal negotiations with the Emperor. A letter is extant from the constable Montmorency, wherein he speaks with the utmost indignation of their practices, using the most unqualified terms as to the dissimulations, lies, and villainous tricks practised in Rome against the King of France.[4]

At length, that he might not lose all his labor, but might gain at least one firm point in the midst of these struggles, the Pope resolved, since Placentia was refused, not to the claims of his house only, but to those of the Church as well, that the duchy should at once be restored to the latter. It was the first time that Paul had conceived any project adverse to the interests of his grandsons, but he felt no doubt of their acquiescence, having always believed himself to exercise an absolute authority over them, and frequently alluding in terms of praise and self-gratulation to their ready obedience. There was, however, a material change of circumstances on this occasion, for whereas he had hitherto been acting constantly with a view to their obvious interests, he was now proposing a measure directly at variance with them.[5] In the first in-

[3] Cardinal Gambara made this proposal to Mendoza, at a private meeting in a church. He said, at least, that "he had written something of the kind to the Pope, who had not taken it ill."

[4] "Le connestable, au Roy, 1 Sept. 1548" (Ribier, ii. 155): "Le pape avec ses ministres vous ont jusques-icy usé de toutes dissimulations, lesquelles ils ont depuis quelque temps voulu couvrir de pur mensonge, pour en former une vraye meschanceté, puisqu'il faut que je l'appelle ainsi." (See the text.)

[5] Dandalo also asserts his positive determination: "His holiness was entirely determined to restore Parma to the Church."

stance they attempted to divert him from his purpose. They
caused it to be notified to his holiness, that the day fixed for
holding the consistory was an unlucky one, being St. Roque's
day. Next they represented that the exchange he contemplated, of Camerino for Placentia, "would not result to the
advantage of the Church." These efforts failing, they retorted on him the arguments he had himself used on a former
occasion; but with all this, they could not prevent the fulfilment of his purpose, and at best effected but a short delay.
The Governor of Parma, Camillo Orsino, was finally commanded by Paul III to hold that city in the name of the Church,
and to deliver it to no other hands. After this declaration,
which left no room for doubt or hope, the Farnesi restrained
themselves no longer. They would on no consideration permit
themselves to be despoiled of a dukedom which placed them on
a level with the independent sovereigns of Italy. In despite of
the pontiff, Ottavio made an attempt to get Parma into his
hands by force or stratagem. The prudence and determination
of Camillo defeated his purpose, but how painful must have
been the feelings of Paul when this attempt was reported to
him! That it should be reserved for him in his old age to see
his grandsons rebelling against him; that those toward whom
he had felt so partial an affection, and on whose account he had
incurred the reproaches of the world, should now become his
enemies, this was bitter indeed. Even the failure of his enterprise did not deter Ottavio from his purpose. He wrote in
plain terms to the Pope, that if Parma were not given into his
possession, he would conclude a peace with Ferrante Gonzaga,
and seek to make himself master of it by aid of the imperial
troops; and in effect, his negotiations with that mortal enemy
of his house, had already proceeded to some extent; a courier
had been despatched with definite proposals to the Emperor.[6]
Loudly did the Pope complain that he was betrayed by his own
kindred, whose conduct was such as must bring him to his
grave. Above all he was most deeply wounded by a report
which prevailed, to the effect that he had himself a secret understanding with Ottavio, in whose enterprise he was taking a
part directly opposed to the spirit of his professions. To the
Cardinal Este he declared that no event of his life had given

him so much pain as this, not even the seizure of Placentia, not even the death of his son Pier Luigi; but that he would not leave the world any doubt as to his real sentiments.[7] His only consolation was, that at least the Cardinal Alessandro Farnese was innocent, and devoted to his interests. Gradually he awoke to the conviction that he also, the man in whom he trusted implicitly, and to whose hands was committed the whole conduct of affairs, was but too well acquainted with these transactions, and but too readily consenting to them. This discovery broke his heart. On the day of All Souls (November 2, 1549) he made it known to the Venetian ambassador in bitter grief of heart. The day following, seeking relief for his troubled thoughts, he went to his vigna on Monte Cavallo, but the repose he hoped for was not to be found. He caused the Cardinal Alessandro to be summoned to his presence; one word led to another, till the pontiff became violently enraged; he tore his nephew's cap from his hand, and dashed it to the ground.[8] The court was already anticipating a change, and it was generally believed that the cardinal would be removed from the administration. But the event terminated differently. So violent an agitation of mind at the advanced age of eighty-three, cast the Pope himself to the earth. He fell ill immediately, and expired in a few days (on the tenth of November, 1549).

All classes of the people crowded to pay respect to his remains and to kiss the foot of their departed sovereign. He was as much beloved as his grandsons were hated; the manner of his death also, which was manifestly caused by those for whose welfare he had been so constantly solicitous, awakened universal compassion.

This pontiff was distinguished by many and varied talents; he possessed extraordinary sagacity, his position was one of supreme elevation; but how impotent, how insignificant does

---

[7] "Hippolyt, Cardinal de Ferrare, au Roy, 22 Oct. 1549," Ribier, ii. p. 248: "S. S. m'a assuré n'avoir en sa vie eu chose, dont elle ait tant receu d'ennuy, pour l'opinion qu'elle craint, qu'on veuille prendre que cecy ait esté de son consentement."

[8] Dandolo: "Il Revmo. Farnese si risolse di non voler che casa sua restasse priva di Roma e se ne messe alla forte.—S. S. accortasi di questa contra-operatione del Revmo. Farnese me la comunicò il dì de' morti, in gran parte con grandissima amaritudine, et il dì dietro la mattina per tempo se ne andò alla sua vigna Monte Cavallo per cercar transtullo, dove si incolerò per tal causa con esso Revmo. Farnese." (See the text.) "Internally he was found in the most healthy state, and as one likely to live some years; but there were three drops of coagulated blood in his heart, judged to have been caused by the movements of anger."

even the most exalted of mortals appear, when placed in contrast with the grand and ceaseless course of events. In all that he proposes or can effect he is limited and held back by the span of time, which bounds his view, and which yet, with its transitory interests, is to him as the weight of eternity; he is besides fettered by the personal considerations incident to his position; these occupy his every hour occasionally perhaps, to his comfort and enjoyment, but more frequently to his sorrow and regret; thus is he but too often overborne by his cares. He departs, but the destinies of humanity make no pause, they move on to their completion.

Section II.—Julius III—Marcellus II

A group of cardinals had assembled around the altar of the chapel during the conclave; they were talking of the difficulties that presented themselves in the choice of a pope. " Take me," said one of the number, Cardinal Monte, " and the next day I will choose you for my favorites and intimates from the whole college of cardinals." " What say you? Shall we really elect him?" inquired another, Sfondrato, as they were about to separate.[1] Monte was considered irascible and impetuous, in many other respects too he was an unlikely choice. " Few bets would be taken on his chance," says a writer of the day. It nevertheless did so happen that he was elected (on the seventh of February, 1550). He had formerly been chamberlain to Julius II, and in memory of that sovereign he took the name of Julius III.

Duke Cosmo had largely contributed to this election; and when it became known at the imperial court, every face was lighted up with joy. For to the high pre-eminence of power and fortune, to which the Emperor had attained, was now to be added the ascent of the papal throne by a man whom he might firmly calculate on finding devoted to his interests. It now seemed probable that public affairs would take the course he should best like to give them.

The Emperor still adhered firmly to his wish for the re-

---

[1] Dandolo, "Relatione," 1551: "Questo Revmo. di Monte se ben subito in consideratione di ogn' uno, ma all' incontro ogn' uno parlava tante della sua colera e subitezza che ne passó mai che di pochissima scommessa." (See the text.)

establishment of the council at Trent, still hoping to compel the attendance of the Protestants and their submission to its authority. The new Pope assented cordially to that proposal. He set forth the difficulties that were in fact inseparable from the whole affair, but was extremely solicitous to prevent his caution from being considered a mere subterfuge; he made repeated declarations that this was not the case, and affirmed that having acted through his whole life without dissimulation, he would continue to do so. He decreed the reassemblage of the council at Trent, and fixed the period in the spring of 1551, intimating that he did so " without compact or condition." [2]

The assent of the Pope was then fully secured, but there was still much to be achieved.

At the instance of Julius, a decree of the Sacred College had reinstated Ottavio Farnese in the possession of Parma; the Emperor was not averse to this, negotiations had been for some time in progress, and there was good hope of a fair understanding between them. But Charles could not resolve on resigning Placentia also, and even retained such places as Gonzaga had seized in the territory of Parma. Thus Ottavio continued to maintain himself in the attitude of war. [3] So many injuries had been committed, so many offences offered by each to the other, that return to mutual confidence was impossible. The death of Paul had doubtless deprived his grandsons of an important support, but it had also given them freedom. No longer compelled to act in accordance with the general interest, or with that of the Church, their measures might now be calculated exclusively with regard to their own advantage. We still find Ottavio possessed by feelings of bitter hatred. He insists that his enemies are seeking to force Parma from " his grasp, and even to rid their hands of his own life," but he declares " that they shall succeed neither in the one nor the other." [4]

It was in this conviction and in such temper that he turned himself to Henry II, who accepted his proposals gladly.

[2] " Lettere del Nunzio Pighino, 12 e 15 Aug. 1550," Inform. Polit. xix.
[3] Gosselini, " Vita di Ferr. Gonzaga," and the justification of Gonzaga, from the accusation of having caused the war (in the third book) give an authentic explanation to this turn of affairs.

[4] " Lettere delli Signori Farnesiani per lo negotio di Parma," Informatt. Pol. xix. The above is from a letter of Ottavio to Cardinal Alessandro Farnese, Parma, March 24, 1551.

Italy and Germany were filled with malcontents. What the
Emperor had already effected, whether in religious or political
affairs, with what it was still expected he would do, had raised
him up innumerable enemies. Henry II determined to carry
forward the anti-Austrian purposes of his father; he gave a
truce to his wars with England, formed an alliance with Ottavio,
and took the garrison of Parma into his pay. French troops
soon appeared in Mirandola also, and the banners of France
were seen to wave in the very heart of Italy.

Pope Julius adhered steadily to the Emperor in this new
complication of affairs. He thought it intolerable "that a
miserable worm, Ottavio Farnese, should presume to contend
with an emperor and a pope." "It is our will," he declares
to his nuncio, "to embark in the same ship with his imperial
majesty, and to intrust ourselves to the same fortune. To him
who has the power and the wisdom we leave the determination
of the course."[5] The desire of the Emperor was, that measures
should be adopted for the immediate and forcible expulsion of
the French and their adherents. The imperial and papal troops
united, soon took the field, an important fortress of the Parmeg-
giano fell into their hands, they laid the whole region in ruins,
and invested Mirandola on all sides.

It was not, however, in these partial hostilities that the
power could be found to suppress those agitations that had
indeed originated here, but were now felt throughout Europe.
Troops were in action on every frontier where the dominions
of France met those of the Emperor. War had broken out by
land and sea. The German Protestants had at length allied
themselves with the French, and the weight they cast into the
scale was something very different from that of the Italians.
From this union there resulted an assault more determined than
any that Charles had ever before sustained; the French were
in force on the Rhine, the elector Maurice appeared in the Tyrol.
The veteran conqueror, who had taken up his position on the
mountain region between Italy and Germany, for the purpose of
holding both in allegiance, suddenly found his post one of the
utmost jeopardy—his enemies were victorious, and himself on
the point of becoming a prisoner.

[5] "Julius Papa III. Manu propria.
Instruttione per voi Monsignor d' Imola
con l'Imperatore. L'ultimo di Marzo."
Informatt. Pol. xii. He gives the cause
of this close union: "Not for any human affection, but because we see that
our cause is one with his imperial
majesty's, more especially in affairs of
religion."

The affairs of Italy were instantly affected by this state of things. " Never could we have believed," said the Pope, " that God would so visit us."[6] He was compelled to make a truce with the enemies in April, 1552.

Mischances sometimes occur that seem not wholly unwelcome to the man they affect; they give pause to a course of action no longer in harmony with his inclinations, they provide him with a legitimate cause, or at least afford an obvious excuse, for departing from it.

It would almost appear that Julius felt his tribulation to be of this character; the sight of his states filled with troops, and his treasury drained of its resources, had already become oppressive and painful to him; nor did he always think himself well treated by the imperial ministers.[7] The council, too, was presenting him with matter for serious uneasiness. Since the appearance of the German deputies, to whom promises of reformation had been given, the proceedings had assumed a bolder aspect. Even so early as January, 1552, Pope Julius complained that efforts were making to despoil him of his authority; the Spanish bishops sought to reduce the chapters to a state of servile subjection on the one hand, while they desired to deprive the holy see of the presentation to benefices on the other. But he affirmed his resolve to endure no invasion of his rights; under the title of an abuse, he would not permit those prerogatives to be torn from him that were no abuse, but an essential attribute of his legitimate power.[8] Affairs standing thus, the attack of the Protestants, by which the council was broken up, could not have been altogether displeasing to the Pope. He lost no time in decreeing the suspension of the assembly, and thus freed himself from disputes and pretensions innumerable.

From that time Julius III never applied himself earnestly to political affairs. It is true that the people of Sienna, whose townsman he was by the mother's side, accused him of supporting Duke Cosmo in his attacks on their freedom; but the falsehood of this accusation was proved by a subsequent

[6] Al Cl. Crescentino, April 13, 1552.
[7] " Lettera del Papa a Mendoza, 26th Dec. 1551," Informatt. Politiche, xix.: " Be it said without pride, we do not stand in need of counsel; we might even help others in that respect: assistance indeed we might require."

[8] " Al Cardinal Crescentio, 16th Jan. 1552: " " It never shall happen, we will never endure it, we will rather set the whole world in ruin."

judicial inquiry. It was rather Cosmo who had cause for complaint, the Pope having taken no steps to prevent the Florentine exiles—the most inveterate enemies of this his ally—from assembling and arming themselves within the States of the Church.

The villa of "Papa Giulio," at the Porta del Popolo, is still visited by the stranger. Restored to the presence of those times, he ascends the spacious steps to the gallery, whence he overlooks the whole extent of Rome, from Monte Mario, with all the windings of the Tiber. The building of this palace, the laying out of these gardens, were the daily occupation and continual delight of Pope Julius. The plan was designed by himself, but was never completed; every day brought with it some new suggestion or caprice, which the architects must at once set themselves to realize.[9] Here the pontiff passed his days, forgetting all the rest of the world. He had promoted the advancement of his connections to a very fair extent: Duke Cosmo had conferred on them the domains of Monte Sansovino, which was the cradle of their race; the Emperor had invested them with Novara; and he had himself bestowed on them the dignities of the ecclesiastical States and Camerino. A certain favorite he had made cardinal, in fulfilment of a promise. This was a young man who had caught the Pope's attention in Parma, when, being but a child, he was seized by an ape, and displayed so much courage, that Julius, pleased with his conduct, adopted and brought him up, always showing him great affection; but unhappily this constituted his only merit.

The pontiff desired to forward the interests of his family, and those of his favorite; but he was not inclined to involve himself in dangerous perplexities on their account. The pleasant and blameless life of his villa was that which, as we have said, was best suited to him. He gave entertainments, which he enlivened with proverbial and other modes of expression, that sometimes mingled blushes with the smiles of his guests. In the important affairs of the Church and State he took no other share than was absolutely inevitable.

Under such circumstances, it is manifest that neither Church nor State could greatly prosper. The discord between the

[9] Vasari. Boissard describes their extent at that time: "It occupies nearly all the heights that stretch from the city to the Milvian bridge." He cele-

two great Catholic powers became ever more and more dangerous and threatening; the German Protestants had recovered themselves effectually from the defeat of 1547, and now displayed a more imposing aspect than they had ever before assumed. Of the Catholic reformation so often looked for, there could now be no further hope; the fact would not permit concealment—the prospects of the Roman Church were, in all directions, ambiguous and gloomy.

But if, as we have seen, there had arisen in the bosom of that Church a more severe spirit of action, a feeling intensely reprobating the whole life and conduct of so many of her chiefs, would not this at length affect the choice of the pontiff? So much was always dependent on the personal character of the pope! for this cause it was that the supreme dignity was made elective; since thus it might be hoped that a man truly representing the prevalent spirit of the Church would be placed at the head of her government.

The .nore strictly religious party possessed no preponderating influence in the Church until after the death of Julius III. The pontiff had frequently felt himself restrained, and his undignified demeanor reproved, by the presence of Cardinal Marcello Cervini. It was on this prelate that the choice fell. He ascended the papal seat on the eleventh of April, 1555, as Marcellus II.

The whole life of the new pontiff had been active, and free from the shadow of reproach; that reform in the Church, of which others only talked, he had exemplified in his own person. "I had prayed," says a contemporary, "that a pope might be granted to us by whom those words of fair import, church, council, reform, might be raised from the contempt into which they had fallen: by this election my hopes received fulfilment, my wish seemed to have become a reality."[10] "The opinion," says another, "entertained of this Pope's worth and incomparable wisdom, inspired the world with hope. If ever it be possible for the Church to extinguish heresy, to reform abuse, and compel purity of life, to heal its divisions, and once again be united, it is by Marcellus that this will be

brates their splendor, and gives us some of their inscriptions; for example: "Let it be lawful that virtuous delights be enjoyed by the virtuous." And especially: "In the neighboring temple, let thanks be given to God and St. Andrew, and let them [visitors] pray for abundant health and eternal life to Julius III, Pontifex Maximus, to Baldwin, his brother, and to their whole family." Julius died on March 23, 1555.

[10] "Seripando al Vescovo di Fiescole," "Lettere di Principi," iii. 162.

brought about."[1] Thus it was that Marcellus commenced his
reign. All his acts were in the same spirit. He would not permit his kindred to approach the capital; he made various retrenchments in the expenditure of the court; and is said to
have prepared a memorial of the different ameliorations that
he proposed to effect in the ecclesiastical institutions. His first
effort was to restore divine worship to its due solemnity; all
his thoughts were of reform, and the council needful to that
effect.[2] In political affairs he determined on a neutrality, by
which the Emperor was perfectly satisfied. "But the world,"
as his contemporaries remark, "was not worthy of him." They
apply to the pontiff those words of Virgil relating to another
Marcellus: "Fate permitted the world to have sight of him
only." On the twenty-second day of his pontificate he died.

We can say nothing of the results produced by so short an
administration. But even this commencement, this election
even, suffices to show the spirit that was beginning to prevail.
It continued predominant in the next conclave, and was exemplified in the choice of the most rigid among all the cardinals.
Giovanni Pietro Caraffa came forth from that assembly as pope,
on the twenty-third of May, 1555.

Section III—Paul IV

Frequent mention has already been made of this pontiff,
who is that same Caraffa, the founder of the Theatines, the
restorer of the Inquisition, and the speaker who so essentially contributed to the confirmation of the ancient doctrines
in the council of Trent. If there were a party whose purpose it was to reinstate Catholicism in all its strictness, not only
was it a member, but a founder and chief of that party who
now ascended the papal throne. Paul IV had already completed his seventy-ninth year, but his deep-set eyes still retained
all the fire of youth: he was extremely tall and thin, walked
with rapid steps, and seemed all nerve and muscle. His personal habits were subjected to no rule or order; frequently
did he pass the night in study, and sleep in the day—woe
then to the servant who should enter the apartment before his

[1] "Lettere di Principi," iii. 141. The
editor is here speaking in his own person.

[2] "Petri Polidori de Vita Marcelli
Commentarius," 1744, p. 119.

bell had rung. In all things it was his custom to follow the impulse of the moment;[1] but this impulse was regulated by a mood of mind formed in the practice of a long life, and become a second nature. He seemed to acknowledge no other duty, no other occupation, than the restoration of the Catholic faith to all its primitive authority. Characters of this description arise from time to time, and are occasionally to be seen even in the present day. Their perceptions of life and the world are gained from a single point of view; the peculiar disposition of their mind is so powerful that all their opinions are tinctured and governed by it; indefatigable speakers, their manner derives a certain freshness from the earnestness of their souls, and the system of thought that, as by a kind of fatality, informs and rules their whole being, is poured forth in a stream inexhaustible. How powerfully do such men act on all around them, when placed in a position wherein their activity is in perfect harmony with their views and sentiments, wherein the power to act is associated with the will! What might men not expect from Paul IV, whose views and opinions had never endured either concession or compromise, but were ever carried out eagerly to their utmost consequences, now that he was raised to the supreme dignity![2] He was himself amazed at having reached this point—he who had in no manner conciliated a single member of the conclave, and from whom nothing was to be expected but the extreme of severity. He believed that his election had been determined, not by the cardinals, but by God himself, who had chosen him for the accomplishment of his own purposes.[3]

"We do promise and swear," says he in the bull that he published of his accession to the holy see, "to make it our first care that the reform of the universal Church, and of the

---

[1] "Relatione di M. Bernardo Navagero (che fu poi cardinale) alla Serma. Repca. di Venetia, tornando di Roma Ambasciatore appresso del Pontefice Paolo IV, 1558:" in many Italian libraries, and in the Informationi Politiche in Berlin: "The complexion of this pontiff is adust and choleric; he has incredible gravity and grandeur in all his actions, and seems really born to command."

[2] It will be readily believed that his character did not secure the approbation of all the world. Aretino's "Capitolo al Re di Francia" describes him thus: "Caraffa, the lazy hypocrite,

who makes a matter of conscience about peppering a thistle."

[3] "Relatione del Clmo. M. Aluise Mocenigo K. ritornato dalla Corte di Roma, 1560" (Arch. Venez.): "Fu eletto pontefice contra il parer e credere di ogn' uno e forse anco di se stesso, come S. S. propria mi disse poco inanzi morisse, che non avea mai compiaciuto ad alcuno e che ne un cardinale gli avea domandato qualche gratia gli avea sempre riposto alla riversa, nè mai compiaciutolo, onde disse: io non so come mi habbiano eletto papa, e concludo che Iddio faccia li pontefici." (See the text.)

Roman Court, be at once entered on." The day of his coronation was signalized by the promulgation of edicts respecting monasteries and the religious orders. He sent two monks from Monte Cassino into Spain, with command to re-establish the discipline of the convents which had become lax and neglected. He appointed a congregation for the promotion of reforms in general; this consisted of three classes, in each of which were eight cardinals, fifteen prelates, and fifty learned men of differing ranks.

The articles to be discussed by them, in relation to the appointments to clerical offices and collation to benefices, were submitted to the universities. It is manifest that the new pope proceeded with great earnestness in the work of reform.[4] The spiritual tendency which had hitherto affected the lower ranks of the hierarchy only, now seemed to gain possession of the papal throne itself, and promised to assume the exclusive guidance of all affairs during the pontificate of Paul IV.

But now came the question of what part he would take in relation to the general movements of the political world.

The principal direction once given to a government, and which has gradually identified itself with its very existence, is not readily susceptible of change.

A desire to deliver themselves from the heavy preponderance of Spain must ever have been uppermost in the minds of the popes; and at the accession of Paul the moment seemed to have come when his wish appeared to be within the possibility of realization. The war proceeding, as we have seen, from the movements of the Farnesi, was the most unfortunate one ever undertaken by Charles V. He was closely pressed in the Netherlands; Germany had deserted his interests; Italy was no longer faithful to him; he could not rely even on the houses of Este and Gonzaga; he was himself ill, and weary of life. I question whether any pontiff, not immediately attached to the imperial party, could have found strength to withstand the temptations presented by this state of things.

In the case of Paul IV they were more than commonly powerful. Born in the year 1476, he had seen his native Italy in all the unrestrained freedom of her fifteenth century, and his very soul clung to this remembrance. He would sometimes

---

[4] Bromato, " Vita di Paolo IV.," lib. ix. § ii. § xvii. (ii. 224, 289).

ompare the Italy of that period to a well-tuned instrument of
our strings—these last being formed by Naples, Milan, Venice,
nd the States of the Church. He would then utter maledictions
n the memory of Alfonso and Louis the Moor: " Lost and
inhallowed souls," as he said, " whose discords had disturbed
hat harmony."⁵ That from their time the Spaniard should
ave become master in the land, was a thought that he could
1 no way learn to bear. The house of Caraffa, whence he de-
ived his birth, was attached to the French party, and had fre-
uently taken arms against the Castilians and Catalonians. In
528 they again joined the French; and it was Giovanni Pietro
Caraffa who advised Paul III to seize Naples in 1547. To this
arty spirit came other causes in aid: Caraffa had constantly
ffirmed that Charles favored the Protestants from jealousy of
he Pope, and that " the successes of those heretics were at-
ributable to no other than the Emperor."⁶ Charles knew
Caraffa well, he once expelled him from the council formed for
he administration of affairs in Naples, and would never per-
iit him to hold peaceful possession of his ecclesiastical
mployments within that kingdom; he had, moreover, made
arnest remonstrance against Caraffa's declamations in the con-
istory. All these things, as may readily be supposed, did but
ncrease the virulence of the Pope's enmity. He detested the
Emperor as Neapolitan and as Italian, as Catholic and as pope:
iere existed in his soul no other passions than that for reform
f the Church and his hatred of Charles.

The first act of Paul was to lighten various imposts, and to
ermit the importation of corn. A statue was erected to him
or these benefits, and it was not without a certain sense of
elf-complacency that he viewed this—while in the midst of
is splendid court, and surrounded by a glittering body of
Neapolitan nobles, proffering him the most obsequious obe-
ience—he received the homage of ambassadors who came
rowding from all countries to his presence. But scarcely had
e felt himself well-seated on the pontifical chair, than he com-
nenced a series of disputes with the Emperor. That monarch
ad complained to the cardinals of his party, that a pope so

⁵" Who first spoiled that noble in-
trument Italy."—Navagero.
⁶" Memoriale dato a Annibale Ru-
ellai, Sept. 1555 " (Informatt. Pol.

tom. xxiv.) " He freely called his imperial majesty a favorer of schismatics
and heretics."

inimical to himself had been chosen; his adherents held suspicious meetings; some of them even carried off certain ships from Civita Vecchia, that had previously been taken from them by the French.[7] The Pope at once breathed fire and flames. Such of his vassals, and the cardinals, as were imperialists, he arrested instantly, confiscating the whole property of those who fled. Nor was this enough. That alliance with France which Paul III never could resolve on completing, was entered into with little hesitation by Paul IV. He declared that the Emperor designed to "finish him by a sort of mental fever," but that he, Paul, was "determined on open fight. With the help of France he would yet free this poor Italy from the tyrannies of Spain, and did not despair of seeing two French princes ruling in Naples and Milan." He would sit for long hours over the black thick fiery wine of Naples, his usual drink (it was of a sort called mangiaguerra, champ-the-war) [8] and pour forth torrents of stormy eloquence, against those schismatics and heretics, those accursed of God, that evil generation of Jews and Moors, that scum of the world, and other titles equally complimentary, bestowed with unsparing liberality on everything Spanish;[9] but he consoled himself with the promise, "thou shalt tread upon the lion and adder, the young lion and the dragon shalt thou trample under foot." The time was now come when the Emperor Charles and King Philip should receive the punishment due to their iniquities. He, the Pope, would inflict it, and would free Italy from their grasp. If others would not listen to nor support him, the future world should at least have to tell, how an old Italian, so near to his grave, and who should rather have been employed in preparing for it, had entertained these lofty purposes. We will not enter into the details of the negotiations which he carried on under

[7] "Instruttioni e Lettere di Monsignor della Casa a nome del Cl. Caraffa, dove si contiene il principio della rottura della guerra fra Papa Paolo IV. e l'Imperatore Carlo V., 1555." Also in the Informatt. Polit. xxiv.

[8] Navagero: "His custom is to eat twice a day, he must be served very delicately; and in the beginning of his pontificate, twenty-five dishes were not sufficient for his table: he drinks much more than he eats; his wine being strong and brisk—it is a black wine, grown in the kingdom of Naples, that they call 'champ-the-war,' and is so thick that one may almost cut it. After his meals he drinks malmsey, and this his people call 'washing his teeth.' He used to eat in public like other popes, till his last indisposition, which was considered mortal—once he had lost his appetite. He often spent three hours at table in talk of various matters, according to the occasion, and in the heat of this he sometimes uttered things of secrecy and importance."

[9] Navagero: "Deploring the misfortune of Italy, compelled to serve a race so abject and vile." The despatches of the French ambassadors are full of these outbreaks; those, for example, of De Lansac and D'Avançon, in Ribier, ii. 610-618.

ie influence of these feelings. When the French concluded truce with Spain,[10] unmindful of an agreement that they had ntered into with himself, he sent his nephew, Carlo Caraffa, ɔ France, where the different parties contending for power in nat country were gradually gained over to his interests. The Iontmorencies and the Guises, the wife of the French King nd his mistress, were equally won to aid the pontiff in pro-ioting a new outbreak of hostilities.[1] Paul secured a vigorous talian ally also in the person of the Duke of Ferrara; nothing ·ss was talked of than completely revolutionizing Italy. Jeapolitan and Florentine exiles filled the Curia; their ·storation to their homes seemed now approaching; the papal scal instituted a legal process against the Emperor Charles nd King Philip, in which the excommunication of those rinces, and the release of their subjects from their oath of alle-iance, was roundly threatened. The Florentines always eclared that they held positive evidence of a design to include ie house of Medici in the downfall of the Spanish power.[2] .ctive preparations were everywhere made for war, and the ·hole character of the century seemed about to suffer change, nd become matter of question.

But meanwhile how different a position was this pontificate ssuming from that which it had been expected to take up! .ll purposes of reform were set aside for the struggles of war, nd these last entailed consequences of a totally opposite naracter.

The pontiff, who as cardinal, had most sternly opposed the buses of nepotism, and had denounced them, even to his own eril, was now seen to abandon himself entirely to this weak-ess. His nephew, Carlo Caraffa, who had passed his whole fe amidst the excesses and license of camps,[3] was now raised ɔ the rank of cardinal, though Paul himself had often declared f him, that " his arm was dyed in blood to the elbow." Carlo

[10] The account of the incredulity ex-essed by the Caraffas, when this truce is first named to them, as given by avagero, is extremely characteristic: Asking the Pope and Cardinal Caraffa they had received intelligence of the uce, they looked at each other laugh-g, as if they would say, as indeed the ntiff openly said to me afterward, at there was but slight hope of that; t the next day came the news, which annoyed the Pope and cardinal (though it confronted all Rome), that they could not conceal their rage, and Paul said, "This truce will be the ruin of the world."
[1] Rabutin, "Mémoires," "Collect. Univers.," tom. xxxviii. Especially "Mémoires," Villars, ib. tom. xxxv. 277.
[2] Gussoni, "Relatione di Toscana."
[3] Babon, in Ribier, ii. 745. Villars, p. 255.

had found means to gain over his superannuated relative; he contrived to be occasionally surprised by him in seeming prayer before the crucifix, and apparently suffering agonies of remorse,[4] but still further was the uncle propitiated by the virulent enmity of his nephew to the Spaniards; this was their true bond of union. Carlo Caraffa had taken military service with the Emperor in Germany, but complained that he had met with neglect only as his reward. A prisoner, from whom he expected a large ransom, had been taken from him, nor had he been suffered to hold possession of a priory belonging to the order of Malta, to which he had been nominated. All these things had awakened his hatred and made him thirst for vengeance. This state of feeling, Paul allowed to stand in the place of all the virtues Carlo wanted; he could find no words eloquent enough to praise him, declaring that the papal seat had never possessed a more efficient servant; he made over to him the greater part, not only of the civil, but even of the ecclesiastical administration, and was perfectly satisfied that he should be regarded as the author of whatever acts of favor were received from the court.

On his other nephews the pontiff would not for some time bestow a glance of kindness; it was not until they had evinced their participation in his anti-Spanish mania, that they were received to his grace.[5] Never could anyone have anticipated what he next did. Declaring that the Colonnas, "those incorrigible rebels against God and the Church," however frequently deprived of their castles, had always managed to regain them, he now resolved that this should be amended; he would give those fortresses to vassals who would know how to hold them. Thereupon he divided the possessions of the house of Colonna among his nephews, making the elder Duke of Palliano and the younger Marquis of Montebello. The cardinals remained silent when he announced these purposes in their assembly; they bent down their heads and fixed their eyes to the earth. The Caraffas now indulged in the most ambitious projects: the daughters of their family should marry into that of the French King, or at least into the ducal house of Ferrara; the sons thought of

[4] Bromato.
[5] " Extract from the trial of Cardinal Caraffa. The Duke of Palliano also deposes, that until he declared against the imperialists, the Pope never showed him a fair countenance, or viewed him with a good eye."

nothing less than the possession of Sienna. To one who spoke jestingly concerning the jewelled cap of a child of their house, the mother of the nephews replied, " We should rather be talking of crowns than caps."[6]

And indeed everything was now depending on the events of the war which then broke out, but which certainly assumed no very promising aspect even from the commencement.

On that act of the fiscal before alluded to, the Duke of Alva had pressed forward from the Neapolitan territory into the States of the Church. He was accompanied by the Roman vassals, whose confederates also aroused themselves. The papal garrison was driven out of Nettuno, and the troops of the Colonnas recalled. Alva seized Frosinone, Anagni, Tivoli in the mountains, and Ostia on the sea. Rome was thus invested on both sides.

The Pope had first placed his reliance on his Romans, and reviewed them in person. They marched from the Campofiore, three hundred and forty columns armed with harquebuses, two hundred and fifty with pikes. In each rank stood nine men admirably appointed, presenting á most imposing aspect, and commanded by officers who were exclusively of noble birth. These troops passed before the castle of St. Angelo, which saluted them with its artillery, to the piazza of St. Peter, where the pontiff had stationed himself at a window with his nephews, and as each caporion and standard-bearer passed, his holiness bestowed his blessing.[7] All this made a very fair show, but these were not the men by whom the city was to be defended. When the Spaniards had approached near the walls, a false alarm, occasioned by a small body of horse, was sufficient to throw them into such perfect confusion, that not one man was found remaining by his colors. The Pope saw that he must seek elsewhere for effectual aid, and after a time Pietro Strozzi brought him the troops that were serving before Sienna. With these he succeeded in recovering Tivoli and Ostia, thus averting the most imminent danger.

But what a war was this!

There are moments in the history of the world when it would seem that the actions of men are influenced by motives

[6] Bromato, ix. 16; ii. 286: literally: "This is no time to talk of caps, but of crowns."

[7] "Diario di Cola Calleine Romano del rione di Trastevere dall' anno 1521 sino all' anno 1562," MS.

in direct opposition to the principles and ideas that usually
govern their lives and conduct.

The Duke of Alva might, in the first instance, have conquered Rome with very little difficulty; but his uncle, Cardinal
Giacomo, reminded him of the unhappy end to which all had
come who had taken part in the conquest under Bourbon
Alva, being a good Catholic, conducted the war with the utmost
discretion; he fought the Pope, but did not cease to pay him
reverence; he would fain take the sword from his holiness, but
had no desire for the renown of a Roman conqueror. His soldiers complained that they were led against a mere vapor, a
mist and smoke that annoyed them, but which they could neither
lay hold on nor stifle at its source.

And who were those by whom the Pope was defended
against such good Catholics? The most effective among them
were Germans, and Protestants to a man! They amused themselves with the saintly images on the highways, they laughed
at the mass in the churches, were utterly regardless of the fast
days, and did things innumerable, for which, at any other time,
the Pope would have punished them with death.[8] I even find
that Carlo Caraffa established a very close intimacy with that
great Protestant leader, the margrave Albert of Brandenburg.

Contradictions more perfect, a contrast more complete, than
that displayed by these circumstances, could be scarcely
imagined. On the one side we have the most fervent spirit
of Catholicism, which was at least exemplified in the leader
(how different were his proceedings from those of the old
Bourbon times!) ; on the other, was that secular tendency of the
popedom, by which even Paul IV, however earnestly con-
demning it, was seized and borne forward. Thus, it came to
pass that the followers of his faith were attacking him, while
it was by heretics and seceders that he found himself defended! But the first preserved their allegiance, even while
opposing his power; the latter displayed their hostility to and
contempt for his person even while in arms to protect him.

It was not until the French auxiliaries crossed the Alps
that the contest really began; these consisted of ten thousand

---

[8] Navagero: "The Germans were considered the best disciplined and most serviceable troops—the Gascons were most insolent; they committed offences against female honor, and were great plunderers. The injured publicly cursed him who was the cause of these disorders."

foot and a less numerous, but very brilliant body of cavalry. Their leader would most willingly have directed his force against Milan, which he believed to be unprepared for defence, but he was unable to resist the impulse by which the Caraffas forced him toward Naples. The latter were fully confident of finding numberless adherents in their own country, they counted on the assistance of the exiles, and hoped for the rising of their party; if not throughout the kingdom, yet certainly in the Abruzzi and round Aquila and Montorio, where their ancestors had always exercised an important influence, both on the paternal and maternal side.

It was manifest that affairs must now arrive at a crisis, in whatever manner this might terminate. The papal power had been too often excited into hostility against the Spanish predominance, not eventually to burst forth without restraint.

The Pope and his nephews were determined that matters should proceed to extremity, not only had Caraffa accepted the aid of the Protestants, he had even made proposals to Solyman. These were to the effect that the Turkish sovereign should abstain from prosecuting his wars in Hungary, and throw himself with all his force on the two Sicilies.[9] Thus was a pontiff entreating the help of infidels against a Catholic monarch.

In April, 1557, the papal troops crossed the Neapolitan frontier, Holy Thursday was signalized by the conquest and atrocious pillage of Compli, which was full of treasure, in part belonging to the town, but also much was there beside that had been carried thither for safety. This done, Guise also crossed the Tronto, and besieged Civitella.

But he found the kingdom fully prepared to baffle his efforts. Alva knew well that there would be no insurrection among the people, so long as he should retain the upper hand in the country; he had received a large grant of money from a parliament of the barons. Queen Bona of Poland, of the ancient family of Aragon, and a bitter enemy of the French, who had shortly before arrived in her duchy of Bari, with much treasure, supplied him with half a million of scudi. The ecclesiastical revenues that should have been sent to Rome he poured into

[9] His confessions in Bromato, " Vita di Paolo IV.," tom. ii. p. 360. Bromato also gives us good information respecting the war; which he takes often word for word—a fact he does not conceal—from a voluminous MS. by Nores, which treats circumstantially of this war, and is to be found in many Italian libraries.

his military chest instead, and even seized the gold and silver
of the churches, with the bells of the city of Benevento, all
which he appropriated to his own purposes.[10]   Thus furnished,
he proceeded to fortify the towns of the Neapolitan frontier, as
also those of the Roman territory that still remained in his hands.
His army was composed in the usual manner of Germans,
Spaniards, and Italians, but was an extremely formidable one.
He also raised Neapolitan centuries under the command of the
native nobles.   Civitella was bravely defended by Count Santafiore, who had succeeded in rousing the inhabitants to active co-
operation, and even to repel an attempt made to take the place
by storm.

While the kingdom of Naples thus held firmly to King
Philip, and displayed only devotion to his service, the assailants,
on the contrary, were weakened by animosities and dissensions.
French and Italians, Guise and Montebello, all were in the utmost discord.   Guise complained that the Pope did not perform
his part in the contract between them, and neglected to send him
the promised supplies.   When the Duke of Alva appeared with
his army in the Abruzzi, toward the middle of May, Guise found
it advisable to raise the siege, and retreat across the Tronto;
operations were then again transferred to the Roman territories.
And now was seen a war in which both sides advanced and then
retreated; invested towns only to resign them, made great movements, in short, but on one occasion only did they come to a
serious engagement.

Marc Antonio Colonna made demonstrations against Palliano, which had been taken from him by the Pope; seeing
which, Giulio Orsino hurried to its relief with provisions and
troops; 3,000 Swiss had arrived in Rome under the command
of a colonel from Unterwalden.   The Pope received them with
great delight, decorated their officers with gold chains and
knightly titles, and declared that this was a legion of angels
sent by God for his behoof.   These were the troops that, together with a few companies of Italian cavalry and infantry,
marched under the command of Giulio Orsino.   They were met
by the forces of Marc Antonio Colonna, and once more ensued

[10] Giannone, " Istoria di Napoli," lib.
xxxiii. c. 1. Gosselini and Mambrino
Roseo, " Delle Historie del Mondo,"
lib. vii., who give a minute account of
this war, with other writers, agree in
attributing to Ferrante Gonzaga a large
share in the most able measures taken
by Alva.

one of those bold battles in the manner of the Italian wars of 1494–1531, the papal troops against those of the empire, a Colonna opposing an Orsino; the German lanzknechts, under their distinguished leaders, Caspar von Feltz and Hans Walther, stood face to face, as they so often had done, with their ancient antagonists the Swiss. Once again the combatants on either side arrayed themselves for a cause in which neither felt the slightest interest, but for which they none the less fought with determined bravery.[1] Hans Walther at length, " tall and strong," say the Spaniards, " as a giant," threw himself into the midst of a Swiss company. With a pistol in one hand and his naked sword in the other, he rushed upon the standard-bearer, whom he brought down, shooting him in the side, at the same moment that he dealt him a fatal blow on the head. The whole troop fell upon him, but his lanzknechts were already at hand for his support. The Swiss were completely broken and dispersed, their banners, on which had been inscribed in large letters, " Defenders of the faith and of the Holy See," were trampled in the dust, and of the eleven captains that went forth, their commander led two only back to Rome.

While this miniature war was in progress here, the great armies were in action on the frontier of the Netherlands. The battle of St. Quintin ensued, wherein the Spaniards gained a complete victory. In France men even wondered that they did not at once press forward to Paris, which at that moment they might certainly have taken.[2]

Hereupon Henry II writes to Guise, " I hope," he remarks, " that the Pope will do as much for me in my need as I did for him in his straits." [3] So little could Paul now hope from the aid of the French, that it was he on the contrary who was called on to help them. Guise declared, " that no chains would now avail to keep him in Italy," [4] and he instantly hurried with all his forces to the aid of his embarrassed sovereign.

No force remaining that could oppose an obstacle to the imperialists and troops of Colonna, they advanced toward Rome, whose inhabitants once more saw themselves threatened with conquest and plunder. Their condition was all the more des-

[1] I find the details of this little encounter in Cabrera, " Don Felipe Segundo," lib. iii. p. 189.
[2] Monluc, " Mémoires," p. 116.
[3] " Le Roy à Mons. de Guise," in Ribier, ii. p. 750.
[4] " Lettera del Duca di Palliano al Cl. Caraffa," Informatt. Polit. xxii.

perate from the fact that they had little less to fear from their defenders than from their enemies. During many nights they were compelled to keep lights burning in every window, and through all the streets. A skirmishing party of Spaniards which had reached the gates was frightened back by this demonstration, which was, however, a mere precaution against the papal troops; everyone murmured. The Romans wished their Pope in his grave a thousand times, and demanded that the Spanish army should be admitted by a formal capitulation.

So far did Paul IV permit his affairs to come. It was not until every enterprise had completely failed, till his allies were beaten, his States for the greater part invested by the enemy, and his capital a second time menaced with ruin, that he would bend himself to treat for peace.

This was accorded by the Spaniards in the same spirit by which they had been actuated throughout the war. They restored all such fortresses and cities of the Church as had been taken, and even promised compensation for Palliano, which the Caraffas had lost.[5] Alva came to Rome; with the most profound reverence did he now kiss the foot of his conquered enemy, the sworn adversary of his King and nation. He was heard to say that never had he feared the face of man as he did that of the pontiff.

This peace seemed in every way favorable to the papal interest; it was nevertheless utterly fatal to all the projects hitherto cherished by the popedom. Any further attempt to throw off the Spanish yoke must now be abandoned, and accordingly, none such has ever (in the old sense and manner) been again brought forward. The influence of the Spaniards in Milan and Naples had proved unassailable. Their allies were more than ever powerful. There had been hope among the Caraffas of expelling Duke Cosmo from Florence; but this prince had not only held firm his grasp, but had seized on Sienna likewise, and was now the possessor of an important sovereignty. By the restitution of Placentia, the Farnesi had been gained over to Philip II. Marc Antonio Colonna had made himself a brilliant reputation, and had fully restored the ancient lustre of his family. For the pontiff there was nothing left but to resign

---

[5] A convention was made between Carlo Caraffa and the Duke of Alva, regarding Palliano, and this was kept secret; not from the public only, but from the Pope himself.—Bromato, ii. 385.

himself to this position of affairs. Bitter as was this necessity
to Paul IV, he yet felt that he must submit; with what feelings
it is not difficult to imagine. Philip II being on some occasion
called his friend, " Yes," he replied, " my friend who kept me
beleaguered, and who thought to have my soul! " It is true
that in the presence of strangers he compared Philip to the
prodigal son of the gospel, but in the circle of his intimates he
took care to mark his estimation of those pontiffs who had designed to raise the kings of France to the imperial throne,[6] for
others he had no praise. His sentiments were what they had
always been, but the force of circumstances controlled him.
There was nothing more to be hoped for, still less to be undertaken; he dared not even bemoan himself, unless in the closest
secrecy.

When once an event is indeed accomplished, it is altogether
useless for a man to struggle against its consequences. Even
Paul IV felt this, and after a certain time his thoughts took
another direction; he experienced a reaction which was of most
effective importance, whether as regarded his own administration, or the general transformation brought about in the papal
position and system.

Other pontiffs had promoted and favored their nephews from
family affection, or mere selfish ambition to raise the house they
sprang from; the nepotism of Paul had a totally different origin: his nephews were favored because they assisted his efforts
against Spain, and because in this contest he considered them
his natural allies; that once over, the utility of the nephews was
at an end. It is only by success that a man is maintained in a
position of great eminence, more especially if it be not acquired
in a manner altogether legitimate. Cardinal Caraffa had
undertaken an embassy to King Philip, principally to promote
the interests of his own house, for which he desired to receive
the compensation promised in lieu of Palliano. He returned
without having accomplished any material purpose, and from
that time the Pope became ever colder and colder toward him.
The cardinal soon perceived that he could no longer decide, as
he had hitherto done, who should or should not be about the

[6] " L'Evesque d'Angoulesme au Roy, 11 Juin, 1558," Ribier, ii. 745. The Pope has said: " That you, sire, must not degenerate from your predecessors, who were always conservators and defend-ers of the holy see; while King Philip, on the contrary, was descended of a race who desired to destroy and con-found it utterly."

person of his uncle; he could no more exclude those who were inimical to himself, and rumors reached the pontiff, by which his unfavorable impressions of former days were revived; a serious illness once seized the cardinal, and on this occasion his uncle paid him a visit unexpectedly, when he found certain persons with him whose reputation was of the worst possible character. "Old people," said Paul, "are mistrustful, and I there saw things that opened a wide field before me." It is obvious that only very slight provocation was needed to arouse the storm within him, and this was presented by an occurrence otherwise of little importance. In the new year's night of 1559, there was a tumult in the streets, during which the young Cardinal Monte, that favorite of Pope Julius before mentioned, drew his sword. This was related to the pontiff the very next morning, and he felt greatly offended with the Cardinal Caraffa for not naming the circumstance to himself. He waited some days, but finding no word said, he then expressed his displeasure. The court, ever delighted with change, caught eagerly at this mark of disgrace. The Florentine ambassador, on whom the Caraffas had inflicted mortifications innumerable, now made his way to the presence, and uttered the most bitter complaints. The Marchese della Valle, one of the pontiff's family, but who had never been allowed access to him, found means to get a note placed in his breviary, in which certain of his nephew's misdeeds were described; "if his holiness should desire further explanations," said this paper, "he has but to sign his name." The Pope gave the required signature, and the promised information did not fail to appear. Thus, well provided with causes for resentment, Paul appeared on the ninth of January at the assembly of the Inquisition. He first spoke of that nocturnal riot, reproved Cardinal Monte with extreme severity, and repeatedly thundered forth "Reform! Reform!" The cardinals, usually so silent, had this time the courage to speak. "Holy father," said Cardinal Pacheco, interrupting the sovereign, "reform must first of all begin among ourselves!" The Pope was silenced; those words struck him to the heart; the half-formed convictions that had been gradually gaining power within him, were at once changed to palpable certainty; he said nothing more of Cardinal Monte's offences, but shut himself up in his apartment, burning with

ge, and thinking only of his nephews. Giving immediate
irections that no order proceeding from Cardinal Caraffa
ould be complied with, he sent to demand that minister's
apers. Cardinal Vitellozzo Vitelli, who was believed to be
a possession of all the Caraffa secrets, was immediately sum-
oned, and compelled to swear that he would disclose all he
new. Camillo Orsino was called from his palace in the Cam-
agna, for the same purpose. Those of the more austere party,
ho had long remarked the proceedings of the nephews with
isapproval, now made themselves heard. The old Theatine,
on Geremia, who was held to be a saint, passed long hours
ith his holiness, who was made acquainted with circumstances
at he had never suspected, and which equally excited his detes-
tion and horror. He fell into a state of pitiable agitation,
ould neither eat nor sleep, and passed ten days consumed by
ver, resulting from distress of mind. At length he was re-
olved; and then was seen to occur an event forever memorable,
pope, with self-inflicted violence, tearing asunder the ties that
ound him to his kindred. On the twenty-seventh of January
consistory was summoned, wherein the evil lives of his
ephews were denounced with passionate emotion by the griev-
g pontiff, who called God and the world to bear witness that
e had never known of these misdoings, but had been con-
antly deceived by those around him. He deprived the accused
f all their offices, and condemned them to banishment, together
ith their families. The mother of the nephews, seventy years
ld, bent with age, and sinking beneath her infirmities, en-
eated for them, throwing herself at the Pope's feet as he en-
red the palace; but, though she was herself blameless, he
assed her by with harsh words. The young Marchesa Monte-
ello arrived in Rome from Naples at this time; she found her
alace closed against her, at the inns they refused to receive her,
e went from door to door in the rainy night, and could find
o shelter, until in a remote quarter, to which no order had
een sent, an innkeeper was found who permitted her to take
efuge beneath his roof. Cardinal Caraffa vainly offered to
onstitute himself the Pope's prisoner, and required to have his
onduct investigated. Paul commanded the Swiss guard to
pel not himself only, but all who, having been in his service,
ould venture to approach the palace. He made but one ex-

ception; this was in favor of the young man, the son of Montorio, whom he loved greatly, and made cardinal in his eighteenth year; this youth he permitted to remain about his person, and take part in his devotional exercises; but he was never allowed to name his banished family, still less to implore their forgiveness; he dared not even hold the slightest intercourse with his father. The misfortunes of his house affected him all the more painfully from this restraint, and the suffering that he was not permitted to express in words, was yet manifest in his face, and legible in his whole person.[7]

And would it not be supposed that occurrences of this character must react on the mind of the pontiff?

He proceeded as though nothing had happened. Immediately after having pronounced sentence against his kindred with stormy eloquence in the consistory, he betook himself to other business, and while most of the cardinals were paralyzed by fear and astonishment, the pontiff betrayed no emotion. The foreign ambassadors were amazed by this coolness of demeanor. "In the midst of changes so unexpected and so complete," they remarked, "surrounded by ministers and servants all new and strange, he maintains himself steadfastly, unbending and imperturbable; he feels no compassion, and seems not even to retain a remembrance of his ruined house." Henceforth it was to a totally different passion that he surrendered the guidance of his life.

This change was most certainly of the highest importance, and of ever memorable effect. His hatred to the Spaniards, and the hope of becoming the liberator of Italy, had hurried even Paul IV into designs and practices utterly worldly; these had led him to the endowment of his kinsmen with the lands of the Church, and had caused the elevation of a mere soldier to the administration even of ecclesiastical affairs. They had plunged him into deadly feuds and sanguinary hostilities. Events had compelled him to abandon that hope, to suppress that hatred, and then were his eyes gradually opened to the reprehensible conduct of those about him. Against these of-

[7] Much valuable information as to these events may be found in Pallavicini, still more in Bromato. In the Berlin "Informationi" there is also, vol. viii., a "Diario d'alcune attioni più notabili nel Pontificato di Paolo IV. l'anno 1558, sino alla sua morte" (beginning from September 10, 1558). This was not known to either of the above writers; it was composed from personal observation, and has supplied me with much information altogether new.

fenders, after a painful combat with himself, his stern justice prevailed, he shook them off, and from that hour his early plans of reformation were resumed, he began to reign in the manner that had at first been expected from him. And now, with that impetuous energy which he had previously displayed in his enmities, and in the conduct of his wars, he turned to the reform of the State, and above all to that of the Church.

All secular offices, from the highest to the lowest, were transferred to other hands. The existing podestas and governors lost their places, and the manner in which this was effected was occasionally very singular. In Perugia, for example, the newly appointed governor arrived in the night; without waiting for daylight, he caused the anziani to be called together, produced his credentials, and commanded them forthwith to arrest their former governor, who was present. From time immemorial, there had been no pope who governed without nepotism: Paul IV now showed this example. The places hitherto monopolized by his kinsmen were bestowed on Cardinal Carpi, Camillo Orsino who had held so extensive a power under Paul III, and others. Nor were the persons only changed, the whole system and character of the administration were changed also. Important sums were economized, and taxes to a proportional amount were remitted; the pontiff established a chest, of which he only held the key, for the purpose of receiving all complaints that any man should desire to make; he demanded a daily report from the governor. The public business in general was conducted with great circumspection; nor were any of the old abuses permitted to remain.

Amidst all the commotions prevailing through the early part of his pontificate, Paul IV had never lost sight of his reforming projects; he now resumed them with earnest zeal and undivided attention. A more severe discipline was introduced into the churches: he forbade all begging; even the collection of alms for masses, hitherto made by the clergy, was discontinued; and such pictures as were not, by their subjects, appropriate to the Church, he removed. A medal was struck in his honor, representing Christ driving the money-changers from the temple. All monks who had deserted their monasteries were expelled from the city and States of the Church; the court was enjoined to keep the regular fasts, and all were com-

manded to solemnize Easter by receiving the Lord's Supper.
The cardinals were even compelled to occasional preaching, and
Paul himself preached! Many abuses that had been profitable
to the Curia he did his best to set aside. Of marriage dispensations, or of the resources they furnished to the treasury, he
would not even hear mention. A host of places that, up to his
time, had been constantly sold, even those of the clerks of the
chamber [8] (chiericati di camera), he would now have disposed
of according to merit only. Still more rigidly did he insist on
the worth and clerical endowments of all on whom he bestowed
the purely ecclesiastical employments. He would no longer endure those compacts by which one man had hitherto been allowed to enjoy the revenues of an office, while he made over its
duties to another, by whom, for some mean hire, they were performed, well or ill, as might chance. He had also formed the
design of reinstating the bishops in many rights which had been
wrongfully withheld from them; and considered it highly
culpable that everything should be absorbed by Rome which
could in any way be made to yield either profit or influence.[9]

Nor were the reforms of Paul confined to the mere abolition
of abuses. Not content with a negative effect only, he proceeded
to practical amendments. The services of the Church were performed with increased pomp; it is to him we are indebted for
the rich ornaments of the Sixtine chapel, and for the solemn
representation of the holy sepulchre.[10] There is an ideal of the
modern Catholic service of the altar, full of dignity, devotion,
and splendor: this it was that floated before the eyes of Paul,
and which he would fain have realized.

He permitted no day to pass over, as he boasts, without the
promulgation of some edict tending to restore the Church to its
original purity. Many of his decrees present the outlines of
those ordinances which were afterward sanctioned by the Council of Trent.[1]

[8] Caracciolo, " Vita di Paolo IV.,"
MS., alludes particularly to these. The
Pope said " that such employments of
justice and government should be given
to those who would perform the duties,
and not be sold to people who would
only want to get back their money from
them."
[9] Bromato, ii. 483.
[10] Mocenigo, " Relatione di 1560 ":
" This pontiff proceeded so gravely

and with so much dignity in the divine
services that he seemed a worthy vicar
of Christ; in matters of religion, also,
greater diligence could not be desired."
[1] Mocenigo: Pope Paul was continually making some new reform, and
always said he had others prepared, so
that there would be little opportunity
and still less necessity for holding a
council.

In the course now adopted, Paul displayed, as might have een expected, all that inflexibility of nature peculiar to him.

Above all other institutions, he favored that of the Inquisition, which he had himself re-established. The days appointed for he "segnatura" and the consistory he would often suffer to ass unnoticed; but never did he miss the Thursday, which was that set apart for the congregation of the Inquisition, and when it assembled before him. The powers of this office he de-ired to see exercised with the utmost rigor. He subjected new lasses of offence to its jurisdiction, and conferred on it the arbarous prerogative of applying torture for the detection of ccomplices. He permitted no respect of persons; the most istinguished nobles were summoned before this tribunal, and ardinals, such as Morone and Foscherari, were now thrown into prison, because certain doubts had occurred to him as to the soundness of their opinions, although these very men had een formerly appointed to examine the contents, and decide the orthodoxy, of important books—the " Spiritual Exercises " f Loyola, for example. It was Paul IV by whom the festival of t. Domenico was established, in honor of that great inquisitor.

Thus did a rigid austerity and earnest zeal for the restoration f primitive habits become the prevailing tendency of the opedom.

Paul IV seemed almost to have forgotten that he had ever ursued other purposes than those that now occupied him; the memory of past times seemed extinguished; he lived and moved in his reforms and his Inquisition, gave laws, imprisoned, excom-municated, and held *autos-da-fé;* these occupations filled up his fe. At length, when laid prostrate by disease, such as would ave caused death even to a younger man, he called his cardinals bout him, commended his soul to their prayers, and the holy ee with the Inquisition, to their earnest care. Once more would he fain have collected his energies: he sought to raise imself, but the disease prevailed; his strength had failed him —he fell back and expired (August 18, A.D. 1559).

In one respect, at least, are these determined and passionate haracters more fortunate than men of feebler mould; they re, perhaps, blinded by the force of their feelings—the vio-ence of their prejudices, but they are also steeled by this force; this violence it is that renders them invincible.

The Roman people did not forget what they had suffered under Paul IV so readily as he had done—they could not forgive him the war he had brought on the State; nor, though they abhorred his nephews, did their disgrace suffice to the resentment of the multitude. On his death being made known, large crowds assembled in the capital, and resolved that, as he had not deserved well either of Rome, or of the world, so would they destroy his monuments. Others attacked the buildings of the Inquisition, set fire to them, and roughly handled the servants of the holy office; they even threatened to burn the Dominican convent of Maria alla Minerva. The Colonnas, the Orsini, Cesarini, Massimi, and other nobles whom Paul had mortally offended, took part in these tumults. The statue that had been erected to this Pope was torn from its pedestal, broken to pieces, and the head, bearing the triple crown, was dragged through the streets.[2]

It would, nevertheless, have been fortunate for the papal see had it met with no more serious reaction against the enterprises of Paul IV than was intimated by this outbreak.

Section IV.—Remarks on the Progress of Protestantism During the Pontificate of Paul IV

It will have become obvious to the reader that the earlier dissensions between the papacy and the imperial or Spanish power, had contributed more than any other external cause to the establishment of Protestantism in Germany. Yet a second breach was not avoided, and this produced results still more comprehensive and important.

The recall of the papal troops from the imperial army by Paul III, and his transfer of the council from Trent to Bologna, may be considered as the preliminary steps. Their importance was at once made evident: there was no impediment to the subjugation of the Protestants so effectual as that presented by the policy, active and passive, of Paul III at that period.

[2] Mocenigo: "Viddi il popolo correr in furia verso la casa di Ripetta deputata per le cose dell' Inquisitione, metter a sacco tutta la robba ch' era dentro, si di vittualie come d'altra robba, che la maggior parte era del Revmo. Cl. Alessandrino sommo Inquisitore, trattar male con bastonate e ferite tutti i ministri dell' Inquisitione, levar le scritture gettandole a refuso per la strada, e finalmente poner foco in quella casa. I frati di S. Domenico erano in tant' odio a quel popolo che in ogni modo volevan abbruciar il monastero della Minerva." (See the text.) He goes on to declare that the nobles were principally to blame in this affair, and says that similar outbreaks occurred in Perugia.

The great and permanent results of these measures were, however, not obvious until after the death of the pontiff. That connection with France, into which he led his nephews, occasioned a universal war; and in this the German Protestants not only achieved that memorable victory by which they secured themselves forever from the Pope, Emperor, and council, but also gained important progress for their opinions by the contact into which the Protestant soldiers, who fought on both sides, were forced with those of France and the Netherlands. This contact caused the extensive acceptance of the new doctrines in those countries, their introduction being favored by the prevalence of a confusion, occasioned by the war, which rendered vigilant precaution impossible.

Paul IV ascended the papal throne. It was for him to have taken a clear view of things as existing before his eyes, and, above all, his first efforts should have been turned to the restoration of peace: but with all the blindness of passion, he plunged himself into the tumult, and it thus came to pass that he, the most furious of zealots, was in fact a more effectual promoter of that Protestantism, which he so abhorred and persecuted, than any one of his predecessors.

Let us examine the influence of his conduct on England alone.

The first victory gained by the new opinions in that country was for a long time incomplete: nothing further was required than a retrogression of the government, and the presence of a Catholic sovereign would at once have determined the Parliament to subject the national church once more to the dominion of the Pope—but then the latter must proceed cautiously; he must not wage open war with those innovations that had arisen from the present and recent state of things. This had been at once perceived by Julius III. His first nuncio having instantly remarked the potency of those interests that were connected with the confiscated property of the Church,[1] he magnanimously resolved to make no effort for its restitution. Indeed, the legate was not permitted to land on the English soil until he had given satisfactory assurances in this respect. It was to these declarations that his extensive influence was

[1] "Lettere di Mr. Henrico, Nov. 1553," in a MS. entitled "Lettere e Negotiati di Polo," in which there is much besides of importance to this history. See also Pallavicini as to this matter, xiii. 9, 411.

attributable—to them was he indebted for the principal part of
his success.[2] This legate, with whom we are already acquainted,
was Reginald Pole—the man, above all others, best fitted to
labor successfully for the restoration of Catholicism in England—a native of the country, of high rank, acceptable equally
to the Queen, the nobles, and the people; moderate, intelligent,
and raised far above all suspicion of sordid or unworthy purposes. Affairs proceeded most prosperously, as might have
been expected from such guidance. The accession of Paul IV
to the papal throne was followed by the arrival of English
ambassadors, who assured him of that nation's obedience.

Thus Paul had not to acquire the allegiance of England, he
had merely to retain it. Let us see by what measures he sought
to effect this.

First, he declared the restitution of all church property to
be an indispensable duty, the neglect of which entails everlasting damnation; he next attempted to re-establish the tax
called "Peter's pence."[3] But, apart from these ill-considered
measures, could he have adopted any method better calculated
to prevent the return of the English to the Catholic pale than
the indulgence of his rancorous hostility to Philip II, who, if
a Spanish prince, was also King of England? In the battle
of St. Quintin, so influential in Italy as well as France, English soldiers assisted to gain the victory. Finally, he persecuted Cardinal Pole, whom he never could endure, deprived
him of his dignity as legate, an office that no man had ever
borne with greater advantage to the Holy See, and appointed
an aged inefficient monk to succeed him, whose principal recom-
mendation was that he shared the prejudices of the pontiff.[4]
Had it been the purpose of Paul to impede the work of restoration, he could not have adopted more effectual measures.

There can be no wonder that the opposing tendencies should
immediately act with renewed violence on the unexpected
death of the Queen and cardinal. This result was powerfully
accelerated by the religious persecutions, which Pole had
condemned, but which his bigoted antagonists approved and
promoted.

[2] He did not hesitate to acknowledge the right of those in possession.—"Letteræ Dispensatoriæ Clis. Poli." "Concilia M. Britanniæ," iv. 112.
[3] He was exclusively occupied with these ideas. He published his bull.

"Rescissio Alienationum" (Bullarium iv. 4, 319), in which he annulled all alienation of church property without any exception.
[4] Godwin's "Annales Angliæ," etc., p. 456,

Once more had the Pope an opportunity of deciding the question whether England should be Catholic or Protestant, and this decision demanded all the more serious consideration from the fact that it must inevitably affect Scotland also. In that country likewise the religious parties were in fierce contest, and accordingly as matters should be regulated in England would assuredly be the future condition of Scotland.

How significant then was the fact that Elizabeth showed herself by no means decidedly Protestant in the beginning of her reign,[5] and that she caused her accession to be instantly notified to the Pope. There were even negotiations in progress for her marriage with Philip II, and the world of that day believed this event very probable. One would have thought that no state of things could be more satisfactory to the pontiff.

But Paul was incapable of moderation; he returned a repulsive and contemptuous reply to the ambassador of Elizabeth: "First of all," said he, "she must submit her claims to the decision of our judgment."

We are not to believe the pontiff moved to this entirely by his sense of what was due to the dignity of the Apostolic See—other motives were in action. The French desired to prevent this marriage from national jealousy, and contrived to persuade Paul, through the pious Theatines, that Elizabeth was entirely Protestant at heart, and that no good could result from such a marriage.[6] The Guises were particularly interested for the success of this affair. Should the claims of Elizabeth be rejected by the Holy See, the next title to the English crown would be possessed by their sister's daughter, Mary Stuart, dauphiness of France and Queen of Scotland. Could her right be established the Guises might hope to rule in her name over all the three kingdoms. And, in fact, that princess did assume the English arms. She dated her edicts with the year of her reign over England and Ireland, while preparations for war were commenced in the Scottish ports.[7]

Thus, had Elizabeth not been disposed to the opinions of the Protestants, the force of circumstances would have com-

[5] Nares, also, in his "Memoirs of Burleigh," considers her religious principles "at first liable to some doubts."
[6] Private narrative of Thuanus.
[7] In Forbes's "Transactions" there is a "Responsio ad Petitiones D. Glasion. et Episc. Aquilani," by Cecil, which sets forth all these motives in the most lively manner.

pelled her to adopt that party. This she did with the most
decided resolution, and succeeded in obtaining a Parliament
having a Protestant majority,[8] by which all those changes that
constitute the essential character of the English Church were
in a few months effected.

The influence of this turn of things necessarily affected
Scotland also. In that country the French-Catholic interest
was resisted by a party that was at once Protestant and
national; Elizabeth lost no time in allying herself with this,
and was even exhorted to the measure by the Spanish ambassador himself.[9] The treaty of Berwick, which she concluded
with the Scottish opposition, gave the predominance in Scotland to the Protestants. Before Mary Stuart could land in
her own kingdom, she was compelled not only to renounce her
claim to the crown of England, but even to ratify the acts of
a Parliament guided by Protestant influence, and one of which
forbade the performance of mass under penalty of death.

To a reaction against the designs of France then, which the
proceedings of the Pope had favored and promoted, was in a
great measure to be attributed the triumph gained to Protestantism in Great Britain, and by which its ascendancy there
was secured forever.

There is no doubt that the inward impulses of those who
held Protestant opinions had their origin in causes much more
deeply seated than any connected with political movements,
but for the most part the outbreak, progress, and decision of
the religious struggle very closely coincided with the various
contingencies of politics.

In Germany, also, a measure adopted by Paul IV was in
one respect of peculiar importance; incited by his old aversion
to the house of Austria, he had opposed the transfer of the
imperial crown, which obliged Ferdinand I to be more attentive than he had hitherto been to the maintenance of friendly
relations with his Protestant allies; the affairs of Germany
were thenceforward governed by a union of the moderate
princes belonging to both confessions, and under their influence it was that the transferrence of ecclesiastical foundations

[8] Neal, " History of the Puritans," i. 126: " The court took such measures about elections as seldom fail of suc- cess."

[9] Camden, " Rerum Anglicarum An- nales," p. 37.

in Lower Germany to Protestant administrations was eventually accomplished.

We are warranted in declaring that the Popedom seemed destined to suffer no injury, to which it had not itself conduced in one way or another by its tendency to interference in political affairs.

And now, if we survey the world from the heights of Rome, how enormous were the losses sustained by the Catholic faith! Scandinavia and Great Britain had wholly departed; Germany was almost entirely Protestant; Poland and Hungary were in fierce tumult of opinion; in Geneva was to be found as important a central point for the schismatics of the Latin nations and of the West as was Wittenberg for those of Germanic race and the East, while numbers were already gathering beneath the banners of Protestantism in France and the Netherlands.

Only one hope now remained to the Catholic confession. The symptoms of dissent that had appeared in Spain and Italy had been totally suppressed, and a restorative strictness had become manifest in all ecclesiastical institutions. The administration of Paul had been doubtless most injurious from its secular policy, but it had at least achieved the introduction of a determined spirit of reform into the court and palace. The question now was, would this have force to maintain itself there; and, in that case, would it then proceed to pervade and unite the whole Catholic world?

Section V.—Pius IV

We are told that Alessandro Farnese, making one at a banquet of cardinals, gave a wreath to a boy who possessed the art of improvisation to the lyre, desiring him to offer it to that one among them who should one day be pope. The boy, Silvio Antoniano, afterward a distinguished man, and himself a cardinal, went instantly to Giovanni Angelo Medici; and, first singing his praises, presented to him the wreath. This Medici was the successor of Paul, and took the name of Pius IV.[1]

[1] Nicius Erythræus relates this anecdote in the article on Antoniano, "Pinacotheca," p. 37. Mazzuchelli also has it. The election took place on December 26, 1559.

He was of mean birth. His father Bernardino had settled
in Milan, where he had acquired a small property by government contracts.[2] The sons had nevertheless to do the best
they could for their own support: the elder, Giangiacomo, betook himself to the trade of arms, and at first entered the
service of a nobleman: the second, Giovan Angelo, devoted
himself to study, but with very slender means. The origin of
their prosperity was as follows: Giangiacomo, naturally reckless and enterprising, had rendered himself useful to the then
rulers of Milan by ridding them of one of the Visconti family,
called Monsignorino, who was their rival; but no sooner was
this murder accomplished than those who devised it were
anxious to be delivered from the tool they had employed. To
this end they sent the young man to the castle of Mus, on the
lake of Como, with a letter to the governor containing orders
for his own immediate death; but Giangiacomo felt suspicions
of evil, opened the letter, saw what was prepared for him, and
at once resolved on the measures to be taken. He gathered a
number of trusty comrades, gained admission to the castle by
means of the letter he bore, and succeeded in taking possession
of it. From that time he assumed the position of an independent prince. Secure in his fortress, he kept the Milanese,
Swiss, and Venetians, who were his neighbors, in perpetual
activity by his ceaseless incursions. After a time, he took the
white cross and entered the imperial service. He received the
title of Marchese di Marignano, served as chief of artillery in
the war against the Lutherans, and commanded the Emperor's
forces at Sienna.[3] His shrewdness was not inferior to his
daring; his undertakings were invariably successful, but he
was altogether without pity; many a wretched peasant, who
was attempting to carry provisions into Sienna, did he destroy
with his iron staff. Scarcely was there a tree far and near on
which he had not caused some one of them to be hanged. It
was computed that he had put to death at least five thousand
men. He took Sienna, and founded a considerable house.

The advance of his brother, Giovan Angelo, had kept pace
with his own. This last took the degree of doctor-in-law, and

[2] Hieronymo Soranzo, " Relatione di
Roma ": " Bernardino, the father of
his holiness, was considered an excellent man, and very industrious; though
poor and of low condition he came to
Milan, and set himself to farming the
taxes."

[3] Ripamonte, " Historia Urbis Mediolani." " Natalis Comes Hist."

gained some reputation as a jurist; he then purchased an office in Rome, and rapidly acquired the confidence of Paul III. When the Marchese di Marignano, his brother, was married to an Orsina, the sister of Pier Luigi Farnese's wife,[4] he was himself made cardinal. After this we find him in the administration of papal cities, charged with the conduct of political negotiations, and more than once intrusted with the commissariat of papal armies. Cardinal Medici ever proved himself discreet, intelligent, and kindly disposed; but Paul IV detested him, and once burst into violent invectives against him in full consistory. Medici then thought it best to leave Rome, and resided sometimes at the baths of Pisa, sometimes in Milan, where he raised many splendid buildings, beguiling his exile by literary occupations, and by the exercise of a beneficence so magnificent as to procure him the name of " Father of the Poor." It was very probably the extreme contrast he exhibited to Paul IV that principally contributed to his election.

This contrast was indeed more than commonly striking.

Paul IV was a Neapolitan, highly born, of the anti-Austrian faction, a zealot, a monk, and an inquisitor. Pius IV was the son of a Milanese tax-gatherer, firmly attached to the house of Austria, by his brother and some other German connections; a lawyer, a man of the world, and fond of enjoyment. Paul IV stood aloof and inaccessible, never deposing his majesty for even the least dignified occasions. Pius was all cordiality and condescension. He was seen daily in the streets on foot or on horseback, and sometimes almost without attendants; he conversed freely with all. The Venetian despatches make us perfectly acquainted with him.[5] The ambassadors find him writing or transacting business in a large cool room; he rises and walks with them up and down this hall; or he is perhaps about to visit the Belvedere; he seats himself without laying the stick from his hand, hears what they have to say, and continues his walk in their company. While

[4] Soranzo: " Nato, 1499, took his degree of doctor, 1525, vivendo in studio così strettamente che il Pasqua suo medico, che stava con lui a dozena, l'accommodò un gran tempo del suo servitore e di qualche altra cosa necessaria. Del 1527 comprò un protonotariato. Servendo il Cl. Farnese [Ripamonte mentions his good understanding with Paul III] colla più assidua diligenza, s'andò mettendo in anzi: ebbe diversi impieghi, dove acquistò nome di persona integra e giusta e di natura officiosa." The marriage of the marquis follows, with the promise of a cardinalate to himself.

[5] " Ragguagli dell' Ambasciatore Veneto da Roma, 1561." By Marco Antonio Amulio (Mula, Informatt. Pol., xxxvii.

treating them with this pleasant intimacy, however, he desired
to meet respect and politeness in return. The clever expedients
occasionally proposed to him by the Venetians were sure to
elicit his smiles and praises; but all his fidelity to the Austrian
cause could not prevent him from disliking the formal imperious manners of the Spanish envoy Vargas. Unwilling to
be encumbered with details, which instantly wearied him, his
attention was readily given to the really important matter, and
while this was kept in view he was always good-tempered
and most easy to deal with. On such occasions he would pour
forth a thousand friendly protestations; declare himself to be
by nature a lover of justice, and to hate bad men with all his
heart; that he would not willingly restrict the freedom of any
man, would fain show kindness and good-will toward all, but
most especially was resolved to labor heartily for the good of
the Church, and trusted in God that he might accomplish something useful to its interests. How easily can we bring him
before us; a portly old man, still active enough to reach his
country-house before sunrise. His countenance was cheerful,
his eyes were bright and keen; lively conversation, the pleasures of the table, and perhaps a harmless jest—these were his
recreations: recovering once from an illness that had been
thought dangerous, he mounted his horse at the first possible
moment, rode away to a house where he had dwelt in his cardinalate, and stepping firmly up and down the stairs, "No,
no," he exclaims, "we don't mean to die just yet!"

But this pontiff, so joyous, of so worldly a temperament—
was he precisely the head of the Church required under the
difficult circumstances of the moment? Was it not to be feared
that he would depart from the course so lately entered on by
his predecessor? I will not say that his character might not
have led him to do this, yet in fact the event was not so.

He had certainly no love for the Inquisition in his heart.
The monkish severity of its proceedings was most uncongenial
to his nature; he seldom or never appeared in the congregation, but neither did he seek to lessen the power of its officers.
He declared himself to understand nothing of the matter, said
that he was no theologian, and permitted them to exercise all
the influence they possessed under Paul IV.[6]

---

[6] Soranzo: "It is well known that the pontiff dislikes the great severity with which the inquisitors handle those accused. He makes it known that it

He made a fearful example of the nephews of his predecessor. The atrocities committed by the Duke of Palliano, even after his fall, among others that of murdering his wife in a fit of jealousy, facilitated the efforts of their enemies, who thirsted for revenge; a criminal process was commenced against them, and they were accused of the most detestable crimes; robberies, forgeries, and assassinations, together with the most tyrannical abuse of the powers intrusted to them, and the most systematic duplicity practised against their aged uncle, the late pontiff. Their defence is still extant, and is not altogether without an appearance of justification.[7] But their accusers prevailed. The Pope caused all the evidence to be read before him; with this he was occupied in the consistory from early morning till late at night, when the accused were condemned, and received sentence of death. These were the cardinal and the Duke of Palliano, with Count Aliffe and Leonardo di Cardine, two of their nearest connections. Montebello and some others had before taken flight. The cardinal had perhaps expected banishment, but had never thought of death. He received the announcement of his sentence in the morning before he had risen: when it was no longer possible to doubt the fact, he buried his face in the bed-clothes for a time, then raising his head he clasped his hands together, uttering those words that, while sounding like resignation, are in fact but the expression of the deepest despair from the lips of an Italian: "Bene! Pazienza"—"It is well! let us take patience!" His usual confessor was not permitted to attend him, but to the one accorded he had as may be imagined much to say, and his confession continued a long time. "Make an end, Monsignore," exclaimed an officer of police, "we have other affairs to settle."

And so perished the nephews of Paul IV. They were the last who aspired to independent principalities, and excited general commotions for the furtherance of their own purposes in politics. From the time of Sixtus IV we have Girolamo

would better please him were they rather to proceed with gentlemanly courtesy than monkish harshness; yet he either will not or dare not oppose their decisions."

[7] Bromato gives particular details of these events, which he takes principally from Nares. In the Informatt we also find the letters of Mula; for example, July 19, 1560: The occurrence of the death of the Caraffas, with the declaration, and the manner in which they died. "La Morte de Cl. Caraffa" (Library at Venice, vi. n. 39) is the MS. that Bromato had before him, in addition to that of Nares.

Riario, Cæsar Borgia, Lorenzo de' Medici, Pier Luigi Farnese, and the Caraffas, who, as we said, were the last. The kindred of popes have made themselves conspicuous in later times, but in a totally different manner. The old forms of nepotism have appeared no more.

How could Pius IV, for example, have conferred on his own family a power, for the exercise of which he had so heavily visited the Caraffas? He was, besides, disposed by the peculiar activity of his character to the retention of affairs in his own hands; all important business was carefully examined by himself; he weighed the evidence, and determined by his own judgment. He was considered to rely too little rather than too much on the aid of others. This disposition was, perhaps, confirmed by the fact that of his two nephews, the one, Federigo Borromeo, whom he might have wished to advance, died young; the other, Carlo Borromeo, was not the man for worldly aggrandizement, and would never have accepted it. This last, indeed, regarded his connection with the pontiff, and the contact into which it brought him with the most weighty affairs of the government, not as involving the right to any personal advantage or indulgence, but rather as imposing duties that demanded his most assiduous care. To these, then, did he devote himself with equal modesty and perseverance; earnestly were his best energies applied to the administration of the state; he gave audience with the most unwearied patience. It was for the more effectual performance of his duties that he called around him that "collegium" of eight learned men, whence was afterward formed the important institution of the "Consulta." He lent valuable aid to the Pope, and is that same Borromeo who was afterward canonized. No life could be more noble and blameless than was that of this cardinal. "In so far as we know," says Geronimo Soranzo, "he is without spot or blemish, so religious a life and so pure an example, leave the most exacting nothing to demand. It is greatly to his praise that in the bloom of youth, nephew to a Pope whose favor he entirely possessed, and living in a court where every kind of pleasure invites him to its enjoyment, he yet leads so exemplary a life." His recreation was to gather round him in the evenings a few learned and distinguished men; with these he would at first discuss profane literature, but from

THE HISTORY OF THE POPES

Epictetus and the Stoics, whom Borromeo, then young, did
not despise, the conversation even in those, his leisure moments, soon turned to theological subjects.[8] If a fault could
be found in him, it was not of deficiency in uprightness of
purpose, or steadiness of application, but perhaps in some degree as regarded his talents. His servants indeed thought it
a defect that they could no longer count on those rich marks
of favor which were conferred in former times by the papal
nephews.

And thus did the qualities of the nephew make amends for
whatsoever might be thought wanting by the more severely
disposed in the character of the uncle. In any case, all things
proceeded in their established course; affairs spiritual and
temporal were conducted with good order and due attention
to the interests of the Church, nor was the work of reform
neglected. Pius admonished the bishops publicly to reside in
their dioceses, and some were seen at once to kiss his foot and
take their leave. Ideas that have once become widely prevalent assume an irresistible force of coercion. The seriousness
of spirit now prevailing in religious matters had gained the
mastery in Rome, and the Pope himself could no longer depart
from its dictates.

But if the somewhat worldly dispositions of Pius IV were
not permitted to impede the restoration of strict discipline to
the ecclesiastical habits, it is certain that they contributed infinitely toward the composing of that discord, and the removal
of those animosities by which the Catholic world had been so
long afflicted.

It had been the full conviction of Paul IV that a pope was
created for the subjugation of emperors and kings; thus it
was that he plunged himself into so many wars and enmities.
Pius perceived the error of this notion all the more clearly
because it was committed by his immediate predecessor, and
one to whom he felt that he was in many ways directly con-
trasted. "Thereby did we lose England," would he say—
"England that we might have retained with perfect ease, had
Cardinal Pole been supported in his measures; thus too has
Scotland been torn from us; for during the wars excited by

[8] These are the "Noctes Vaticanæ," mentioned by Glussianus, "Vita Caroli
Borromei," i. iv. 22.

these severe proceedings the doctrines of Germany made their
way into France." He, on the contrary, was desirous of peace
above all things; even with the Protestants he would not
willingly have war. An ambassador from Savoy came solicit-
ing his aid for an attack on Geneva. He repeatedly interrupted his speech: "What sort of times are these," said he,
"for making such proposals?" He declared that nothing was
so needful to him as peace.[9] Fain would he have been on
good terms with all the world. He dispensed his ecclesiastical
favors liberally; and when compelled to refuse anything, always did so with gentleness and consideration. It was his
conviction that the authority of the papacy could no lcnger
subsist without the support of the temporal sovereigns, and
this he did not seek to conceal.

In the latter part of the pontificate of Paul IV, a council
was again universally demanded; and it is certain that Pius IV
would have found it very difficult to resist this call. He
could not urge the pretext of war, as had previously been
done, since peace was at length established throughout Europe.
A general council was indeed imperatively needful to his own
interests, for the French were threatening to convoke a national council, which might possibly have led to a schism. But,
apart from all this, my own impression is, that he honestly desired this measure. Let us hear what he says himself of the
matter: "We desire this council," he declares, "we wish it
earnestly, and we would have it to be universal. Were it
otherwise, we could throw obstacles before the world that
might hinder it for years, but we desire on the contrary to
remove all hinderances. Let what requires reformation be reformed, even though it be our own person and our own affairs.
If we have any other thought than to do God service, then
may God visit us accordingly." He sometimes complained
that the sovereigns did not duly support him in so great an
undertaking. One morning the Venetian ambassador found
him still in bed, disabled by gout, but deeply cogitating this
momentous affair. "Our intentions are upright," he remarked
to the ambassador, "but we are alone." "I could not but com-

[9] Mula, February 14, 1561. Pius requested him to say, "That we desire
to remain at peace; we have no idea of
these fancies of the Duke of Savoy;
this is no time for an undertaking
against Geneva, or for the appointment
of generals; write that we are determined to remain at peace."

passionate him," observes the Venetian, "seeing him thus in his bed, and hearing him complain that he was alone to bear so heavy a burden;" the affair was nevertheless making progress. On January 18, 1562, so many bishops and delegates had assembled in Trent, that the twice-interrupted council could for the third time be opened. Pius IV had the most important share in bringing this about.

"Without doubt," says Girolamo Soranzo, who does not usually take part with this pontiff, "his holiness has in this matter given proof of all the zeal that was to be expected from so exalted a pastor; he has neglected nothing that could forward so holy and so needful a work."

Section VI.—Later Sittings of the Council of Trent

How materially had the state of the world altered since the first sittings of this council! No more had the Pope now to fear lest a mighty emperor should avail himself of its powers to render himself lord paramount over the Holy See. Ferdinand I was entirely divested of influence in Italy, nor was any important error as to essential points of doctrine to be apprehended.[1] These dogmas, retaining the form they had received from the first sittings of the council, though not yet entirely developed, had become predominant throughout the greater part of the Catholic world. To reunite the Protestants with the Church was no longer a thing that could be brought into question. In Germany they had now gained a position wholly unassailable. In the north their ideas as to ecclesiastical affairs had entered even into the civil policy; a change that was in process of accomplishment in England also. When the Pope declared that the present council was but a continuation of the former one, he had in fact abandoned all hope that the event would verify his assertion, although he had succeeded in silencing the dissentient voices; for how in fact was it possible that the free Protestants should acquiesce in a council which, in its earlier edicts, had condemned the

---

[1] It was thus that Ferdinand I considered the matter. "Litteræ ad Legatos, 12 Aug. 1562," in Le Plat, "Monum. ad Hist. Conc. Tridentini," v. p. 452: "For to what end shall we discuss those dogmas, respecting which there is now no dissension among Catholics, whether princes or private individuals ?"

most essential articles of their creed?[2] Thus, the influence of the council was limited from its commencement to the now greatly contracted circle of the Catholic nations. Its purposes must be confined to the arrangements of disputes between these last and the supreme ecclesiastical authority, to the precise determination of such tenets as were not distinctly settled; and, but this most especially was its great end, to the completion of that reform in the Church which had already commenced, and to the setting forth rules of discipline that should possess universal authority.

These duties were closely limited, yet their fulfilment was surrounded by various difficulties, and there soon arose among the assembled fathers most animated controversies and disputes.

Whether the residence of bishops in their dioceses were by divine command, or prescribed simply by human authority, was a question mooted by the Spaniards; though this might seem but an idle discussion, since all agreed on the fact that residence was imperative. The Spaniards, however, further maintained the episcopal authority to be no mere emanation from that of the pontiff, but to have its origin immediately from divine appointment. Hereby they struck at the very heart's core of the whole ecclesiastical system; for by the admission of this principle, that independence of the subordinate grades in the hierarchy, which the popes had so earnestly labored to subdue, must necessarily have been restored.

Already had the council fallen into eager disputes on this topic, when the imperial ambassadors arrived. Most especially remarkable are the articles of their proposing. One of them is to the effect that, "The Pope, following the example of Christ, should humble himself, and submit to a reform in his own person, his state, and curia. The council must reform the appointment of cardinals, as well as the conclave." "How is it possible that the cardinals should choose a good pope," inquired Ferdinand, "seeing that they are not good themselves?" For the reform that should satisfy him, he desired

---

[2] The principal argument urged by the Protestants in their protest: "Causæ cur Electores Principes aliique Augustanæ confessioni adjuncti status recusent adire concilium."—Le Plat, iv. p. 57. They remark, in the first proclamation, those alarming words: "Omni suspensione sublata." They recall to mind the condemnation formerly passed on their most essential doctrines, and enlarge at great length on "What will lie concealed beneath that confirmation."

to have the resolutions proposed by the Council of Constance (but which had not received effect) as the basis; the plan to be prepared by deputations from the different countries. But, besides this, he demanded also the cup for the laity, the marriage of priests, the remission of the fasts for some of his subjects, the establishment of schools for the poor, the purification of the breviary, legends, and homilies; more intelligible catechisms, the use of German in Church singing, and the reform of the monasteries; the last for this special reason, "that their great wealth might no longer be expended in so profligate a manner."[3] Most important proposals these, without doubt, and such as, being conceded to, must have led to a thorough change in the whole system of the Church. The Emperor urged the consideration of them, in repeated letters.

Finally, the Cardinal of Lorraine appeared with the French prelates, and cordially supported the German propositions. He also demanded, most especially, that the cup should be conceded to the laity. He required the administration of all sacraments in the mother tongue, that the mass should be accompanied by preaching and instruction, and that the psalms might be allowed to be sung in the French language in full congregation; concessions from all which the most desirable results were anticipated. "We are fully assured," said the King, "that the accordance of the cup to the laity will restore quiet to many troubled consciences, will recall to the Church whole provinces now severed from her communion, and be to us an effective assistance in appeasing the troubles of our kingdom."[4] But the French were, moreover, desirous again to bring forward the decrees of the Council of Basle; and by these it was determined, that the authority of the Pope is subordinate to that of a council.

It is true that the Spaniards would in no wise support these demands of the Germans and French; the accordance of the cup to the laity, and the marriage of priests, were altogether

[3] Pallavicini has almost entirely overlooked these requirements, xvii. 1, 6. They are not to his mind, indeed they never have been made known in their proper form. They lie before us in three extracts. The first I find in P. Sarpi, lib. vi. p. 325; also, with no other variation than that they are in Latin, in Rinaldus and Goldast. The second is in Bartholomæus de Martyribus, and is somewhat more extensive. The third has been taken by Schelhorn from the papers of Staphylus. They do not strictly agree. I should think the original might be found in Vienna, and it would certainly be a remarkable document. I have adhered to the extract in Schelhorn. Le Plat gives them all, together with the reply.
[4] "Mémoire baillé à M. le Cl. de Lorraine, quand il est parti pour aller au concile de Trent."—Le Plat, iv. 562.

abhorrent in their eyes, and condemned without remission.
No agreement could possibly be arrived at in the council, as
regarded these points; all that could be gained was, the reference of such proposals to the pontiff, who was to decide on
the expediency of granting them. There were certain matters, nevertheless, as to which all three nations concurred in
opposition to the claims of the Curia. All found it insuffer-
able that the legates alone should have the right of proposing
resolutions; and not this only, but that these legates should
further require the approbation of the Pope for every decree,
and suffer none to pass but at his good pleasure. This seemed
to all an affront to the dignity of the council. "If things
are to proceed thus," said Ferdinand, "there will be two
councils; one at Trent, the other, which is indeed the true one,
in Rome."

Had the votes been taken by nations, what extraordinary
decrees might there not, in this state of opinions, have ema-
nated from this assembly!

But since this was not done, the three nations still remained
in a minority, even when their forces were united; for the
Italians were more numerous than all the rest put together,
and they supported the Curia, on which they were for the
most part dependent, with but little regard to the question of
right or wrong. This awakened much bitterness of feeling.
The French amused themselves with a story of how the Holy
Spirit had come to Trent in a cloak-bag. The Italians spoke
of Spanish leprosies, and French diseases, by which all the
faithful were infected, one after another. The Bishop of Cadiz
declared, that there had been bishops of great fame, nay
excellent fathers of the Church, who had been appointed by
no pope; on which the Italians burst forth in unanimous
vociferations, demanded his instant expulsion, and even spoke
of anathema and heresy. The " heresy " was sent them back
with interest, by the Spaniards.[5] Parties would frequently
assemble in the streets, shouting each its watchword of " Spain
Spain! " " Italy! Italy! " and blood was seen to flow on the
ground that had been consecrated to the establishment of peace

[5] Pallavicini, xv. v. 5. Paleotto, Acta:
" Alii prælati ingeminabant, clamantes,
' Exeat, exeat '; et alii, ' Anathema sit,'
ad quos Granatensis conversus respon-
dit, ' Anathema vos estis.' "—Mendham
" Memoirs of the Council of Trent," p
251.

For ten months it was found impossible even to proceed to a
session. But could this be wondered at? or is it surprising
that the first legate should dissuade the Pope from going to
Bologna, on the ground of the remarks that all would make,
if, in spite of his presence, the council could still be conducted
to no satisfactory end, but must after all be dissolved?[6] Yet
a dissolution, nay, even a suspension, or a mere translation,
which had often been thought of, would have been extremely
dangerous. In Rome they dared hope for nothing but evil;
a council was there considered much too violent a remedy for
the grievously debilitated constitution of the Church, and all
feared that ruin must ensue, both for Italy and the hierarchy.
"In the beginning of the year 1563," says Girolamo Soranzo,
"and but a few days before my departure, Cardinal Carpi,
dean of the college, and a man of great foresight, assured me,
that in the last illness he had suffered, his prayers had been
constantly that God would grant him permission to die, and
not survive to see the downfall and burial of Rome. Other
distinguished cardinals equally bemoan their evil destiny, and
clearly perceive that no hope of escape remains to them, unless the hand of God should be mercifully extended for their
protection."[7] All the misfortunes that had ever been anticipated from a council by his predecessors, were now believed
by Pius IV to hang over his own head.

The persuasion that in seasons of difficulty, and, above all,
in cases of grave errors in the Church, an assembly of her
principal shepherds will avail to remove all evil, is at once
consoling and sublime. "Let its deliberations proceed," says
Augustine, "without presumption or envy, and in Catholic
peace. Having profited by wider experience, let the concealed be made obvious, and let all that was shut up be brought
to the light of day." But, even in the earliest councils, this
ideal was far from being realized. It demanded an uprightness of purpose, a freedom from all extraneous influences—a

[6] "Lettere del Cle. di Mantua, Legato
al Concilio di Trento, scritta al Papa
Pio IV. li. 15 Gen. 1563": "Quando si
avesse da dissolversi questo concilio,
per causa d' altri e non nostra, mia
piaceria più che Vra. Beatitudine fusse
restata a Roma."
[7] "Li Cardinali di maggior autorità
deploravano con tutti a tutte l'ore la
loro miseria, la quale stimano tanto
maggiore che vedono e conoscono assai
chiaro, non esservi rimedio alcuno se
non quello che piacesse dare al Sr. Dio
con la sua santissima mano." Soranzo
himself adds, "It must needs be feared,
most serene prince, that our poor Italy,
afflicted by so many curses, will have
to suffer from this also, and so do all
wise men see and know."

purity of soul, in short, that man has not yet obtained. Still less could these now be hoped for, when the Church was involved in so many contradictory relations with the State. If, notwithstanding their imperfections, general councils had still retained the respect of nations, and were still looked to with hope, and demanded as remedial, this must be attributed to the necessity existing for imposing some restraint on the papal influence; but the present state of affairs seemed confirmatory of what the pontiffs had constantly maintained: namely, that in times of great perplexity, church councils tended rather to increase than remove the evil. All Italy took part in the fears of the Curia. "The council," said the Italians, "will either be continued, or it will be dissolved. In the first case —and more especially if the Pope should die pending its duration—the ultramontanes will arrange the conclave according to their own interests, and to the disadvantage of Italy; they will lay so many restrictions on the pontiff, that he will be little more than the mere bishop of Rome; under pretence of reforms, they will render all offices worthless, and ruin the whole Curia. On the other hand, should the council be dissolved without having produced any good effect, even the most orthodox would receive great offence, while those whose faith is wavering will stand in peril of being utterly lost."

That any essential change could be produced in the opinions of the council itself, seemed, as matters now stood, altogether impossible. The legates, guided by the Pope, with the Italians who were closely bound to him, were confronted by the prelates of France, Spain, and Germany, who, on their side, were led, each by the ambassador of his sovereign. What arrangement of differences—what middle term, could be devised? There seemed none: even in February of 1563 the state of things appeared to be desperate, the most vehement contentions prevailed, each party obstinately adhering to the opinions it had adopted.

But when all these affairs were examined with more earnest attention, there appeared the possibility of an escape from the labyrinth.

The discordant opinions only met and combated in Trent; their origin and guides were in Rome, and at the courts of the respective sovereigns. If these dissensions could ever be

healed, it must be by proceeding to their sources. Pius IV
had declared that the papacy could no longer support itself
without the aid of the temporal princes: it was now the moment to act upon the principle thus laid down. The Pope
had once thought of receiving the demands of the different
courts himself, and granting them without the intervention of
the council; but this would have been a half-measure only.
The best thing now to be done was to bring the council to a
close, in concert with the other great powers: no other resource
presented itself.

Pius IV determined to attempt this. The most able and
statesmanlike of his cardinals, Morone, gave him effectual aid.

In the first instance, Ferdinand I must be gained—this was
of the highest importance, for not only had the French concurred with him in opinion, as before related, but he had, also,
much influence with Philip of Spain, his nephew, who deferred
to him on most occasions.

Cardinal Morone had been chosen president of the council,
but well assured that nothing effectual could be accomplished
in Trent, he proceeded to Inspruck, in April, 1563, permitting
no other prelate to accompany him, for the purpose of meeting the Emperor, who was in that city. He found Ferdinand
highly offended—in extreme discontent, fully persuaded that
no serious intentions of reform were entertained in Rome, and
resolved in the first place to procure perfect freedom for the
council.[8]

An extraordinary exercise of address, or, as we should now
say, of " diplomatic skill," was required on the part of the
legate, in order to propitiate the irritated monarch.[9]

The Emperor was, above all, offended because his own project of reform had been set aside, and had not even been made
the subject of serious discussion; but Morone found means to
persuade him that there were very sufficient reasons why the
formal discussion of his plan had been deferred, but that, in
fact, its more important points had not only been considered

[8] To this place belongs also the " Relatione in scr. fatta dal Comendone ai
Sri. Legati del Concilio sopra le cose
ritratte dall' imperatore, 19 Feb. 1563 ":
" They seem to think that they shall
find ways and means to have more influence and authority in this council,
so as to secure all their desires con-
jointly with the French."

[9] The most important paper I have
found in regard to the Council of Trent
is Morone's " Report of his Legation ":
it is brief but conclusive. Neither Sarpi
nor even Pallavicini has noticed it.
" Relatione sommaria del Cl. Morone
sopra la Legatione sua." Bibl. Altieri,
in Roma, vii. f. 3.

but even adopted. Next, Ferdinand complained that the council was led by Rome, the legates proceeding entirely according to the instructions received from the pontiff. To this Morone replied, and the fact was incontrovertible, that the ambassadors from all the courts received their instructions from home, and were constantly furnished by their sovereigns with new suggestions.

The cardinal had long possessed the confidence of the house of Austria, and he so contrived as to get over this delicate negotiation very happily—he smoothed away the unfavorable impressions that Ferdinand had received, and applied himself skilfully to the effecting a compromise on those points which were most eagerly contested by the prelates in council. He was resolved never to permit the essential authority of the Pope to be in any wise diminished; the principal object was, as he tells us himself, " to hit upon such expedients as that Ferdinand might consider himself satisfied without really compromising the power either of pope or legate." [10]

The first point in dispute was, that exclusive right of presenting resolutions, which, being vested in the legates, was maintained to be an infringement on the liberty of the council. Here Morone remarked, that the right to the initiative, if possessed by the prelates generally, would be frequently used in opposition to the interest of princes: of this fact he had no difficulty in convincing the Emperor, for would not the bishops, once possessed of this privilege, be very prone to use it for the purpose of proposing resolutions inimical to the existing rights of States? thus infinite confusion might arise from such a concession. It was needful, nevertheless, to meet the wishes of the temporal princes in some way, and the expedient adopted for this purpose is sufficiently remarkable. The cardinal promised that he would himself propose whatever the ambassadors should suggest to him from their sovereigns; or, on his failing to do so, they should then have the right of proposing for themselves. This compromise was significant of the spirit that now began to prevail in the council: the legates agreed to renounce the initiative in a case supposed, but rather

[10] " Fu necessario trovare temperamento tale, che paresse all' imperatore di essere in alcuno modo satisfatto, et insieme non si pregiudicasse all' autorità del papa nè de' legati, ma restasse il concilio nel sao possesso." (See the text.)

in favor of the ambassadors, than in that of the fathers in council.[1] It follows, then, that to the sovereigns only was accorded a portion of that authority hitherto enjoyed exclusively by the pontiffs: to the council no benefit whatever accrued.

The demand, that the committees wherein the decrees were prepared should be permitted to assemble according to their several nations, was the second question to be mooted. To this Morone replied that the practice had always been so; but that, since the Emperor desired it, a more rigid attention should be given to this rule, which should for the future be established as invariable.

Then came the third point—reform: and here the Emperor conceded that the expression " Reform of the Head," as also that old question of the Sorbonne, as to whether Pope or council were superior, should be avoided; in return for which, the cardinal promised a searching reform through every department; and in the plan drawn up to this intent even the conclave was included.

These more important points once arranged, the secondary questions were soon agreed on; many demands at first made by Ferdinand were withdrawn, and his ambassadors were enjoined to maintain a good understanding with the papal legates. Having successfully accomplished his mission, Morone again traversed the Alps. " When people became fully aware of the Emperor's friendly dispositions," says he, " and of the concord established between his ambassadors and those of the Pope, the council presently changed its aspect, and was much more easily managed."

Other circumstances contributed to this result.

The French and Spaniards had fallen into dissensions about the right of their respective ambassadors to precedence in the council: thus they no longer continued to act in concert.

Special negotiations had also been entered into with each of these powers.

[1] " Summarium eorum quæ dicuntur Acta inter Cæsaream Majestatem et Illustrissimum Cardinalem Moronum," in the " Acts of Torellus "; also, in Salig, " Geschichte des tridentinischen Conciliums," iii. A. 292; where this is expressed as follows: " His majesty reserves to himself to cause the proposal of measures, either by the said legates, or, if they feel aggrieved by this, through his own servants." I confess that I should not have inferred such a negotiation as Morone describes, from these words, although it may be implied in them.

A cordial understanding with the Pope was most essential to Philip II, whose authority in Spain, being founded in a great measure on ecclesiastical interests, it was his policy to keep these carefully in his hands. This fact was perfectly well known to the Court of Rome, and the nuncio from Madrid often said that a friendly termination of the council was quite as desirable for the King of Spain as for the Pope. The burdens imposed on church property had already been brought into question by the Spanish prelates in Trent, but the sums furnished by ecclesiastical foundations formed an important portion of the public revenue, and the King, much alarmed, requested the Pope to forbid these offensive discourses.[2] Could he then be desirous of procuring for his prelates the right of proposing resolutions? He was anxious, on the contrary, to restrict the privileges they already possessed. The pontiff complained of the vehement opposition he had continually to endure from the Spanish bishops, and Philip promised to adopt such means as should keep them within the limits of obedience: suffice it to say, that the Pope and King became assured that their interests were absolutely identical. Other negotiations must also have taken place: the Pope threw himself wholly into the arms of the King, who promised, on his part, that whatever difficulty should assail the pontiff, he, Philip, would come to his aid with the whole force of his kingdom.

The French also were in the meanwhile approaching more cordially to the Pope. The Guises, whose powerful influence prevailed equally in the Council at Trent as in their government at home, had in both places adopted a policy that was decidedly and increasingly Catholic. It was wholly attributable to the compliant dispositions of Cardinal de Guise, that after ten months of delay and eight adjournments, the council did at length hold a session. In addition to this an alliance of the closest character was proposed by his eminence. He desired to form a congress of the leading Catholic sovereigns, the Pope, the Emperor, and the Kings of France and Spain.[3] For the better discussion of this project he proceeded himself to Rome, and the Pope could find no words sufficiently eloquent to praise " his Christian zeal for the service of God and the public tranquillity,

[2] Paolo Tiepolo, " Dispaccio di Spagna, 4th Dec. 1562."
[3] " Instruttione data a Mons. Carlo Visconti, mandato da Papa Pio IV. al Re catt. per le cose del concilio di Trento (ultimo Ottobre, 1563)," Bibl Barb. 3007.

not in matters touching this council only, but also in others affecting the common weal." [4] The proposed congress would have been exceedingly agreeable to the Pope, who sent ambassadors on the subject to both Emperor and King.

It was therefore rather at the respective courts, and by means of political negotiations, than at Trent, and by the assembled fathers, that all discords were eventually composed, and all obstacles to a peaceful close of the council removed. Cardinal Morone, to whom this was principally attributable, had besides found means to conciliate the prelates individually, bestowing on each all the deference, praise, and favor that he desired and thought his due.[5] His proceedings furnish a striking example of the much that may be effected by an able and skilful man, even under the most difficult circumstances; when he has thoroughly mastered the position of affairs, and proposes to himself such an aim only as is compatible with that position. To him more than to any other man is the Catholic Church indebted for the peaceful termination of the council.

The path was now freed from its encumbrances; there now only remained, as he has himself remarked, to contend with those difficulties that were inseparable from the nature of the subject.

The first that presented itself was the old controversy as to the divine right of bishops, and that of the necessity of their residence. Long did the Spaniards remain immovably fixed in the defence of their tenets; even so late as July, 1563, they maintained them to be as infallible as the ten commandments. The Archbishop of Granada desired that all books upholding contrary doctrines should be prohibited.[6] They consented, nevertheless, that these their favorite tenets should be omitted from the decree that was at length drawn up, a form being adopted that left them a pretext for defending the same at any future time. Lainez makes this ambiguity of the decree a special subject of eulogy.[7]

No very dissimilar course of proceeding was that adopted

---

[4] " Il beneficio universale." " Lettera di Papa Pio IV. 20 Ottobre, 1562."
[5] I have not yet seen the life of Ayala by Villaneuva, in which, as I find, there must be some account of this; but the assertion of Morone himself is quite sufficient. " The prelates," says

he, " being caressed, praised, flattered, and favored, became more tractable."
[6] " Scrittura nelle Lettere e Memorie del Nuncio Visconti," ii. 174.
[7] " Ejus verba in utramque partem pie satis posse exponi:" Paleotto, in Mendham's " Memoirs of the Council of Trent," p. 262.

in regard to the next point in dispute, the initiative namely, *proponentibus legatis*. The Pope announced that everyone should be free to ask and to say whatever, by the decrees of ancient councils, it had been permitted to ask and to say, but he carefully abstained from using the word " propose." [8] Thus an expedient was formed by which the Spaniards were contented, although the Pope had not in fact made the slightest concession.

The difficulties arising from political considerations thus removed, the questions that had caused so much bitterness and wrangling were treated, not so much in the hope of deciding them, as with a view to evade their spirit by some dexterous compromise.

The less weighty matters were very easily accommodated in this disposition of the council, and its proceedings had on no occasion made more rapid progress. The important tenets respecting clerical ordination, the sacrament of marriage, indulgences, purgatory, the adoration of saints, and in fact all the principal measures of reform adopted by the assembly, were decided on in the last three sessions of the latter half of the year 1563. The congregations, as well on the one side as the other, were composed of different nations, the project of reform being discussed in five separate assemblies, one French, which met at the house of Cardinal de Guise, one Spanish, at that of the Archbishop of Granada, and three Italian. [9]

The questions were for the most part agreed upon with little difficulty; two only presented an exception, the first was the exemption of chapters, the second the plurality of benefices; and as regarded both these, private interest took a large share in the contest.

The first of these questions more particularly affected Spain, where the chapters had already lost some portion of the extraordinary immunities they had once enjoyed. These they sought eagerly to regain, while Philip was as eagerly bent on restricting them still further; holding the nomination of bishops himself, he had a personal interest in the extension of episcopal authority. But the Pope took part with the chapters, because

[8] Pallavicini, xxiii. 6, 5.
[9] The best accounts touching this matter are to be found where one would scarcely think of seeking them—in Baini, " Vita di Palestrina," i. 199; they are from authentic letters. The " Diary of Servantio," used by Mendham (p. 304), also names it.

the influence he exercised over the Spanish Church would have been materially diminished by the absolute subjection of chapters to the bishop. Again then were these two powerful interests brought into direct collision, and it became a question which was to command the majority. The Spanish King was exceedingly strong in the council, a delegate had been sent by the chapters to watch over their rights, but his ambassador had found means to exclude him. Philip had so extensive a church patronage at his disposal, that all wished to keep on good terms with him; hence it resulted that opinions were not favorable to the chapters when the votes were taken orally, but the device adopted by the papal legates for escape from that dilemma also is worthy of remark. They resolved that the votes should on this occasion be given in writing. For though the voices, pronouncing in the presence of so many adherents of Philip were restrained by considerations for him, the written opinions being for the legates' hands only, were freed from that influence, and this contrivance did in fact recover an important majority for the papal wishes, and the chapters. Thus supported, and by the intervention of Cardinal de Guise they proceeded to further negotiations with the Spanish prelates, who contented themselves eventually with a much less important extension of their powers than they had hoped to obtain.[10]

The second article, regarding plurality of benefices, was yet more important to the Curia; a reform in the institution of cardinals had been talked of from time immemorial, and many thought the degeneracy of that body the primary cause of all abuses. In their hands was accumulated a vast number of benefices, and the intention was to restrict the cardinals in that matter by the most stringent laws. It will be readily believed that on this point the Curia would be most sensitive; they dreaded the slightest innovation in such a direction, and shrank from even deliberating upon the question; very peculiar is here also the expedient contrived by Morone for evading the subject so feared. He mingled the reform of the cardinals with the articles respecting the bishops. " Few perceived the importance

[10] Sarpi, viii. 816, is not very distinct on this subject. The authentic explanation of Morone is extremely valuable. The affair of the canons and their exemptions was at first carried in favor of the ultramontane party, but the votes being afterward taken in writing, which was not customary, opinions changed, and the contrary prevailed; at length the decrees were issued as they exist, by means of Lorraine, who had returned from Rome, full of devotion to his holiness and to the purposes of the council.

of this proceeding," as he remarks himself, " and so the rocks and shoals were all avoided.

Pius IV having thus successfully accomplished the preservation of the Roman Court in the form it had hitherto maintained, did not evince any great rigor as regarded the proposed reformation of the temporal sovereigns; he permitted this subject to drop, in compliance with the suggestions of Ferdinand.[1]

The proceedings were in fact such as those of a mere friendly conference might have been, while questions of subordinate interest were left to be formed into general decrees by the divines; the more important affairs were discussed by the courts. Couriers were incessantly flying in all directions, and one concession was requited by another.

And now the most earnest desire of the Pope was to bring the convocation to an early close. For some time the Spaniards were unwilling to accede to this; they were not satisfied with the reforms that had been effected, and the envoy of Philip even made a demonstration of protesting; but the Pope declared his readiness to call a new synod in case of need,[2] and all perceived the great inconvenience that would be caused by protracting the proceedings till a vacancy of the papal throne might occur while the council was still sitting; and as, besides, everyone felt tired and longed to return home, even the Spaniards at length resigned their objections.

The spirit of opposition was essentially overcome. Even to the last, the council evinced an extreme subserviency. It even condescended to solicit from the Pope a confirmation of its edicts, and expressly declared that all canons of reform, whatever might be implied in their words, were prepared with the perfect understanding that no portion of them should be construed to affect the dignity of the Holy See.[3] How far was the Council of Trent from renewing the demands of Constance or Basle to superiority over the papal power! In the proclamations by which the sittings were closed, and which were prepared by Cardinal de Guise, the universal bishopric of the Pope was distinctly recognized.

Thus prosperous was the conclusion; the council so eagerly

[1] That a searching reform of the Curia, the cardinals, and the conclave did not take place, is in close connection with the omission of that intended for the sovereigns. Extracts from the correspondence of the legates, in Pallavicini, xxiii. 7, 4.
[2] Pallavicini, xxiv. 8, 5.
[3] Sessio xxv. c. xxi.

demanded and so long evaded; twice dissolved, and agitated by so many political tempests; which had even in its third assembly been assailed by dangers so imminent, now closed amidst the universal accord of the Catholic world. It will be readily comprehended that the prelates, as they came together for the last time on the fourth of December, 1563, should feel themselves affected by emotions of gladness. Former antagonists were now seen offering mutual gratulation, and tears were observed in the eyes of many among those aged men.

But seeing, as we have shown, that this happy result had been secured only by the utmost pliancy, the most astute contrivance, the most dexterous policy, may we not inquire if the efficiency of the council had not been impaired thereby?

The Council of Trent, if not more important than all other general assemblies of the Church, is indubitably more so than any that have been called in later times.

Its importance is comprised in two momentous periods:—

The first, to which we have already alluded, was during the war of Smalkalde, when the tenets of Rome, after many fluctuations, became separated forever from the Protestant opinions. From the doctrine of justification as then set forth, arose the whole system of dogmatic theology, as it is professed even to the present day by the Catholic Church.

In the second, which we have been just considering, and after the conferences of Cardinal Morone with Ferdinand in the summer and autumn of 1563, the hierarchy was established anew, theoretically by the decrees respecting clerical ordination, and practically by the resolutions touching measures of reform.

These reforms were most important at the moment, nor have they ever yet lost their efficacy.

For the faithful were again subjected to the uncompromising severity of church discipline, and even in extreme cases, to the sword of excommunication. Seminaries were established, wherein the youth preparing for the Church were carefully trained in habits of austerity and the fear of God. Parishes were regulated anew, preaching and the administration of the sacraments were subjected to fixed ordinances, and the co-operation of the conventual clergy was regulated by determined laws. The most rigid performance of their duties was enjoined on the bishops, more especially of that involving the supervision

of the clergy, according to their different grades of consecration.
It was besides of the most essential efficacy that these prelates
had solemnly bound themselves, by a particular " confession of
faith," subscribed and sworn to by each, in a compact of obedience to the ordinances of Trent, and of absolute subjection
to the Pope.

And this was the result of the council by which it had unquestionably been contemplated to restrict the authority of the
pontiff. An object far from being obtained, that authority having in effect received extent and confirmation from the acts of
the assembly. Reserving to himself the exclusive right of
interpreting the decrees of Trent, the Pope held the power of
prescribing the rule of faith and life. Discipline was restored,
but all the faculties of directing it were centred in Rome.

But the close circumscription of her limits was now also
perceived and acknowledged by the Catholic Church. On the
East and the Greek confession she now resigned all claim;
while she drove Protestantism from her borders with anathemas
innumerable. In the bosom of the earlier Catholicism, a certain
element of the Protestant creed was included, this was now cast
forth for ever; but if the Catholic profession had received
limitations, it had also concentrated its forces, and braced all its
energies well together.

Results so effectual were achieved by the concurrence and
aid of the great Catholic sovereigns only, and it is in this alliance of the Church with monarchies, that one of the primary
conditions to her subsequent development will be found. This
is in some degree analogous with the tendency of Protestantism
to combine the episcopal and sovereign rights. It was only by
degrees that this displayed itself among Catholics. There is
manifestly involved in it a possibility of new divisions, but of
such a result there was then no immediate apprehension. The
decrees of the council were readily admitted in one province
after another. It is the having effected these things that has
procured for Pius IV an important station in the history of the
world. He was the first pontiff by whom that tendency of the
hierarchy to oppose itself to the temporal sovereigns, was deliberately and purposely abandoned.

Having secured this important result, Pius now believed that
the labors of his life were brought to a close. On the dispersion

of the council it is remarked, that the tension of his mind was relaxed. It was thought that he became negligent of religious services, and devoted himself too earnestly to the pleasures of the table. He increased the splendor of his court, gave rich entertainments, and erected magnificent buildings. The more zealously disposed perceived a difference between himself and his predecessor, of which they loudly complained.[4]

Not that any reaction of the general feeling was likely to ensue; a tendency had displayed itself in Catholicism that was no longer to be repressed or turned aside.

When once the spirit is fully aroused, there is no presuming to prescribe the path it shall pursue; a very trifling violation of its dictates on the part of those who should represent it in its utmost force, is productive of the most extraordinary symptoms.

It was thus that the spirit of rigid Catholicism, which had gained possession of the age, became instantly perilous to the existence of Pius IV.

There lived in Rome a certain Benedetto Accolti, catholic to enthusiasm, who was constantly speaking of a mystery intrusted to him by God himself, and which he was to make known. In proof that he was declaring the truth only, he offered to walk unhurt in presence of the assembled people, through a burning pile that was to be prepared on the Piazza Navona.

His mystery was this:—he believed himself to have received a revelation, to the effect that the Greek and Roman churches were about to be united, and that this combined Catholic Church would then subdue the Turks and all heretics; that the pontiff would be a holy man, would attain universal monarchy, and restore truth and justice to the human race. By these ideas he was possessed to fanaticism. He was now convinced, however, that Pius IV, whose worldly living and being were infinitely remote from his ideal of holiness, was not formed to carry out this divine mission, and that he, Benedetto Accolti, was selected by God to deliver Christendom from so unsuitable a chief.

He conceived the design of putting the Pope to death, and found an associate whom he made his own by the promise of

---

[4] Paolo Tiepolo: "After this (the council) was at an end, freed from great anxiety, and rendered bold in his confirmed authority, he began to act more freely according to his inclina- tions, so that one clearly saw in him the mind of a prince assured of his own affair, rather than that of a pontiff regardful of the welfare of others." Panvinius makes the same remark.

rewards from God himself, as well as from their future holy
sovereign. One day they set forward on their purpose, and
soon perceived the pontiff approaching. He was in the midst
of a procession, within reach of their hands—tranquil, free from
suspicion, and without defence.

But instead of rushing on the sovereign, Accolti began to
tremble and changed color. The solemnity of attendance on
the person of a pope has something too imposing to fail of im-
pressing so fanatical a Catholic as was this man. The Pope
passed on his way.

Accolti had, however, been meanwhile remarked by others.
The companion whom he had gained over, Antonio Canossa,
was not a person of firm resolution—at one moment he would
suffer himself to be persuaded into a second attempt, at the
next he felt tempted himself to denounce their intended crime.
Neither of them preserved a perfect silence, and they were at
length arrested and condemned to death.[5]

This will serve to show what feelings were astir in those
agitated times. Pius IV had done much for the reconstruc-
tion of the Church; yet were there many to whom all seemed
insufficient, and whose views went much further than anything
that had yet been accomplished. Pius died on the ninth of
December, 1565.

Section VII.—Pius V

The partisans of a more rigid system in the Church had now
secured a great and almost unhoped-for advantage: a pope was
elected whom they might safely consider one of themselves, this
was Pius V.

I will not repeat the more or less credible stories related of
his election by the book on the conclaves, and by some of the
histories of his time. We have a letter from Carlo Borromeo,
which sufficiently informs us on this point: " I was determined," says he (and the large share he had in the election
is well known), " to consider nothing so much as religion and

---

[5] I take these notices, which I have
not found elsewhere, from a MS. of the
Corsini library in Rome, No. 674, with
the title of " Antonio Canossa " : " This
is my deposition of the cause for which
I die; your holiness will deign to send
it to my father and mother."

purity of faith. I was well acquainted with the piety, irreproachable life, and devout spirit of the Cardinal of Alessandria, afterward Pius V; I thought none could more fitly administer the Christian commonwealth, and used my best efforts in his favor." [1] In a man of so entirely spiritual a character as that possessed by Carlo Borromeo, no other motives could be supposed. Philip of Spain, who had been won over to the interest of the same cardinal by his ambassador, sent his express thanks to Borromeo for having promoted the election. [2] Pius V was precisely the man then believed to be required. The adherents of Paul IV, who had kept themselves retired during the last pontificate, considered themselves most fortunate: " To Rome, to Rome!" writes one of them to another: " come confidently and at once, but with all modesty; God has awakened up for us our fourth Paul again!'

Michele Ghislieri, now Pius V, was of humble extraction; he was born at Bosco, near Alessandria, in 1504, and entered a convent of Dominicans at the age of fourteen. Here he resigned himself, body and spirit, to the devotion and monastic poverty enjoined by his order. Of the alms he gathered, he did not retain so much for himself as would have bought him a cloak for the winter, and against the heats of summer he thought severity of abstinence the best preservative. Though confessor to the Governor of Milan, he always travelled on foot with his wallet on his back. When he taught, his instructions were given with zeal and precision: when, as prior, it was his office to administer the affairs of a monastery, he did this with the utmost rigor and frugality—more than one house was freed from debt by his government. The formation of his character was effected during those years when the strife between Protestant innovation and the ancient doctrines had extended into Italy: he took earnest part with those who upheld the established creed in its most rigid acceptation, and of strictly disputed points maintained by him in Parma during the year 1543, the

---

[1] Clis. Borromeus, Henrico Cli. Infanti Portugalliæ, Romæ, d. 26 Feb. 1566. Glussiani, " Vita C. Borromei," p. 62. Compare with Ripamonti, " Historia Urbis Mediolani," lib. xii. p. 814.
[2] I find this in a despatch of Soranzo, ambassador in Spain. " The qualities of his holiness, while yet cardinal, were not known to this most serene king; but the said commendator (Luigi Reque- sens, Comm. maggior) always praised him highly, declaring that he well deserved the pontificate; so that his majesty was moved to give orders that he should be supported with all his power." Thus the story related by Oltrocchi, in his remarks on Guissano, falls to the ground. The election took place January 8, 1566.

greater part related to the papal authority, and were opposed to the new opinions. He was early invested with the office of inquisitor, and was called on to perform his duties in places of peculiar danger, as were Como and Bergamo for example.[3] In these cities an intercourse with Germans and Swiss was not to be avoided: he was also appointed to the Valteline, which, as belonging to the Grisons, was in like manner infested by heretics. In this employment he displayed the obstinacy and the courage of a zealot. On entering the city of Como, he was sometimes received with volleys of stones; to save his life he was frequently compelled to steal away like an outlaw, and conceal himself by night in the huts of the peasantry: but he suffered no personal danger to deter him from his purposes. On one occasion the Conte della Trinita threatened to have him thrown into a well. " As to that, it shall be as God pleases," was the Dominican's reply. Thus did he take eager part in the contest of intellectual and political powers then existing in Italy; and as the side he had chosen was victorious, he, too, advanced in importance. Being appointed commissary of the Inquisition in Rome, he was soon remarked by Paul IV, who declared Fra Michele an eminent servant of God, and worthy of higher honors. He promoted him to the bishopric of Nepi, and, by way of placing " a chain round his foot," as Michele himself tells us, " that he might not again creep back to the repose of his cloister," [4] in 1557 he nominated him cardinal. In this new dignity Ghislieri continued, as ever, poor, austere, and unpretending. He told his household that they must fancy themselves living in a monastery: for himself, his sole interest was still centred in devotional exercise and the business of the Inquisition.

In a man of this character, Philip of Spain, Cardinal Borromeo, and all the more rigid party, believed they had found the salvation of the Church. The people of Rome were not so perfectly satisfied. Pius was told this, and he remarked in reply: " All the more shall they lament for me when I am dead."

[3] Paolo Tiepolo, " Relazione di Roma in Tempo di Pio IV. et V." : " In Bergamo was taken from him by force a certain principal heretic, Giorgio Mondaga, whom he had thrown into the prisons of the convent of St. Domenico, then used for criminals, and whom he and his monks strove to keep, to their own great peril. In the same city he afterward labored to institute a process against the then bishop of Bergamo."

[4] Catena, " Vita di Pio V.," whence we draw most of our information, has this also. It was related by Pius himself to the Venetian ambassadors, Mich. Serviano and Paul Tiepolo, as they tell us (October 2, 1568).

He maintained all the monastic severity of his life even when Pope: his fasts were kept with the same rigor and punctuality; he permitted himself no garment of finer texture [5] than his wont —heard mass every day and frequently said it himself. Yet was he careful that his private devotions should offer no impediment to his public duties, and, though rising with the first light of day, he would not indulge himself with the customary siesta. Could any doubt exist as to the reality of his religious feelings, we may consider this proved by what he has himself declared of the papacy: it was not conducive to his advance in piety, as he complains, and the progress of his soul toward salvation and the joys of paradise was impeded by its duties, to his infinite lamentation. "But for the support of prayer, he believed the weight of that burden would be more than he could endure." He enjoyed the happiness of a fervent devotion to his last hour— it was the only kind of happiness of which he was capable, but he found it perfect. The warmth of his devotion often brought tears to his eyes, and he constantly arose from his knees with the persuasion that his prayers had been heard. When the people beheld him in the processions, barefoot, and with uncovered head, his face beaming with unaffected piety, and his long white beard sweeping his breast, they were excited to enthusiastic reverence; they believed so pious a pope had never before existed, and stories were current among them of his having converted Protestants by the mere aspect of his countenance. Pius was, moreover, kindly and affable; his manner toward his old servants was extremely cordial. How admirable, too, was the remark with which he received that Conte della Trinita, who, after having threatened to drown him, was now sent ambassador to his court. "See, now," he exclaimed, when he recognized his old enemy, "thus it is that God helps the innocent:" in no other way did he show the count that the past was remembered. He had always been exceedingly charitable, and now kept a list of the poor in Rome, whom he regularly assisted in accordance with their station.

Humble, resigned, and child-like are men of this character, in their ordinary state; but when irritated or wounded, they kindle into violent anger, and their resentment is implacable.

[5] Catena, Tiepolo: " Nor has he even left off the coarse shirt that he began to wear when he became a monk. He performs his devotions most devoutly, and frequently with tears."

An adherence to their own modes of thought and proceeding appears to them the most imperative duty, and they are exasperated by its neglect. Pius V felt an immovable conviction, that the path he had chosen was the only right one; its having conducted him to the papal throne gave him so complete a self-reliance, that doubt or fear as to the consequences of his own actions was a pain unknown to his experience.

It follows, that his adhesion to his own opinions was most obstinate; the most cogent reasons availed nothing toward making him retract or alter them. Easily provoked by contradiction, he would redden deeply on being opposed, and break forth into expressions of the utmost violence.[6] But slightly acquainted with the affairs of the world, or with politics, and suffering his judgment to be warped by accidental and secondary circumstances, it was extremely difficult to bring matters of business well through with him.

It is true that he did not permit himself to act on his first impressions, as regarded individuals, and those with whom he came into contact; but having once made up his mind about any man, whether for good or evil, nothing could afterward shake his opinion.[7] He was, nevertheless, more disposed to think people deteriorated, than that they became better, and there were few whom he did not regard with suspicion.

Never would he mitigate a penal sentence; this was constantly remarked of him; rather would he express the wish that the punishment had been more severe!

He was not satisfied to see the Inquisition visiting offences of recent date, but caused it to inquire into such as were of ten or twenty years' standing.

If there were any town wherein few punishments were inflicted, he did not believe the place any the better for that, but ascribed the fact to the negligence of the officials.

The severity with which he insisted on the maintenance of church discipline is entirely characteristic. "We forbid," says he, in one of his bulls, "that any physician, attending a patient

---

[6] "Informatione di Pio V." (Bibl. Ambrosiana at Milan, F. D. 181): "His holiness is naturally cheerful and kindly (though sometimes accidentally seeming otherwise), so that he readily enters into pleasant talk with Mr. Cirillo, his house-steward, and he, being a prudent as well as polished man, delights his holiness, while he gains advantages both for himself and others."

[7] "Informatione di Pio V.:" "It is more difficult to free him from a bad impression than a good one; especially with regard to people of whom he knows but little."

confined to his bed, should visit him longer than three days, without receiving a certificate that the sick person has confessed his sins anew." [8] A second bull sets forth the punishments for violation of the Sabbath, and for blasphemy. These were fines for the rich; but, " for the common man, who cannot pay, he shall stand before the church-door, for one whole day, with his hands tied behind his back, for the first offence; for the second, he shall be whipped through the city; but his tongue, for the third, shall be bored through, and he shall be sent to the galleys."

This was the general spirit of his ordinances. How frequently did it become necessary to remind him, that he had to govern mere men, and not angels! [9]

To defer to the secular powers was now acknowledged to be most needful; but no consideration of this kind was permitted to affect the severities of Pius V. The princes of Europe had constantly complained of the bull, " In Cœnâ Domini." This he not only proclaimed anew, but even rendered it more onerous, by adding special clauses of his own, wherein there was a disposition shown to refuse the temporal sovereign all right of imposing new taxes.

It will be manifest, that proceedings so violent were calculated to produce reactions, and so it happened; not merely because the demands made by a man of so rigid an austerity never can be complied with by the generality of mankind, but also because, in this case, a deliberate resistance was provoked, and various misunderstandings arose. Even Philip of Spain, though usually so devout, was once moved to warn the pontiff, that he would do well to avoid the trial of what a prince was capable of doing when driven to the last extremity.

Pius V, on his part, felt this very deeply. He was sometimes most unhappy in his high station, and declared himself " weary of living." He complained, that the having acted without respect to persons had made him enemies, and that he had never been free from vexations and persecutions since he had ascended the papal throne.

[8] "Supra gregem dominicum," Bull. iv. ii. p. 218.
[9] In the Informationi, for example, is found an epistle to the holy father, expatiating largely on this subject, and exhorting him to endure the Jews and courtesans. The Caporioni entreated the Pope at least to tolerate these last; but Pius replied, that "rather than connive at what was wrong he would leave Rome himself."

But, however this may have been, and though Pius V could no more give satisfaction to the whole world than other men, it is yet certain that his demeanor and habits did exercise incalculable influence over his contemporaries, and the general development of his Church. After so long a train of circumstances—all concurring to call forth and promote a more spiritual tendency—after so many resolutions had been adopted, to make this tendency universally dominant, there needed a pope of this character, in order to secure that it should not only be widely proclaimed, but also practically enforced. To this effect, the zeal and example of Pius V were alike efficacious.

That reformation of the court, so often promised, was at length commenced in fact and reality, if not in the forms at first proposed. The expenditure of the papal household was greatly reduced. Pius V required little for his own wants, and was accustomed to say, that " he who would govern others must begin by ruling himself." For such of his servants as he believed to have served him truly throughout his life, not from hope of reward, but affection, he provided well; but his dependents generally were held within closer limits than had ever been known under any other pope. He made his nephew, Bonelli, cardinal, but only because he was told that this was expedient to his maintaining a more confidential intercourse with the temporal princes. He would, however, confer on him only a very moderate endowment; and when the new cardinal once invited his father to Rome, Pius commanded that he should quit the city again, not that same night only, but that very hour. The rest of his relations he would never raise above the middle station; and woe to that one among them whom he detected in any offence, for the least falsehood, never would he forgive him— he was driven without mercy from the pontiff's presence. How different was all this from that favoritism of nephews which had, for centuries, formed so significant a fact in the papal histories! In one of his most severely energetic bulls, Pius V forbade any future alienation of church property, under whatever title, or with whatever pretext; he even declared everyone to be excommunicated who should even counsel such an act, and made all the cardinals subscribe this edict.[10] He proceeded zeal-

[10] " Prohibitio alienandi et infeudandi civitates et loca S. R. E.: Ad. monet nos; 1567, 29 Mart."

ously to the removal of all abuses. Few dispensations were granted by him, still fewer compositions; even such indulgences as had been issued by his predecessors were partially recalled. His auditor-general was commanded to proceed against all bishops and archbishops who should neglect to reside in their dioceses, and to report the refractory to himself in order to their instant deposition.[1] He enjoined all parish priests to remain in their parishes, under heavy penalties for disobedience, or for the neglect of divine service, recalling whatever dispensations had been granted to them in this behalf.[2] Not less earnest were his labors for the restoration of conventual order and discipline. To all monasteries he confirmed, on the one hand, their exemption from taxes and other burdens, as, for example, that of quartering troops; he would not permit their tranquillity to be disturbed: but, on the other hand, he forbade monks to receive confessions without examination by, and permission from, the bishops: this examination might be repeated by every new bishop.[3] He commanded both monks and nuns to remain in the strictest seclusion. This was not universally commended. The orders complained that he enforced on them rules of more stringent severity than those to which they had bound themselves. Some fell into a sort of desperation; others fled their cloisters.[4]

These regulations were first enforced in Rome; but afterward throughout the States of the Church. He bound the secular as well as the ecclesiastical authorities to the observance of his religious ordinances,[5] while he himself provided for a rigorous and impartial administration of justice.[6] Not content with earnestly enforcing on all magistrates a strict attention to their duties, he held himself a public sitting with the cardinals, on the last Wednesday in every month, when any person, who might consider himself aggrieved by the ordinary tribunals, was

---

[1] " Cum alias, 1566, 10 Junii." Bull. iv. ii. 303.

[2] " Cupientes, 1568, 8 Julii." Bull. iv. iii. 24.

[3] " Romani, 1571, 6 Aug." Bull. iv. iii. 177.

[4] Tiepolo: " Always proceeding in extremes, he sometimes fell into a greater evil, while seeking to avoid a smaller one."

[5] Bull. iv. iii. 284.

[6] " Informatione della qualità di Pio V., e delle cose che da quelle dependono " (Berlin Library): " He confers favors without that respect of persons, which might sometimes be necessary for weighty causes; nor will he change one tittle in affairs of justice, even though other popes have given the example, and it may be done without causing scandal." Soriano says that he granted no favor without an admonition, " which appears to me precisely the fashion of a confessor, who reproves the penitent severely when about to bestow absolution."

at liberty to make his plaint to the sovereign in person. Besides all this, he gave audience with the most indefatigable assiduity. He remained seated for this purpose, from the first hours of morning, nor was anyone refused admission to his presence. The consequence of all these efforts was, in fact, an entire reform of external life in Rome. We have a remark of Paolo Tiepolo to this effect. " In Rome," says he, " matters proceed in a fashion very unlike what we have hitherto seen. Men here have become a great deal better—or at least they have put on the appearance of being so.

Something similar was, more or less, to be seen over all Italy. Church discipline had been rendered more strict, in most places, by the promulgation of the decrees of the council; and the pontiff received a readiness of obedience such as none of his predecessors had enjoyed for a long period.

Duke Cosmo of Florence gave up to him, without hesitation, whosoever had been condemned by the Inquisition. Carnesecchi, another of the men of letters who had participated in those early movements toward Protestantism, which we have described as made in Italy, had hitherto remained uninjured. But neither his personal credit, the position of his family, nor his connection with the reigning house itself, could longer save him. He was given up bound to the Roman inquisition, and suffered death at the stake. Cosmo was entirely devoted to the Pope; he assisted him in all his enterprises, and did not hesitate to admit all his spiritual claims. Pius was moved by this to crown him grand duke of Tuscany. The right of the Papal See to take such a step was very doubtful, and the immoral character of Cosmo caused it to be seen with just resentment; but the obedience he displayed toward the Holy See, and the severity of ecclesiastical regulation that he enforced throughout his dominions, were merits that stood above all others in the eyes of the Pope.

Those ancient rivals of the Medici, the Farnese, now emulated their proceedings in this particular; even Ottavio Farnese made it his glory to show that every papal command found unquestioning obedience at his hands.

Not altogether so friendly were the terms on which the Pope stood with the Venetians. They were not sufficiently virulent against the Turks, they were less favorable toward monastic odies, and, above all, less cordial to the Inquisition than Pius would have had them be. He nevertheless took great pains to avoid a rupture with them. " The republic," he declared to be " firmly seated in the faith—ever had she maintained herself most Catholic—she alone had been exempt from the incursions of barbarians, the honor of Italy reposed on her head;" and he declared that " he loved her." The Venetians, too, conceded more to him than they had ever done to any other pontiff. The unhappy Guido Zanetti of Fano, whose religious opinions had become suspected, and who had fled to Padua, they resigned into his hands, a thing never before recorded in their annals. The clergy of their city had previously troubled themselves but little with strict ecclesiastical discipline—they were now brought into very tolerable order. The churches of Verona, being placed under the guidance of Matteo Giberti, became models of discipline. Giberti was held up as affording an example of what the life of a true bishop should be;[7] his plans and regulations have been accepted as exemplars by the whole Catholic world, and many of them were adopted by the Council of Trent. Carlo Borromeo caused his portrait to be taken, and had it hung in his cabinet, that he might have constantly before his eyes the face of him whose life and conduct he so greatly venerated.

Still more effectual was the influence exercised by Carlo Borromeo himself. From his numerous dignities and offices, that of grand penitentiary among others, and as chief of the cardinals nominated by his uncle, he might have held the most brilliant position in Rome; but he resigned these advantages, and refused all, to devote himself to his duties as Archbishop of Milan. These he performed, not with energy and conscience only, but with a sort of passion. He was incessantly occupied in the pastoral visitation of his diocese, which he traversed in every direction; there was no village, however remote, that he had not visited two or three times; the highest mountains, the most secluded valleys, all were alike known and cared for. He was usually preceded by a " Visitator," whose report he then took with him, examining and verifying all with his own eyes; all punishments were adjudged by himself, all improvements pro-

[7] " Petri Francisci Zini, boni pastoris, exemplum ac specimen singulare ex Jo. Matthæo Giberto episcopo expressum atque propositum." Written in 1536, and originally intended for England.— " Opera Giberti," p. 252.

ceeded under his own directions.[8]   His clergy was instructed
to pursue similar methods.   Six provincial councils were held
under his presidency.   In addition to all this he performed the
usual clerical functions with indefatigable zeal.   He preached
and read mass, passed whole days in administering the Lord's
Supper, ordaining priests, presiding at the profession of nuns,
and consecrating altars.   The consecration of an altar was a
ceremony of eight hours' duration, and he is said to have consecrated three hundred.   It is true that many of his arrangements relate to matters merely external, such as the restoration
of buildings, harmonizing of the ritual, exposition and adoration
of the host, etc.   The most efficient result of his labors was perhaps the severity of discipline to which he held his clergy, and
which they, in their turn, enforced on the people.

Nor was he unacquainted with the best modes of procuring
obedience for his ordinances.   In the Swiss districts of his
diocese it was his custom to visit all places of ancient and venerated sanctity; to the people he would distribute gifts; those
of better station were invited to his table.   He was prepared
on the other hand, with measures suitable to the refractory; passing on a certain occasion through the Val Camonica, the peasantry stationed themselves along the road to receive his blessing;
but they had not for a long time paid their tithes, and the archbishop passed along without moving a hand or turning his eyes
on one of them; the people, shocked and terrified by this pri-
vation, were glad to return to their accustomed duty.[9]   He
nevertheless did sometimes meet with a more obstinate and rancorous opposition.   He had resolved to reform the order of
Umiliati, whose members had entered it only to expend the great
wealth of the order in a life of licentiousness.[10]   These men were
so exasperated by his purpose of reforming them, that they
made an attempt to destroy him; a shot was fired at him when
he was praying in his chapel.   But no event of his life was more
useful to his influence than this attack; the people considered

[8] Glussianus, " De Vita et Rebus ges-
tis S. Caroli Borromæi Mediol," p. 112,
is very explicit in regard to the " ritus
visitationis " and all such matters.
[9] Ripamonte, " Historia Urbis Mediolani," in Grævius, ii. i. p. 864.   Ripamonte has also dedicated all the second
part of his history, lib. xii. xvii. to St.
Charles Borromeo.

[10] They had altogether ninety-four
houses, of which each could accommo-
date a hundred men; but the brethren
were so few that two would occupy a
whole house; the order was suppressed,
and their riches were divided between
the endowments of Borromeo and the
society of Jesuits.

his escape a miracle, and from that time it was that they first began to regard him with veneration.

This feeling increased from day to day, as constant proofs of his excellence were seen. His zeal was as pure and unsullied by worldly motive as it was warm and persistent. When the plague raged in Milan, in that hour of utmost peril, his solicitude for the temporal and eternal welfare of those committed to his care was incessant, and his conduct marked an utter disregard for his own life; no one act of this excellent archbishop but proved his piety, and under his governance the city of Milan assumed a new aspect. " How shall I find words sufficient to praise thee, most beautiful city!" exclaims Gabriel Paleotto toward the close of the archbishop's administration; "thy sanctity and religion excite my veneration; in thee I behold a second Jerusalem!" However we may suppose the Milanese nobility led by policy to praise their spiritual chief, we cannot believe exclamations so enthusiastic to have been without cause. The Duke of Savoy also offered a solemn congratulation to Borromeo on the success of his exertions. It was now the care of the latter to secure the future stability of his regulations; to this end a congregation was established, whose office it was to maintain the uniformity of the ritual. A particular order of regular clergy, called Oblati, devoted themselves wholly to the service of the archbishop and his church, the Barnabites received new rules, and from that time their labors have been consecrated to assisting the bishops in the cure of souls; first, in that diocese, and afterward wherever their order made a home.[1] These regulations were a repetition of those established in Rome, but on a smaller scale. A *Collegium Helveticum* was also founded in Milan, intended to promote the restoration of Catholicism in Switzerland, as the *Collegium Germanicum* of Rome was erected in that city for the same purpose as regarded Germany. All this could only corroborate and confirm the dignity and consideration of the Pope, since Borromeo, who never received a papal brief but with uncovered head, would infallibly communicate his own reverential devotedness to his Church.

Pius V had meanwhile acquired an unusual degree of in-

---

[1] Ripamonte, 857. He calls the first founders, Beccaria, Ferraria, and Mo-   rigia: Giussano, p. 442, gives the usual names.

fluence in Naples also; in the earliest days of his pontificate
he had summoned to his presence Tomaso Orfino da Foligno,
whom he had sent on a visitation of reform to the Roman
churches. This mission being accomplished, he had nominated Orfino to the bishopric of Strongoli, and despatched him
with the same view to Naples. Amidst a great concourse of
that devout people the new bishop completed his visitation in
the capital, and afterward proceeded through a great part of
the kingdom.

It is true that the Pope had, not unfrequently, disputes with
the different authorities in Naples as well as in Milan. The
King was aggrieved by the bull "In Cœnâ Domini"; the
Pope would not hear mention of the "Exequatur Regium."
The former accused the ecclesiastical functionaries of doing
too much; the latter thought the royal officers did too little.
Extreme dissatisfaction often prevailed, as we have said, at
the Court of Madrid, and the King's confessor made bitter
complaints, but no positive quarrel ensued. Either sovereign
attributed the principal blame to the officers and advisers of
the other; they remained personally on very friendly terms.

When Philip on a certain occasion was ill, the Pope raised
his hands to Heaven, imploring God to deliver him from that
malady: the aged pontiff prayed that the Almighty would
take some years from his own life and add them to that of
the King, on whose existence so much more depended than on
his own.

And it was entirely in the spirit of the new ecclesiastical
regulations that Spain was now governed. Philip had for a
moment hesitated whether to permit the entire recognition of
the edicts issued by the Council of Trent or not. Gladly would
he have limited the papal power, so far as regarded its right
to make concessions at variance with those edicts; but the religious character of his monarchy was opposed to all attempts
of this kind; he perceived that even the semblance of any serious difference with the Holy See must be carefully eschewed,
if he would remain secure in the allegiance due to himself.
The decrees of the council were therefore promulgated through
the dominions of Philip, and the consequent regulations were
strictly enforced. Here the principles of the rigidly Catholic
party obtained the ascendancy. Carranza, Archbishop of To-

ledo and the first ecclesiastic in Spain, was himself given over
to the mercies of the Inquisition, spite of his many claims to exemption; one of the members of the Council of Trent, he had
also contributed more than any other person, Pole only excepted,
to the restoration of Catholicism in England, under Queen
Mary. "I have no other object in life," he says of himself,
"than that of suppressing heresy, and my efforts have received
the divine aid; I have converted many who had departed from
the faith; the bodies of certain men who were leaders in heretical opinions I have caused to be dug up and burnt; I have been
called Chief Defender of the Faith, whether by Catholics or
Protestants." But all these claims to reverence, all these unquestionable proofs of Catholicism, were not permitted to avail
him against the claims of the Inquisition. Sixteen articles were
discovered in his works, intimating an approximation toward
Protestant opinion, especially in regard to justification; he suffered a long imprisonment in Spain, and underwent all the torments of a protracted trial; he was finally taken to Rome. Thus
removed from the grasp of his personal enemies, he appeared
to be receiving a great favor, but even in Rome he could not
escape: the Inquisition condemned him to death.[2]

If such were the modes of procedure toward a person of
so exalted a character, and in a case so doubtful, it will be
obvious that little hope would remain for those whose heter-
odoxy admitted of no question, and whose station was less
distinguished. Instances of such were still occasionally found
in Spain, and all the relentless cruelty with which the traces
of Judaic and Mahometan tenets had formerly been hunted
down, was now turned against the Protestant opinions. One
auto-da-fé followed close upon another, till every germ of the
hated belief was extirpated. From the year 1570, few besides
foreigners were brought before the Court of Inquisition as
guilty of Protestantism.[3]

The Spanish government was not favorable to the Society
of Jesus. Its members were said to be for the most part aliens
to the pure blood of Spain, Jewish Christians, who were suspected of nourishing projects of revenge, to be taken at some

[2] Llorente has devoted three long chapters of his "History of the Inqui-sition" to the circumstance of Carran-za's trial.—"Hist. de l'Inquisition," vol. iii. 183-315.

[3] M'Crie's "History of the Progress and Suppression of the Inquisition in Spain," p. 336.

future time, for all the miseries their unhappy race had been made to endure. The Jesuits were on the contrary all-powerful in Portugal, where they had made their rule absolute under the name of King Sebastian. Being also in the highest favor at Rome under Pius V, they made their influence in that country subservient to the views of the Curia.

Thus did the pontiff rule both peninsulas with an authority more unlimited than had been known for long periods by his predecessors; the decrees of the Council of Trent were in practical activity through all Catholic countries. Every bishop subscribed the "*professio fidei,*" wherein the substance of those dogmatic decisions promulgated by the council was contained, and Pius published the Roman catechism, in certain parts of which these same propositions are more diffusely expressed. All breviaries, not expressly issued by the Papal See, or which had not been in use upward of two hundred years, were abolished, and a new one was composed on the model of that used in the earliest periods by the principal churches of Rome. This the pontiff desired to see adopted universally.[4] A new missal was also prepared, " according to the rule and ritual of the holy fathers," [5] and appointed for general use. The ecclesiastical seminaries received numerous pupils, monastic institutions were effectually reformed, and the Court of Inquisition devoted itself with untiring vigilance and merciless severity, to guard the unity and inviolability of the faith.

Governed by ordinances thus uniform, a strict alliance ensued between all these countries and States. This position of things was further promoted by the circumstance that France, involved in civil wars, had either renounced her former hostility to Spain, or was unable to give it effect. A second consequence also resulted from the troubles in France. From the events of any given period, certain political convictions of general influence are always elicited, which convictions then became a practical and motive power throughout the world over which they extend. Thus the Catholic sovereigns now believed themselves assured, that any change in the religion of a country involved the danger of destruction to the State. Pius IV had said that the Church could not support herself without the aid of the

[4] " Be those removed that are of doubtful and unknown origin."—" Quoniam nobis: 9 Julii, 1568."

[5] " Collated with all the oldest MSS. in our Vatican Library, and with other uncorrupted MSS. from all quarters."

temporal princes, and these last were now persuaded that union with the Church was equally requisite to their security. Pius V did not fail to preach this doctrine continually in their ears, and in effect he lived to see all southern Christendom gathered around him for the purposes of a common enterprise.

The Ottoman power was still making rapid progress. Its ascendancy was secured in the Mediterranean, and its various attempts, first upon Malta, and next on Cyprus, rendered obvious the fact, that it was earnestly bent on the subjugation of the yet unconquered islands. Italy herself was menaced from Hungary and Greece. After long efforts, Pius succeeded in awakening the Catholic sovereigns to the perception that there was indeed imminent danger. The idea of a league between these princes was suggested to the Pope by the attack on Cyprus; this he proposed to Venice on the one hand, and to Spain on the other.[6] " When I received permission to negotiate with him on that subject," says the Venetian ambassador, " and communicated my instructions to that effect, he raised his hands to heaven, offering thanks to God, and promising that his every thought, and all the force he could command, should be devoted to that purpose."

Infinite were the troubles and labors required from the pontiff before he could remove the difficulties impeding the union of the two maritime powers: he contrived to associate with them the other States of Italy, and although in the beginning he had neither money, ships, nor arms, he yet found means to reinforce the fleet with some few papal galleys. He also contributed to the selection of Don John of Austria as leader, and managed to stimulate alike his ambition and religious ardor. From all this resulted a battle, the most successful in which Christendom had ever engaged with the Turks, that of Lepanto. The pontiff's mind was so intensely absorbed by the enterprise, that on the day of the engagement, he believed himself to witness the victory in a kind of trance. The achievement of this triumph inspired him with the most lofty self-confidence and the boldest prospects. In a few years he believed that the Ottoman power would be utterly subdued.

[6] Soriano: " Having received the resolution, I went instantly to seek audience, though it was night, the hour inconvenient, and his holiness wearied by the events of the day, arising out of the coronation of the Duke of Florence, and the imperial ambassador's protest (against it). But when I had made known my business, his holiness was mightily rejoiced."

It would have been well if his energies had always been devoted to works so unquestionably legitimate, but this was not
the fact; so exclusive, so imperious were his religious feelings,
that he bore the very bitterest hatred to all who would not accept his tenets. And how strange a contradiction! the religion
of meekness and humility is made the implacable persecutor of
innocence and piety! But Pius V, born under the wings of the
Inquisition, and reared in its principles, was incapable of
perceiving this discrepancy; seeking with inexhaustible zeal to
extirpate every trace of dissent that might yet lurk in Catholic
countries, he persecuted with a yet more savage fury the avowed
Protestants, who were either freed from his yoke or still engaged in the struggle. Not content with despatching such military forces as his utmost efforts could command, in aid of the
French Catholics, he accompanied this with the monstrous and
unheard-of injunction [7] to their leader, Count Santafiore, to
" take no Huguenot prisoner, but instantly to kill everyone that
should fall into his hands." When trouble arose in the Netherlands, Philip of Spain was at first undetermined as to the manner in which he should treat those provinces. Pius recommended an armed intervention, " for," said he, " if you negotiate without the eloquence of arms, you must receive laws;
with arms in your hands, it is by yourself that they are imposed."
The sanguinary measures of Alva were so acceptable to the
Pope, that he sent him the consecrated hat and sword as marks
of his approval. There is no proof that he was aware of the
preparations for the massacre of St. Bartholomew, but he did
things that leave no doubt of his approving it as cordially as
did his successor.

How wonderful is this union of upright purpose, elevation
of mind, austerity toward himself, and devout religious feeling,
with morose bigotry, rancorous hatred, and sanguinary eagerness in persecution!

Such were the dispositions in which Pius IV lived and died.[8]
When he felt that death was approaching, he once more visited
the seven churches, " in order," as he said, " to take leave of
those holy places." Thrice did he kiss the lowest step of the
Scala Santa. He had promised at one time not only to expend

[7] Catena, " Vita di Pio V.," p. 85:
" He complained of the count for not
having obeyed his command to slay instantly whatever heretic fell into his
hands."
[8] He died on May 1, 1572.

the whole treasure of the Church, the very chalices and crosses included, on an expedition against England, but even to appear himself at the head of the army. Certain fugitive Catholics from England presenting themselves on his way, he declared that " fain would he pour forth his own blood for their sakes." The principal subject of his last words was the league, for the prosperous continuation of which he had made all possible preparations ; the last coins he sent from his hand were destined for this purpose. His fancy was haunted to the last moment by visions of his different undertakings. He had no doubt of their success, believing that, of the very stones, God would, if needful, raise up the man demanded for so sacred a work.[9]

His loss was felt more immediately than he had himself anticipated ; but also, there was a unity established ; a force called into existence, by whose inherent power, the course into which he had directed the nations would inevitably be confirmed and maintained.

[9] " Informatione dell' infirmità de Pio V.: " "Having in his chamber a casket containing 13,000 scudi, intended for alms to be distributed by his own hand, he sent for the treasurer to the Camera, two days before his death, bidding him take them, for they would be useful to the league."

BOOK IV

STATE AND COURT—TIMES OF GREGORY XIII AND SIXTUS V

WITH renewed and concentrated forces did Catholicism now advance to confront the Protestant faith.

Comparing these two mighty antagonists, we perceive that Catholicism possessed an immense advantage, inasmuch as that all its movements were directed by a common chief, and tended toward a common centre.

And not only could the popes combine the strength of other Catholic powers for one common effort, but they had also dominions of their own sufficiently extensive and powerful to contribute largely toward a successful result.

It is in a new aspect that we are henceforth to consider the States of the Church.

This sovereignty had been founded by the struggles of different pontiffs to exalt their families to princely dignity, or to secure paramount influence for themselves among the temporal powers, those of the Italian States more particularly. In neither of these purposes did they succeed to the extent of their wishes, and the renewal of these struggles had now become altogether impossible. The alienation of church property was forbidden by a special law, while the Spaniards were now too powerful in Italy to leave hope of a successful competition with them. The temporal sovereignty had on the other hand become auxiliary to the Church, and the financial resources presented by the former were of the utmost importance to the general development and welfare; but, before proceeding further, it will be needful to examine more closely the administration of the Papal See, in that form which it gradually assumed during the course of the sixteenth century.

261

Section I.—Administration of the States of the Church

A finely situated, rich, and noble territory had fallen to the lot of the popes.

The writers of the sixteenth century can find no words that suffice them to extol its fertility. How fair are the plains around Bologna and through Romagna! How brightly does a rich productiveness combine with beauty adown the slopes of the Apennines! "We travelled," say the Venetian ambassadors in 1522, "from Macerata to Tolentino, through a district of surpassing loveliness. Hills and valleys were clothed with grain through an extent of thirty miles; nothing less rich might be seen. Uncultivated land we could not find for the breadth of a foot. We thought it impossible to gather so vast a quantity of corn, how then shall it be consumed?" In Romagna 40,000 stara of corn were yearly produced beyond what was required for consumption; for this there was a great demand, and after supplying the mountain districts about Urbino, Tuscany, and Bologna, 35,000 stara were sometimes exported by sea. On the one coast, Venice was supplied from Romagna and the March,[1] whilst Genoa on the other, and sometimes even Naples, were provided for by the territory of Viterbo and the Patrimony (of St. Peter). In one of his bulls for 1566, Pius V exalts the divine favor, by whose permission it is that Rome, who was formerly not able to subsist without foreign corn, had now not only abundance for herself, but could also come in aid of her neighbors, and even of foreigners, by land and sea, with the produce of her own Campagna.[2] In the year 1589, the exports of corn from the States of the Church were estimated at the annual value of five hundred thousand scudi.[3] The various districts were also famed, each for its peculiar production; as Perugia for hemp; Faenza for flax; Viterbo for both;[4] Cesena for its

[1] Badoer, "Relatione," 1591. The friendship of Romagna for Venice was based on the recollection of "what an excellent city it was to sell your corn and wine in, your fruits, your nuts, and many another commodity, for which one brings back good money."
[2] "Jurisdictio consulum artis agriculturæ urbis, 9 Sept. 1566: " "Bullar. Cocquel." iv. ii. 314.
[3] Giovanni Gritti, "Relatione," 1589: "Romagna and the March alone have sometimes 60,000 rubbia of wheat and more than 30,000 rubbia of other grain.

The Roman Campagna and the transalpine states supply food almost every year to Genoa and other surrounding places: it is said that in return for the grains of the ecclesiastical states there go at least 500,000 scudi into the country; they, on their part, have little need of foreign goods, except some few things of small value and importance, wares for the apothecary and grocer, with stuffs for the dress of the nobles and great personages."
[4] "Voyage de Montaigne," ii. 488.

wine, which was exported; Rimini for its oil; Bologna for woad; San Lorenzo for manna. The vintage of Montefiascone was known and esteemed the world over. In the Campagna was then produced a breed of horses but little inferior to those of Naples. Around Nettuno and Terracina there was excellent hunting, especially of the wild boar. There were lakes abounding in fish. They had besides salt-works, alum-works, and marble quarries. In a word, the country supplied whatever could be desired for the enjoyment of life in the richest profusion.

This fine territory was equally well situated for general intercourse with the world. Ancona possessed a flourishing trade. "It is a beautiful place," say those same ambassadors of 1522, "full of merchants, principally Greeks and Turks; we were assured that of these, some had transacted business in preceding years to the amount of five hundred thousand ducats." In the year 1549, we find two hundred Greek families settled there as merchants, and who had a church of their own. The harbor was full of caravels from the Levant. There were Armenians, Turks, Florentines, Lucchese, Venetians, and Jews from East and West. The wares exposed by the dealers consisted of silks, wool, leather, Flemish lead and cloths. Luxury increased, house-rent became high, physicians and schoolmasters were more numerous, and better paid than at any previous time.[5]

It is not however so much on the commercial readiness and activity of the papal subjects as on their bravery, that writers of the period love to dwell. Not unfrequently are the inhabitants of each district set before us, distinguished by the varying shades of their military character. The people of Perugia are "steady soldiers"; those of Romagna, "brave but improvident." The inhabitants of Spoleto are fertile in expedients and the arts of strategy; those of Bologna full of courage, but difficult to hold in discipline; the men of the March are given to plunder; the people of Faenza surpass all others in firmness when charged in battle, or in the sustained pursuit of the retreating enemy. The Forlivese excel in the execution of difficult manœuvres; the dwellers of Fermo in the use of the lance.[6] The whole population, says one of the Venetians before referred

[5] Saracini, "Notizie istoriche della Città d'Ancona," Roma, 1675, p. 362.
[6] Landi, "Quæstiones Forcianæ," Ne-

apoli, 1536; a book filled with minute and remarkable notices of the state of Italy at that time.

to, is apt for the uses of war, and martial by nature. No sooner
do they leave their homes than they are fitted for any mode of
service. They are equally good in sieges as in the open field,
and bear with little difficulty the toils and privations of a campaign.[7] Venice ever drew her best troops from the March and
from Romagna; therefore it was that the republic always prized
so highly the good-will of the dukes of Urbino; we constantly
find officers from that district in their service. It was said of
this country, that captains for all the princes in the world might
he found in it. The fact was frequently alluded to, that from
these lands had gone forth that company of St. George, with
whose aid Alberic of Barbiano had extirpated the hordes of foreign mercenaries, and restored the fame of Italian arms. It
was still the same race of men as that whence had proceeded
the legions who of old had so largely contributed to the establishment of the Roman Empire.[8] They have not indeed continued to merit these emphatic encomiums through all periods of
their history, yet the last great military leader, by whom these
men were employed beyond their own frontiers, is known to
have preferred them to any other of his Italian troops, nay, even
to a considerable part of his French soldiery.

These rich and populous territories, with their brave inhabitants, were now subjected to the peaceful and spiritual
government of the popes. It is for us to examine the basis and
organization of this ecclesiastical state as it developed its resources under their rule.

It was founded, as were most of the Italian sovereignties,
on the more or less rigid limitation of that independence to which
the municipalities had, in the course of the century, almost
everywhere attained.

Even during the fifteenth century, the priors of Viterbo,
seated on their stone seats before the door of the town-hall, received the oath of the podestà, sent them by the pontiff or his
representative.[9]

When the city of Fano placed itself under the immediate

[7] Soriano, 1570: "As to the soldiers, it is generally believed that those of the Papal States are the best in Italy, or, indeed, in all Europe."

[8] Lorenzo Priuli, "Relatione," 1586: "The state abounds with the necessaries of life, so that it can supply its neigh- bors; it has also wealth of warlike men." He specifies the families of Genga, Carpagna, and Malatesta. "They all seem born for war, and are quickly brought together by the beat of the drum."

[9] Feliciano Bussi, "Istoria di Viter- bo," p. 59.

sovereignty of the Papal See, in 1463, it made certain conditions:
first, that " to all future time " the city should hold " immediately " of the papal throne; next that it should select its own
podestà, whose appointment should need no further confirmation, and that for twenty years it should be subjected to no
new impost; finally, it stipulated for all benefits arising from
the sale of salt, with various other immunities.[10]

A prince, so arbitrary as was Cæsar Borgia, could yet not
avoid the grant of certain privileges to the cities constituting
his principality. Thus he resigned revenues to the town of
Sinigaglia, which till then had invariably been claimed by the
sovereign.[1]

How much more, then, would these concessions be expected
from Julius II, whose ambition it was to present himself as a
liberator from tyranny. He reminded the Perugians himself
that the best years of his youth had been passed within their
walls. When he drove Baglione from Perugia, he did not refuse to recall the exiles or to reinstate the peaceful magistrates, " the *priori*"; he conferred increased emoluments on the
professors of the university, and invaded no one of the ancient
immunities of the city: for a long time it paid a few thousand
ducats only as a recognition of his sovereignty; and, even under
Clement VII, I find a calculation of how many troops Perugia
could bring into the field, precisely as though it had been a completely free municipality.[2]

Nor was Bologna more closely restricted. Together with
the forms of municipal independence, it retained many of the
essential attributes: the administration of the town revenues
was entirely in its own hands, it maintained troops of its own,
and the papal legate received a salary from the city.

The towns of Romagna were seized by Julius II during the
Venetian war; but he did not annex a single one to the pontificate without first consenting to restrictive conditions, or conferring new and fixed rights; these stipulations were always
referred to in later times. The political relation with the Church
into which they had entered by these treaties received the title
of " Ecclesiastical Freedom."[3]

[10] Amiani, " Memorie istoriche della Città di Fano."
[1] Siena, " Storia di Sinigaglia," App. n. 6.
[2] Suriano, " Relatione di Fiorenza," 1533.

[3] Rainaldus alludes to this, but very briefly. Touching Ravenna, see " Hie-ronymi Rubei Historiarum Raven-natum," lib. viii. p. 660.

Thus constituted, the State as a whole bore a certain resemblance to that of Venice. In each, the political power had at one time resided in the commune, and this had for the most part subjected other smaller communities over which it held sway. In the Venetian States these paramount municipalities had submitted themselves under conditions strictly defined, and without resigning the whole of their independence to the control of the nobili of Venice. In the States of the Church these same municipalities became subject to the commonwealth of the Curia; for as in Venice it was the nobility that formed the commonwealth, so in Rome this was represented by the court. The dignity of the prelacy was not indeed absolutely indispensable as a qualification, even for the supreme powers of the municipalities, during the first half of this century; secular vice-legates were frequent in Perugia, while in Romagna it seemed to be almost an established rule that a lay president should direct the administration. It would sometimes happen that laymen would acquire an almost unlimited power and influence, as did Jacopo Salviati under Clement VII, but in such cases they were ever connected in some manner with the Curia; they belonged in one way or another to the Pope, and were thus members of that corporation.

At this period the towns would seem to have had no liking for secular governors; they preferred and requested to be ruled by prelates, as holding it more honorable to obey an ecclesiastic of high rank. Compared with a German principality, and its carefully organized system of well-defined grades, the Italian looks at first sight little better than a mere anarchy; but in point of fact the partition of rights and privileges was quite as clearly understood, and as rigidly adhered to in the latter as in the former. The supreme authorities of a city, for example, were held in check by the nobles, the nobles by the burghers (cittadini), the subjugated commune kept jealous watch over the acts of its superior, and the rural populations over the towns. It is a striking fact that the establishment of provincial governments was in no one instance adopted in Italy; certain provincial assemblies were indeed held in the Papal States, and even received the imposing name of " parliament," but there must have been something adverse to institutions of this character in the manners or modes of thought of Italians, since no one of them ever attained to effectual or enduring influence.

From what has been said, it will be obvious that if the municipal constitution had acquired that complete development of which it was susceptible, and toward which it seemed to tend (by the limitation which on the one hand it imposed on the governing authority, and that presented to the powers of the communes, and the multitude of individual privileges on the other), it would then have exhibited the principle of stability in its most significant aspect; a political system, based on prerogatives clearly defined, and on checks that were reciprocally effectual.

Considerable progress toward a constitution of this character was made by the Venetian States, and certain steps, but much less decided ones, were taken in the same direction by those of the Church.

This difference was inevitable from the diversity of origin in each government. In Venice the reins were held by a corporation, self-governing and hereditary, which considered the supreme power as its legitimate property. The Roman Curia, on the contrary, was in continual fluctuation, every new conclave infusing new elements, the compatriots of each successive pope invariably obtained a large portion of the public business. Among the Venetians, appointments to office proceeded from the corporation itself; in Rome they were to be gained only from the favor of the Pope. The rulers of Venice were held to their duties by rigorous laws, close inspection, and regard to the honor of their body. The Roman authorities were rather incited by hope of promotion than restrained by fear of punishment; both depending principally on the favor and goodwill of the pontiff, they thus enjoyed a more extensive freedom of action.

We shall proceed to show that the papal government had from the first secured to itself a larger degree of authority.

Of this fact we find convincing proof by a comparison of the concessions made to the municipalities they conquered, by Rome and Venice respectively; a favorable opportunity for such comparison presents itself in the case of Faenza. This city, which had capitulated to Venice some years before its surrender to the ecclesiastical State, had made conditions with each government.[4] It had, for example, demanded from both

---

[4] "Historie di Faenza, fatica di Giulio Cesare Tonduzzi," Faenza, 1675, contains, p. 562, the capitulations concluded with the Venetians in 1501, and those agreed to by Julius II in 1510.

that no new impost should ever be laid on them, but with
consent of the majority in the great Council of Faenza. To
this the Venetians agreed without reserve; whereas the pontiff
added the significant clause, "unless it shall appear to him
advisable to do otherwise for good and sufficient causes." I
will not multiply instances; a similar state of matters prevailing throughout; one other fact in proof shall suffice. The
Venetians had assented without hesitation to the demand that
all criminal judgments should be referred to the podestà and
his court (Curia). The Pope confirms this privilege in its
general import, but makes the important exception, "In
cases of high-treason or of similar crimes, circulated to cause
popular irritation, the authority of the governor shall step
in." It is obvious then that the papal government assumed
from the very outset a much more effective exercise of the
sovereign authority than did that of Venice.[5]

But it must also be admitted that this extension of the
ecclesiastical powers was greatly facilitated by the municipalities
themselves.

In these subjugated towns, and in that day, the middle
classes, the burghers, traders, and artisans, while their gains
sufficed to procure them the means of life, remained peaceable
and obedient; but the patricians, the nobles in whom the
municipal authority was vested, were in perpetual commotion
and tumult; they practised no arts, they paid little attention
to agriculture, had no disposition to intellectual improvement,
and did not greatly care even for skill in arms; they were
wholly devoted to the pursuit of their particular feuds and enmities. The old factions of Guelfs and Ghibellines were still
in existence, they had been revived by the late wars, in which
victory was sometimes with one and sometimes with the other;
all the families belonging to these two parties were well known,
with the side they adopted. In Faenza, Ravenna, and Forli, the
Ghibellines had the upper hand, in Rimini the Guelfs were the
stronger. But in all these towns the weaker party still maintained itself alive. In Cesena and Imola they were nearly bal-

[5] Its mode of employing this authority may be gathered from Paul III, who tells us in 1547 that "those who have newly attained the papacy have come to it poor, loaded with the promises they have made, and compelled to large ex-penses before they can assure them-selves in the lands of the Church. Their outlay is for some years beyond their profits."—The Cardinal de Guise to the King of France, in Ribier, ii. 77.

anced. Among these then, even in times of external peace, a secret warfare was incessantly proceeding; each man was specially occupied in seeking to depress his opponent of the adverse faction, and to cast him into the shade.[6] The leaders had always adherents from the lowest classes at their command; wild, determined bravoes, of fierce and wandering habits, who were ever prepared with offers of service to those whom they knew to be in fear of enemies, or to have injuries demanding vengeance; these men were always ready to commit murder for a sum of money.

The result of these incessant feuds was, that the cities became less vigilant in the maintenance of their rights, for as each party distrusted the other, so neither would permit authority to rest in its opponent's hands. On the arrival of the president or legate in the province, the question was not whether the municipal rights would be respected, but rather which party would be favored by the new functionary. It would be difficult to describe the exultation of the successful party, or the dismay of its rivals, when this was ascertained. Infinite prudence was required on the part of the legate, the most influential men were ready to attach themselves to his side, they did their utmost to render themselves acceptable to him, affected earnest zeal for the interest of the State, and acquiesced in all the plans he might propose for its advantage; but all this was frequently for no other purpose than that of placing themselves well with the governor, and by gaining his confidence, become all the better enabled to persecute the party they abhorred.[7]

The position of the provincial barons was somewhat different. They were for the most part very poor, but ambitious, and liberal to prodigality, usually keeping open house, although it was known that their expenditure largely exceeded their income, and this without exception. They had always adherents in the towns, and sometimes employed these men for the most

[6] "Relatione della Romagna" (Bibl. Alt.) : "The nobles have numerous dependents, of whom they avail themselves in the councils to obtain offices, either for themselves or others; also to further their own purposes and hinder their neighbors'; these aid them even in their suits before the tribunals, or bear witness for them, and take part in their quarrels, or procure them revenge; some too, about Ravenna, Imola, and Faenza, are in the practice of smuggling grain."

[7] "Relatione di Monsre. Revmo. Giov. P. Ghisilieri, al P. Gregorio XIII., tornando egli dal presidentato di Romagna." From Tonduzzi ("Historie di Faenza," p. 673) we see that Ghisilieri went into the province in 1578.

illegal purposes; but their principal care was to preserve a perfect understanding with their peasantry, in whose hands remained the greater part of the soil, which constituted all their wealth. The advantages of high birth, and the prerogatives of gentle blood, were sufficiently appreciated on the one part, and held in profound reverence on the other, through all the lands of the south; but distinction of ranks was not marked in the same manner as in northern countries, presenting no obstacle to a close personal intimacy. The peasants lived with their barons in a sort of fraternal subordination, nor could it easily be told whether the peasantry were more ready to offer service and obedience, or the barons to render aid and protection; their connection had a character that was even patriarchal.[8]   One cause for this probably was, that the baron abstained from giving his peasantry any cause for appeal to the state authorities, being but little disposed to regard with reverence the feudal supremacy of the Papal See; as to the peasants, they considered this supremacy, and the legate's claim to jurisdiction (not in cases of appeal only, but also in the first instance), by no means as claims of right, but rather as the consequence of an unfortunate political conjuncture, that would soon pass away.

There were also found in certain districts, more especially in Romagna, independent communities of peasants.[9]   These were large clans, descending from a common stock; lords in their own villages, generally half-savage, all well armed, and especially practised in the use of the arquebus, they may perhaps be best compared with the free Greek and Sclavonian communities, who had preserved their privileges among the Venetians; or with those of Candia, the Morea, and Dalmatia, who had regained their lost independence from the Turks. In the States of the Church these peasants also adhered to one or other of the different factions; thus, the Cavina clan, with the Scardocci and Solaroli, were Ghibellines; the Manbelli, Cerroni, and Serra were Guelphs. In the district of the Serra clan there was a hill, which served as an asylum for those who had committed any offence. The most important of these clans was the Cerroni, whose numbers had extended across the fron-

[8] " Relatione della Romagna: " " Each bending to the humor of the other."
[9] The peasants also sometimes freed themselves from the yoke of the towns (see Ghisilieri), " withdrawing as a body from those cities, they govern themselves by separate laws, under a president chosen by themselves, and who has power to decide in all their affairs."

tier into the Florentine territory; they were divided into two branches, the Rinaldi and Ravagli, between whom, spite of their common origin, there existed a bitter feud. They maintained a sort of hereditary connection with many among the noblest families of the towns, and also with certain eminent jurists, by whom the faction was supported in all questions with the laws. Throughout Romagna, there was no single family, however distinguished, that might not have been injured by these banded peasants. The Venetians took care to have always an interest in one or other of their chiefs, for the purpose of securing their aid in case of war.

If these populations, as we have before remarked, had been well united, the Roman prelates would have found it difficult to assert their authority, but in their dissensions the government found its strength. To this effect a president of Romagna, writing to Gregory XIII, expresses himself, as I find, in his report: "Very difficult is the task of governing, when the people hold themselves too closely together; let them be disunited, and the mastery is then easily gained."[10] There was, besides, another circumstance acting in favor of government. This was the formation of a party consisting of those peaceable men of the middle classes who desired to live tranquilly, and were not attached to either faction. In Fano this party entered into an association called the "Holy Union," compelled to this, as the record of their institution sets forth, "because all the town is become full of robbers and murderers, so that, not only are those in jeopardy who join themselves to the several feuds, but also those who would fain eat their bread in the sweat of their brow." They bound themselves, by an oath in the Church, as brethren for life and death, to maintain the tranquillity of the town, and to exterminate those who sought to disturb it.[1] They were favored by the government, from whom they received permission to carry arms, and we find them throughout Romagna under the name of the *Pacifici*. From this body was gradually constituted a kind of plebeian magistracy. Adherents of government might also be found among

---

[10] Ghisilieri: "Siccome il popolo disunito facilmente si regge, cosi difficilmente si regge quando è troppo unito." (See the text.)
[1] They were not unlike the Hermandad. Amiani, "Memorie di Fano," ii.

146, gives us their formula founded on the text: "Blessed are the peacemakers, for they shall be called the children of God." From this their name in other towns may have been derived.

the free peasants; the Manbelli, for example, attached themselves to the court of the legate; they arrested banditti, and
acted as wardens of the frontiers, a service that procured them
increased estimation among the neighboring clans.[2]   Local
jealousies, the contests arising between cities and the surrounding villages, with various other internal differences, all contributed to increase the power of the government.

Here, then, in place of that respect for law, good order, and
stability, which, judging form its theory only, we should have
expected this constitution of the State to produce, we find the
turbulent strife of factions, intervention of the government so
long as these remained at variance, reaction and opposition of
the municipalities when they are again united; violence acting
in support of the law, violence opposed to the law; every man
trying to what extent he might rebel with impunity.

Immediately after the accession of Leo X, the Florentines,
who had obtained a large share in the administration, exercised
the rights of the Curia with the most oppressive violence.
Deputations from the cities were seen to arrive in Rome, one
after another, entreating relief from their burdens.   Ravenna
declared itself prepared to surrender to the Turks, rather than
endure the continuance of such a system.[3]   During vacancies of
the pontificate, it frequently happened that the ancient feudal
lords would return to power, and were not expelled by the new
Pope without considerable difficulty.   The cities, on the other
hand, dreaded the being alienated from the Papal See.   A cardinal, a connection of the Pope, or perhaps some neighboring
prince, would occasionally offer a sum of money to the
"camera," for the right of governing one or other of these
towns.   Aware of this, the towns, on their part, had agents
and envoys at Rome, whose office it was to discover all projects of this sort on the instant of their formation, and to
interpose for their defeat; in this they were most frequently
successful; they were, however, sometimes compelled to em-

[2] According to the "Relatione della
Romagna," they also called themselves
"men of Sciato," from their dwelling-
place.   "Men," says the same, "who
made themselves much respected, they
are Guelfs, and the Court of Romagna
found them very useful, particularly in
capturing banditti, and preventing the
cattle from being carried off from the
mountains."

[3] Marino Zorzi, "Relatione of 1517":
"The country of Romagna is in great
commotion, little justice is done there:
I who speak, have seen as many as ten
deputations going to Cardinal Medici,
lamenting the state of things there;
and, above all, loudly bewailing the
lawless conduct of their rulers."

ploy force against the papal authorities, and even against the
pontiff's troops. In the history of nearly all these towns are
found instances of very determined insubordination. It once
happened in Faenza that the citizens had a regular battle with
the Swiss guards of Leo X. This was in the summer of 1521.
They fought furiously in the streets, and the Swiss had succeeded in gathering themselves into one body on the market-
place (piazza) ; but the townsmen having barricaded all the
avenues leading from it, the Swiss were content to depart
quietly, since they could do so unmolested, when one of the
barriers had been removed. The anniversary of this day was
long afterward celebrated in Faenza with religious solemnities
and rejoicings.[4] Jesi, again, though by no means a town of
importance, had yet courage to attack the vice-governor in his
palace, on the twenty-fifth of November, 1528. He had demanded certain marks of honor, which the inhabitants refused.
The peasants united themselves to the citizens, they took into
their pay a hundred Albanians who chanced to be in the neighborhood, and drove the vice-governor, with his followers, from
the town. The chronicler of Jesi, in other respects a most devout Catholic, relates this fact with infinite complacency. " My
native town," says he, " now seeing herself restored to her
primitive freedom, resolved solemnly to celebrate the anniversary of this day, at the public expense." [5]

But other results were sure to proceed from these acts of
violence ; new oppressions for example, punishments, and closer
restrictions. All such occasions were gladly seized by the government, as affording a pretext for depriving the towns that
still retained any efficient part of their ancient independence, of
its last traces, and reducing them to entire subjection.

Of this we have remarkable examples in the histories of
Ancona and Perugia.

From Ancona the pontiffs received a very small annual
tribute only, as a mere recognition of their sovereignty. The
insufficiency of this became all the more apparent as the town
advanced in riches and prosperity. The revenues of Ancona
were estimated by the court at 50,000 scudi, and it was found
to be intolerable that the local nobility should divide so large

---

[4] Tonduzzi, " Historie di Faenza," p.
609.
[5] Baldassini, " Memorie istoriche dell'

antichissima Città di Jesi "; Jesi, 1744,
p. 256.

a sum among themselves. It chanced that the city not only refused the payment of new imposts, but also took forcible possession of a castle to which it had claims. This occasioned a violent misunderstanding. The mode of asserting their rights sometimes adopted by governments in that day is worthy of notice. The papal officers drove off the cattle from the march of Ancona, by the way of levying the new taxes. This they called making reprisals.

But Clement VII was not content with these " reprisals." He waited only for a favorable opportunity to make himself really master of Ancona, and this he made no scruple of employing artifice to bring about.

Declaring that the Turkish power, emboldened by its recent successes in Egypt and Rhodes, and the extent of its influence in the Mediterranean, might be daily expected to attack Italy, he caused a fortress to be erected in Ancona. Many Turkish ships were constantly at anchor off Ancona, and the pontiff expressed extreme apprehension for its safety, defenceless as it was alleging this as the only motive for raising the fortress. He sent Antonio Sangallo to construct the works, which proceeded with excessive rapidity, and a small garrison soon after appeared to take possession. This was the moment that Clement had awaited: matters having arrived so far, the governor of the march, Monsignore Bernardino della Barba, who, though a priest, was a man of martial character, arrived before Ancona one morning in September of 1562, with an imposing force which the jealousy of the neighboring cities had supplied to him. Having seized one of the gates, he marched to the market-place and drew up his troops before the palace. Suspecting no evil, the Anziani, but recently chosen by lot, were peaceably abiding here, with the badges of the supreme dignity around them; Della Barba entered with his escort of officers, and with little ceremony informed them that " the Pope had determined to take the uncontrolled government of Ancona into his own hands." There was no possibility of opposing effectual resistance, for though the younger nobles hastily gathered a few bands of devoted adherents from the neighboring villages, the elders, perceiving that the papal troops were prepared by their new fortifications for every emergency, refused to expose the city to devastation and ruin: they submitted, therefore, to what they saw was unavoidable.

The Anziani vacated the palace, and immediately after appeared the new legate, Benedetto degli Accolti, from whom the *Camera Apostolica* had received promise of twenty thousand scudi annually for the right of government in Ancona.

And now its position was changed entirely: all arms were required to be surrendered, and sixty-four of the principal nobles were banished; the magistracy was placed in different hands; portions of the administration were intrusted to persons who were not noble, and to the inhabitants of the districts surrounding. The old statutes were no longer suffered to form the rule of government.

Woe to him who ventured to deviate from the new regulations. Some of the principal nobles incurred the suspicion of conspiracy—they were instantly seized, condemned, and beheaded. On the following day a carpet was spread in the market-place; on this were laid the bodies, each with a burning torch beside it; and thus they remained through the whole day.

The inhabitants of Ancona were indeed relieved by Paul III from some portion of the severe restrictions they at first suffered, but their subjection was none the less complete; their former independence he was by no means inclined to restore.[6]

This pontiff was, in fact, more disposed to fix than to remove the fetters of the conquered cities in most instances, as for example in that of Perugia, for whose subjugation he employed that same Bernardino della Barba.

The price of salt being doubled by Paul III, the people of Perugia declared that they were justified by their privileges in refusing to pay it. For this the Pope excommunicated them; and the citizens assembling in the churches, elected a magistracy of " twenty-five defenders." They laid the keys of their town before a crucifix in the market-place, and both sides took up arms.

A general commotion was excited by the revolt of so important a city, and very grave consequences would doubtless have ensued had there been war in any other part of Italy; but as all was tranquil, the assistance on which the inhabitants had calculated from surrounding States, could not be rendered.

Accordingly, when Pier Luigi Farnese appeared before the

[6] Sarancinelli, " Notizie istoriche della Città d' Ancona," Roma, 1675, ii. xi. p. 335.

town with an army of 10,000 Italians and 3,000 Spaniards, Perugia, though possessing considerable power, had yet not wherewith to oppose a force so considerable. The government of the twenty-five, too, was rather distinguished by violence and tyranny than by prudence and careful measures for the defence of the town; they did not even provide money to pay the troops brought to their aid by a member of the Baglione family. Ascanio Colonna, who also resisted the same impost, was their only ally, and he confined himself to driving off cattle from the domains of the Church, nor could he be prevailed on to afford a more effectual assistance.

Thus Perugia, after a brief enjoyment of liberty, was again reduced to subjection, and surrendered on the third of June, 1540. Clothed in long mourning dresses, with ropes round their necks, the deputies of the city presented themselves beneath the portico of St. Peter, and kneeling at the feet of the pontiff, entreated his pardon.

This was not refused; but their liberties were entirely destroyed, and all their rights and privileges repealed.

And now Bernardino della Barba arrived in Perugia, and dealt with that city as he had done with Ancona. The inhabitants were compelled to deliver up their arms; the chains with which they had been accustomed to close their streets were taken away; the houses of the "twenty-five," who had themselves escaped in time, were razed to the ground, and on the site of that inhabited by the Baglioni a fortress was constructed. The citizens were obliged to pay the expense of all. A chief magistrate was now appointed, whose name sufficiently denotes the character of his duties; he was called "the conservator of ecclesiastical obedience." The ancient title of "prior" was, indeed, restored to the functionary by a subsequent pontiff, but the restitution of its former powers did not accompany it.[7]

By the same force that had subjugated Perugia, Ascanio Colonna was also put down and expelled from all his strongholds.

These repeated and successful achievements effected an immense augmentation of the papal authority in the States of the

---

[7] Mariotti, "Memorie istoriche civili ed ecclesiastiche della Città di Perugia e suo contado," Perugia, 1806, gives us authentic and minute accounts of these events, vol. i. p. 113-160, and again refers to them on p. 634.

Church—neither city nor baron dared now presume to oppose it. The independent municipalities had submitted one after another, and the Roman Court had at length drawn the entire resources of the country into its own hands, to be disposed of for the furtherance of its own purposes.

Let us now examine the manner in which these resources were administered.

Section II.—Finances

In the first instance we must proceed to make ourselves acquainted with the system of the papal finances, and the rather as this system is important, not only as regards the Roman States, but also because of the example furnished by it to all Europe.

We have first to observe that the system of exchanges adopted in the Middle Ages originated chiefly in the nature of the papal revenues, which, due from all parts of the world, were to be transmitted to the Curia from every separate country: but it is equally worthy of remark, that the system of national debt by which we are even now enveloped, and which maintains so important an influence on the operations of commerce, was first fully developed in the States of the Church.

There has doubtless been justice in the complaints raised against the exactions of Rome during the fifteenth century, but it is also true that of the proceeds a small part only passed into the hands of the Pope. Pius II enjoyed the obedience of all Europe, yet he once suffered so extreme a dearth of money that he was forced to restrict his household and himself to one meal a day! The 200,000 ducats required for the Turkish war that he was meditating had to be borrowed; and those petty expedients, adopted by many popes, of demanding from a prince, a bishop, or a grand-master, who might have some cause before the court, the gift of a gold cup filled with ducats, or a present of rich furs,[1] only show the depressed and wretched condition of their resources.

There is no doubt that money reached the court, if not in

[1] Voigt, "Voices from Rome respecting the papal court in the fifteenth century," in F. von Raumer's "Historichen Taschenbuch for 1833," contains numerous remarks on this subject. Whoever has access to the work, "Silesia vor und seit dem Jahre 1740," will find there, ii. 483, a satire of the fifteenth century, not badly done, on this monstrous system of present-making: "The passion of our lord the Pope, according to the mark of gold and silver."

those extravagant sums that many have believed, yet to a very considerable extent; but, arrived so far, it was at once dispersed through channels innumerable. A large portion, for example, was absorbed by the revenues of those offices, which it had long been the practice to dispose of by sale. The income of these offices was principally derived from perquisites and fees, and but slight restraint was imposed on the exactions of those who had purchased them. The price at which each of these appointments was resold as it became vacant, was all that recurred to the papal coffers.

If then the pontiff desired to undertake any costly enterprise, he was compelled to find some extraordinary expedient for procuring the means; jubilees and indulgences were thus most welcome auxiliaries; incited by these, the piety of the faithful secured him an ample resource. He had also another mode of gaining supplies at his need. He had but to create new offices, when the sale of these was sure to afford him a respectable amount. This was an extraordinary sort of loan, and one for which the Church paid heavy interest, which had to be provided for by an increase of the imposts. The practice had long prevailed; an authentic register existing in the house of Chigi enumerates nearly six hundred and fifty salable offices, of which the income amounted to about one hundred thousand scudi.[2] These were for the most part, procurators, registrars, abbreviators, correctors, notaries, secretaries, nay, even messengers and doorkeepers, whose increased numbers were continually raising the expense of a bull or brief. It was indeed for that very purpose that their offices took the particular form assigned them, as to the duties connected with each, these were little or nothing.

It will be readily imagined that succeeding popes, involved as they were in the politics of Europe, would eagerly have recourse to so convenient a method of replenishing their coffers. Sixtus IV, proceeding by the advice of his prothonotary, Sinolfo, founded whole colleges, the places in which he sold for a few hundred ducats each; most curious are the titles that some of them bore. There was the college, for example, " of the hun-

[2] " Gli uffici più antichi," MS. Bibliotheca Chigi, No. ii. 50. There are 651 offices and 98,340 scudi, before the creation of Sixtus IV. So little truth is there in the assertion of Onuphrius Panvinius, that Sixtus IV was the first pontiff who sold them.

dred Janissaries, " who were nominated for 100,000 ducats, and
whose appointments were then paid from the profits arising
on bulls and the proceeds of the first-fruits (annates).[3] " No-
tariats " and " prothonotariats," the office of procurator to the
" camera " ; everything, in short, was sold under Sixtus IV,
who carried this system to such an extent that he has frequently
been called its founder, nor indeed was it completely organized
until his time. A new college of twenty-six secretaries, with a
complement of other officers, was founded by Innocent VIII for
60,000 scudi; the embarrassments of this pontiff were such
that he was compelled to give even the papal tiara as security.
Alexander VI named eighty writers of briefs, each of whom
paid 750 scudi for his place; Julius II added one hundred
" writers of archives " at the same price.

Meanwhile the sources whence all these hundreds of officers
drew their emoluments were not inexhaustible. We have seen
how almost all Christian States made efforts, and very frequently successful efforts, to limit the encroachments of the
Papal Court. This happened, too, precisely when the popes
had been led into a vast expenditure by the magnitude of their
undertakings.

This disposition of other countries made the circumstance of
their obtaining so great an extension of their own territories
extremely fortunate; for though their government was in the
first instance very mild, they nevertheless drew large sums from
these sources, and we cannot be surprised at finding this income
administered in the same manner as the ecclesiastical funds.

When Julius II secured the salaries of the above-mentioned
" writers," by an assignation on the annates, he added a further
security charged on the customs and exchequer. He also instituted a college of 141 presidents of the Annona, all of whom
were paid from the public chest; he made the surplus revenue
of the country serve as a basis for contracting loans. The most
distinguishing characteristic of this pope in the eyes of foreign
powers was that he could raise what money he pleased; that
was, in a certain measure, the foundation of his policy.

Still more urgent were the demands of Leo X than those

---

[3] There were also Stradiotes and
Mamelukes, who were, however, afterward suppressed. " Cautioners, without
whom no papers were considered complete." Onuphrius Panvinius. According to the register (" Uficii Antichi "),
this creation appears to have brought
only 40,000 ducats.

of Julius had been; he was equally involved in war, was much less provident, and more dependent on the political aid of his family, which last required to be paid for. " That the Pope should ever keep a thousand ducats together was a thing as impossiole," says Francesco Vettori of this pontiff, " as that a stone should of its own will take to flying through the air." He has been reproached with having spent the revenues of three popes : that of his predecessor, from whom he inherited a considerable treasure, his own, and that of his successor, to whom he bequeathed a mass of debt. Not content with selling existing offices, his extraordinary nomination of cardinals brought him in important sums; and having once got on the beaten path of establishing offices for no other purpose than to sell them, he proceeded along it with the most pertinacious boldness. More than 1,200 of these appointments were created by him alone,[4] the one point in which all these *portionarii, scudieri, cavalieri di S. Pietro,* and whatever other strange name they bore, agreed, was this, that all paid a sum of money for their offices, and drew the interest of it for life by virtue of these titles. Their appointment had no other signification. Some slight prerogative was sometimes conferred in addition to the interest. It was, in fact, a kind of life annuity; from such sales Leo is said to have drawn 900,000 scudi.

The interest was indeed extremely high, amounting annually to an eighth of the capital,[5] which was to a certain extent provided for by a slight increase of ecclesiastical dues, but the larger portion came from the newly conquered provinces. This latter part of the general sum proceeded, first from the surplus funds of the municipal administrations, which were paid into the coffers of the State, next from the alum works, and then from the salt trade. The remainder was supplied by the Roman custom-house. The number of salable appointments was increased by Leo to 2,150, the annual income of which was estimated at 320,000 scudi, and was a burden both on Church and State.

But however blamable this prodigality might in itself have

[4] "Sommario di la Relation di M. Minio, 1520." " He never has ready money; he is too liberal, and cannot keep any; then the Florentines, who either are or pretend to be his relations, will not leave him a penny, and those Florentines are greatly detested at court, for in every man's business shall come the hand of a Florentine." .

[5] The 612 portionarii di ripa—added to the college of presidents—paid 286,200 ducats, receiving yearly 38,816. The 400 cavaliers of St. Peter paid 400,000, and annually received 50,610 ducats.

been, yet Leo was undoubtedly confirmed in it, by perceiving that for the time its effects were rather beneficial than injurious. If Rome at this period acquired so unusual an elevation and prosperity, it must be attributed principally to the monetary system we have described. In no city could the capitalist of that day invest his money to so much advantage; the number of new appointments, the vacancies and reappointments, kept up a continual movement in the Curia; so that each man could easily find his opportunity for advancement.

By these operations the necessity for imposing new taxes was also avoided. The States of the Church were unquestionably less burdened with imposts at that moment than any other; and Rome, as compared with other cities, was equally fortunate as to amount of taxation. It had long before been represented to the Romans, that, whereas other cities were loaded by their lords with heavy loans and vexatious imposts, they on their parts were rather made rich by their sovereign the Pope. A secretary of Clement VII who wrote an account of the conclave by which that pontiff was elected, expresses his surprise that the Roman people were not more devoted to the Holy See, the lightness of their burdens considered. "From Terracina to Placentia," he exclaims, "the Church is in possession of a broad and fair portion of Italy, her dominion extends far and wide, yet all those flourishing lands and rich cities, which under any other sovereign would be burdened for the support of large armies, pay no more to the popes than just so much as will meet the expense of their own administration." [6]

But this state of things could last only, as is evident, so long as there was surplus money in the public coffers. Leo himself did not succeed in funding all his loans; he had borrowed 32,000 scudi from Aluise Gaddi, and 200,000 from Bernardo Bini. Salviati, Ridolfi, and others, of his servants and connections, had done their utmost to procure him money; their hopes of repayment and of future rewards were founded

[6] Vianesius Albergatus, " Commentarii Rerum sui temporis " (the description of the conclave rather): " opulentissimi populi et ditissimæ urbes, quæ, si alterius ditionis essent, suis vectigalibus vel magnos exercitus alere possent, Romano pontifici vix tantum tributum pendunt, quantum in prætorum magistratuumque expensam sufficere queat " (see text). In the " Relation of Zorzi,"

1517, the united revenues of Perugia, Spoleto, the March and Romagna, are set down at 120,000 ducats, after a calculation by Francesco Armellino. The half of this went into the papal treasury. " Di quel somma la mità è per terra per pagar i legati et altri officii, e altra mità ha il papa." Unfortunately there are numerous errors in the copy of this report as given by Sanuto.

on his known liberality, and on his comparatively early years.
By his sudden death they were all utterly ruined.

The financial operations of Leo X left his dominions in a
state of exhaustion, the consequences of which were very soon
felt by his successor.

The universal hatred drawn upon himself by the unlucky
Adrian, was indeed caused in a great measure by the direct
taxes he was compelled to impose. He found himself in the
most urgent need, and laid the tax of half a ducat on each
hearth;[7] this was not much, but was most unpopular with
the Romans, to whom demands of this character were almost
unknown.

Neither could Clement VII avoid the imposition of new
taxes; he chose indirect ones: yet much complaint arose against
Cardinal Armellino, who was believed to have invented them.
The increased duties levied at the city gates, on articles of daily
necessity, occasioned great dissatisfaction, but all were obliged
to endure them.[8] Affairs were indeed in such a condition that
much more important supplies than these were demanded, and
could not be dispensed with.

Up to this time, loans had been raised under the form of
salable offices; an approximation to the system of direct loans
was first made by Clement VII on the decisive occasion of his
armament against Charles V in 1526.

In the method by offices, the capital was lost on the death
of the purchaser, unless his family could make interest to recover it from the treasury; but Clement now raised a capital
of 200,000 ducats, which did not yield so high an interest as
the places, though still a large one, ten per cent. namely;
but which continued the property of the heirs. This is a
monte non vacabile, the *monte della fede*. The interest was
charged on the customs, and was further secured by a provision
that each creditor should receive a share in the direction of the
dogana (customs). The old form was not however entirely
abandoned, these *monti* being also incorporated as were colleges.
There were certain contractors for the loan, who paid the sum

[7] "Hieronymo Negro a Marc Antonio
Micheli, 7 April, 1523," "Lettere di
Principi," i. p. 114.
[8] Foscari, " Relatione." 1526: " There
is some murmuring in Rome on account
of Cardinal Armellino, who has devised
new schemes for raising money: he has
made new taxes, so that if a man do
but bring a few thrushes or other eat-
ables for sale, he must pay something:
this tax brings in 2,500 ducats."

required to the treasury, and then divided it in shares among the members of the college.

And now are we to say that these creditors of the State, in so far as they had a lien on the general income, or the produce of the common labor, had also an indirect share in the government? It was certainly so understood in Rome, and without the form of such a participation, no man would lend his money.

But this, as we shall see, was the commencement of widely extensive financial operations.

These were entered into with a certain moderation by Paul III. He contented himself with diminishing the interest of the *monti* established by Clement, and being successful in making new assignments of it, he increased the capital by nearly one-half. He establish no new *monti*, but for this moderation he was amply indemnified by the creation of 600 new places. The measures by which this pontiff rendered himself memorable in the history of papal finance, were of a somewhat different character.

The commotions occasioned by his increase of the price of salt, we have already noticed. This source of income he relinquished; but in its stead he imposed the direct tax of the *sussidio*, solemnly promising, however, that it should not be permanent. It is this impost that was levied in so many of the southern States at that time. In Spain it was called the *servicio*, in Naples the *donativo*, in Milan the *mensuale*, and in other places it was known under different titles. It was originally introduced into the States of the Church for three years only, and was fixed at 300,000 scudi. The contribution of each province was determined in Rome; the provincial parliaments then assembled to divide this sum among the several towns, and the local governments again apportioned it between themselves, and the surrounding districts. No one was exempt. All the lay subjects of the Roman Church, whatever their privileges and immunities, marquises, barons, feudal tenants, and public officers not excepted, are enjoined by the bull for this tax to contribute their share of the burden.[9]

Payment was nevertheless not made without urgent remon-

[9] Bullar. In the year 1537 he declares to the French ambassador, " the scantiness of the Church's revenues, as well as city, for she has not 40,000 crowns a year really disposable."

strance, more especially when it was found that this *sussidio* was continually renewed from one period of three years to another; it was indeed never formally repealed, but neither was it ever perfectly collected.[10] Bologna had been rated at 30,000 scudi, but her inhabitants had the foresight to compound for perpetual freedom from this impost by the payment of one large sum. Parma and Placentia were alienated, and did not pay; of what took place in other cities, that of Fano will afford us an example: this town refused for some time to pay the share apportioned to it, under pretext of being rated too highly, and Paul agreed for once to remit the arrears, but on condition that the full amount should be applied to repair the defences of the city. Subsequently too they were always allowed a third of their contingent for the same purpose. The descendants of these men nevertheless continued to declare that they were rated too highly; the rural populations also uttered incessant outcries on the large share the towns imposed on their shoulders; these last sought to emancipate themselves from the rule of the town council; and as this body asserted its supremacy, they would fain have had recourse to the protection of the Duke of Urbino. But we should be led too far from our subject were we to pursue these local disputes into their details; what we have said will suffice to explain the fact, that little more than half of the sum fixed on for the *sussidio* was ever realized.[1] In the year 1560, the whole proceeds did not surpass 165,000 scudi.

But, notwithstanding all these things, the income of the Roman States was largely increased by this pontiff. Under Julius II the revenues were valued at 350,000 scudi; under Leo, at 420,000; under Clement VII, in the year 1526, at 500,-000; immediately after the death of Paul III, we gather, from authentic statements procured from the Roman treasury by the Venetian ambassador, Dandolo, that the amount had risen to 706,473 scudi.

His successors were, nevertheless, but slightly benefited by

[10] Bullar, "Decens esse censemus," September 5, 1543: Bullar, "Cocq." iv. i. 225.
[1] Bull of Paul IV, "Cupientes Indemnitati," April 15, 1559; Bullar, "Cocq." iv. i. 225: "Because of the various exceptions, privileges, and immunities from the payment of the subsidy, granted to divers communities, cities, universities, and individuals, as also to lands, towns, and other places in our ecclesiastical territories; and because of the many remissions and donations made from the said subsidy, we have had brought to our treasury but barely half the gross sum of the 300,000 crowns demanded."

this rise. Julius III, in one of his instructions, complains that his predecessor had alienated the entire revenue. He must certainly have meant to except the subsidy, which being, nominally at least, to be paid but for three years, could not of course be alienated; but he furthermore bewails, that a floating debt of 500,000 scudi had also been bequeathed to him by the same pontiff. [2]

But as Julian III was not withheld by this state of his affairs from plunging into wars with the French and the Farnesi; the utmost embarrassment was inevitable, whether for himself or the State. The imperialists paid him what, for those times, was a very large sum; but his letters are, nevertheless, filled with complaints. " He had hoped to receive 100,000 crowns from Ancona, and has not received half as many pence. Instead of 120,000 scudi from Bologna he has had 50,000 only. The money-changers of Genoa and Lucca had made promises, but had withdrawn them before they were well spoken. Whoever possessed a groat (carline) kept it safe in his fingers, and would hear nothing of speculating with it." [3]

The Pope, desiring to keep an army on foot, was compelled to the adoption of more effectual measures, and resolved on founding a new *monte*. The manner in which he proceeded on this occasion became the model which has been almost invariably pursued in later times.

A new impost of two carlines was laid on every rubbio of flour, and this produced him, when all deductions had been made, the sum of 30,000 scudi, which was appropriated to the payment of interest on a capital raised forthwith: thus did he originate the *monte della farina*. It will be remarked, that this operation is closely analogous to the measures of finance adopted in earlier times. New ecclesiastical offices had on previous occasions been created, and their salaries made payable on the increasing revenues of the Curia, merely that they might be sold to procure the sum required by the demand of the moment. On this occasion the revenues of the State were increased by a new tax; but this was employed solely as interest for a large capital that could not otherwise have been raised. This practice has been continued by all succeeding

[2] " Instruttione per voi Monsignore d' Imola, ultimo di Marzo, 1551," Inform. Polit. tom. xii.   [3] " Il Papa, a Giovamb. di Monte, 2 April, 1552."

pontiffs. These *monti* were sometimes *non vacabili*, like the Clementine; at other times they were *vacabili*, the interest ceasing, that is, on the death of the lender, but then the percentage was much higher, and the collegiate character of the *monte* brought the plan nearer to that of salable offices. Paul IV established the *monte novennale de' frati*, founding it on a tax which he imposed on the regular monastic orders. Pius IV levied half a farthing (a quattrino) on every pound of meat, applying the produce to the foundation of the *monte pio non vacabile*, which brought him in about 170,000 scudi. Pius V added a second quattrino on the pound of meat, and on this he established the *monte lega*.

The general importance of the Roman States becomes intelligible to our perceptions in proportion as we keep the development of this system clearly in view: by what class of necessities were the popes compelled to a mode of raising loans that burdened their territories with so direct a weight of imposts? We reply, that these necessities arose chiefly from the demands of Catholicism. The time had passed by when the purposes of the popes could be purely political; those of an ecclesiastical character could alone be now attempted, with any hope of success. The desire to come in aid of Catholic sovereigns, in their struggle with the Protestants, or in their undertakings against the Turks, was now almost invariably the immediate inducement to new financial operations. The *monte lega* received that name from Pius V, because the capital derived from it was applied to the war against the Turks, undertaken by that pontiff in his " league " with Spain and Venice. This becomes ever more and more observable; the Papal States were affected in their finances by almost every commotion arising in Europe. There were few of these occasions when the popes could escape the necessity of exacting new efforts from their own subjects for the maintenance of ecclesiastical interests. Thus was the possession of extensive dominions of vital importance to the ecclesiastical prosperity of the popes.

Not that they were content with the produce of their *monti;* they still continued the former practices. New offices, or *cavalierate*, were still created, with more or less of privilege attached; whether it was that the salaries were provided for as before, by new imposts, or that the depression which then took place in the value of money caused larger amounts to be paid into the treasury. [4]

It resulted from this, that the revenues of the papacy, excepting only a short period of diminution, occasioned by the war under Paul IV, were continually rising in nominal value; even during his life they increased again to 700,000 scudi. Under Pius they were estimated at 898,482 scudi. Paul Tiepolo is surprised to find them, after an absence of five years, augmented by 200,000 scudi, and risen to an amount of 1,100,000 scudi. Yet the popes did not, in effect, receive a larger income. This, though an extraordinary circumstance, was yet a necessary consequence of the system; for, as the taxes increased so did the alienations. Julius III is said to have alienated 54,000; Paul IV, 45,960; and Pius IV, who found all means good that gave him money, is calculated to have disposed of 182,550 scudi. This latter pontiff increased the number of salable offices to 3,500, and this did not include the *monti*, which were not considered to belong to the offices. [5] He raised the amount of the alienated funds to 450,000 scudi, and this now increased continually. In the year 1576 it was 530,000 scudi; the increase of the revenue had been also large, but the half of its total amount was, nevertheless, absorbed by these alienations. [6] The registers of the papal revenues present an extraordinary aspect in these times. The contracts made with the farmers of the revenue were generally for a period of nine years; after specifying, article by article, the sums these men had agreed to pay, the registers also state what portion of each is alienated. In 1576, and the following years, the Roman customs, for example, brought in the considerable amount of 133,000 scudi, but of this 111,170 were alienated; other deductions having also to be made, the treasury received in effect 13,000 only. There were some taxes, as on corn, meat, and wine, of which the whole were swallowed up by the *monti*. From many provincial chests, called treasuries, which had also to provide for the exigencies of the provinces, not one sixpence reached the papal coffers;

[4] Thus about 1580 many of these "luoghi di monte" stood at 100, instead of 130; the interest of the "vacabili" was reduced from 14 to 9, so that on the whole a great saving was effected.
[5] "Lista degli Uffici della Corte Romana, 1560," Bibl. Chigi, N. ii, 50. Many other separate lists of different years.

[6] Tiepolo calculates that in addition to 100,000 scudi for salaries, 270,000 were expended on fortifications and offices of legates; the Pope had 200,000 left. He tells us that of 1,800,000 received under pretext of the Turkish war, 340,000 only were applied to that purpose.

the March and Camerino may serve as examples of this fact, yet the *sussidio* was often applied to the same purpose; nay, so heavy were the incumbrances laid on the alum-works of Tolfa, which had usually been a valuable source of income, that their accounts displayed a deficiency of 2,000 scudi.[7]

The personal expenses of the pontiff and those of his court, were principally charged on the dataria, which had two distinct sources of income; the one was more strictly ecclesiastical, as arising from compositions, fixed payments for which the datary permitted *regresses,* "reservations," and various other clerical irregularities, in the course of translation from one benefice to another. The rigid severity of Paul IV had greatly diminished this source of profit, but its value was gradually restored. The other part of the dataria's income proceeded from the appointments to vacant *cavalierate,* salable offices, and places in the *monti vacabili,* it increased as the number of these appointments was augmented, and was, as is obvious, of a more secular nature than the portion first described.[8] About the year 1570, however, both united did but just suffice to meet the daily expenses of the papal household.

The position of things had become greatly changed by these financial proceedings of the Roman States, which, from having been famed as the least burdened in Italy, was now more heavily taxed than most of them.[9] Loud complaints were heard from all quarters; of the ancient municipal independence scarcely anything remained; the administration gradually became more uniform. In former times the rights of government had frequently been ceded to some favorite cardinal, or other prelate, who made no inconsiderable profit from them. The compatriots of popes, as, for example, the Florentines under the Medici, the Neapolitans under Paul IV, and the Milanese under Pius IV, had in turn held possession of the best places. Pius V put an end to this practice. The governments thus committed to favorites had not been adminis-

[7] For example, " Entrata della Reverenda Camera Apostolica sotto il Pontificato di N. S. Gregorio XIII., fata nell' Anno 1576." MS. Gothana, No. 219.
[8] According to Mocenigo, 1570, the dataria had at one time yielded between 10,000 and 14,000 ducats per month. Under Paul IV the proceeds fell to 3,000 or 4,000 ducats.

[9] Paolo Tiepolo, " Relatione di Roma in tempo di Pio IV. e Pio V.," already remarks: " The incumbrances of the Papal States are nearly insupportable, being aggravated by various causes; no further alienation of Church revenues is possible; for all certain sources are already alienated, and no one would advance money on those that are uncertain."

tered by them, but had always been deputed to some doctor of laws, chosen for that purpose;[10] these doctors, Pius V himself appointed, appropriating to the treasury those advantages that had previously accrued to the favorites. Everything proceeded more tranquilly and with better order; in earlier times a militia had been established, and 16,000 men enrolled. Pius IV had besides maintained a body of light cavalry. Pius V dispensed with both; the cavalry he disbanded, and suffered the militia to fall into disuse; his whole armed force amounted to less than 500 men, of whom 350, principally Swiss, were in Rome. Had there not been still some need of protection along the coast from the incursions of the Turks, the people might have forgotten the use of arms. This population, once so warlike, seemed now disposed to live in undisturbed peace. The popes desired to rule their territory like a large domain, applying a certain portion of its rents to the expenses of their household, but disposing of the largest part in the service of the Church exclusively.

In the pursuit of this design also, we shall see that they encountered no slight difficulty.

[10] Tiepolo, ibid.: " Some legations or governments were valued at 3,000, 4,000, or perhaps 7,000 or more scudi per annum; but almost all those appointed to them were glad to receive the money, and made a doctor perform the duties of the office.

THE TIMES OF GREGORY XIII AND SIXTUS IV

Section III.—Gregory XIII

GREGORY XIII, Hugo Buoncompagno of Bologna, who had raised himself to eminence as a jurist and in the civil service, was cheerful and lively in disposition. He had never married, but before the assumption of any clerical dignity he had a son born to him, of whom we shall hear further. Later in life his habits became serious and regular; not that he was at any time particularly scrupulous; on the contrary, he displayed a certain dislike of all sanctimonious acerbity, and seemed more disposed to take Pius IV as an example than his more immediate predecessor.[1] But in this pontiff was exemplified the force of public opinion; a hundred years earlier, he would have governed at the most as did Innocent VIII. It was now on the contrary made obvious, that even a man of his dispositions could no longer resist the rigidly ecclesiastical tendency of the times.

This tendency was maintained by a party in the court, whose first object was to prevent it from declining. Jesuits, Theatines, and their adherents, were its members; those more conspicuously active were Monsignori Frumento and Corniglia, with the bold and fearless preacher Francesco Toledo, and the datary Contarelli. Their influence over the Pope was acquired all the more readily and preserved the more securely, from the fact that they all acted in concert. They represented to him that the high consideration enjoyed by his predecessor had arisen principally from the severity of his personal character and conduct; in all the letters that they read aloud to him, the memory of Paul's holy life and virtues with the fame of his reforms, was the subject principally dwelt on; whatever was not to this effect they passed over. By thus

[1] His reign was expected to be different from that of his predecessor; "of a more conciliating and milder character." "Commentarii de rebus Gregorii XIII." (MS. Bibl. Alb.)

proceeding, they gave to the ambition of Gregory XIII a character most thoroughly spiritual.[2]

He had it greatly at heart to promote the son we have mentioned, and to raise him to princely dignity. But at the first act of favor he showed him, the naming him *castellan* of St. Angelo and *gonfaloniere* of the Church, these rigorous counsellors alarmed the conscience of the Pope; and during the jubilee of 1575, they would not permit him to suffer the presence of Giacomo (his son) in Rome. When this was over, they did indeed allow him to return, but only because the disappointment of the aspiring young man was injuriously affecting his health. Gregory then caused him to marry, and induced the republic of Venice to enrol him among its *nobili*,[3] he also prevailed on the King of Spain to nominate him general of his *hommes d'armes*, not, however, relaxing the close restraint in which he held him. But on a certain occasion the young man attempted the liberation of a college friend who had been arrested, when his father again sent him into exile, and was about to deprive him of all his offices; this was prevented only by the young wife, who threw herself at the pontiff's feet, and at length obtained her husband's pardon. The time for more ambitious hopes was however long since past.[4] Giacomo Buoncompagno had never any very serious influence with his father until the life of the latter was drawing to a close, nor even then was it unlimited in state affairs of moment.[5] If any one requested his intercession in these matters, his reply was to shrug his shoulders, as one who would say, "how hopeless is the case!"

Being thus rigid in regard to his son, it will be manifest

[2] "Relatione della corte di Roma a tempo di Gregorio XIII." (Bibl. Corsini, 714), February 20, 1574, is full of instruction on this subject. Of the Pope's character the author says, "he has never been either scrupulous or dissolute, and regards all misconduct with displeasure."

[3] They were not a little puzzled for a description of his origin on this occasion, and it is thought creditable to Venetian address that he was called simply "Signor Boncompagno, nearly related to his holiness." The evasion was invented by Cardinal Como. The affair being in discussion, the ambassador asked the minister if Giacomo should be called the son of his holiness. "His excellency then making many excuses for his holiness, to whom this son was born before he had taken orders, suggested that the youth might be called 'Sr. Giacomo Boncompagno of Bologna, closely connected with his holiness.'"

[4] Antonio Tiepolo, "Dispacci, Agosto, Sett. 1576." In the year 1583, March 29, one of these papers remarks that Signor Giacomo is not permitted to interfere in matters of state.

[5] It is only in the latter part of the life of Gregory that this opinion of him is correct; it has, however, taken firm hold, and I find it again, for example, in the "Memoirs" of Richelieu: "He was a mild-tempered and benevolent prince, and better as a man than as pope." It will be seen that this was only partially true.

that he was little likely to favor more distant relations. It
is true that he did raise two of his nephews to the cardinalate
(and Pius V had done as much), but when a third, encouraged
by their promotion, came to court with the hope of equal fortune, he was refused an audience, and commanded to quit Rome
within two days. The brother of Gregory had left his home,
and was on the road to see and enjoy the honor that had visited
his family, but arrived at Orvieto, he was met by a papal mes-
senger, who desired him to return. Tears rose to the old man's
eyes, and he was tempted to go yet a little further toward Rome;
but, receiving a second intimation to desist, he obeyed it and
returned to Bologna.[6]

These things suffice to show that this pontiff is not charge-
able with nepotism, or the advancing his own family to the
offence of the laws. On one occasion, when a newly appointed
cardinal declared that he should be ever grateful " to the family
and nephews of his holiness," Gregory struck the arms of the
chair he sat on with both hands, exclaiming, " Be thankful
rather to God, and to the Holy See!"

To this extent was he already influenced by the serious
tendency of the time. Not only did he seek to equal the piety
of demeanor[7] so lauded in Pius V, he even desired to surpass
it; in the early years of his pontificate he read mass three times
a week, never omitting to do so on the Sundays: his life and
deportment were not only irreproachable but even exemplary.

There were certain duties of the papal office that no pontiff
ever performed with more zeal and propriety than Gregory
XIII. He had a list of all those men, of whatever country, who
were proper to the office of bishop; evinced an accurate
knowledge of the character and qualifications of all who were
proposed to his acceptance, and exercised the most anxious care
in the nomination to these important offices.

His most earnest endeavors were especially given to the securing a strict system of ecclesiastical education. His liberality

[6] The good man complained that the election of his brother was more in-jurious than useful to him, since it compelled him to an expenditure which was beyond the allowance that Gregory granted him.
[7] " Seconda Relatione dell' Ambascia-tore di Roma Clmo. M. Paolo Tiepolo, Cavre, 3 Maggio 1576: " " In religion he tries not to imitate only, but to go beyond Pius V; he usually says three masses in the week. He has taken great care of the churches, not only adorning them with new buildings, but he fills them also by a large concourse of priests at the performance of divine ser-vice."

in assisting the progress of Jesuit colleges was almost without bounds. He made rich presents to the house of the "professed" in Rome, caused whole streets to be closed up, purchased many buildings, and assigned a large income, to aid the completion of the college in that form which we see it bear even to our days. Twenty lecture-rooms, with 360 cells for students, are enumerated in this building, which was called "the Seminary of all Nations." Even on its first foundation, measures were taken to make it clear that this college was meant to embrace the whole world — twenty-five speeches being pronounced in as many different languages, each accompanied by a Latin interpretation.[8] The *Collegium Germanicum*, which had been founded some years before, was falling into decay from want of means; to this, also, Gregory gave a palace, that of St. Apollinare, and added the revenues of San Stefano on Monte Celio, together with the sum of 10,000 scudi, charged on the *Camera Apostolica*. He may indeed be regarded as the true founder of this institution, whence, year after year since his time, a whole host of champions for the Catholic faith has been poured into Germany. He found means to erect and endow an English college in Rome; he assisted those of Vienna and Grätz from his private purse; and there was not, perhaps, a single Jesuit school in the world which he did not in some way contribute to support. Following the counsels of the Bishop of Sitia, he also established a Greek college, into which boys from thirteen to sixteen were admitted. And not only were they received from countries already under Christian rule, as Corfu and Candia, but also from Constantinople, Salonichi, and the Morea. They had Greek instructors, and were clothed in the Kaftan and Venetian *barret;* they were upheld in all Greek customs, and never permitted to forget that it was in their native country they were preparing to act. They retained their own rites [9] as well as language, and their religious education was conducted according to those doctrines of the council, and in those principles, whereon the Greek and Latin churches were of one accord.

The reform of the calendar, accomplished by Pope Gregory XIII, was another proof of that assiduous care which he ex-

[8] "Dispaccio Donato, 13 Genn. 1582."
[9] "Dispaccio Antonio Tiepolo, 16 Marzo, 1577:" "So that when grown up they may declare the truth to their Greek countrymen with affectionate zeal."

tended over the whole Catholic world. This had been greatly desired by the Council of Trent, and it was rendered imperatively necessary by the displacement of the high festivals of the Church from that relation to particular seasons of the year which had been imposed on them by the decrees of councils. All Catholic nations took part in this reform.

A Calabrian, else little known, Luigi Lilio, has gained himself immortal renown by the suggestion of the most efficient method for overcoming the difficulty. All the universities, among them the Spanish—those of Salamanca and Alcala —were consulted as to his proposed plan; favorable opinions came from all quarters. A commission was then appointed in Rome (its most active and learned member being the German Clavius).[10] By this body it was minutely examined and finally decided on. The learned Cardinal Sirleto had exercised the most important influence over the whole affair; it was conducted with a certain degree of mystery, the calendar being concealed from all, even from the ambassadors, until it had received the approval of the different courts;[1] Gregory then proclaimed it with great solemnity, vaunting this reform as a proof of God's illimitable grace toward his Church.[2]

The labors of this pontiff were, however, not always of so peaceable a character; could he have decided the question, that "league" by which the battle of Lepanto had been gained, would never have been dissolved; and it was a source of grief to him when the Venetians made peace with the Turks, and when Philip of Spain afterward agreed to a truce with them. A wide field was afforded to his exertions by the disturbances in France and the Netherlands, as also by the collision of parties in Germany. He was inexhaustible in expedients for the destruction of Protestantism; and the insurrections that Elizabeth had to contend with in Ireland were almost all excited or encouraged by Rome. The Pope made no secret of his desire to bring about a general combination against England: year after year was this subject pressed by his nuncios on Philip II and the house of Guise. A connected history of all these labors and projects would be no uninteresting occupation for him who

---

[10] Erythræus: "Wherein Christopher Clavius obtained the chief place."
[1] "Dispaccio Donato, 20 Dec. 1581;"

"2 Giugno, 1582." He praises the cardinal as "a man of really great learning."
[2] Bull of February 13, 1582, 12.—Bullar, "Cocq." iv. 4, 10.

should undertake it: they were for the most part unknown to those whose destruction they were intended to accomplish, but did at length produce the great enterprise of the Armada. With the most eager zeal were all the proceedings forwarded by Gregory, and it was to his connection with the Guises that the French league, so dangerous to Henry III and IV, is indebted for its origin.

We have seen that this pontiff did not load the State too heavily for the benefit of his family, as so many of his predecessors had done, but the comprehensive and costly works in which he constantly engaged compelled him to lay his hand with equal weight on the public revenues. Even for the expedition of Stukeley, though comparatively insignificant, and which terminated so unhappily in Africa, he expended a very large sum. To Charles IX he once sent 400,000 ducats, the proceeds of a direct impost levied on the towns of the Roman States; he also frequently aided the Emperor and the grandmaster of Malta with sums of money. His pacific enterprises equally demanded extensive funds: he is computed to have spent two millions on the support of young men in the pursuit of their studies.[3] How heavy, then, must needs have been the cost of those twenty-two Jesuit colleges which owed their origin to his munificence.

When we consider the financial condition of the State, which, spite of its increasing income, had never presented a disposable surplus, it becomes obvious that he must often have suffered considerable embarrassment.

The Venetians attempted to persuade him into granting them a loan very soon after his accession to the see. Gregory listened to the representations of the ambassador with increasing attention; but having arrived at the drift of his proposals, he at once interrupted him. "What do I hear, my lord ambassador?" he exclaimed; "the congregation sits every day to devise means of raising money, but never does one man among them contrive any available expedient for doing so."[4]

The mode in which Gregory should administer the re-

[3] Calculation of Baronius. Possevinus in Ciacconius, "Vitæ Pontificum," iv. 37. Lorenzo Priuli considers him to have expended 200,000 scudi annually on works of piety. On this subject the extracts given by Cocquelinus at the close of Maffei's "Annals," from the report of cardinals Como and Muscotti, are most authentic and copious.
[4] "Dispaccio, 14 Marzo, 1573:" "It is a congregation deputed for the raising of money."

sources of the State was now a question of paramount importance. The evil of alienations had at length become clearly apparent to all; new imposts were considered impolitic and highly censured — the doubtful, nay, the pernicious consequences of such a system were clearly perceived and fully appreciated. Gregory imposed on the congregation the task of procuring him money, but they were to make no ecclesiastical concessions, lay on no new taxes, and permit the sale of no church revenues.

How, then, were they to proceed? The means devised, in reply to this question, were sufficiently remarkable, as were also the results eventually produced by them.

Gregory XIII was not to be restrained from the pursuit of what he considered a right, and he believed himself to have discovered that many prerogatives of the ecclesiastical principality yet remained to be put in force; these he thought had only to be asserted in order to their supplying him with new sources of income.[5] It was not in his character to respect the privileges that might stand in his way: thus, among others, he abolished, without hesitation, that possessed by the Venetians, of exporting corn from the March and Ravenna, under certain favorable conditions, declaring that it was fair to make foreigners pay equal duty with the natives.[6] Since the Venetians did not instantly comply, he caused their magazines in Ravenna to be opened by force, the contents to be sold by auction, and the owners imprisoned. This was but a small affair, it is true, but served to intimate the path he intended to pursue. His next step was of much more lasting importance: believing that a crowd of abuses existed among the possessions of the aristocracy in his own territories, he decided that the reform of these would be highly beneficial to his treasury. His secretary of the *Camera*, Rudolfo Bonfigliuolo, proposed a comprehensive renewal and extension of feudal rights, which had hitherto scarcely been thought of; he affirmed that a large part of the estates and castles held by the barons of the State had lapsed to the sovereign, either by failure in the direct line of succession, or because the dues to which they were liable had

[5] Maffei, " Annali di Gregorio XIII.," i. p. 104. He calculates that the States of the Church had a clear income of 160,000 scudi only.

[6] " Dispaccio Antonio Tiepolo, 12 April, 1577."

not been paid.[7] The Pope had already acquired some domains that had either lapsed or were purchased, and nothing could be more agreeable to him than to continue doing so. He at once set earnestly to work. From the Isei of Cesena he wrested Castelnuovo in the hills of Romagna, and from the Sassatelli of Imola he gained Coreana. Lonzano, seated on its beautiful hill, and Savignano in the plain, were taken from the Rangoni of Modena. Alberto Pio resigned Bertinoro, to escape the process preparing against him by the treasury; but this did not suffice, and he was divested of Verrucchio and other places. Seeing this, he tendered his arrears of rent on every festival of St. Peter, but they were never afterward accepted. All this occurred in Romagna alone, and the other provinces did not fare better. It was not only to estates on which the feudal services remained unpaid that the court asserted a claim, there were other domains which had originally been mortgaged to certain barons, but this so long since that the mode of their tenure had been forgotten; the property had descended from hand to hand as freehold, and had often largely increased in value. The Pope and his secretaries now chose to redeem the mortgages; in this manner they gained possession of Sitiano, a castle that had been pledged for 14,000 scudi; that sum they laid down, but it was greatly below the value of the property, which, being considered freehold, had received extensive improvement.

Gregory congratulated himself continually on these proceedings; he believed he had established a new claim to the favor of heaven with every addition, were it only of ten scudi, that he succeeded in adding to the income of the Church, provided it were done without new imposts. He calculated with infinite pleasure that he should soon have made an addition of 100,000 scudi to the revenues of the State, and all by legitimate proceedings. How greatly would his means for proceeding against infidels and heretics be thus increased! His measures were, for the most part, much approved by the court. " This Pope is called the 'vigilant' " (Gregorius signifies vigilant), says the Cardinal of Como; " by his vigilance will

[7] " Dispaccio A. Tiepolo, 12 Genn. 1579:" " The commissary of the Camera seeks diligently for all writings that may enable him to recover whatever has been given in pledge by former popes; and, perceiving that his holiness encourages this, he is disposed to excuse no one."

he recover his own." [8]   But the feeling of the provinces on this subject was altogether different from that of the court; on the aristocracy the impression produced was most unfavorable.

Estates that had long been considered their own, and held by the most legitimate claims, were now torn from the best families of the land; a like calamity was impending over others, daily search among old papers was made in Rome, new claims were continually founded on them, no man could believe himself secure, and many resolved to defend their property by force of arms, rather than resign it to the commissioners of the treasurer. One of these feudal tenants told Gregory to his face, " If a thing is lost, it is lost; but there is always a satisfaction in arming one's self for the defence of one's own."

But from all this there arose the most violent fermentation, the influence of the barons on the peasantry and on the *nobili* of the neighboring towns, awakened extreme indignation throughout the country at the pontiff's new measures.

In addition to these unpopular proceedings, came the fact that certain towns had suffered heavy losses by other injudicious expedients of the Pope. He had, for example, raised the port-dues of Ancona, believing that these would fall, not upon the country, but the foreign merchant. An injury was nevertheless inflicted on that city from which it has never recovered. Its commerce suddenly departed, nor could the removal of the obnoxious impost avail to bring it back; even the restoration of their ancient privileges to the Ragusans, did not suffice to make up the loss.

Equally unexpected and peculiar were the consequences that ensued from the policy that Gregory had adopted.

In all countries (but more especially in one of so pacific a character as that now displayed by the Papal States) obedience to the government is based on voluntary subordination. In the Roman territories, the elements of dissension were neither destroyed nor removed, they were simply concealed by the mantle of authority extending over them; accordingly, the principle of subordination being disturbed on one point, these all pressed forward together and burst into open conflict. The land seemed

[8] " Dispaccio, 21 Ott. 1581:" " It is many years since the Church has had a pontiff of this name, ' Gregory,' which, according to its Greek etymology, means ' vigilant.' This, then, being ' Gregory,' is ' Vigilant,' he determines to watch and recover what is due to the see, and thinks he has done good service when he has got back anything, however small."

suddenly to remember how warlike, how well skilled in arms,
and how unfettered in its parties it had remained for whole
centuries. It began to feel contempt for this government of
priests and men of law, and returned to the condition most
natural to it.

It is true that no direct opposition was offered to the government, no general revolt ensued; but the old feuds reappeared
in every part of the country.

Once again was the whole of Romagna divided by these factions; in Ravenna the Rasponi and the Leonardi were arrayed
against each other; in Rimini, the Ricciardelli and the Tignoli;
in Cesena, the Venturelli and the Bottini; in Furli, the Numai
and the Sirugli; in Imola, the Vicini and the Sassatelli. The
first named of these families were Ghibellines, the others
Guelphs; however completely the interests originally connected
with these appellations had altered, the names still survived.
These parties often held possession of different quarters of the
city, and different churches; they were distinguished by slight
signs, as for example, that the Guelphs wore the feather on the
right side of his hat, the Ghibelline on the left.[9] These divisions reigned even in the smallest villages; a man would not
have spared the life of his brother, had he belonged to the opposite faction; and some were known who had destroyed their
wives, that they might be at liberty to marry into families of
their own party. In these disorders, the "Pacific" could
avail nothing; and their influence was all the more completely
lost, from the fact that favoritism had placed unsuitable members among their body. The factions took the administration
of justice into their own hands; certain persons who had been
condemned by the tribunals, they declared innocent, and liber-
ated them by breaking open their prisons; their enemies on the
contrary they sought in the same place and by the same means,
but it was to place their heads around the fountains, where, on
the day following their capture, they were frequently to be
seen.[10]

Public authority being thus enfeebled, troops of bandits as-

[9] The "Relatione di Romagna" describes the difference as existing "in
the cutting of their clothes, mode of
wearing the belt, the feather, tassel, or
flower worn on the cap or at the ear."

[10] In the MS. "Sixtus V. Pontifex
Max." (Altieri Library in Rome) this
state of things is minutely described.
(See App. No. 52.)

sembled in the March, the Campagna, and indeed all the provinces; these outlaws very soon amounting to small armies.

At the head of these bands were Alfonso Piccolomini, Roberto Malatesta, and other young men of the most illustrious families; Piccolomini seized the Town-house of Monte Abboddo, had all his enemies hunted out, and put them to death before the eyes of their mothers and wives; nine of the name of Gabuzio were thus destroyed, Piccolomini's followers dancing in the market-place while the execution was proceeding. He marched through the country as lord of the land: an attack of ague seized him, but was not suffered to impede his progress; when the fever-fit came on, he would cause himself to be carried in a litter at the head of his troops. He sent a message to the inhabitants of Corneto, advising them to make good speed with their harvest, because he meant himself to come and burn the crops of his enemy Latino Orsino. In his personal conduct, Piccolomini affected to deal with a certain sort of honor; he would take the letters of a courier, but the gold borne by him would remain untouched; to the rapacious brutality of his followers, however, he set no bounds; from all sides messengers were sent by the different cities to Rome, entreating protection.[1] The Pope increased his military forces, and invested Cardinal Sforza with powers for the repression of this violence, surpassing any that had ever been conferred since the time of Cardinal Albornoz. Not only was he empowered to proceed without respect to privileges, by whomever or however possessed; but he was also at liberty to act without regard to any forms of law, without even the ceremony of a trial, *manu regiâ*.[2] Giacomo Buoncompagno took the field, and they did certainly succeed in dispersing these bands, and in clearing the country; but no sooner were their backs turned, than the outlaws instantly sprang up as actively as ever in their rear, and all the previous disorders recommenced.

That these evils should thus become incurable, is attributable to a particular circumstance that must be related.

[1] "Dispacci Donato," of 1582, throughout.

[2] Brief for Sforza, given in the "Dispacci": He has every sort of power, authority, and absolute discretion against bandits of whatsoever kind, with their favorers, receivers, or followers; also against communities, universities, and cities, domains and castles, barons and dukes of whatsoever pre-eminence; against persons in any authority, and that without form of process, to punish them all and each, with royal power, as well in their property as in their persons."

Pope Gregory XIII, who is so frequently described as good-natured to excess, had yet asserted his ecclesiastical as well as secular rights with extremity of rigor,[3] and in doing this he regarded no man's interest or feelings.   He spared neither the Emperor nor the King of Spain, and to his more immediate neighbors he showed as little deference.   With Venice he was involved in disputes interminable; some regarded the affair of Aquileja, some the visitation of their churches, and various other points.   The ambassadors can find no words to describe the heat with which he spoke of these matters, the acerbity that he displayed on their being even alluded to.   With Tuscany and Naples affairs were not more peaceably arranged, nor did Ferrara find greater favor.   Parma had but lately lost large sums of money in legal disputes with the pontiff.   It thus happened that all his neighbors exulted at seeing the Pope involved in perplexities so painful, and gave a ready asylum to his outlaws, who took the first opportunity of returning to their country.   It was in vain that Gregory entreated them to discontinue this connivance; they chose to consider it extraordinary that Rome should treat all other States with indifference and contempt, but should nevertheless set up a claim to service and respect at the hands of all.[4]

Thus it came to pass that Gregory could never make himself master of these bandits.   The taxes remained unpaid, and the *sussidio* could not be collected; a feeling of discontent took possession of the whole country; even cardinals were mooting the question whether it would not be advisable to attach themselves to some other State.

The further prosecution of the measures suggested by the secretary of the *Camera* was out of the question in this position of things; in December, 1581, the Venetian ambassador made it publicly known that his holiness had commanded the discontinuance of all proceedings in the confiscation of lands.

Perhaps even more painful was the necessity to which the

---

[3] So early as 1576 Paolo Tiepolo remarks this: "The more he seeks to acquire the name of a just man, the less is he likely to retain that of a gracious prince, conferring fewer especial favors than any pontiff for many years past; besides this, he does not succeed in winning those around him, partly because he has a natural incapacity for express-ing himself, and because of the very few words he uses on all occasions—thus he gains but little personal attachment."
[4] "Dispaccio Donato, 10 Sett. 1581:" "It is a strange thing, that giving satisfaction to no one, he should yet desire every sort of obsequiousness from all others in matters touching the State."

pontiff was also reduced, of permitting Piccolomini to appear in the capital, and present a petition for pardon.[5] A deep shudder passed over him as he read the long list of murders and other atrocities that he was called on to forgive, and he laid the paper from his hand; but he was assured that one of three things must happen, either his son Giacomo would receive his death from the hand of Piccolomini, or he must himself condemn Piccolomini to death, or resolve on granting him a pardon. The father confessors of St. John Lateran declared, that though they dared not violate the secrets of the confessional, yet thus much they were permitted to say, a great calamity was impending, and unless something were speedily done, would inevitably ensue: Piccolomini was besides publicly favored by the Grand Duke of Tuscany, and was at that moment lodged in the Medici palace. Seeing all these things, the pontiff at last submitted, but with a deeply mortified spirit, and the brief of absolution received his signature.

This did not, however, suffice to restore tranquillity to the country; his own capital was filled with the outlaws, and matters got to such a pass that the city magistracy of the *conservators* was compelled to act in aid of the Pope's police, which could not secure obedience. A pardon being offered to a certain bandit called Marianazzo, he refused it, declaring that his life " was more secure while remaining an outlaw, to say nothing of the increased advantage! "[6]

Worn out and weary of life, the aged pontiff raised his hands to heaven and cried, " Thou wilt arise, O Lord, and have mercy upon Zion! "

Section IV.—Sixtus V

It would sometimes seem that even in confusion itself there exists some occult force, by which the man capable of steering through its mazes is formed and brought forward.

Hereditary principalities or aristocracies transmit their power from generation to generation throughout the world, but the

---

[5] Donato, April 9th, 1583: " The desire to save expense and secure Signor Giacomo's safety, with that of escaping the disturbances daily arising between him and Florence, has led his holiness to this decision."

[6] That living as an outlaw turned to better account, and was of greater security. Gregory XIII reigned from May 13, 1572, to April 10, 1585.

sovereignty of the Church has this peculiarity, that its throne may be attained by men from the lowest ranks of society. It was from a station among the most humble that a pope now appeared, by whom those qualities, intellectual and moral, demanded for the suppression of the prevalent disorders, were possessed in their highest perfection.

When the provinces of Illyria and Dalmatia first became a prey to the successful armies of the Ottomans, many of their inhabitants fled into Italy. Arriving in melancholy groups, they might be seen seated on the sea-shore, and raising their hands imploringly toward heaven; among these fugitives would most probably have been found a Sclavonian by birth, named Zanetto Peretti; this was the ancestor of Sixtus V. Sharing the frequent lot of exiles, neither Zanetto nor his descendants, who had settled in Montalto, could boast of any great prosperity in the country of their adoption. Peretto Peretti, the father of the future pope, was driven by his debts from Montalto, and it was only by marriage that he was enabled to rent a garden at Grotto a Mare, near Fermo; the place was a remarkable one: amidst the plants of the garden were seen the ruins of a temple to Cupra, the Etruscan Juno; rich fruits of the South grew up around it, for the climate of Fermo is milder and more beneficent than that of any other district in the March. Here a son was born to Peretti, on the eighteenth of December, 1521; but a short time before this birth, the father had been consoled by the voice of a divinity, which, speaking to him in a dream, as he bemoaned his many privations, assured him that a son should be granted to him, by whom his house should be raised to high fortunes. On this hope he seized with all the eagerness of a visionary temperament, further excited by want, and naturally disposed to mysticism. He named the boy Felix.[1]

---

[1] Tempesti, "Storia della Vita e Geste di Sisto V.," 1754, has given the archives of Montalto, as authority for the origin of his hero. The "Vita Sixti V.," ipsius manu emendata, is also authentic. MS. of the Altieri Library in Rome. Sixtus was born while his father cultivated the garden of Ludovico Vecchio of Fermo, and his mother gave aid to the domestic duties of Diana, a very virtuous matron and the housekeeper of Ludovico. This Diana, when in extreme old age, was witness to the pontificate of Sixtus: "The feeble old woman desired to be carried to Rome, that she might offer veneration to him, now at the summit of all greatness, but whom she had nurtured on mean fare in her house, where he was born, he being the son of her gardener." Further: "The people of Piceno relate that the boy tended sheep, and he does not conceal, but rather boasts that this was so." In the "Ambrosiana," R. 124, there is, F. Radice dell' Origine di Sisto V., an Information, dated Rome, May 4, 1585, but it is not of great importance.

That the family was not in prosperous circumstances, appears from what is related, among other things, of the child falling into a pond, when his aunt, " who was washing clothes at this pond," drew him out; it is certain that he was employed to watch the fruit, and even to attend swine. His father was not able to spare even the five bajocchi (three-pence) demanded monthly by the nearest schoolmaster; thus Felix had to learn his letters from the primers that other boys left lying beside him as they passed through the fields in their way to and from school. There was happily one member of the family who had entered the Church, Fra Salvatore, a Franciscan; this relative at length permitted himself to be prevailed on to pay the schoolmaster. Felix could then go to receive instruction with the other boys; he had a piece of bread for his dinner, and this he ate at midday by the side of a stream, which supplied him with drink for his meal. These depressed circumstances did not prevent the hopes of the father from being shared by the son. In his twelfth year he entered the order of the Franciscans, for the Council of Trent had not then forbidden the vows to be taken thus early, but did not resign his name of good omen, and continued to be called Felix.

Fra Salvatore kept him in very strict order, joining the authority of an uncle to that of a father; but he sent him to school. The young Felix passed long evenings in conning his lessons, without supper, and with no better light than that afforded by the lantern hung up at the crossing of the streets; and when this failed him, he would go to the lamp that burnt before the host in some Church. He was not remarked for any particular tendency to religious devotion, or profound researches in science; we find only that he made rapid progress, as well at the school of Fermo, as at the universities of Ferrara and Bologna. His particular talent seemed rather for dialectics, and he became a perfect master of that monkish accomplishment, the dexterous handling of theological subtleties. At the general convention of the Franciscans, in the year 1549, which commenced with an exhibition of skill in literary disputation, he was opposed to a certain Thelesian, Antonio Persico of Calabria, who was at that time in high repute at Perugia; on this occasion he acquitted himself with a presence of mind and intelligence, that first procured him notice and a certain degree of distinction;[2] from this time Cardinal Pio of Carpi, protector of the order, took a decided interest in his fortunes.

But it is to another circumstance that his progress is principally to be attributed.

In the year 1552, he was appointed Lent preacher in the Church of the Holy Apostles in Rome, and his sermons were very well received; his style was found to be animated, copious, fluent, and free from meretricious ornament; his matter was well arranged, his manner impressive, his utterance clear and agreeable. While preaching to a full congregation, he one day came to that pause in the sermon, customary among Italian preachers; and when he had reposed for a time, he took up the memorials, which are usually prayers and intercessions only: while reading these, he perceived a paper lying sealed in the pulpit, and containing matter of a totally different character; all the main points of the sermons hitherto preached by Peretti, especially those touching the doctrine of predestination, were here set down, and opposite to each were written in large letters the words, "Thou liest." The preacher could not wholly conceal his amazement, he hurried to a conclusion, and instantly on reaching home despatched the paper to the Inquisition.[3] Very shortly afterward the grand inquisitor, Michele Ghislieri, entered his room; the most searching examination ensued: in later times Peretti often described the terror caused him by the aspect of this man, with his stern brow, deep-set eyes, and strongly-marked features; but he did not lose his presence of mind, answered satisfactorily, and betrayed weakness on no point whatever. When, therefore, Ghislieri saw that there was no shadow of suspicion, that the friar was not only guiltless, but also well versed in the Catholic doctrines, and firmly fixed in the faith, he became a totally different person, embraced Peretti with tears, and was his second patron.

. From that time Fra Felice attached himself with a firm hold

---

[2] "Sixtus V. Pontifex Maximus," MS. of the Altieri Library: "Persico, with high reputation among scholars, was teaching philosophy at Perugia after the principles of Thelesius; he brought forward a doctrine then new, which he marvellously illustrated by the light of his genius. Then Montalto defended positions from universal theology, inscribed to the Cardinal of Carpi, and this to the admiration of all who heard him."

[3] Relation taken from the same MS.:

"Jam priorem orationis partem exegerat cum oblatum libellum resignat, ac tacitus, ut populo summam exponat, legere incipit. Quotquot ad eam diem catholicæ fidei dogmata Montaltus pro concione affirmarat, ordine collecta continebat singulisque id tantum addebat, literis grandioribus, 'Mentiris.' Complicatum diligenter libellum, sed ita ut consternationis manifestus multis esset, ad pectus dimittit, orationemque brevi præcisione paucis absolvit." (See text.)

to the severe party just then beginning to gain ascendancy in the Church; with Ignazio, Felino, and Filippo Neri, all of whom received the title of saints, he maintained the most intimate intercourse. It was of particular advantage to him that he was driven out of Venice by the intrigues of his brethren, for having attempted to reform the order. This greatly enhanced his credit with the representatives of the more rigid opinions, then fast acquiring the predominance. He was presented to Paul IV, and sometimes called to give an opinion in cases of difficulty. At the Council of Trent he labored with the other theologians, and was consultor to the Inquisition. He had a considerable share in the condemnation of Archbishop Carranza, patiently submitting to the labor of seeking through the Protestant writers for all those passages which Carranza was accused of embodying in his works. He gained the entire confidence of Pius V, who appointed him vicar-general of the Franciscans, with the express understanding that his authority extended to the reformation of the order. This, Peretti carried into execution with a high hand. The principal offices of the order had hitherto been controlled by the commissaries-general. These functionaries he deposed, restored the primitive constitution according to which the supreme power was vested in the provincials, and made the most rigorous visitations. The expectations of Pius were not only fulfilled, they were surpassed. He considered his inclination for Peretti as an inspiration from above; refused all credence to the calumnies by which his favorite was persecuted, bestowed on him the bishopric of St. Agatha, and in the year 1570 exalted him to the College of Cardinals.

The bishopric of Fermo was also conferred on the successful monk. Robed in the purple of the Church, Felix Peretti returned to the abode of his fathers; to that place where he had once guarded the fruit-trees and followed the swine; yet were neither the predictions of his father nor his own hopes entirely accomplished.

The various artifices employed by Cardinal Montalto, so was Peretti now called, to obtain the papal tiara, have been described and repeated, much and often. The affected humility of his deportment; how he tottered along leaning on his stick, bent to the earth, and coughing at every step; but to him who reflects, no evidence will be requisite to prove that in all this there is but little truth. It is not by such means that the highest dignities are won.

Montalto kept guard over his own interests by a life of tranquil frugality and industrious seclusion. His recreations were, the planting of vines and other trees in his gardens near the Church of Santa Maria Maggiore, which are still visited by the stranger, and doing such service as he could to his native town. His hours of labor he devoted to the works of St. Ambrose; an edition of which he published in the year 1580. He bestowed great pains on this work, but has not always been sufficiently conscientious in adhering to the meaning of his author. In other respects his character does not appear to have been so guileless as it is occasionally represented. So early as 1574, he is described as learned and prudent, but also crafty and malignant.[4] He was doubtless gifted with remarkable self-control. When his nephew, the husband of Vittorie Accorambuona, was assassinated, he was himself the person who requested the Pope to discontinue the investigation. This quality, which was admired by all, very probably contributed to his election; when, having been put in nomination, principally by the intrigues of the conclave, in 1585, he was nevertheless elected. The authentic narrative of the proceedings assures us also that his comparatively vigorous years were taken into account, he being then sixty-four, and possessing a firm and healthy constitution; for all were persuaded that a man of un-

---

[4] A discourse concerning those who are eligible to the papacy under Gregory XIII, speaks thus of Montalto: "His character, considered to be ferocious, arrogant, and imperious, is but little calculated to win regard." Here we see that the dispositions he displayed as pope, were already obvious in the cardinal. Gregory XIII often remarked to those of his immediate circle, that they should beware of that great charnel-box ·of a gray friar. The author of "Sixtus V. P. M." makes Farnese observe, on seeing Peretti between the two Dominicans, Trani and Justinian, who also entertained hopes of ascending the papal throne: "That Picenian pack-horse will take a magnificent spring some day, if ever he can shake off those two sacks of coals that he carries so awkwardly one on each side." He further added that it was precisely this conviction, by which the daughter of Accorambuona was induced to marry Montalto's nephew. The grand duke Francis of Tuscany had also a large share in determining the election of Peretti. In a despatch from the Florentine ambassador, Alberti, of May 11, 1585 (Roma, Filza, n. 36), is this remark: "Your highness alone will enjoy the fruit of this work (the election), and so is it right, since it is your own; in case of war, you and no other will have the friendship of the pontiff." In another Florentine despatch occurs the following: "The Pope replied that the grand duke had cause to wish him well, being like the husbandman, who, when he has planted a tree, rejoices to see it thrive and live long, adding, that his highness alone had conducted this matter, under God, and that he, the Pope, knew well in what gratitude he was bound to him by this, though he could not speak to many on that subject." It is obvious that much was here behind the scenes of which we know little or nothing. The election took place on April 24, 1585.

impaired energies, whether physical or mental, was imperatively demanded by the circumstances of the times.

And thus did Fra Felice see himself at the summit of his
wishes. It was doubtless with a feeling of proud satisfaction
that he beheld the accomplishment of desires so noble and so
legitimate. Every incident of his life in which he had ever
believed himself to perceive an intimation of his exalted destiny,
now recurred to his thoughts. The words he chose for his
motto were these: "Thou, O God, hast been my defender,
even from my mother's womb."

In all his undertakings he believed himself, from this time,
to possess the immediate favor of God. At his first accession
to the throne, he announced his determination to exterminate
all the bandits and evil-doers. He was persuaded that in the
event of his own powers failing, God would send him legions
of angels for so good a work.[5]

To this difficult enterprise he at once addressed himself with
deliberate judgment and inflexible resolution.

Section V.—Extirpation of the Banditti

The memory of Gregory XIII was regarded with intense
dislike by his successor. Pope Sixtus departed instantly from
the measures of the previous pontiff. He disbanded the greater
part of the troops, and reduced the number of *sbirri* by one-
half. He determined, on the other hand, to visit with relentless
severity whatever criminals should fall into his hands.

A prohibition had for some time existed against carrying
short weapons, and more especially a particular kind of rifle.
Four young men of Cora, nearly related to each other, were
nevertheless taken with arms of this description about them.
The day following was that of the coronation, and an occasion
so auspicious was seized by their friends for entreating their
pardon from the pontiff. "While I live," replied Sixtus,
"every criminal must die."[1] That very day the four young

[5] "Dispaccio, Priuli, Maggio 11, 1585:"
Speech of Sixtus in the Consistory:
"He named two things that engaged
his attention, the administration of justice and the securing abundance for his
people; and to these he had resolved to
give his utmost care, trusting that God
would send him legions of angels, if his
own strength and the aid of others
should not suffice, to punish the male-
factors and reprobates. He exhorted the
cardinals not to use their privileges for
the shelter of criminals, and spoke very
bitterly of his predecessor's inconsid-
erate proceedings."
[1] "Se vivo, facinorosis morlendum
esse."

men were seen hanging on one gallows near the bridge of St. Angelo.

A youth of the Trastevere was condemned to death for having offered resistance to the *sbirri*, who were proceeding to take his ass from him. On sight of the poor boy led weeping to the place where he was to die for so venial an offence, all were moved to pity. His youth was represented to the Pope, who is said to have replied, " I will add a few years of my own life to lengthen his," and he caused the sentence to be executed.

The rigor of these first acts of the pontiff impressed all with terror; immediate obedience was secured by it to the commands he next sent forth.

Barons and communes were enjoined to clear their castles and towns of banditti; the losses sustained by the bands of outlaws were at once to be made good by the noble or commune within whose jurisdiction they might take place.[2]

It had been customary to set a price on the head of a bandit; Sixtus now decreed that this should no longer be paid by the public treasury, but by the relations of the outlaw; or, if these were too poor, by the commune wherein he was born.

It is manifest that his purpose in this proceeding was to engage the interests of the barons, the municipalities, and even the kinsmen of the outlaws on the side of his wishes; he made an effort to enlist that of the banditti themselves in the same cause, promising to any one of them who should deliver up a comrade, living or dead, not his own pardon only, but also that of some of his friends whom he was at liberty to name, with a sum of money in addition.

When these commands had been carried into effect, and certain examples of their rigorous enforcement had been exhibited, the condition of the outlaws was presently seen to assume a very different character.

It happened fortunately for the purpose of Sixtus, that pursuit had from the beginning been successfully directed against some of the most formidable chiefs of large bands.

He declared that sleep had forsaken his eyes, because the priest Guercino, who called himself King of the Campagna, was still continuing his depredations, and had just committed new deeds of violence. This man had laid his commands on

*Bull. t. iv. p. iv. p. 137. Bando, in Tempesti, i. ix. 14.

the subjects of the Bishop of Viterbo to pay no further obedience to their lord; Sixtus prayed, as we are told by Galesinus, "that God would be pleased to deliver the Church from that robber"; and the following morning intelligence arrived that Guercino was taken. A gilded crown was placed on the severed head, which was instantly set up on the castle of St. Angelo. The man who brought it received its price of 2,000 scudi, and the people applauded his holiness for so effectual a mode of administering justice.

Spite of all these severities, another leader of outlaws, called Della Fara, had the boldness to present himself one night at the Porta Salara; he called up the watchmen, declared his name, and desired them to present a greeting on his part to the Pope and the Governor. Hearing this, Sixtus sent an order to those of the outlaw's own family, commanding them to find and bring him in, under pain of suffering death themselves. In less than a month from the date of this order, the head of Della Fara took its place beside that of Guercino.

It was on some occasions rather cruelty than justice that was now employed against the bandits.

Some thirty of them had intrenched themselves on a hill at no great distance from Urbino. The duke caused mules laden with provisions to be driven near their hold; the robbers did not fail to plunder this rich train; but the food had been poisoned, and they all died together. "When intelligence of this was carried to Sixtus V," says one of his historians, "the Pope received thereby an infinite contentment."[3]

In the capital, a father and son were led to death, though they persisted in declaring their innocence; the mother presented herself, entreating for a postponement only of the execution, when she could bring proof of innocence both for her husband and son: this the Senator refused to grant. "Since you thirst for blood," she exclaimed, "I will give you enough of it!" Saying which, she threw herself from the window of the Capitol. The victims meanwhile arrived at the place of execution, neither could endure to see the other suffer, each implored permission to die first; seized with compassion, the people called aloud for mercy, while the savage executioner reproached them for causing useless delay.

[3] " Memorie del Ponteficato di Sisto V.: " " Ragguagliato Sisto ne prese gran contento."

The ordinances of Sixtus permitted no respect of persons;
a member of one of the first families in Bologna, Giovanni
Count Pepoli, was known to have taken part in the excesses
committed by the outlaws; he was strangled in prison, his
estates and every other species of property being confiscated.
No day passed without an execution: over all parts of the
country, in wood and field, stakes were erected, on each of
which stood the head of an outlaw. The Pope awarded praises
only to those among his legates and governors who supplied
him largely with these terrible trophies, his demand was ever
for heads: there is a sort of oriental barbarism in this mode of
administering justice.

Such of the outlaws as escaped the officers of the pontiff,
were destroyed by their own comrades. The promises of forgiveness and reward before alluded to had carried dissension
into their bands; none dared trust even his nearest connection
—they fell by the hands of each other.[4]

In this manner, and before the year had come to an end,
the disturbances that had so harassed the Roman States, if not
extinguished at the source, were yet suppressed at the outbreak; intelligence was received in the year 1586, that Monte-
brandano and Arara, the two last leaders of the bandits, had
been put to death.

It was matter of great pride and rejoicing to the Pope, when
ambassadors now arriving at his court, assured him that "in
every part of his States through which their road had led,
they had travelled through a land blessed with peace and security."[5]

Section VI.—Leading Characteristics of the Administration

It was not only to the absence of vigilant control that those
disorders against which the pontiff contended owed their birth,
there were others also; and it is principally to his measures
with regard to these, that the decided success of his efforts
must be attributed. It has been common to regard Sixtus V

[4] "Disp.," Priuli, so early as June 29, 1585, says "The new brief has caused the banditti to fall upon each other."
[5] "Vita Sixti V.," i. m. em.: "Such is the peace and tranquillity, that in this great city, in this assemblage of na-tions, this vast concourse of strangers and travellers, among all these wealthy and magnificent nobles, there is no one who needs endure injury or offence, however feeble his condition, however abject his state." According to Gual-terius, "Vita Sixti V.," the latter ap-plied the text: "The wicked fleeth, though no man pursueth."

as the sole founder of that judicial system by which the Ecclesiastical States are governed; laws and institutions are ascribed
to him that were in fact existing long before his day. He is
extolled as an incomparable master of finance, a statesman,
wholly free from prejudice, and an enlightened restorer of antiquity. This arises from the fact that his natural qualities
were such as readily impress themselves on the memory of
man, and dispose him to the credence of fabulous and hyperbolical narrations.

We are not then to believe all that we find related of this
pontiff's regulations. It is nevertheless perfectly true, that
his administration was an extremely remarkable one.

It was in certain particulars directly opposed to that of his
predecessor. Gregory XIII was severe and energetic, but not
clear-sighted in his general measures; individual cases of disobedience he readily overlooked. The attacks he made upon
so many different interests on the one hand, with the unexampled impunity that he permitted to various offences on the other,
gave rise to those miserable perplexities that he lived to bewail.
Sixtus, on the contrary, was implacable toward individual
cases of crime. His laws were enforced with a rigor that bor-
dered on cruelty; but the character of his regulations generally
was mild, conciliatory, almost indulgent. Under Gregory, the
obedient were not rewarded, nor were the refractory punished.
Under Sixtus, the insubordinate had everything to fear, but
whoever sought to gain his approbation might safely depend
on receiving proofs of his favor. This mode of proceeding
was admirably calculated for the promotion of his purposes.

We have seen the many disquietudes suffered by Gregory
from the claims he sought to enforce on his neighbors regarding ecclesiastical affairs; these Sixtus would in no case
pursue. He declared that it was incumbent on the head of
the Church to uphold and extend the privileges of the temporal powers. In accordance with this principle, he restored
the Milanese to their place in the Rota, of which Gregory had
sought to deprive them. When the Venetians succeeded in
bringing to light a brief by which their claims were definitively established in the affair of Aquileja, they did not themselves experience a more decided satisfaction than was evinced
by the Pope. He determined on suppressing the clause so

much complained of in the bull "In Cœnâ Domini." The Congregation taking cognizance of ecclesiastical jurisdiction in foreign countries, from whose interposition it was that the greater part of the disputes between the Papal See and its neighbors had originated, Sixtus abolished entirely.[1] There is doubtless a certain magnanimity in the voluntary cession of contested rights; in the pontiff's case this course of proceeding was instantly productive of effects the most satisfactory. He received an autograph letter from the King of Spain, who informed him that he had commanded his ministers in Milan and Naples to receive the papal ordinances with obedience no less implicit than that paid to his own. This moved the Pope even to tears, "That the most exalted monarch of the world should," as he said, "so honor a poor monk." The Tuscan State declared itself devoted to the Church. Venice expressed entire satisfaction. These powers now adopted a different line of policy. The outlaws who had found refuge within their frontiers were given up to the Pope. Venice prohibited their return into the Papal States, and forbade such of her ships as should touch the Roman coasts to receive them on board. This delighted the Pope. He declared that, to use his own words, "He would think of Venice for this some other day; he would suffer himself to be flayed alive for the republic, and would shed his blood for her." The bandits now found aid and refuge from no quarter, so that he no longer found it difficult to master them completely.

The unpopular measures by which Gregory had sought to enrich the treasury were wholly abandoned by Sixtus. He did not fail to punish the rebellious feudatories, but as earnestly set himself to conciliate and attach the great body of the nobles. Pope Gregory had deprived the Colonna family of its fortresses; Sixtus, on the contrary, made them advances of money, and assisted them to regulate the expenditure of their households.[2] Those ancient enemies, the Colonna and the Orsino, he united by marriages between their respective houses, and with his own. He gave one of his grand-nieces to the Constable Marc Antonio

[1] Lorenzo Priuli, "Relatione," 1586] "This is a pontiff who does not so readily embark in quarrels with princes; to avoid them he has abolished the congregation of ecclesiastical jurisdiction [in another place he says this was chiefly from consideration for Spain], thinking that so he shall the more easily bring affairs to a conclusion, or in any case shall suffer less indignity when matters are treated secretly and by himself alone."
[2] "Dispaccio degli Ambasciatori estraordinarii, 19 Ott., 25 Nov. 1585."

Colonna, and another to the Duke Virginio Orsino. The dower bestowed with each was of equal value, and their husbands received similar marks of favor. Their claims to precedence he adjusted by according it to the elder of either house. Highly exalted was the position now taken up by Donna Camilla, the pontiff's sister, surrounded as she was by her children, her noble sons-in-law and grand-daughters so magnificently allied.

The Pope derived extreme gratification from the power he possessed of conferring benefits and privileges.

He proved himself more particularly a good and open-handed fellow-countryman to the people of the March. He restored many of their ancient immunities to the inhabitants of Ancona. In Macerata he instituted a supreme court of justice for the whole province. The college of advocates in that district he distinguished by the grant of new privileges. Fermo he erected into an archbishopric, and Tolentino into a bishopric. The little village of Montalto, where his ancestors had first taken up their abode, he raised by a special bull to the rank of an episcopal city; "for here," said he, "did our race take its fortunate origin." During his cardinalate he had established a school of science there, and he now founded a "college of Montalto" in the University of Bologna, for fifty students from the March; Montalto holding presentations for eight, and even the little Grotto a Mare receiving the right to send two.[3]

Loreto also he resolved to elevate into a city. Fontana pointed out to him the difficulties that opposed this plan: "Give yourself no uneasiness about it, Fontana," said the Pope, "the execution of this project will not cost me so much as the resolving on it has done." Portions of land were bought from the people of Recana, valleys were filled up, hills levelled, and lines of streets marked out. The communes of the March were encouraged to build houses; Cardinal Gallo appointed new civic authorities for the holy chapel; by all which, the patriotism of Sixtus and his devotion to the Blessed Virgin were equally satisfied.

[3] He included even the neighboring villages as part of Montalto—"Vita Sixti V." ipsius manu emendata. "Porcula, Patringoro, and Mintenoro, being respectively but about a bow-shot from Montalto, and being all connected with it by interests of trade, by frequent intermarriages, and by some community in their lands, were beloved and aided by Sixtus, as portions of his native place; thus he bestowed favors on all in common, hoping they might one day draw together into one city."

His solicitude was extended in different degrees to the several cities of all the provinces; he made arrangements for preventing the increase of their debts, and for the control and limitation of their mortgages and alienations; he caused a strict inquiry to be made into the management of their finances, and made regulations of various character, but all conducing to restore the lost importance and well-being of the communes.[4]

Agriculture was equally indebted to the cares of Sixtus V: he undertook to drain the Chiana (swamp or pool) of Orvieto and the Pontine marshes, which last he visited in person. The river Sixtus (Fiume Sisto), which, until the time of Pius VI, was the best attempt made for draining the Pontine marshes, was cut across them by his command.

Neither was he negligent with regard to manufactures: a certain Peter of Valencia, a Roman citizen, had offered his services for the establishment of a silk manufacture. The thorough-going measures by which Sixtus attempted to forward his plans are extremely characteristic of that pontiff. He commanded that mulberry-trees should be planted throughout the States of the Church, in all gardens and vineyards, in every field and wood, over all hills, and in every valley— wherever no corn was growing, these trees were to find place; for it was fixed that five of them should be planted on every rubbio of land, and the communes were threatened with heavy fines in case of neglect.[5] The woollen manufactures, also, he sought earnestly to promote, "in order," as he says, "that the poor may have some means of earning their bread." To the first person who undertook this business he advanced funds from the treasury, accepting a certain number of pieces of cloth in return.

But we must not attribute dispositions of this kind to Sixtus alone; this would be unjust to his predecessors. Agriculture and manufactures were favored by Pius V and Gregory XIII

---

[4] Gualterius: "Five members of the apostolic chamber were sent to examine into the condition of the universities, with power to reform and reorganize." The "Memorie," also, give evidence that these measures were of great utility. These arrangements were the commencement of a better state of things among the communes of the Ecclesiastical States, which recovered the more readily because Clement VIII continued these judicious measures.

[5] "Cum sicut accepimus, 28 Maji, 1586," Bull. Cocq. iv. 4, 218: "The art of making glass, and of working in silk and wool, with the culture of silkworms, were either brought into the city, or extended by him; but to promote the silk trade, he ordered mulberry-trees to be planted throughout the States. A certain Jew, called Main, produced two cocoons from the worm in each year, and promised to make great improvements in the manufacture; to him, therefore, he accorded large privileges."

also. It was not so much by the adoption of new paths that Sixtus distinguished himself from earlier pontiffs, as by the energy and decision with which he pursued those on which they had already entered. Therefore it is that his actions have remained fixed in the memory of mankind.

Neither is it to him that the " congregations " of cardinals are wholly indebted for their origin—the seven most important, those for the Inquisition, namely, the Index, the affairs of councils, of the bishops, the monastic orders, the *segnatura,* and the *consulta,* were already in existence. Nor were affairs of State left altogether unprovided for by these earlier congregations, the two last-named having cognizance of judicial and administrative affairs. Sixtus added eight new congregations to these, of which two only were for ecclesiastical matters —one relating to the erection of new bishoprics, the other charged with the renewal and maintenance of church usages:[6] the remaining six received the management of various departments in the government, as the inspection of roads, the repeal of oppressive imposts, the building of ships of war, the corn-laws (*Annona*), the Vatican press, and the Roman university.[7] The Pope's disregard of all system in these arrangements is most obvious—partial and transient interests are placed on a level with those most permanent and general; his plans were nevertheless carried well out, and his regulations have, with very slight changes, been persisted in for centuries.

With regard to the personal character of the cardinals, he fixed a very high standard. " Men of true distinction, of morals most exemplary, their words oracles, their whole being a model and rule of life and faith to all who behold them; the salt of the earth, the light set upon a candlestick." [8] Such was the cardinal in the theory of Sixtus: in his practice these demands were not always strictly adhered to. He had, for example, nothing better to plead in behalf of Gallo, whom he had raised to that dignity, than that he was his servant, for whom he had many reasons to feel regard, and who had once received him

---

[6] " Congregation of sacred rites and ecclesiastical ceremonies, holding cognizance also of the erection of new cathedrals."

[7] " Sopra alla grascia et annona—sopra alla fabbrica armamento e mantenimento delle galere—sopra gli aggravi del popolo — sopra le strade, acque, ponti e confini — sopra alla stamperia Vaticana [he gave the first manager of the ecclesiastical press a residence in the Vatican, and 20,000 scudi for ten years]—sopra l'università dello studio Romano." (See text.)

[8] Bulla, " Postquam verus ille; 3 Dec. 1586." Bullar. M. iv. iv. 279.

very hospitably when on a journey.[9] He nevertheless established a rule even in this department of his government, which if it has not been adhered to invariably, has yet much affected the subsequent practice; he limited, namely, the number of cardinals to seventy. " As Moses," he remarks, " chose seventy elders from among the whole nation, to take counsel with them."

This pontiff has also received the credit of having abolished nepotism; but, considering the question more closely, we find that this was not done by him. The habit of unduly exalting the pontifical house had greatly declined under Pius IV, Pius V, and Gregory XIII; the favors bestowed on the papal nephews had sunk to insignificance. Pius V more especially deserves commendation in this particular, since he forbade the alienation of church property by an express law. The earlier forms of nepotism were then extinct before the times of Sixtus V, but among the popes of the succeeding century it reappeared under a different form. There were always two favored nephews or kinsmen, of whom one, raised to the cardinalate, acquired the supreme administration of affairs, ecclesiastical and political; the other, remaining in a secular station, was married into some illustrious family, was endowed with lands and " luoghi di monte," established a *majorat*, and became the founder of a princely house. If we now ask by whom this mode of nepotism was introduced, we shall find that though its rise was gradual, yet it grew to maturity under Sixtus V. Cardinal Montalto, whom the Pope loved so tenderly that he even put a restraint on the impetuosity of his temper in his favor, gained admission to the *consulta*, and a share at least in the administration of foreign affairs: his brother Michele became a marquis, and founded a wealthy house.

We are yet not to conclude that Sixtus thus introduced a system of governing by nepotism. The marquis possessed no influence whatever, the cardinal none over essential interests.[10] To have allowed them any, would have been wholly at variance

[9] Though Sixtus could endure no other form of contradiction, he could not escape that from the pulpit. The Jesuit Francis Toledo said, with regard to this, in one of his sermons, that a ruler sinned who bestowed a public office as reward for private services: " not because a man is a good carver or cup-bearer can we prudently commit to him the charge of a bishopric or a cardinalate." It was precisely a cook that Cardinal Gallo had been. (" Memorie della Vita di Sisto V.")

[10] Bentivoglio, " Memorie," p. 90: " There was scarcely a single person who had any participation in the government."

with the pontiff's mode of thinking. There was something
cordial and confiding in the favors he bestowed, and they procured him the good-will not of individuals only, but of the
public also. The helm of government was, however, in no case
resigned to another hand; he was himself sole ruler. He appeared to regard the " congregations " with very high consideration, and pressed the members to give their free unfettered
opinions; but whenever any one of them did so, he became
irritated and impatient.[1] Obstinately did he persist in the execution of his own will. " With him," says Cardinal Gritti, " no
man has a voice, even in counsel—how much less then in
decision? "[2] His personal and provincial attachments were
never permitted to interfere with his general government,
which was invariably rigid, thorough-going, and above all arbitrary.

These characteristics were exhibited in no department more
strikingly than in that of finance.

Section VII.—Finances

The Chigi family in Rome are in possession of a small
memorandum-book, kept by Sixtus in his own handwriting
while yet but a poor monk.[1] With the utmost interest does the
reader turn over the leaves of this document, wherein he has
noted all the important interests of his life: the places he
preached in during Lent, the commissions he received and executed, the books that he possessed, in what manner they
were bound, whether singly or together, are here noted down;
finally, all the details of his small monkish housekeeping are
given with the utmost exactitude. We read in these pages
how Fra Felice bought twelve sheep of his brother-in-law
Baptista; how he paid first twelve florins, and afterward two
florins and twenty bolognins for these sheep, so that they became his own property; how the brother-in-law kept them,
receiving half the profits, as was the custom of Montalto, with
many other matters of like character. We perceive with how

[1] Gualterius: " Although he referred
affairs to the congregations and others,
he yet had cognizance of all himself,
and took part in the execution. With
great zeal did he investigate the proceedings of all magistrates, whether in
the city or the provinces, likewise the

conduct of all others who had rule,
throughout the Apostolic See."
[2] Gritti, " Relatione," " Not only is
there no one who decides for him, but
there is scarcely anyone whom he will
even consult."
[1] Sisto V.

close an economy he guarded his small savings, how minutely
he kept account of them, and how at length they amounted to
some hundred florins; all these details one follows with
interest and sympathy, remarking throughout, the same eco-
nomical exactitude which this Franciscan afterward brought to
bear on the government of the Papal States. His frugality is
a quality for which he gives himself dūe praise in every bull
that affords him opportunity for introducing the subject; and
even in many of his inscriptions; it is certain that no pope,
either before or after him, administered the revenues of the
Church with so good an effect.

The treasury was utterly exhausted when Sixtus V ascended
the papal chair, and he complains bitterly of Pope Gregory,
whom he accuses of having spent the treasures of his predecessor and his successor, as well as his own:[2] he conceived so
bad an opinion of this pontiff, that he ordered masses to be said
for his soul, having seen him in a dream enduring the torments
of the other world. The revenues of the State were found to
be anticipated up to the following October.

All the more earnestly did he set himself to the task of replenishing the public coffers, and in this he succeeded beyond
his expectations. In April, 1586, at the close of the first year
of his pontificate, he had already gathered 1,000,000 scudi in
gold. To this he added a second million in November of 1587,
and in the April following a third. Thus an amount of more
than 4,500,000 of silver scudi was laid up by the early part
of 1588. When Sixtus had got together 1,000,000, he deposited it in the castle of St. Angelo, dedicating it, as he
says, " to the Holy Virgin, the mother of God, and to the holy
apostles Peter and Paul." In this bull he tells us that he " not
only surveyed the billows on which the little bark of St. Peter
was now sometimes tossing, but also the storms that are threatening from the distance. Implacable is the hatred of the
heretics; the faithful are menaced by the power of the Turk,
Assur, the scourge of God's wrath." The Almighty, in whom
he trusted, had taught him that " even by night also shall the

[2] " Vita e Successi del Cardinal di
Santaseverina," MS. Bibl. Alb.:
" When I spoke to him of the colleges of the neophytes and Armenians,
both needing aid, he replied angrily,
that there was no money in the castle
and no revenue, for the last Pope had
squandered his income as well as that
left by Pius V; he bewailed aloud that
evil state wherein he had found the
Apostlic See."

father of the family be watchful, and shall follow that example
given by the patriarchs of the Old Testament, who had ever
large treasures stored in the temple of the Lord."

He decided, as is well known, on what contingencies those
were, that would make it lawful to have recourse to this fund.
They were the following: a war undertaken for the conquest
of the Holy Land, or for a general campaign against the Turks;
the occurrence of famine or pestilence; manifest danger of
losing any province of Catholic Christendom; hostile invasion
of the Ecclesiastical States; or the attempt to recover a city
belonging to the Papal See. He bound his successors, as they
would shun the wrath of Almighty God, and of the holy apostles
Peter and Paul, to confine themselves within the limits thus
assigned them.[3]

The merit of this arrangement we leave for the moment
unquestioned, to inquire by what means the pontiff contrived
to amass a treasure so astonishing for the times he lived in.

The direct revenues of the Papal See could not account for
it; these, as Sixtus himself informs us, were not in their net
product more than 200,000 scudi a year.[4]

The savings of the Pope were considerable, but not equal
to this amount. His retrenchments were certainly very close,
the expenses of his table being reduced to six pauls a day
(nearly three shillings of our present money). He abolished
many useless offices of the court, and disbanded a part of the
troops. But we have the authority of the Venetian Delfino for
the fact that all this did not lessen the expenditure of the
Camera by more than 150,000 scudi; and we learn, besides,
from Sixtus himself, that his reduction of expense was to the
amount of 146,000 scudi only.[5]

We find then that with all his economy and by his own
showing the net revenue was increased to 350,000 scudi, and
no more. This would scarcely suffice for the buildings he was
engaged in; what then would it do toward the amassing of so
enormous a treasure?

The extraordinary system of finance established in the States

---

[3] " Ad Clavum," April 21, 1586, Cocq.
iv. iv. 206.
[4] " Dispaccio Gritti, 7 Giugno, 1586."
The Pope blames Henry III, because,
with an income of 3,000,000, he saves
nothing. Bringing forward his own example, who has no more than 200,000
scudi, when the interest on debts contracted by earlier popes, and other in-
cidental expenses are paid.
[5] " Dispaccio Badoer, 2 Guigno, 1589."

of the Church has been already considered; we have seen the continued increase of imposts and burdens of all sorts, without any corresponding increase of the real income; we have observed the multiplicity of loans by the sale of offices and by *monti*, with the ever-augumenting incumbrances laid on the State for the necessities of the Church. The many evils inseparable from this system are manifest, and, hearing the eulogies so liberally bestowed on Sixtus V, we at once infer that he found means to remedy those evils. What then is our amazement, when we find that he pursued the same course in a manner the most reckless; nay, that he even gave to this system so fixed a character as to render all future control or remedy impossible!

In the sale of offices it was that Sixtus found one chief source of his treasures. He raised in the first instance the prices of many that had been obtained by purchase only from periods long before his own. Thus the office of treasurer to the *Camera*, of which the price till now had been 15,000 scudi, he sold for 50,000 to one of the Giustiniani family; and, having raised him to the College of Cardinals, he sold it again to a Pepoli for 72,000 scudi. This second purchaser being also invested with the purple, Sixtus appropriated one-half the income of the office, namely 5,000 scudi, to a *monte;* and thus mulcted, he sold it once more for 50,000 golden scudi. In the next place he began to sell certain employments that up to his time had always been conferred gratuitously; as, for example, the notariates, the office of fiscal, with those of commissary-general, solicitor to the *Camera*, and advocate of the poor: for all these he now obtained considerable sums; as 30,000 scudi for a notariate, 20,000 for a commissariat-general, etc. Finally, he created a multitude of new offices, many of them very important ones, as were those of treasurer to the *dataria*, prefect of the prisons, etc., and some others. Of his invention are, besides, the "twenty-four referendaries," from which, as from notariates in the principal cities of the State, and from " 200 cavalierates," he derived very large sums of money.

When all these means are taken into account, the mode by which Sixtus amassed his treasure is no longer problematical. The sale of offices is computed to have brought him 608,510 golden scudi, and 401,805 silver scudi, making together nearly a million and a half of silver scudi;[6] but if this sale of places had before caused undue pressure on the State, from their involving, as we have shown, a share in the rights of government under plea of a loan, which rights were most rigorously enforced against the tax-payer, while the duties of these offices were never performed, how greatly was this evil now augmented! Offices were, in fact, considered as property conferring certain rights, rather than as an obligation demanding labor.

In addition to all this, an extraordinary increase was made by Pope Sixtus in the number of the *monti;* of these he founded three *non vacabili*, and eight *vacabili*, more than any one of his predecessors.

The *monti* were always secured, as we have seen, on new taxes; to this expedient Sixtus was at first most reluctant to have recourse, but he could devise no other. When he brought forward in the consistory his project of an investment of treasure for the Church, Cardinal Farnese opposed the idea, by observing that his grandfather Paul III had thought of this plan, but had resigned it on prceiving that it could not be accomplished without imposing new taxes. The Pope turned on him fiercely; the intimation that a previous pontiff had been wiser than himself put him in a fury. "That," he retorted, "was because there were certain great spendthrifts under Paul III, who by the blessing of God are not permitted to exist in our times." Farnese reddened and made no reply,[7] but the result showed that he was right.

In the year 1587, Sixtus would no longer endure restraint from considerations of this kind: he laid heavy imposts on the most indispensable articles of daily use, such as firewood, and the wine sold by retail in the wine-shops of the city, as also on the most toilsome occupations, that of towing barges up the Tiber by means of buffaloes or horses, for example: with the money thus gained he established *monti*. He debased the coinage, and a small money-changing trade having arisen

---

[6] "Calculation of the Roman Finances under Clement VIII," in a detailed MS. of the Bibl. Barberini in Rome.

[7] Changing countenance as Farnese spoke, the Pope replied angrily, "There is no marvel, Monsignore, if in the time of your grandfather the ordinary receipts and revenues were insufficient to found a treasure for the Church, because in that day there were many and great squanderers ['scialaquatori,' a word he was very fond of using], but we have, thank God, none of them in our times." He remarked bitterly on the multitude of sons, daughters, and nephews of all kinds surrounding Paul III. At all this Farnese colored somewhat, and remained silent.

from this fact, he turned even that circumstance to account, by
selling permission to those who stationed themselves at the cor-
ners of the streets with a view to such traffic.[8] His attachment
to the March did not prevent him from burdening the trade of
Ancona by a duty of two per cent. on her imports. Even the
manufactures, which were but just commencing their existence,
he compelled to afford him at least an indirect advantage.[9] In
these and similar operations his principal adviser was one Lopez,
a Portuguese Jew, who had fled his country from fear of the
Inquisition, and having gained the confidence of the datary and
of Signora Camilla, at length obtained that of the pontiff himself. The mode in which Cardinal Farnese had been silenced,
rendered the whole college very cautious in their opposition of
the Pope; when the wine-tax just referred to was discussed in
the consistory, Albano of Bergamo remarked, " Whatever
pleases your holiness, I approve; but should this impost dis-
please your holiness, I shall approve still more."

By all these means so many new sources of income were
rendered available, that the pontiff was enabled to take up a
loan of 2,500,000 scudi (or to be exact 2,424,725), and pay interest thereon.

It must be admitted, however, that in this system of finance
there is something exceedingly difficult to comprehend.

The country was most oppressively burdened by these taxes
and by the multitude of places. Of the latter the salaries were
made to depend on perquisites and fees, which must of necessity
embarrass the course of justice and the administration. The
taxes were imposed on the trade of the country, wholesale and
retail, and could not but seriously impair its activity. And to
what end was all this suffering inflicted?

If we add the proceeds of the *monti* to those of the offices,
we shall find that the whole sum thus produced to the *Camera*
was about equal to the treasure shut up by Sixtus in the castle
of St. Angelo—4,500,000 scudi, and very little more. All the
undertakings for which this Pope has been so highly praised

[8] For an old Giulio, besides ten bajocchi of the coin of Sixtus, a premium
of from four to six quatrini was demanded.
[9] Here we have an eloquent example
of his administration: He exacted that
no silk or wool, raw or woven, should
be sold without permission from officers appointed by him, nor come into
the market without their license: this
prevented fraud; but, better still, it
aided the treasury, because the fees on
licenses and stamps brought large sums
to the purse of the pontiff. This was
but little likely to promote the welfare
of trade.

might very well have been accomplished with the amount of
his savings.

To collect and hoard superfluous revenues is a proceeding
sufficiently intelligible: to raise a loan for some present necessity is also easily comprehended, and in the course of things;
but to borrow money and impose heavy imposts, merely for the
purpose of locking up the proceeds in a fortress, as a treasure
for some future contingency, this is altogether foreign to the
general practice of governments. Such was nevertheless the
process which has gained the admiration of the world for the
government of Sixtus V.

There was doubtless much tyranny and many unpopular
characteristics in the administration of Gregory XIII. The
reaction of these was most pernicious; but I am decidedly of
opinion that if he had succeeded in rendering the papal treasury independent of new loans and imposts for the future, the
result would have been highly beneficial to the Roman States,
and would probably have rendered their progress much more
prosperous.

But the energy required to carry the views of Gregory into
all their consequences, was not fully possessed by that pontiff;
it was more especially wanting in the last year of his life.

This practical force it was, this power of executing what
he willed, that characterized Sixtus V. His accumulation of
treasure by means of loans, imposts, and venal offices, did but
add burden to burden; nor shall we fail to perceive the consequence, but the world was dazzled by his success, which,
for the moment, did certainly give the Papal See increased importance. For the States surrounding those of the Church
were in most cases always pressed for money, and the possession of wealth inspiring the pontiffs with a more perfect
confidence in themselves, procured for them a more influential position in the eyes of their neighbors.

This mode of administering the State was indeed an essential part of the Catholic system of those times. Gathering
all the financial strength of the realm into the hands of the
ecclesiastical chief, it first rendered him the complete and exclusive organ of spiritual influence. For to what purpose
could all this treasure be applied, if not to the defence and
extension of the Catholic faith?

And in projects having these ends in view did Sixtus live, move, and have his being. His enterprises were sometimes directed against the East and the Turks, but more frequently against the West and the Protestants. Between these two confessions, the Catholic and Protestant, a war broke out, in which the pontiffs took most earnest part and interest.

This war we shall treat of in the following book: for the present let us remain a little longer with Rome herself, which now made her influence once more felt by the whole world.

Section VIII.—The Public Works of Sixtus V

Even in her external form, the city now assumed for the third time the aspect of capital of the world.

The splendor and extent of ancient Rome are familiar to all; its ruins and its history have alike contributed to bring it clearly before our eyes: these have been zealously explored, nor would the Rome of the Middle Ages less richly repay our diligence. This too was a noble city. The majesty of her basilicas, the divine worship ever proceeding in her grottoes and catacombs, the patriarchial temples of her pontiffs, preserving as they did the most revered monuments of early Christianity, all aided to render her august and imposing. The palace of the Cæsars, still magnificent, and then possessed by the German kings, with the many fortresses erected by independent races, as if in defiance of those numerous powers by which they were surrounded, added further to the interest awakened.

But during the absence of the popes at Avignon, this Rome of the Middle Ages had fallen into decay, equally with the long-ruined Rome of antiquity.

In the year 1443, when Eugenius IV returned to Rome, the city was become a mere dwelling of herdsmen; her inhabitants were in no way distinguished from the peasants and shepherds of the surrounding country. The hills had been long abandoned, and the dwellings were gathered together in the levels along the windings of the Tiber: no pavements were found in the narrow streets, and these were darkened by projecting balconies and by the buttresses that served to prop one house against another. Cattle wandered about as in a

village. From San Silvestro to the Porta del Popolo all was
garden and marsh, the resort of wild-ducks. The very
memory of antiquity was fast sinking; the capital had become
" the hill of goats," the Forum Romanum was " the cow's
field." To the few monuments yet remaining the people attached the most absurd legends. The church of St. Peter was
on the point of falling to pieces.

When Nicholas at length regained the allegiance of all
Christendom, and had become enriched by the offerings of
those pilgrims who had flocked to Rome for the jubilee, he
determined to adorn the city with buildings that should compel all to acknowledge her as the capital of the world.

To effect this was, however, no work for the life of one man;
the popes succeeding him, also labored at it for centuries.

Their exertions are sufficiently described by their respective
biographers, and I do not repeat the details; the most effective
and remarkable laborers, not as to the consequences only, but
also as to the contrasts they presented, were Julius II and
that Sixtus whose pontificate we are now considering.

When Sixtus IV had built the simple but substantial bridge
of Travertine which bears his name, thus forming a more
convenient communication between the two shores of the Tiber,
the inhabitants began to build on either bank with considerable
activity. The lower city, which had now withdrawn to these
banks of the river, was entirely restored under Julius II. Not
content with his enterprise of St. Peter's church on the southern
side, which was rising in great majesty under his direction, Julius also restored the palace of the Vatican, and across the decliv-
ity that separated the old buildings from the villa of Innocent
VIII, called the Belvedere, he laid the foundation of the Loggie,
one of the most admirably conceived works in existence. At
no great distance from these erections, his kinsmen of the Riario
family and his treasurer, Agostini Chigi, were all building
palaces of great beauty, each in emulation of the other. Of
these, the Farnesina, that of Chigi, is unquestionably the superior, admirable for the perfection of its plan and the grace
of its construction, but most of all for the rich decorations it
received from the hand of Raphael. To the north of the Tiber,
Julius also displayed his munificence by completing the Can-
cellaria with its fine court (*cortile*), which from the purity

and harmony of its proportions is considered the most beautiful in the world. The example he gave was eagerly followed by his cardinals and nobles; among them Farnese, the magnificent entrance of whose palace has gained it the reputation of being the finest in Rome; and Francesco del Rio, who boasted of his house that " it should last till a tortoise had completed the tour of the globe." The Medici meanwhile filled their dwellings with the most varied treasures of art and literature; while the Orsini dorned their palace on the Campofiore with painting and sculpture both within and without.[1] The remains of that magnificent period, when the noble works of antiquity were so boldly rivalled, do not receive all the attention they merit, from the stranger who passes them in his walks around the Campofiori and across the Piazza Farnese. The genius, emulation, and fertility of spirit characterizing this bright epoch produced a general prosperity in the city. In proportion with the increase of the people, buildings were erected on the Campo Marzo, and around the mausoleum of Augustus. These were further extended under Leo X. Julius had previously constructed the Lungara on the southern shore, and opposite to the Strada Giulia on the northern bank. The inscription still remains wherein the conservators boast that Julius had traced out and given to the public these new streets, " in proportion with the majesty of his newly acquired dominions."

The plague and the sack of the city occasioned a large decrease of the population; which again suffered during the troubles under Paul IV. It did not recover from these injuries until some time after, when an increase of the inhabitants was seen to accompany the return of the Catholic world to its allegiance.

The reoccupation of the deserted hills had been contemplated by Pius IV. The palace of the conservators on the Monte Capitolino was founded by him; and it was for the same pontiff that Michael Angelo erected the church of Santa Maria degli Angeli, on the Viminal, with a portion from the ruins of the Baths of Dioclesian, and on a small part of their site. The Porta Pia, on the Quirinal, still bears his name and

---

[1] See " Opusculum de Mirabilibus novæ et veteris Urbis Romæ, editum a Francisco Albertino," 1515; more especially the second part, " De novâ urbe."

inscription;[2] additions were made to the same quarter by Gregory XIII.

But these were all vain labors only, so long as the hills remained destitute of water.

And here it was that Sixtus V achieved a well-merited glory. He has distinguished himself from all other pontiffs, and rivalled the ancient Cæsars, by supplying the city with pure streams of water, brought into it by means of colossal aqueducts. This he did, as he tells us himself, "that these hills, adorned in early Christian times with basilicas, renowned for the salubrity of their air, the pleasantness of their situation, and the beauty of their prospects, might again become inhabited by man." "Therefore," he adds, "we have suffered ourselves to be alarmed by no difficulty, and deterred by no cost." He did in fact declare to the architects from the first commencement, that he desired to produce a work whose magnificence might compete with the glories of imperial Rome. He brought the Aqua Martia from the Agro Colonna, a distance of two-and-twenty miles, to Rome; and this in defiance of all obstacles, carrying it partly underground and partly on lofty arches. How great was the satisfaction with which Sixtus beheld the first stream of this water pouring its bright wealth into his own vine-garden (*vigna*)! still further did he then bear it onward to Santa Susanna, on the Quirinal. From his own name he called it the "Acqua Felice," and it was with no little self-complacency that he placed a statue by the fountain, representing Moses, who brings water, streaming from the rock, at the touch of his staff.[3]

Not only the immediate neighborhood, but the whole city, drew at once great advantage from that aqueduct. Twenty-seven fountains were supplied by the Acqua Felice, which gives 20,537 cubic metres of water every twenty-four hours.

From this time, building on the hills was resumed with great activity, which Sixtus further stimulated by the grant of special privileges. He levelled the ground about the Trinità de Monti, and laid the foundation of the steps descending

[2] Luigi Contarini, "Antichità di Roma," bestows high praise on the efforts of Pius IV: "Had he lived four years longer," he remarks. "Rome would have been another city as to its buildings."

[3] We have stanzas by Tasso, "All' Acqua Felice di Roma" ("Rime,") ii. 311), describing how the water at first flows along a gloomy path, and then bursts joyously forth to the light of day to look on Rome as Augustus beheld it.

to the Piazza di Spagna, which offer the most direct line of communication between that height and the lower city.[4] Along the summit he laid out the Via Felice and the Borgo Felice, opening streets that even to our day continue to be the great thoroughfares from all directions to Santa Maria Maggiore. It was his purpose to connect all the other basilicas by spacious avenues with this church. The poets boast that Rome had nearly doubled her extent, and was again resuming her old abodes.

These fine constructions on the heights were not the only works by which Sixtus distinguished himself from earlier popes. His designs were, in some respects, directly opposed to the purposes and ideas of his predecessors.

Under Leo X, the ruins of ancient Rome were regarded with a species of religious veneration. The presence of a divine genius was hailed in these relics with rapturous delight; with a ready ear did that sovereign listen to him who exhorted to the preservation of " the all that yet remains to us of our city; that ancient mother of the greatness and renown of Italy."[5]

Distant as earth from heaven were all the ideas of Sixtus from these modes of view and feeling; for the beauties of antiquity, this Franciscan had neither comprehension nor sympathy. The Septizonium of Severus, a most extraordinary work, could find no favor in his eyes, though surviving the storms of so many centuries. He demolished it entirely, and carried off a part of its columns for the church of St. Peter.[6]

[4] Gualterius: "That he might form a more convenient road from the lower part of the city to the Pincian mount, and between that and the Esquiline, he lowered the Pincian hill before the Church of the Most Holy Trinity, so that carriages might pass; he built steps also, convenient as well as beautiful, which lead to the Pincian hill and to that church, where there is a most pleasant and fair prospect."

[5] Passages from Castiglione's well-known letter to Leo X, "Lettere di Castiglione," Padova, 1796, p. 149. But I can find no intimation here of a plan for excavating the ancient city; rather it seems to me that this is the preface to a description of Rome, with a plan, reference being frequently made both to the plan and description. It is highly probable that the works of Raphael himself were to be introduced by this preface, an opinion that is strengthened by the similarity of certain expressions in this letter with those of the well-known epigram on the death of Raphael: " vedendo quasi il cadavero di quella nobil patria cosi miseramente lacerato;" " urbis lacerum ferro igni annisque cadaver ad vitam revocas." This certainly does intimate a restoration, but in idea only, in a description, not more; an opinion not essentially at variance with those before expressed—it is rather confirmatory of them. I think we may conclude that the work with which Raphael occupied the latter part of his life was far advanced, since a dedication of it was already composed in his name. What a name to add to the list of describers of cities (astyographers)! These papers, with the plan, may have fallen into the hands of Fulvius, who probably took an active part in the researches.

[6] Gualterius: "Above all he caused the Septizonium of Severus to be demolished, to the infinite grief of the

His rage for destruction seemed equal to his zeal in building, and great fears were entertained that he would go beyond all bounds of moderation in both. Let us hear what
Cardinal Santa Severina relates as to this matter—were it not
the testimony of an eye-witness, we should find it incredible:
" When it was perceived," he tells us, " that the Pope seemed
resolving on the utter destruction of the Roman antiquities,
there came to me one day a number of the Roman nobles,
who entreated me to dissuade his holiness with all my power
from so extravagant a design." They addressed their petition
to that cardinal, who was then, without doubt, himself considered as a confirmed zealot. Cardinal Colonna united
his prayers to theirs. The Pope replied that he would " clear
away the ugly antiquities," but would restore all others that required restoration. And now for an instance of those he found
" ugly." That tomb of Cecilia Metella, which was even then
one of the most valuable relics of the republican times, and
a monument of admirable sublimity—this it was among his
purposes to destroy! How much may not have perished beneath his hand!

He could not persuade himself to endure the Laocoon and
the Apollo Belvedere in the Vatican without great difficulty,
and would not suffer those ancient statues with which the
Roman citizens had enriched the Capitol to retain their places.
He thereatened to destroy the Capitol itself if they were not
removed. These were a Jupiter Tonans between Apollo and
Minerva; the two first-named were in fact removed, and the
Minerva was permitted to remain only because Sixtus had
contrived to invest her with the character of Rome,[7] and
Rome christianized, by taking the spear of the goddess from
her hand and replacing it with a gigantic cross.

The columns of Trajan and of Antonine he restored in the
same spirit, removing the urn which was believed to contain
the ashes of the Emperor from the former, which he dedicated
to St. Paul. The column of Antonine was in like manner
assigned to St. Peter, and from that time the statues of the
two apostles have stood confronting each other on that airy

Romans, using its columns and mar-
bles for his works; and in many places
of the city might excavations be seen
where he had extracted various mar-
bles."

[7] Passage from the life of Sixtus V,
ipsius manu emendata, given in Bun-
sen's " Description of Rome," i. p. 702.

elevation, overlooking the dwellings of men. The pontiff thought that he had thus secured a triumph for Christianity over paganism.[8]

He had set his heart on erecting the obelisk before the church of St. Peter, principally because " he desired to see the monuments of unbelief subjected to the cross on the very spot where the Christians had formerly suffered the bitter death of crucifixion."[9]

This was indeed a magnificent design, but his mode of conducting it was highly characteristic, evincing a singular mixture of despotism, grandeur, pomp, and bigotry.

He threatened to punish the architect, Domenico Fontana, who had worked his way up under his own eyes from the condition of a mason's apprentice, should the enterprise fail, or the obelisk sustain injury.

The task was one of exceeding difficulty: to lift this monument from its base near the sacristy of the old church of St. Peter, lower it to a horizontal position, remove it to the place assigned, and fix it on a new basis.

The work was undertaken with a consciousness in those concerned, that their enterprise was one which would be famed throughout all ages. The men employed, 900 in number, began by hearing mass, confessing and receiving the sacrament. They then entered the enclosure set apart for their labors, the master placing himself on a raised platform. The obelisk was defended by straw mats and a casing of planks firmly secured by strong iron bands. The monstrous machine which was to upheave it with thick ropes, received motion from thirty-five windlasses, each worked by two horses and ten men. When all was ready, the signal was given by sound of trumpet. The first turn proved the efficacy of the means employed. The obelisk was lifted from the base on which it had rested during 1,500 years. At the twelfth turn it had risen two palms and three-quarters, where it was held fast. The architect saw the ponderous mass (weighing, with its defences, more than 1,000,000 Roman pounds) in his power. This took place, as

---

[8] This at least is the opinion of J. P. Maffei, among others, " Historiarum ab excessu Gregorii XIII," lib. i. p. 5.
[9] Sixti V," i. m. e.: " Ut ubi grassatum olim suppliciis, in Christianos et passim fixæ cruces, in quas innoxia natio sublata teterrimis cruciatibus necaretur, ibi supposita cruci, et in crucis versa honorem cultumque ipsa impietatis monumenta cernerentur." (See text.)

was carefully recorded, on April 30, 1586, at the twentieth hour (about three in the afternoon). A salute was fired from the castle St. Angelo. All the bells of the city pealed forth, and the workmen carried their master round the enclosure in triumph, uttering joyous and reiterated acclamations.

Seven days were suffered to elapse, when the obelisk was lowered to the desired level with similar skill. It was then conveyed on rollers to its new destination; but it was not till the hot months had passed that they ventured to attempt the re-erection.

The day chosen by Sixtus for this undertaking was September 10th, a Wednesday (which he had always found to be a fortunate day), and that immediately preceding the festival of the Elevation of the Cross, to which the obelisk was to be dedicated. The workmen again commenced their labors by commending themselves to God, all falling on their knees as they entered the enclosure. Fontana had profited by the description given in Ammianus Marcellinus of the last raising of an obelisk for making his arrangements, and was, besides, provided with a force of 140 horses. It was considered peculiarly fortunate that the sky chanced to be clouded that day: all succeeded perfectly. The obelisk was moved by three great efforts, and an hour before sunset it was seen to sink upon its pedestal, formed by the backs of four bronze lions that seem to support it. The exulting cries of the people filled the air, and the satisfaction of the pontiff was complete. This work, which so many of his predecessors had desired to perform, and which so many writers had recommended, he had now accomplished. He notes in his diary that he has achieved the most difficult enterprise conceivable by the mind of man. He struck medals in commemoration of this event, received poems of congratulation in every language, and sent official announcements of his success to foreign powers.[10]

[10] The despatches of Gritti of May 3 and 10, July 12, and October 11, allude to this elevation of the obelisk. The effect is well described in the "Vita Sixti V.," ipsius manu emendata: He held the eyes of the whole city fixed on the spectacle of a new thing, or rather one repeated after a lapse of more than 1,500 years; when either he raised the mass, after wrenching it from its site by the force of thirty-five capstans, or that he slowly suffered it to fall while thus suspended, and extended it along the ground on a huge tray formed of beams to receive it. Then on cylinders, wooden columns rounded and smooth, it was dragged along by four windlasses over the line which had been built and elevated to the level of the base whereon it was to stand; and lastly, being again set up and poised exactly, it was fixed on the place newly assigned it."

The inscription he affixed has a strange effect; he boasts of having wrested the monument from the emperors Augustus and Tiberius, to consecrate it to the holy cross; and a cross was erected on the obelisk, enclosing within it a piece of the supposed true cross. This proceeding is an eloquent expression of his whole mode of thought. The very monuments of paganism were to be made ministers to the glory of the cross.

Sixtus devoted himself with his whole spirit to his architectural undertakings. A herd-boy, brought up among fields and gardens, for him the city had peculiar attractions. He would not hear mention of a villa residence; his best pleasure, as he declares himself, was " to see many roofs." He doubtless meant that his highest satisfaction was derived from the progress of his buildings.

Many thousand hands were kept constantly employed, nor did any difficulty deter him from his purpose.

The cupola of St. Peter's was still wanting, and the architects required ten years for its completion. Sixtus was willing to give the money, but he also desired to gratify his eyes by the completed building. He set 600 men to work, allowing no intermission even at night. In twenty-two months the whole was finished, the leaden covering to the roof alone excepted; this he did not live to see.

The arbitrary and impetuous character of the pontiff was manifest even in labors of this kind. He demolished without remorse the remains of the papal *patriarchium*, which were by no means inconsiderable, and were singularly interesting. These antiquities were connected with the dignity of his own office, but he destroyed them nevertheless to erect his palace of the Lateran on their site; a building not at all wanted, and which excites a very equivocal interest, solely as one of the earliest examples of the uniform regularity of modern architecture.

How complete was the revolution which then took place in the relations of the age to antiquity! As in former times men emulated the ancients, so did they now; but their earlier efforts were directed toward an approach to their beauty and grace of form; now they sought only to vie with, or exceed them, in extent and magnitude. Formerly the slightest trace of the antique spirit was reverenced in however trifling a monument;

now the disposition seemed rather to destroy these traces. One sole idea held predominance among the men of this day; they would acknowledge no other. It was the same that had gained ascendancy in the Church—the same that had succeeded in making the State a mere instrument of the Church. This ruling idea of modern Catholicism had penetrated throughout the being of society, and pervaded its most diversified institutions.

Section IX.—General Change in the Intellectual Tendency of the Age

It is not to be supposed that the Pope alone was subjected to the dominion of the spirit we have seen to prevail; toward the close of the sixteenth century, a tendency became obvious in every manifestation of intellect directly opposed to that which had marked its commencement.

Highly significant of this change is the fact that the study of the ancients, which in the first part of the century had been a primary condition to all knowledge, had now greatly declined. Another Aldus Minutius had indeed appeared in Rome, and was professor of eloquence; but neither for his Greek nor Latin did he find admirers. At the hour of his lectures he might be seen pacing up and down before the portal of the university with one or two hearers, the only persons in whom he found congeniality of sentiment or pursuit. How rapid a progress was made by the study of Greek in the early part of this century! yet there did not exist at its conclusion one single Hellenist of reputation in all Italy.

Not that I would assert this change to be altogether symptomatic of decline; it was in a certain sense connected with the necessary progress of science and literature.

For if in earlier times all science had been immediately derived from the ancients, this was now no longer possible. How enormous was the mass of knowledge brought together by Ulisses Aldrovandi, for example; during the labors of his long life and extensive travels, in comparison with anything that could be possessed by the ancients! In the construction of his museum he had labored to produce completeness, and wherever the natural object was unattainable, had supplied its place by drawings, carefully appending to each specimen an elaborate description. How far, too, had the knowledge of geography extended beyond what had even been imagined by those best informed in the ancient world! A more profound and searching spirit of investigation had arisen; mathematicians had in earlier days sought only to fill up the chasms left by the ancients; as for example, Commandin, who, believing he had discovered that Archimedes had either read or written some treatise on gravitation, which was afterward lost, was led by this supposition, himself to investigate the subject. But by this very process men were conducted to more extensive observations; even while seeking to pursue the light offered by the ancients, the mind of the student became freed from their tutelage. Discoveries were made that led beyond the circle prescribed by them, and these again opened new paths to further inquiries.

More especially did the study of nature attract zealous and self-relying students. For a moment men wavered between an acquiescence in the mysteries attributed to natural phenomena and the bold, deep-searching examination of those phenomena; but the love of science soon prevailed. An attempt was already made to produce a rational classification of the vegetable kingdom. In Padua, the science of anatomy was zealously pursued; and a professor of that university was called "the Columbus of the human body!" Inquirers marched boldly forward in all directions, and knowledge was no longer restricted to the works of the ancients.

It followed, if I am not mistaken, as a matter of course, that antiquity, being no longer studied with so exclusive an attention as regarded the subject, could no longer exert its earlier influence with reference to form.

Writers of learned works began now to think principally of accumulating material. In the beginning of the century, Cortesius had embodied the essence of the scholastic philosophy, spite of the intractable nature of his subject, in a well-written classical work, full of wit and spirit. But at this time, the subject of mythology, well calculated to call forth and to repay the most genial and imaginative treatment, was handled by Natal Conti in a dull and uninviting quarto. This author also wrote a history composed almost entirely of sentences quoted directly from the ancients; the passages whence he has borrowed being cited; but he does not possess one qualification for giving a genuine description; a mere heaping together of the bare facts seemed sufficient for his contemporaries. We may safely affirm that a work like the Annals of Baronius, so entirely destitute of form—written in Latin, yet without one trace of beauty or elegance, even in detached phrases—could not have been thought of at the commencement of the century.

Nor was this departure from the track of the ancients, in science, in form, and in expression, the only change; others took place in all the social habits of the nation; changes by which an incalculable influence was exercised both on literature and art.

Republican and independent Italy, on whose peculiar circumstances the early development of her people, intellectual and social, had depended, was now no more; all the freedom and simplicity of intercourse proper to the earlier days had departed. It is worthy of note that titles came into use at this time. As early as the year 1520, it was remarked with disgust that all desired to be called " Sir ": this was attributed to the influence of the Spaniards. About the year 1550, the old forms of address, so noble in their simplicity, were encumbered, whether in speech or writing, by ponderous epithets of honor; at the end of the century duke and marquis were titles everywhere prevailing; all wished to possess them, every man would fain be " Excellency." Nor are we permitted to consider this a mere trifle; even in the present day, when this system of titles is become old and familiar, they still have their effect; how much more then when all were new? In every other respect also, society became more rigid, stiff, and exclusive; the cheerful easy tone of manner, the frank intercourse of earlier times were gone forever.

Be the cause of this where it may—whether a change incident to the nature of the human mind—thus much is manifest, that so early as the middle of the century a different spirit pervaded all productions; new wants were making themselves felt in the external forms, as in the living essence of society.

We find evidence of this change in many striking phenomena, and perhaps one of the most remarkable is the remodelling of Bojardo's " Orlando Innamorato," by Berni. It is the same work, and yet altogether different; all the freshness and charm of the original have disappeared. On a more rigid examination, we shall find that Berni has invariably displaced the individual to substitute the universal; he has obliterated the unfettered expression of a lovely and most vivid nature, for the conventional decorums then and now demanded by Italian manners.[1] His success was perfect, the manufacture he presented was received with incredible approbation, and entirely superseded the original poem. How rapidly too, for it was not yet fifty years since Bojardo had first published his work.

This essential change, this infusion of a different spirit, may be traced through most of the productions of that period.

If the longer poems of Alamanni and Bernardo Tasso are tedious and uninviting, this does not proceed entirely from the absence of talent, in the case of the latter more especially. But the very conception of these works is cold. In compliance with the demands of a public that was certainly not very virtuous, but had put on manners of serious sedateness, both these writers chose immaculate heroes. Bernardo Tasso selected Amadis, of whom the younger Tasso says, "Dante would have retracted his unfavorable opinion of chivalric romance, had he known the Amadis of Gaul or of Greece; characters so full of nobleness and constancy." The hero of Alamanni was Giron le Courtoys, the mirror of all knightly virtues. His express purpose was to show youth by this example, how hunger and night-watching, cold and heat, were to be endured; how arms should be borne; how justice and piety were best to be exemplified; how enemies were to be forgiven, and mercy extended to all. Proceeding with this their moral and didactic aim, entirely after the manner of Berni, and intentionally divesting the fable of its poetic basis, the result they have gained is a work of infinite prolixity and insipid dulness.

The nation would seem, if we may venture on the expression, to have worked out and used up the whole amount of the poetical conceptions, descending to it from its by-gone history, and from the ideas proper to the Middle Ages; it had even lost the power of comprehending them. Something new was sought for, but the creative genius would not come forth, nor did the life of the day present any fresh material. Up to the middle of

[1] In the Academical Treatise before alluded to, I have endeavored to pursue this subject in a more detailed form.

the century, Italian prose, though from its nature didactic, was yet imaginative, life-like, flexible, and graceful. Gradually prose also became rigid and cold.

And as with poetry, so was it with art. She lost the inspiration derived from her connection with religion, and soon after that which had informed her more profane efforts. Some few traces of it yet lingered in the Venetian school alone. How entirely had the disciples of Raphael, with one exception only, degenerated from their master. While they sought to imitate him, they lost themselves in artificial beauties, theatrical attitudes, and affected graces. Their works sufficiently show in how total an absence of feeling and with how feeble a sense of beauty they were conceived. With the scholars of Michael Angelo it fared no better. Art no longer comprehended her object; the ideas that she had formerly taxed her powers to clothe with form were now abandoned. There remained to her only the externals of method.

In this state of things, when antiquity was deserted; when its forms were no longer imitated; when its science was left in the background, and far overpassed; when the old national poetry and all religious modes of conception were despised and rejected by literature and art, the resuscitation of the Church commenced. It obtained the mastery over the minds of men, either with their consent or in spite of their resistance, producing a radical change in the whole being and system of art and of literature.

Its influence was equally obvious in science, but if I am not mistaken, the effect was in this case of a totally different character from that exercised over art.

Philosophy, and indeed all science, now passed through a very important epoch. Having restored the genuine Aristotle, men soon began to set themselves wholly free from his authority in matters of philosophy, as had happened in other branches of knowledge and with other ancient writers, and proceeded to the unfettered investigation of the most recondite and highest problems. But from the very nature of things it was impossible that the Church could favor this freedom of inquiry, she lost no time in laying down first principles in a manner that permitted no doubt. The adherents of Aristotle had not unfrequently expressed opinions, such as the Church had never sanctioned, and which were derived from the light of nature only; might not something similar be apprehended from those who set themselves to oppose that philosopher? for their purpose was, as one of them expressed it, to compare the tenets of former teachers, with the original handwriting of God, the world and nature. This was a project of which it was difficult to determine the probable result; but whether discoveries or errors ensued, they could not fail to be deeply perilous; the Church, consequently, extinguished this evil in the germ. Telesius did not suffer his speculations to pass beyond the domain of physical science; he was nevertheless confined through his whole life to his small native town. Campanella was subjected to torture, and compelled to live in exile. The most profound thinker of all, Giordano Bruno, a true philosopher, after many persecutions and long wanderings, was at last seized by the Inquisition, was sent to Rome, imprisoned and condemned to the flames, " not only," as the legal record sets forth, " because himself a heretic, but as a dangerous heresiarch, who had written things affecting religion, and unseemly."[2] How could men find courage for earnest investigation with such examples before them? One only of those who ventured on innovations found favor with Rome, and he did so, because his attacks on Aristotle were confined to the accusation that his principles were opposed to the Church and to Christianity. This was Francesco Patrizi. He believed himself to have discovered a genuine philosophical tradition, descending from the pretended Hermes Trismegistus, and which he traced through all succeed-

[2] In a Venetian MS. now in the Archives of Vienna, under the Rubric Roma, Espositioni, 1592, will be found the original of a protocol respecting the surrender of Giordano Bruno. There appeared before the college the vicar of the patriarch, the father inquisitor, and Tommasso Morosini, the assistant of the Inquisition. The vicar stating that there had been arrested within the last few days, and was then in the prison of the Inquisition, a certain Giordano Bruno of Nola, accused not of heresy only, but also as an heresiarch, he having written various books wherein he spoke in terms of praise of the English queen and other principal heretics; and also had said divers things concerning religion, which were not becoming, even though he spoke philosophically; that this man was besides an apostate, having been a Dominican friar, but had lived many years in Geneva and in England: of these things he had also been accused in Naples and other places; that his arrest being communicated to the authorities in Rome, the most illustrious cardinal Santa Severina had written and commanded that he should be sent to Rome by the first safe opportunity. Such an opportunity these officers now had. To this application they received no immediate reply; and, in the afternoon, the father inquisitor again appeared; but the Savi replied that the matter was of weight, and demanded reflection; that the affairs of the state were pressing and numerous, so that they had not yet been able to come to any decision. The inquisitor was very earnest for their reply, because the boat was about to depart. But this time it had to go without the prisoner, whether his being afterward surrendered was in consequence of further application I have not been able to ascertain.

ing ages. This tradition contradicted the views of Aristotle, and gave a clearer explanation of the Trinity than was to be found even in the Mosaic records. Patrizi was anxious to restore it, and to substitute its tenets for those of the Aristotelian philosophy. In all the dedications of his works he alludes to this purpose, and insists on the utility and necessity of its execution. His mind was peculiarly constituted; he was not without critical discernment, but evinces this quality, rather in what he has rejected than in what he adopts. He was invited to Rome, and maintained himself there in high credit, not by the influence of his works, which was extremely insignificant, but because the peculiarities of his opinions and the tendency of his labors were in harmony with the views of the Church.

The investigation of physics and natural history was at that time almost inseparably connected with philosophical inquiry. The whole system of ideas as previously accepted was called in question; there was indeed among the Italians of that period an earnest tendency toward the vigorous pursuit of truth, a zeal for progress, a noble loftiness of anticipation. Who shall say to what glorious results this might have led? But the Church set up a barrier which they must not overpass; woe to him who should be found beyond it!

That the restoration of Catholicism produced unfavorable effects on science it is impossible to deny. Poetry and art on the contrary received benefit from its renovation; a living subject, a prolific material was needful to them, and this they once more received from the Church.

Of the dominion exercised by the regenerated spirit of religion over the minds of men, we have an example in Torquato Tasso. His father Bernardo, had chosen a hero of blameless moral character; he took a step further in the same direction. The crusades had been selected as the subject of a poem by another writer of that day, on the ground that " it is better to handle a true argument in a Christian fashion, than to seek a little Christian fame from an argument without truth." Torquato Tasso did likewise. He sought his hero not in fable, but history, and Christian History. Godfrey is more than Æneas, he is like a saint satiated with the world and with its passing glories. The work would nevertheless have been very tedious and dry, had the poet contented himself with the mere representation of such a personage; but Tasso seized on all the resources offered by the sentimental and enthusiastic portion of religious feeling; this harmonized most happily with the fairy world, whose rainbow tints he has wrought into the fabric of his poem. The work is perhaps occasionally somewhat prolix, the effect is not always fully made out, yet on the whole it is replete with feeling and fancy, national spirit, and truth of character. The love and admiration of his countrymen were secured by it to the author, and have been continued to his memory even down to our own days. But what a contrast does he present to Ariosto! At an earlier period the art of poetry had fallen off from the Church. Religion, now rising in the might of her renovated empire, subjected poetry once more to her allegiance.

At no great distance from Ferrara, where Tasso composed his poem, at Bologna namely, there soon after arose the school of the Caracci, the origin of which marks a general revolution in painting.

When we ask whence this change proceeded, we are assured that it was due to the anatomical studies of the Bolognese academy—to their eclectic imitation, and their learned style of art. There was, unquestionably, great merit in the zeal with which they sought, in their manner, to approach the truth of nature: but the subjects they selected, and the spirit in which these were treated, appear to me no less important.

The most earnest efforts of Ludovico Caracci were devoted to a realization of the ideal of Christ. He is not always successful; but in the Calling of St. Matthew he has indeed most happily presented the mild and serious man, full of truth and fervor, of grace and majesty. This, as is well known, has become the model of many succeeding painters. He has doubtless imitated earlier masters, but in a manner entirely characteristic of himself. The Transfiguration of Raphael was evidently in his mind; but even while appropriating this, he infuses his own idea, and the hand of Christ is raised toward Moses as in the act of teaching. The master-piece of Agostino Caracci is without doubt his St. Jerome. The old man is on the very point of death: he has lost all power of movement, but aspires with his last breath in fervent longing toward the host about to be presented to him. The Ecce Homo of Annibale Caracci in the Borghese palace, with its deep shadows, its delicate, transparent skin and tearful eyes, is the ideal of Ludovico, but raised to a more exalted sublimity. Admirably is this exemplified, once more, in the Dead Christ; the rigidity of death has not concealed the grandeur and freedom of conception that distinguish this fine work; the tragical event just completed is expressed as it was conceived—with new and characteristic feeling. The lunettes of the Doria palace present us with landscapes rendered eloquently vivid by the simple expression of human events in the sacred histories.

These masters, then, though not refusing profane subjects, yet devoted themselves with peculiar earnestness to sacred ones; they are not indebted wholly to their technical and external merits for the rank they maintain; this is secured to them principally by the fact that they once more caught the full inspiration of their subject—the religious representations they set before us had once more significance to themselves.

Their pupils are distinguished by a similar tendency. That ideal of St. Jerome, which Agostino Caracci had originated, was elaborated by Dominichino with such felicitous industry, that in variety of grouping and perfection of expression he has perhaps gone beyond his master. His head of St. Nilus appears to me a noble work, from its mingled expression, suffering, and reflection. His Sibyls, too, how youthful and innocent, yet how profoundly meditative! Dominichino delighted in contrasting the joys of heaven with the sufferings of earth, as we find them in his Madonna del Rosario—the Divine Mother, rich in grace and beauty, as opposed to the feeble and wretched mortal.

Guido Reni, also, has occasionally presented us with this contrast: the Virgin, radiant with immortal beauty, is placed together with monkish saints attenuated by fast and vigil. Guido displays vigorous force of conception and originality of manner. How sublime is his Judith, exulting in the deed she has accomplished, and glowing with gratitude for the aid bestowed by heaven! Who but will remember his Madonnas—exalted— wrapt in the ecstasy of their devotion? Even in his saints he embodies an ideal of enthusiastic reverie.

Certain other characteristics of this tendency in art remain to be described, but of less attractive quality. The invention of these painters is occasionally deformed by a fantastic incongruity. In the fine group of the Holy Family, for example, is found a St. John ceremoniously kissing the foot of the Divine Infant, or the apostles are brought in to condole with the Virgin, and are deliberately preparing to wipe away their tears. The horrible, too, is expressed with needless frequency, and without the slightest mitigation. We have the St. Agnes of Dominichino, with the blood starting beneath the sword! Guido, has set the Slaughter of the Innocents before us in all its atrocity—the women with their mouths all open pouring forth shriek on shriek—the savage executioners whose hands are dyed with the blood of their victims!

Religion had resumed her empire over the minds of men, but the mode of her influence was no longer that of earlier times: in the older periods her external manifestations were pure and simple; in this later epoch ·they became fantastic, forced, and conventional.

The talents of Guercino are admitted and admired by all, but what a St. John is that of the Sciarra gallery—those large muscular arms, those bare gigantic knees—that face too, inspired without doubt, but darkened by a gloom that makes it difficult to decide whether the inspiration be not rather of earth than heaven. His St. Thomas lays so heavy a hand on the wounds of Christ, that we fancy the Redeemer suffering from so rude a touch. Guercino has depicted Peter Martyr at the very moment when the sword cleaves his head. By the side of the Duke of Aquitaine, whom St. Bernard is investing with the cowl, stands a monk, busily occupied with the conversion of a squire belonging to the duke, and the spectator is inexorably consigned to a scene of premeditated devotion.

This is not the place to inquire how far the limits of art were overstepped by this mode of treating the subject—now extravagantly ideal, now unnaturally hard; it will suffice to say, that over the restored art of painting the Church acquired complete dominion; by the inspiration of poetry, and the principles of a positive religion, she doubtless infused new life into it, but she also imposed on it a character essentially ecclesiastical, sacerdotal, and dogmatic.

This was effected with greater ease in architecture, which was more immediately vowed to her service. I am not certain that anyone has investigated the progress of modern architect-

ure, from the imitation of antiquity to the canon devised by
Barozzi for the construction of churches, and which has been
observed in Rome and through all Catholic countries to the
present day. Here, too, the lightness and cheerful freedom distinguishing the early part of the century were abandoned for
pompous solemnity and religious magnificence.

As regarded one art 'only, did the question long remain
doubtful whether or not it could be made subservient to the
purposes of the Church.

This was music, which toward the middle of the sixteenth
century had become lost in the most artificial intricacies. Variations, imitations, proportions, and fugues formed the reputation of composers; the meaning of the words was no more regarded. Masses of that period may be found in great number,
of which the themes are furnished by well-known profane melodies. The human voice was treated as a mere instrument.[3]

We cannot be surprised that the Council of Trent should
take offence at the introduction of music thus arranged in the
churches. In consequence of the discussion there commenced,
Pius IV appointed a commission to inquire into the subject,
and to settle definitely whether music should be admitted to the
divine service, or banished from it entirely. The decision was
very doubtful. The Church required that the words sung
should be intelligible, and that the musical expression should
be in harmony with the sense. The professors of music
asserted that this was unattainable, according to the rules of
their art. Cardinal Borromeo was in the commission, and the
known rigor of that eminent churchman rendered an adverse
decision extremely probable.

Happily the right man once more presented himself, and he
appeared at the right moment.

Among the Roman composers of that day was Pier-Luigi
Palestrina. This master was married, and the severity of Paul
IV had driven him on that account from the papal chapel. After
his expulsion he lived retired and forgotten, in a wretched hut
among the vine-grounds of Monte Celio. But his was a spirit
that could to yield to adverse fortune. Even in this abandon-
ment he devoted himself to his art with a singleness of purpose

[3] Giuseppe Baini, "Memorie storico-
critiche della Vita e delle Opere di Giovanni Pier-Luigi di Palestrina, Roma,
1828," supplies the information of
which I have made use.

that secured the originality of his conceptions, and the free action of that creative force with which he was endowed. It was here that he wrote the "Improperie" which to this day ennoble the solemnities of Good Friday in the Sistine Chapel. The profound significance of a scriptural text, its symbolic import, its power to move the soul, and its application to religion, have perhaps in no instance been more truly appreciated by any composer.

If the experiment, whether his method were applicable to the grand and comprehensive purposes of the mass, could be successfully made by any man, that man was Palestrina; to him accordingly the commission intrusted it.

Deeply conscious that on this trial was now depending the life or death of the grand music of the mass, it was with earnest tension of all his powers that the composer proceeded to his task. The words "O Lord, open thou mine eyes," were found written on his manuscript.

His success was not immediate; the first two attempts failed. At length, however, the happy moment arrived, and the mass known as "the mass of Pope Marcellus" was completed. All expectation was far surpassed by this composition. Full of simple melody, it will yet bear comparison in rich variety with any work preceding it. Choruses separate and again blend. The meaning of the words received the most eloquent expression. The Kyrie is all submission, the Agnus humility, the Credo majesty. Pope Pius IV, before whom it was performed, was enchanted. He compared it with those heavenly melodies that St. John may have heard in his ecstatic trance.

The question was set at rest forever by this one great example; a path was opened, pursuing which, works the most beautiful and most touching, even to those who are not of the Romish creed, have been produced. Who can listen to them without enthusiasm? Nature herself seems to have acquired voice and utterance; it is as if the elements spoke; and the tones breathing through universal life, poured forth in blended harmony of adoration; now undulating, like the waves of the sea, now rising in songs of triumph to the skies. Amidst the consenting sympathies of creation, the soul is borne upward to the region of religious entrancement.

It was precisely this art, at one time alienated more completely perhaps than any other from the Church and her service, that was now to become one of her most efficient handmaids. Few things could more effectually promote the interests of Catholicism. Even in its dogmas, the Church, if we are not mistaken, had embodied some portion of that enthusiasm and reverie which form the leading characteristic of its devotional books. Spiritual sentimentality and rapture were favorite subjects for poetry and painting. Music, more direct, more penetrating, more resistless than any other exposition, or any other art, now embodied the prevailing tendency, in language more pure and appropriate, fascinating and subjecting the minds of men.

Section X.—The Curia

While all the elements of social life and of intellectual activity were seized and transformed by the ecclesiastical spirit, the Court of Rome, in which these varying elements met, was also greatly changed.

This change was remarked under Paul IV, and it was essentially promoted by the example of Pius V. Under Gregory XIII it became palpable to all. " Several pontiffs in succession have been men of blameless lives," says Paolo Tiepolo in 1576, " and this has contributed immeasurably to the welfare of the Church; for all other men have become better, or at least have assumed the appearance of being so. Cardinals and prelates attend diligently at the mass; their households are careful to avoid whatever might give offence. The whole city has indeed put off its former recklessness of manner. People are all much more Christian-like in life and habit than they formerly were. It may even be safely affirmed, that in matters of religion, Rome is not far from as high a degree of perfection as human nature is permitted to attain."

Nor are we by any means to conclude that the court was composed of demure hypocrites or feigned puritans. It was formed, on the contrary, of distinguished men; but these men had in a high degree assimilated themselves to the rigorous tone of manner and opinion prevailing in the Church.

If we represent to ourselves the Papal Court as it existed under Sixtus V, we find many among its cardinals who had taken a considerable share in the politics of the world. Gallio

of Como had conducted the affairs of state as prime minister
during two pontificates, and possessed the art of governing by
address and pliancy. He was now distinguished by the ecclesiastical endowments his large revenues enabled him to
establish. Rusticucci, powerful under Pius V, was not without influence under Sixtus; laborious in his habits, of penetrating mind, and endowed with cordial kindness of heart, he
was, perhaps, rendered more circumspect and irreproachable
in his life, by the hope he entertained of the papal throne.
Salviati had gained reputation by his conscientious government of Bologna; simple and blameless, his manners were not
merely serious, they were austere. Santorio, Cardinal of Santa
Severina, the man of the Inquisition, long commanding influence on all questions of ecclesiastical polity, inflexible in opinion, rigorous to his servants, severe even toward his own family,
still more so toward others, harshly cold and inaccessible to all.
In contrast with him stood Mandruzzi, always deep in the counsels and secrets of Austria, whether of the German or Spanish
lines, and called the Cato of the college; but with reference
to his learning and unclouded virtues only, not to any cen-
soriousness or arrogance, for he was modesty itself. Sirleto
also was still living; beyond question the most profoundly
skilled in science, and the most accomplished linguist of all the
cardinals of his time. Muret calls him a living library; yet,
when he rose from his books, he would gather around him the
poor boys who were carrying a few fagots of wood to the market, give them religious instruction, and then buy their wood.
He was, indeed, a most kindly and compassionate man.[1] The
example of Carlo Borromeo, who was afterward canonized,
could not fail to produce effects of great utility. Federigo Borromeo was by nature impetuous and irritable; but, influenced
by his uncle, he led a religious life, and did not permit the mortifications that he frequently experienced to deprive him of his
self-command. But he who most resembled the excellent Archbishop of Milan, was Agostino Valiere, a man whose nature was
pure and noble, as his learning was extraordinary. Following
implicitly the plan prescribed by his conscience, he had now

[1] Ciaconius, "Vitæ Paparum," iii. p. 978. He also gives the epitaph of Sirleto, where he is described as the "patron of the learned and the poor." Cardella, in his "Memorie storiche de' Cardinali," has nothing more than the notices of Ciaconius translated into Italian.

arrived at extreme old age, and presented a true type of a bishop of the primitive Church.

The remainder of the prelates were careful to regulate their lives by the pattern they received from the cardinals, whose associates they were in the congregation, and whose seats they were one day to occupy.

There were also two men who distinguished themselves highly among the members of the supreme tribunal, the Auditori di Rota. These were Mantica and Arigone, men of equal talent, but of characters entirely opposite. Mantica lived only among books and legal documents; his works on jurisprudence were of authority in the forum and the schools; his manners and address were unstudied and abrupt. Arigone, on the contrary, devoted less time to books than to the world, the court, and public affairs.* He was remarkable for the acuteness of his judgment and the flexibility of his character; but neither of these men yielded to the other in efforts to maintain a high reputation for purity and sanctity of life. Among the bishops about the court, those who had been much employed in legations were especially noticed; as, for example, Torres, who had taken active part in concluding the league that Pius V formed with Spain and Venice against the Turks; Malaspina, who had carefully watched over the interests of Catholicism in Germany and the North; Bolognetti, to whom had been intrusted the arduous visitation of the Venetian churches: all men whose talents and zeal for religion had procured them distinction. Men of learning held a very eminent place in the Roman Court: Bellarmine, professor, grammarian, and the most powerful controversialist of the Catholic Church, whose memory is held in reverence for the apostolic purity of his life. Another Jesuit, Maffei, who wrote a history of the Portuguese conquests in India, with particular reference to the effect produced by them on the diffusion of Christianity through the South and East. He is also the author of a life of Loyola, every phrase labored with the most deliberate prolixity and most studied elegance.[2] Distinguished foreigners were also to be found here; as the German Clavius, who combined profound learning with purity of life, and was the object of universal respect; or Muret, a Frenchman, and the best Latinist of his day. He passed a large

---

[2] " Vita J. P. Maffeji," Serassio Auctore. In the edition of Maffei's Works, Berg. 1747.

part of his life in expounding the Pandects; which he did in an original and classic manner. Muret was famed for wit as well as eloquence; yet, in his old age, he took orders, read mass every day, and devoted the close of his existence to the study of theology. Here also was the Spanish canonist, Azpilcueta, whose " *responsa* " were received as oracles, not in Rome only, but throughout the Catholic world. Pope Gregory would sometimes pass hours in conversation with Azpilcueta, pausing to talk with him before the door of his house, while, at the same time, the Spaniard humbly performed the lowest offices in the hospitals.

But, among these remarkable personages, few acquired so deep and extensive an influence as Filippo Neri, founder of the congregation of the Oratory. This eminent confessor and guide of souls, was of cheerful temper and playful manners; rigid in essentials, he was most indulgent in matters of mere form; it was not his custom to command, but only to advise, or, perhaps, to request. Agreeable and easy of access, he did not lecture or harangue—he conversed. He possessed a penetration that enabled him to discriminate the peculiar bent of every mind. His oratory grew up gradually from visits paid him by young men, whose attachment to his person and teaching made them desire to live with him as his disciples. The most renowned among these is the annalist of the Church, Cæsar Baronius. Perceiving his talents, Filippo Neri induced him to give lectures on ecclesiastical history in the Oratory.[3] For this occupation, Baronius showed but little inclination in the first instance, but he none the less applied himself to it during thirty years; and even when called to the College of Cardinals, he rose constantly before daylight to continue his labors. His meals were taken regularly at the same table with his whole household: humility and piety were displayed in his every action. Baronius was bound in the closest friendship with Tarugi, who was of great eminence as a preacher and confessor in the College of Cardinals, as in the Oratory. This intimacy made the happiness of these eminent men; the life of Tarugi being equally pure and irreproachable with that of his friend; death only interrupted this affection, and they were buried side by side. Silvio Antoniano was also a disciple of Filippo Neri. His early disposi-

[3] Gallonius, " Vita Phil. Nerii, Mog. 1602," p. 163.

tions were rather toward poetry and literature; he distinguished himself in both; and when he was afterward intrusted with the preparation of papal briefs, they were composed in a manner unusually skilful and elegant. He too was remarkable for kindliness of heart, modest affability of demeanor, pure truthfulness, and exalted piety.

All who rose to eminence in the Papal Court at this time, whether in the State, the law, poetry, or art, exhibited the same characteristics.

How widely does all this differ from the Curia of the earlier part of the century! Then the cardinals lived in continual contest with the popes, who on their parts buckled on the sword, and banished from their court and person whatever could remind them of their Christian vocation. How still, how cloisterlike, were now the lives of the cardinals. The failure of Cardinal Tosco, who was once on the point of being elected pope, was principally occasioned by his use of certain proverbs, current in Lombardy, but which were found offensive by the delicacy of Rome; so exclusive was the tendency of the public mind, so sensitive were now its ideas of decorum.

We are nevertheless compelled to admit that a different aspect of things, and one much less consonant to our notions of right, was exhibited in social habits, no less than in art and literature. Miracles, which had not for a long time been heard of, were revived. An image of the Virgin began to speak in the church of San Silvestro, and this event produced so powerful an impression upon the people that the region around the church, hitherto neglected and desolate, was presented covered with dwellings. In the Rione de' Monti, a miraculous image of the Virgin appeared in a haystack; and the people of the district considered this so especial a token of divine favor that they rose in arms to prevent its removal. Similar wonders appeared at Narni, Todi, San Severino, and other parts of the Ecclesiastical States, whence they gradually extended over all Catholic countries. The pontiffs also resumed the practice of canonization, which had been suffered to fall into disuse. Nor were all confessors so judicious and moderate as Filippo Neri; hollow unprofitable works of sanctity were encouraged, and fantastic superstitions were mingled with the representation of things sacred and divine.

There would be consolation in the belief that together with these mistaken ideas the majority had acquired a sincere devotion to the precepts of religion.

But from the very nature of this court it resulted inevitably that the most eager struggle after worldly greatness was mingled with the general effort to promote religious interests.

The Curia was not an ecclesiastical institution only, it was a political government also, and had indirectly to rule a large part of the world in addition to its own State. In proportion as men acquired part in the exercise of this power, they also acquired consideration, riches, influence, and whatever else can best excite the wish of man. Human nature could not so entirely change as that men should limit themselves to spiritual weapons alone in their efforts to attain the great prizes of social life and of the State. Matters proceeded in Rome as in other courts, but with very peculiar modifications imposed by the nature of the arena.

The population of Rome was then more fluctuating than that of any city in the world. Under Leo X it had risen to more than 80,000 souls. The severe measures of Paul drove so many to flight, that in his pontificate it sank to 45,000. In a few years after his death it was found to be increased to 70,000; and under Sixtus V it rose to more than 100,000; the most peculiar circumstance was that the fixed residents bore no proportion to these numbers. To few of its inhabitants was the city a home, their abode in it was rather a long sojourn than a permanent citizenship. It might be said to resemble a fair or diet, having no stability or fixed continuance, no connecting links of family or kindred. Many were there simply because no road to preferment was open to them in the land of their birth; wounded pride drove one man thither, boundless ambition impelled another, some came believing they found more liberty in Rome than elsewhere. But the grand object of all was to advance their own interest in their own manner.

These varying classes did not become amalgamated into one body, the different races were still so distinct that the diversities of national and provincial character were clearly perceptible. The courteous and observant Lombard was readily distinguished from the Genoese, who expected to accomplish all things by his money. Nor was it difficult to discover the Venetian, ever occupied in seeking to penetrate the secrets of others. The frugal and talkative Florentine met here with the sagacious Romagnese, whose eyes were ever bent with instinctive prudence on the path by which his interests might best be secured. The ceremonious and exacting Neapolitan came, together with the simply mannered native of the North, remarked for his love of comfort; even the learned German Clavius was the subject of many a jest, provoked by the abundance of his two substantial breakfasts. The Frenchman kept himself much apart, and relinquished his national habits with more difficulty than any others. The Spaniard, full of personal pretence and projects of ambition, stalked onward, wrapping his cloak about him, and casting looks of scorn on all the rest.

In this court there was no position so eminent, but the most obscure individual might aspire to hold it. People delighted to recall the words of John XXIII, who, being asked why he was going to Rome, said " he meant to be pope," and pope he became. It was from a station among the humblest that Pius V and Sixtus V had been exalted to the supreme dignity. Each man believed himself capable of all, and hoped for everything.

It was a remark frequently made in those days, and a perfectly just one, that there was a sort of republicanism in the character of the prelacy and Curia; this consisted in the circumstance that all might aspire to all; examples were continually presented of men whose origin was most obscure, attaining to positions of the first eminence. The constitution of this republic was nevertheless very singular; to the undisputed rights of the many stood opposed the absolute power of one, from whose arbitrary decision it was that all promotion and every advantage must be derived. And who was this one? It was he who, by some combination, on which it was impossible to calculate, had come forth as victor from the conflict of election. Of small importance hitherto, he was suddenly invested with the supreme authority. Persuaded that he had been raised by the Holy Spirit to this height of dignity, he was but slightly tempted to dissemble his disposition and inclination; thus the pontificate usually commenced with a complete change in all public offices. Legates and governors of provinces were removed. There were certain appointments in the capital that fell as matters of course to the nephews or other kinsmen of the reigning pope; for even when nepotism was under restraint, as was the case in the times

we are describing, there was no pontiff who did not promote
his immediate confidants and old adherents; he would naturally
feel indisposed to resign the society of those with whom he had
previously been passing his life. The secretary who had long
served the cardinal Montalto, was most acceptable to that prelate
when he became Sixtus V. The adherents of their opinions
also were sure to be brought forward by each new pope. Thus
did every accession to the papal chair cause a perfect change
in all prospects and expectations; in the approaches to power,
and in ecclesiastical no less than in temporal dignity. Commendone compares the state of things appearing on a new pontificate, to " a city in which the palace of the sovereign had been
transferred to a new site, and all the streets turned toward this
new centre. How many abodes must be demolished? How
often must the road be carried through a palace; new passages
are opened, and thoroughfares hitherto unfrequented are enlivened by the crowd." The alterations taking place on these
occasions, and the degree of stability possessed by the new arrangements, are not unaptly typified by this description.

But from these peculiarities there necessarily resulted a consequence very singular in its character.

From the fact that a pope attained the sovereignty when
much older than other monarchs, these mutations were so frequent that a new change might at any moment be expected. The
government might be instantly placed in other hands. This
made pepole live as in a perpetual game of chance, wherein
nothing could be calculated, but everything might be hoped for.

To attain promotion, to gain advancement, as everyone desired and trusted to do, this would depend on the degree of
personal favor that each could command; but where all personal influence was in so perpetual a fluctuation, the calculations
of ambition must necessarily assume a similar character, and
sometimes employ very extraordinary devices.

Among our manuscript collections we find a multitude of
regulations for the conduct of those who are sent to the Papal
Court.[4] The varying modes in which each man pursues fort-

[4] For instance: " Instructions to Cardinal Medici on the manner in which
he must guide himself in the Court of
Rome; " " Warnings to Cardinal Montalto as to how he may best govern as
cardinal and as nephew of the Pope; "
" Advice political and most useful for
conduct in the Court of Rome." Sev-
enty-eight maxims of very questionable
morality. " Inform." xxv. The most
important of all is the " Discourse on
the Court of Rome, with its portrait, by
Commendone ": Codd. Rang. 18; this
last is at Vienna.

une present us with a subject not unworthy of observation. Inexhaustible is the plasticity of human nature; the more rigid the limits by which it is restrained, so much the more unexpected are the forms into which it throws itself.

It is manifest that all could not pursue the same path. The man who possessed nothing must be content to forward himself by rendering service to him who had means. A liberal domestication in the houses of princes, secular or temporal, was still accepted by literary men. Whoever was compelled to adopt this mode of life, must then make it his first object to ingratiate himself with the head of the house, to gain merit in his eyes, to penetrate his secrets, and in some way to render himself indispensable to his lord. For this all indignities must be endured; no injustice must be resented. For who could say how soon a change in the papacy might cause the star of his master to rise in the ascendant, and its lustre to be poured on the servant? Fortune ebbs and flows; the man remains the same.

Or to some of those aspirants, the possession of a subordinate office was perhaps the object of desire. From this they might advance to better employments by the exercise of zeal and activity. It was, nevertheless, in Rome as elsewhere, and in those times as in all others, a very critical and dangerous thing to be compelled to consider interest in the first place, and honor only in the second.

Much more favorable was the position of those who had the means of life. The *monti*, in which they purchased shares, gave them a certain income every month. They bought a place by means of which they immediately entered the prelacy; not only attaining an independence, but also acquiring an opportunity for the brilliant display of their talents. To him that hath, it shall be given. At the Roman Court the possession of property was doubly advantageous; for since this possession reverted to the treasury, the Pope himself had an interest in granting promotions.

This state of things did not demand servility of attachment to any one great man; on the contrary, too earnestly declared an adherence might prove an impediment to promotion, if fortune should not happen to be favorable. The grand essential was to beware of making enemies, to give no offence. This precaution was to be departed from in no circumstance of social intercourse, however slight or trivial. It was essential, for example, to offer no man more honor than he was strictly entitled to claim; equality of deportment toward persons of different degrees would be inequality, and might produce an unfavorable impression. Even of the absent, nothing but good was to be spoken, not only because words once uttered are beyond our control, and we know not whither they are borne, but also because few love too keen an observer. If a man possess extended acquirements, let him be moderate in displaying them; and above all, let him never permit them to become tedious. It is not prudent to be the bearer of bad news; the unpleasant impression they make recoils on him who brings them; but in regard to this, there is an error to be avoided—that of maintaining a silence so rigid as would make its motive apparent.

The elevation to higher dignities, even to that of cardinal, conferred no exemption from these observances; they were to be fulfilled with increased caution in his own sphere. Who could venture to betray a conviction that one member of the Sacred College was less worthy than another to ascend the papal·throne? There was none so obscure that the choice might not fall on him.

It was above all important that a cardinal should cultivate the good-will of the reigning pontiff. Fortune and dignity, universal deference and obsequiousness, follow him who has gained this. But more than ever must he be cautious while seeking it; profound silence was to be maintained with regard to the personal interests of the pope, but these must nevertheless be secretly penetrated, and the conduct governed accordingly. It was permitted occasionally to magnify the kinsmen of the pontiff, their fidelity and talents might be lauded; this was for the most part an acceptable subject. To arrive at the secrets of the papal family, it was expedient to employ the monks; these men, availing themselves of religious duties as their pretext, contrive to penetrate further than is possible to any other class of the community.

Ambassadors are imperatively called on by the rapid vicissitudes and extensive importance of personal relations, for the most vigilant watchfulness. Like a skilful pilot, the envoy is attentive to mark from what quarter blows the wind; he must spare no cost to assure himself of those who possess good information, certain that his utmost expenditure would be largely repaid by one single piece of intelligence that enabled him to seize the moment favorable to his negotiation. If he had to present a request to the pontiff, he made incredible efforts imperceptibly to interweave some point that the pope himself desired to carry, with the business he was laboring to promote. Most of all did he seek to gain the favorite nephew or other kinsman to his wishes, by persuading him that more permanent and more important advantages, whether of riches or greatness, were to be obtained from his court than from any other. Neither must he neglect to secure the good-will of the cardinals. He would not promise the papacy to any, but all were to be allured by the hope of it. He displayed devotion to none; but even for those most inimical to his purposes, he would occasionally perform some act of favor. He resembled the falconer, who shows the piece of meat to the hawk, but gives it him in small quantities only; and that morsel by morsel.

Thus did they live, and such was the policy of the Ecclesiastical Court. Cardinals, ambassadors, prelates, princes, those who were the known possessors of power, and those who exercised it in secret. Full of ceremony, of which Rome was the classic soil, of submissive subordination, and reverential observance; but egotists to the very core, all eagerly seeking to attain some object, to accomplish some purpose, to achieve some advantage over his neighbor.

Strange that the struggle for what all desire—power, honor, riches, enjoyment—elsewhere the fruitful source of rancorous feuds, should here assume the aspect of a courteous anxiety to serve. Here every man flattered the hope of his rival, conscious that he nourished something similar, for the purpose of arriving at the possession of what he also is seeking to obtain. Here self-denial was full of eagerness to enjoy, and passion stole onward with cautious footstep.

We have seen the dignity, the seriousness, the religious zeal prevailing in the Roman Court, we have also remarked its worldly aspect, ambition, avarice, dissimulation, and craft.

If it were our purpose to pronounce the eulogy of the Papal See, we should have insisted on the first only of the two elements composing it. Were we disposed to inveigh against it, we should have displayed only the second; but whoever will

raise himself to the level, whence a clear and unprejudiced view
can be obtained, will arrive at an exact perception of the whole
subject; he will see both these elements, but he will also perceive that both are rendered inevitable by the nature of man and
the condition of things.

The period of the world's history that we have just been
considering, was one wherein the prevalent mode of opinion
made pressing demand for external propriety, purity of life,
and religious fervor. This state of public feeling coincided with
the principle of the court, whose position, as regards the rest
of the world, is determined by these qualities. It followed of
necessity that power and eminence were most certainly secured
by men whose characters were in accordance with this demand.
Were it otherwise, public opinion would not only be untrue to
itself, it would destroy its own existence. But that the advantages of fortune should happen to be so immediately consequent on the possession of spiritual qualities, is indeed the most
seductive allurement that could be offered by the spirit of this
world.

We cannot doubt the sincerity of these qualities and sentiments, not unfrequently described by our observant and discreet authorities, but there were doubtless many by whom the
mere appearance of these qualities was adopted for the furtherance of their fortunes; while in others the worldly tendency
may have insinuated itself together with those of more lofty
import, and veiled in the dim uncertainty of motives imperfectly
developed.

The process we have seen taking place in art and literature
may be traced also in the Curia. Here also a desertion from
what the Church demands was most apparent; there was a
laxity approaching to paganism in the modes of thought prevailing. But the march of events reawakened the principle of
the Church, aroused the energies of society as with a new breath
of life, and imparted an altered tone to the existence of the times.
How broad is the difference between Ariosto and Tasso, Giulio
Romano and Guercino, Pomponazzo and Patrizi! A vast epoch
lies between them. They have, nevertheless, something in common, and the later is linked by certain points of contact with the
earlier. With its ancient forms the Curia also retained many
component parts of its old nature, yet this did not prevent it from

being animated by a new spirit. What could not be wholly transferred and assimilated to itself, was at least urged forward by the force of the impulse which that spirit communicated.

While occupied in contemplation of these commingling elements, I recall to mind a scene of nature, that may serve to bring this state of things more vividly before us by the kind of similitude it presents.

At Terni, the Nera is seen tranquilly approaching through wood and field; it proceeds across the distant valley in calm, unruffled course. From the other side comes rushing the Velino; pressed between opposing rocks, it foams onward with resistless speed, till at length its mass of waters are dashed down headlong in magnificent falls that sparkle and glitter with a myriad changing hues. These reach the peaceful Nera; they at once communicate their own wild commotion, raging and foaming; the mingled waters then rush forward on their eager and hurried course.

It was thus that the whole being of society, all literature, and every art, received a new impulse from the reawakened spirit of the Catholic Church. The Curia was at once devout and restless, spiritual and warlike: on the one side replete with dignity, pomp, and ceremony; on the other, unparalleled for calculating subtlety and insatiable love of power: its piety and ambition, reposing on the idea of an exclusive orthodoxy, coincide, and act in harmony for the production of one end—universal domination. The Roman Church once more binds on her armor for the conquest of the world.

COSIMO is a specialty publisher for independent authors, not-for-profit organizations, and innovative businesses, dedicated to publishing books that inspire, inform, and engage readers around the world.

Our mission is to create a smart and sustainable society by connecting people with valuable ideas. We offer authors and organizations full publishing support, while using the newest technologies to present their works in the most timely and effective way.

COSIMO BOOKS offers fine books that inspire, inform and engage readers on a variety of subjects, including personal development, socially responsible business, economics and public affairs.

COSIMO CLASSICS brings to life unique and rare classics, representing a wide range of subjects that include Business, Economics, History, Personal Development, Philosophy, Religion & Spirituality, and much more!

COSIMO REPORTS publishes reports that affect your world, from global trends to the economy, and from health to geopolitics.

COSIMO B2B offers custom editions for historical societies, museums, companies and other organizations interested in offering classic books to their audiences, customized with their own logo and message. **COSIMO B2B** also offers publishing services to organizations, such as media firms, think tanks, conference organizers and others who could benefit from having their own imprint.

CPSIA information can be obtained
at www.ICGtesting.com
Printed in the USA
BVHW081447141022
649471BV00006B/82